John Brown, David Smith

An Exposition of the Epistle of the Apostle Paul to the Hebrews

Vol. 2

John Brown, David Smith

An Exposition of the Epistle of the Apostle Paul to the Hebrews
Vol. 2

ISBN/EAN: 9783337318420

Printed in Europe, USA, Canada, Australia, Japan

Cover: Foto ©Lupo / pixelio.de

More available books at **www.hansebooks.com**

AN EXPOSITION

OF

THE EPISTLE OF THE APOSTLE PAUL

TO THE

HEBREWS.

BY THE LATE

JOHN BROWN, D.D.,

PROFESSOR OF EXEGETICAL THEOLOGY TO THE UNITED PRESBYTERIAN CHURCH,
AND SENIOR PASTOR OF THE UNITED PRESBYTERIAN CONGREGATION,
BROUGHTON PLACE, EDINBURGH.

EDITED BY

DAVID SMITH, D.D.,

BIGGAR.

VOL. II.

EDINBURGH: WILLIAM OLIPHANT AND CO.
LONDON: HAMILTON, ADAMS, AND CO.

MDCCCLXII.

CONTENTS OF VOL. II.

PART II.—PRACTICAL.

	PAGE
SECT. 1. General Exhortation and Warning, x. 19–xii. 29,	1
,, 2. Particular Exhortations, xiii. 1–19,	219
CONCLUSION, xiii. 20, 21,	251
POSTSCRIPT, xiii. 22–25,	272

DISCOURSE I.
The Christian's Privilege and Duty.—Heb. iv. 14–16, . 279

DISCOURSE II.
Christ, the Author of Eternal Salvation, made perfect by Suffering.—Heb. v. 7–9, . 303

DISCOURSE III.
Christ's Character and Ministry as a High Priest.—Heb. ix. 11, 12, . 323

DISCOURSE IV.
The Superior Efficacy of Christ's Sacrifice.—Heb. ix. 13, 14, . 337

DISCOURSE V.
Christ the Mediator of the New Covenant.—Heb. ix. 15, . 353

DISCOURSE VI.
Entrance into the Holiest by the Blood of Christ.—Heb. x. 19–22, . 369

DISCOURSE VII.
The joint Perfection of Old and New Testament Saints in Heaven.—Heb. xi. 39, 40, . 383

CONTENTS.

DISCOURSE VIII.

The Christian Altar.—Heb. xiii. 10, ... 397

DISCOURSE IX.

The Great Shepherd of the Sheep.—Heb. xiii. 20, 21, . . 409

INDEX.

1. Principal Matters, ... 431
2. Greek Words and Phrases remarked on, ... 434
3. Authors referred to, ... 437
4. Texts of Scripture, ... 439

AN EXPOSITION

OF THE

EPISTLE OF THE APOSTLE PAUL

TO THE

HEBREWS.

PART II.

PRACTICAL.

§ 1. *General Exhortation to Perseverance, and Warning against Apostasy.* Chap. x. 19-xii. 29.

THE preceding part of this Epistle has been chiefly occupied with stating, proving, and illustrating some of the grand peculiarities of Christian doctrine; and the remaining part of it is entirely devoted to an injunction and enforcement of those duties which naturally result from the foregoing statements. The paragraph, vers. 19-23, obviously consists of two parts:—a statement of principles, which are taken for granted as having been fully proved; and an injunction of duties, grounded on the admission of these principles. "Having therefore, brethren, boldness to enter into the holiest by the blood of Jesus, by a new and living way, which He hath consecrated for us through the vail, that is to say, His flesh; and having an High Priest over the house of God; let us draw near with a true heart, in full assurance of faith, having our hearts sprinkled from an evil conscience, and our bodies washed with pure water. Let us hold fast the profession of our faith without wavering (for He is

faithful that promised)." The principles stated are these:—
First, "We have boldness to enter into the holiest by the blood
of Jesus;" and secondly, We have a great "High Priest over
the house of God." The duties enjoined are,—"drawing near,"
and "holding fast the profession of our faith," or rather, hope.

The first principle which the Apostle takes for granted as
having been sufficiently proved, is thus expressed in our version:
—"Having therefore, brethren, boldness to enter into the
holiest by the blood of Jesus, by a new and living way, which He
hath consecrated for us through the vail, that is to say, His flesh."

It is not often that there is reason to complain of our translation, that it is not sufficiently literal. It is often so literal as
to be obscure, if not unintelligible. But in the passage before
us there is ground for such a charge. The words, literally rendered, run thus :—" Having therefore, brethren, boldness, or
confidence, in reference to the entrance into the holiest, by the
blood of Jesus—or by blood, of Jesus,—by which entrance[1] He
has opened, or consecrated, for us a new and living way,—
through the vail, that is, of His flesh."[2]

The first question which here suggests itself is, What are
we to understand by the entrance of the holiest? whose entrance is it that is referred to? and what is the nature of this
entrance? It has been common to consider the entrance into
the holiest here as the entrance of believers; and that entrance
has been explained of the thoughts, affections, and devotions of
Christians being fixed on and addressed to a reconciled Divinity,
by which they have all that intercourse of mind with God which
is compatible with a state in which the capacities of the soul are
confined by its union to an earthly body. But to this mode of
interpretation there are very strong objections. Throughout
the whole of this Epistle, the true holy of holies is heaven; and
to enter into this true holy of holies, is just to go to heaven.
Besides, it is plain that the principle which the Apostle states
here is one which he had already illustrated. Now, what the

---

[1] ἥν may be = καθ' ἥν.
[2] Most justly has Valcknaer remarked, " Hic locus paucis videtur intellectus." Εἰς is expressive of a direction of mind towards an object ; παῤῥησία εἰς, 'boldness in reference to;' Matt. xxvi. 10; Acts ii. 25; Rom. iv. 20, xvi. 19, etc., etc. Παῤῥησία and παῤῥησιάζεσθαι are generally construed with the same prepositions as πίστις and πιστεύειν.

Apostle has been illustrating, is neither that Christians have a present spiritual access to God in heaven, nor that they shall have a future real, bodily entrance into heaven; but that Christ, as our High Priest, has really and bodily gone into heaven, the antitype of the holy of holies.[1] I cannot doubt, then, that the entrance here mentioned is the entrance of Jesus Christ, and that the true meaning of the whole phrase is, ' the entrance of Jesus into the holiest by His own blood.'

A few additional remarks on the construction of the passage are necessary, to open the way to our distinct and satisfactory apprehension of its meaning. The words, " by a new and living way, which He hath opened for us," are, literally, " by which entrance He has opened, or consecrated, for us a new and living way,"—and are, I apprehend, parenthetical. The phrase, " through the vail," connects with " the entrance into the holiest through the blood of Jesus ;"—it is a further description of this entrance. The entrance of Jesus by His own blood into the holiest through the vail, is just what is described, chap. ix. 11, 12.

The concluding explicatory clause, " that is, His flesh," has commonly been supposed to refer to the words which immediately precede it—" the vail;" and has been considered as teaching that Christ's body was the antitype of the vail which divided the holy from the most holy place, and that the rending of that vail was emblematical of His death. To this mode of interpretation there are, however, great objections. Throughout this Epistle, as the holy of holies is evidently the heaven of heavens, so the holy place—the tabernacle and its vails—seems as plainly to be the visible heavens, through which our High Priest entered into the heaven of heavens. Besides, though the rending of the vail, taken by itself, and its consequence, the laying open of the holy of holies, may be considered as a fit emblem of the death of Christ, yet the figure does not hold in the point referred to : the high priest left the vail behind when he entered,—Christ carried " His flesh," His human nature, along with Him to heaven.

I am disposed to consider the words, " that is, of His flesh,"

---

[1] The οὖν refers back to what immediately precedes, but especially to chap. ix., where it was shown that Christ has entered into the true holy of holies.—THOLUCK.

as referring to the entrance of our Lord into the holy place,—the word 'entrance' being understood, thus: "that is, the entrance of His flesh;" just as the word 'tabernacle' is understood in the parallel passage,—"a greater and more perfect tabernacle, that is, not the tabernacle of this building." The passage without the parenthesis would read thus :—" Having then, brethren, boldness in reference to the entrance of Jesus by His own blood into the holiest of all, through the vail, that is, the entrance of His flesh."

Having thus endeavoured to ascertain the true construction of this somewhat involved and difficult passage, let us shortly illustrate the glorious truths which it unfolds :—Jesus Christ, our great High Priest, has entered into the holiest; He has done so by His own blood; He has done so through the vail; He has done so bodily; and He has consecrated this entrance for us, a new and a living way. You will observe that these are just the great truths which the Apostle had been stating and illustrating in the preceding section.

Jesus has " entered into the holiest," *i.e.*, into heaven. He is " a great High Priest passed into the heavens,"—a " High Priest set on the right hand of the Majesty in the heavens,"— " He is entered in into the holy place,"—" not the holy places made with hands, but into heaven itself."[1]

He has entered in " with blood," with His own blood; *i.e.*, His entrance into heaven as our High Priest is the result of the all-perfect expiation of our sins, which He effected by the shedding of His own blood. "When He had by Himself purged our sins, He sat down on the right hand of the Majesty on high." " For the suffering of death, He was crowned with glory and honour." " As the Captain of salvation, He was made perfect through suffering." " Having been made perfect through the things which He suffered, He is become the Author of eternal salvation to all who obey Him." " He is entered in, not by the blood of goats and calves, but by His own blood." " After He had offered one sacrifice for sins, He for ever sat down on the right hand of God."[2]

He has entered " through the vail;" that is, through the visible heavens, of which the tabernacle and its vails, as concealing the holy of holies from general inspection, as necessary

[1] Heb. iv. 14, viii. 1, ix 12, 24. [2] Heb. i. 3, ii. 9, 10, v. 9, ix. 12, x. 12.

to be gone through in order to enter it, were emblematical. Our "great High Priest is passed through the heavens." "He is entered into the holy place, through a greater and more perfect tabernacle than the tabernacle of this building."[1]

He has entered bodily into heaven. His entrance is the entrance of His "flesh," or body, *i.e.*, of Him as embodied; just as to "present our bodies living sacrifices," means, 'present ourselves as embodied beings.' Our Lord's entrance is not a metaphorical entrance; it is as real as that of the high priest, which was its emblem. The same God-man Jesus who died on the cross, ascended up through these heavens, far above them, into the heaven of heavens; and there, in human nature, as the representative of His people, He appears in the immediate presence of God.

The only other principle contained in these words is that expressed in the parenthetical clause. This bodily entrance into the holiest by His own blood, through the visible heavens, "He has consecrated for us, a new and living way." The word " consecrate" literally means, 'opened up;' and it matters very little whether you understand it in its primary or secondary sense. The idea which the Apostle here expresses is the same as that brought forward in the 20th verse of the 6th chapter, where Jesus is represented as entering as our " Forerunner"[2] within the vail. The general meaning is plainly this:—' By His bodily entrance through these visible heavens into the heaven of heavens, on the ground of His atoning sacrifice, He has secured that in due time all of us who are His people shall also, through that blood, bodily pass through these heavens into the heaven of heavens.' When He went away He said to His disciples, " In My Father's house are many mansions : if it were not so, I would have told you. I go to prepare a place for you. And if I go and prepare a place for you, I will come again, and receive you unto Myself; that where I am, there ye may be also."[3] He is gone to glory through His own blood, that through that blood He may bring the whole company of the " many sons to glory." Through the power of His atonement it is secured that they shall all, like Him, be raised from the dead, and, like Him, be taken up to heaven. These " vile bodies" being changed, " and made like unto His glorious body,"

[1] Heb. iv. 14, ix. 11, 12.   [2] Πρόδρομος.   [3] John xiv. 2, 3.

they "shall be caught up to meet Him in the air," and go with Him to the heaven of heavens.

This mode of entering heaven, which Christ has opened for us, is "a new and a living way." His entrance to heaven is our way of entering it; and it is a new way—a way totally different from that in which innocent man would have entered heaven—a way belonging to the New Covenant, in which all things are new—a way which man could never have opened up, and newly proclaimed in the doctrine of Christianity. "A living way" seems equivalent to 'a life-giving way—the way of life to life,' in all the extent of meaning which belongs to that peculiarly emphatic term. To have followed the Jewish high priest into the holy place would have been *death*.

Now, concerning this "entrance of our Lord Jesus into the holiest," we have "boldness." This is the same word which in chap. iii. 6 is termed "confidence," and chap. iv. 16, "boldness." It properly signifies 'freedom of speech,' but often is used for that state of firm belief and assured confidence which leads to freedom of speech and determination of action.[1] Here it is, I apprehend, expressive of that state of mental confidence which naturally springs from the knowledge and faith of the truths here referred to. 'Having confidence of mind in reference to our spiritual interests; knowing and being sure, as we are, that Christ as our High Priest has gone bodily to heaven, and that in due time, through His death and exaltation, we shall be taken bodily to heaven also.' This, then, is the first principle which the Apostle takes for granted as having been already abundantly established.

The second is, that "we have a great Priest over the house of God." The word "having" is very properly repeated here to make out the sense. Perhaps the whole phrase, "having boldness," or confidence, should have been repeated. "The house of God" may signify either the family of God, or the temple of God. It is plainly used in the first sense in the beginning of the 3d chapter. Though I cannot speak with perfect conviction on the subject, I think it probable that it here means the temple of God—the celestial temple.[2] We

---

[1] Eph. iii. 12; Heb. iii. 6, iv. 16; 1 John ii. 28, iii. 21, iv. 17, v. 14.

[2] Comp. x. 19, viii. 1, 2, ix. 24, vii. 25, iv. 16. ἐπί used as ch. iii. 6.

know that our Lord Jesus, as our High Priest, is gone to heaven; and we know also, that *there* He is over the temple of God—that everything with respect to the acceptable mode of worship is committed to Him.

The truth here stated, like those formerly referred to, is spoken of as one already established. The greatness of Christ Jesus as a Priest is the grand subject of the third and principal section of the Epistle; and that He is over the celestial temple, is distinctly asserted in the 1st verse of the 8th chapter.

On the foundation of these principles, the Apostle proceeds to exhort the Hebrews to " draw near with a true heart, in full assurance of faith," and to " hold fast the profession of their faith without wavering; for He is faithful that promised."

Since these things are so, and since we have abundant evidence that they are so, " let us," says the Apostle, " draw near with a true heart, in the full assurance of faith, having our hearts sprinkled from an evil conscience, and having our bodies washed with pure water. Let us hold fast the profession of our faith without wavering; for He is faithful who hath promised."

To " draw near" is the same as to "come to God"—to "come to the throne of grace;" and is expressive of worshipping God as a reconciled Divinity. The language in which this idea is expressed is borrowed from the Jewish ritual. In all their religious exercises they looked towards, and in many of them they approached towards, the emblem of Jehovah's favourable presence in the holy of holies. "Let us draw near" is just equivalent to—' let us worship God as the God of peace—let us draw near to Him as propitious to us.'

And let us do so " with a true heart." This phrase seems to me very nearly synonymous with our Lord's description of acceptable worship, John iv. 24: " In spirit and in truth."[1] " Let us draw near to God"—not by mere bodily service, but by the exercise of the mind and heart—not figuratively, but really —" with a true heart,"—with the mind enlightened with the truth, and with the heart made *true, sound, upright*, through the influence of this truth; not under the influence of the " evil

---

[1] It is the Heb. בְּלֵבָב שָׁלֵם, rendered ἀληθινὴ καρδία by the LXX., Isa. xxxviii. 3, and καρδία τελεία, 1 Kings viii. 61, xi. 4, xv. 3. Theophylact thus explains it: ἀδόλου, ἀνυποκρίτου πρὸς τοὺς ἀδελφοὺς, ἀδιαστάκτου, μηδὲν ἀμφιβαλλούσης, μηδὲν ἐνδοιαζούσης περὶ τῶν μελλόντων καὶ διὰ τοῦτο μικροψυχούσης.

heart of error and unbelief," which leads men away from God, but under the influence of the heart of truth and faith, which, by uniting the mind and heart of man to the mind and heart of God, gives real fellowship with Him.

Christians are exhorted thus to draw near to God, " in the full assurance of faith." " The full assurance of faith" is just equivalent to—' the fullest and most assured belief.' The question naturally occurs, The full and most assured belief of what? And the answer is easy : The full and assured belief of that respecting which we have confidence—that Christ as our High Priest has bodily passed through these heavens into the heaven of heavens by His own blood, thereby proving the perfection of His atoning sacrifice, and the efficacy of his intercession ; and thus securing that in due time we shall also enter in a similar way into the heavens; and that in heaven, whither He has entered as our Forerunner, He is a great High Priest over the celestial temple, having everything connected with the acceptable worship of God committed to His management. We ought to draw near to God with this full assurance, because we have the most abundant evidence that these things are true, and because it is the assurance of these things which enables us to draw near. It is the faith of the truth respecting the reality and efficacy of the sacrifice of Jesus Christ, and the hope that rises out of that faith, that enable us to *draw near* to *Him*, from whom, but for this faith and hope, had we just views of His holiness and justice and power, we would seek shelter, if possible, under rocks and mountains.

It is a just and important remark of Dr Owen, respecting the meaning of the phrase, "assurance of faith,"—" The full assurance of faith here respects not the assurance that any have of their own salvation, nor any degree of such assurance ; it is only the full satisfaction of our souls and consciences of the reality and efficacy of Christ's priesthood to give us acceptance with God, in opposition to all other ways and means thereof, that is intended." " Let us draw near in the full assurance of faith," is just—' Let us worship God in the firm faith of these truths.'

The two following clauses have, in later times, very generally been considered as both referring to the exhortation, "let us draw near," and as descriptive of the qualifications of an acceptable worshipper. "Having the heart sprinkled from an evil conscience, and the body washed with pure water," has been considered as just equivalent to such phrases as—"being purified from all filthiness of the flesh and of the spirit,"—"being sanctified in the whole man, soul, body, and spirit;" and the Apostle has been supposed to teach the important truth, that the worship of men living habitually in the indulgence either of internal or external sin cannot be acceptable. I cannot but take a somewhat different view of the matter. This is no doubt an important truth, but it has no particular bearing on the Apostle's argument. The construction of the original text induces me, along with many of the most learned both of ancient and modern expositors, to connect the phrase, "and having our bodies washed with pure water," not with the exhortation, "let us draw near," but with the exhortation, "let us hold fast our profession; thus: "Let us draw near, having our hearts sprinkled from an evil conscience: and having our bodies washed with pure water, let us hold fast the profession of our faith."

The words, "having our hearts sprinkled from an evil conscience," appear to me not so much intended to state that we must be holy in heart if we would acceptably worship God, as to bring forward the truth, that "having a heart sprinkled from an evil conscience, through the full assurance of faith," we may, and we ought, to draw near to God as the God of peace. "An evil conscience" is a conscience burdened and polluted with the sense of unpardoned guilt. A man who has offended God, and knows this, and who has no solid ground of hope of pardon, is totally unfit for affectionate fellowship with God. His mind is a stranger to confidence and love—it is full of jealousy, and fear, and dislike. The man must get rid of this "evil conscience" in order to his coming to God. This is expressed by the Apostle by the "heart being *sprinkled* from this evil conscience." The "evil conscience" occupies the same place, as a bar in the way of spiritually drawing near to God, as ceremonial defilement did in the way of ceremonially drawing near to God; and as ceremonial defilement was removed by the sprinkling of the blood of the ritual expiatory sacrifice, so the "evil conscience" is removed by what he terms the sprinkling of the blood of Christ. That which in the New Covenant corresponds to the sprinkling of the blood, is "the faith of the truth as it is in Jesus," by which the sinner is delivered from the jealousies of guilt, and the tormenting fear of divine vengeance. The words, then, are just equivalent to—'Having obtained freedom from those jealousies and fears which arise out of unpardoned guilt, and keep us at a distance from God,—having obtained freedom from these by the faith of these truths, let us draw near to God.' There is an allusion to the consecration of Aaron and his sons, whose garments were sprinkled with blood that they might enter into the sanctuary. Christians are invited, sprinkled *inwardly*—on the conscience with the blood of the only effectual atoning sacrifice,—not only into the sanctuary, but into the holy of holies, where God is, and where the *Forerunner* is also.

It must be evident to every person who has attentively considered and distinctly understood what has been said, that the Apostle's exhortation naturally rises out of and is strongly enforced by the principles on which it is grounded. 'Since we have the most satisfactory evidence that Christ Jesus has bodily gone through these visible heavens into the heaven of heavens, on the ground of His own meritorious, expiatory death, thus proving at once the perfection of His sacrifice and the prevalence of His intercession; and since He has thus secured that all we, believing in Him, shall in due time enter into the heaven of heavens in the same way,—let us worship Jehovah as the God of peace, with enlightened minds and upright hearts, in the assured faith of these truths, by which we are delivered from those jealousies and fears which a guilty conscience produces, and which prevent us from approaching Jehovah as the propitiated Divinity, reconciling the world to Himself, not imputing to men their trespasses.'

It must be equally plain that the Apostle meant his readers to draw the conclusion—'How much better is the way of drawing near to God which is thus opened up than the way of drawing near to Him by the ritual of Moses, and how foolish as well as criminal would it be to abandon the former and revert to the latter!' The Jews, on the ground of the entrance of their high priest through the tabernacle and its vails into the material holy place by the blood of animal sacrifices, though they had no reason to hope they were ever to be allowed to go into the holiest, were yet encouraged tremblingly to approach towards the emblem of the reconciled Divinity, having their bodies purified from ceremonial defilement by the sprinkling of "the blood of bulls and goats." But we Christians have the most satisfactory evidence that our High Priest has passed through these heavens into the heaven of heavens by His own blood, and has secured that in due time we shall follow Him; and through the faith of this truth, our consciences are freed from those jealousies and fears which prevent spiritual intercourse with God, and therefore we can, and we ought, in the spiritual institutions of our holy faith, to cultivate affectionate and child-like intercourse with Jehovah as our Father, because His Father —as His God, and therefore our God.

The Apostle's second exhortation is in these words: "And having our bodies washed with pure water, let us hold fast the profession of our faith without wavering." The great body of MSS. read, "profession of our hope," which seems to be the true reading. It does not, however, materially alter the sense. "The profession of our hope" is just equivalent to—'the hope we profess, the acknowledgment we have made of our hope.' "Let us hold this fast;" *i.e.*, 'let us not abandon it. Let us not be induced by any worldly motive to apostatize from the faith of Christ, and thus abandon that hope of entering at last into the true holy place by the blood of His sacrifice, of which we have made a solemn acknowledgment.'

That solemn acknowledgment was made when they submitted to baptism; and to this, I apprehend, the Apostle refers when he says, "having your bodies washed with pure water." Some have supposed that the allusion is to the divers washings or immersions under the law, by which both the priests and the people were purified for approaching God in worship, and that the Apostle, as it were, says, 'As you have the substance of which the sprinkling of blood was an emblem, so you have also the substance of which the washing of water was an emblem.' I have already, however, stated to you what appear to me satisfactory reasons for considering the words before us as standing in connection, not with the injunction, "let us draw near," but with the injunction, "let us hold fast." And if this mode of connection is adopted, there can scarcely be any doubt that the reference is to Christian baptism. Submitting to Christian baptism by a Jew was a renunciation of Judaism—

it was a public and solemn acknowledgment of his hope in Christ. It was a declaration that he considered himself as one with Christ—as having died with Him, been buried with Him, been raised with Him—and of his expectation of a personal resurrection and ascension entirely on the ground of what He did and suffered, — the Just One in the room of the unjust." That this was the import of a person's submitting to baptism, seems plain from the words of the Apostle: — "Know ye not, that so many of us as were baptized into Jesus Christ were baptized into His death? Therefore we are buried with Him by baptism into death: that like as Christ was raised up from the dead by the glory of the Father, even so we also should walk in newness of life. For if we have been planted together in the likeness of His death, we shall be also in the likeness of His resurrection: knowing this, that our old man is crucified with Him, that the body of sin might be destroyed, that henceforth we should not serve sin." — "For as many of you as have been baptized into Christ have put on Christ. There is neither Jew nor Greek, there is neither bond nor free, there is neither male nor female: for ye are all one in Christ Jesus. And if ye be Christ's, then are ye Abraham's seed, and heirs according to the promise."[1] The substance, then, of the Apostle's exhortation seems to be,—'Having in your baptism made a solemn acknowledgment of your hope of eternal life through Christ Jesus, hold fast the hope which you have acknowledged, in opposition equally to the threats of persecutors and the sophistical reasonings of false teachers.'

He adds a very powerfully persuasive motive in the words which follow: — "For He is faithful who has promised." God, to give the "heirs of salvation" "strong consolation," has confirmed by an oath that declaration in reference to the everlasting priesthood of Jesus Christ, on which all their hope depends; and He cannot lie—He cannot deny Himself. He can as soon cease to exist as cease to be faithful to His promise. — He is not a man, that He should lie; nor the son of man, that He should repent." And He has proved His faithfulness in accomplishing the promise with regard to our great High Priest. He has brought Him—according to His promise, that "He would not leave His soul in the separate state, nor suffer His Holy One to see corruption,"—He has "brought Him from

[1] Rom. vi. 3–6; Gal. iii. 27–29.

the dead:" and He will in due time fulfil all the promises which He has made to His people, bringing them again from the dead, and giving them that "kingdom prepared for them before the foundation of the world." A consideration of the faithfulness of the Promiser is the principal means of strengthening faith in the promise.

Vers. 24, 25. "And let us consider one another to provoke unto love, and to good works: not forsaking the assembling of ourselves together, as the manner of some is; but exhorting one another: and so much the more, as ye see the day approaching." For the purpose of mutually confirming each other in the hope of the Gospel, the Apostle exhorts the Hebrew Christians to "consider one another, to provoke unto love and good works." Christians are not merely to be concerned about their improvement and safety as individuals, but as members of one body they are to seek to promote each other's best interests. They are to "consider each other." They are to attend to each other's wants, infirmities, temptations, and dangers, and to administer suitable assistance, advice, caution, admonition, and consolation. In this way they are to stir up each other "to love." The word "provoke" is ordinarily used in a bad sense, but here it is just equivalent to "excite." They are to act the part which is calculated to call forth in one another's bosoms the workings of that peculiar affection which all Christians have to each other. By doing offices of Christian kindness, they are to excite Christian love in return. They are required to excite each other "to good works;" i.e., I apprehend, to the "labour of love."¹ They are to "do good to all as they have opportunity," and "especially to those of the household of faith."

Such a course was calculated at once to confirm their own faith and that of their brethren. The faith of the truth, and that holy love which it produces, act and react on each other. Accordingly, the Apostle exhorts the Hebrew Christians to be regular in attending on the stated meetings for instruction and worship: "Not forsaking the assembling of yourselves together."² It is by means of the public assemblies or churches

---

¹ Heb. vi. 10.

² ἐπισυναγωγή.—perhaps in contradistinction to συναγωγή, the name for the ordinary Jewish religious assemblies, as if the new superseded the o.

of the saints that the visible profession of Christ's name is kept up in the world; and the exercises in which Christians there engage — reading, preaching the word, prayer, the Lord's Supper—are all well calculated to strengthen their faith and hope. "Some"[1] of the Hebrew Christians had become negligent in attending to this duty. The Apostle calls on his readers, instead of imitating the conduct of these persons, to "exhort one another." His meaning may be, to exhort one another to attend on these assemblies; or, generally, as chap. iii. 12, 13, to exhort one another to be "stedfast and unmoveable, always abounding in the work of the Lord."

He adds a powerful motive: "And so much the more, as ye see the day approaching." "The day" here referred to seems plainly the day of the destruction of the Jewish State and Church. That day had been foretold by many of the prophets, and with peculiar minuteness by our Lord Himself: "And He said, Take heed that ye be not deceived: for many shall come in My name, saying, I am Christ; and the time draweth near: go ye not therefore after them. But when ye shall hear of wars and commotions, be not terrified: for these things must first come to pass; but the end is not by and by. Then said He unto them, Nation shall rise against nation, and kingdom against kingdom: and great earthquakes shall be in divers places, and famines, and pestilences; and fearful sights and great signs shall there be from heaven. But before all these, they shall lay their hands on you, and persecute you, delivering you up to the synagogues, and into prisons, being brought before kings and rulers for My name's sake."[2] He assures His followers that in that awful destruction they should be preserved. But this security was only to be expected in attending to His cautions, and persevering in faith, and hope, and holiness: "Take heed that ye be not deceived: for many shall come in My name, saying, I am Christ; and the time draweth near: go ye not therefore after them." "Take heed to yourselves, lest at any time your hearts be overcharged with surfeiting, and drunkenness, and cares of this life, and so that day come upon you unawares." "But he that shall endure unto the end, the same shall be saved."[3] These events were now very near; and

---

[1] $\kappa\alpha\theta\dot{\omega}\varsigma$ ἔθος τισὶν, by *meiosis* for πολλοῖς.   [2] Luke xxi. 8-12.
[3] Luke xxi. 8, 34; Matt. xxiv. 13.

the harbingers of their coming were well fitted to quicken to holy diligence the Hebrew Christians, that they might escape the coming desolation. But the Apostle, to impress on their minds still more strongly the infinite importance of perseverance in the faith and profession of the Gospel, lays before them a peculiarly impressive view of the complete and "everlasting destruction" which awaits the final apostate in a future state.

Vers. 26, 27. "For if we sin wilfully after that we have received the knowledge of the truth, there remaineth no more sacrifice for sins, but a certain fearful looking for of judgment and fiery indignation, which shall devour the adversaries."[1]

The first point which here requires our attention is the description of the persons of whom the Apostle is speaking. That description consists of two parts. They are such as "have received the knowledge of the truth;" and such as, "after having received the knowledge of the truth, sin."

They are such as "have received the knowledge of the truth." By *the truth*, we are, without doubt, to understand Christianity, which is not only truth as opposed to falsehood and error, but—what we apprehend, probably, was chiefly in the Apostle's view—is truth, or reality, as contrasted with the shadows of the Mosaic economy. The truth, the reality, of which the shadow was given by Moses in the law, "came by Jesus Christ." The Gospel makes known to us the real High Priest, the real sacrifice, the real holy place. To "receive the knowledge of this truth," is not only to be furnished with the means of obtaining a knowledge of Christian truth, but actually to apprehend its meaning and evidence in some good measure, so as to make a credible profession of believing it. To "receive the knowledge of the truth," seems just the same thing as the "being enlightened," which is spoken of in the 6th chapter.

Now, it is taken for granted that persons who "have received the knowledge of the truth" may *sin*. The persons who are here described are persons who, "after they have received

---

[1] Vers. 26-31. These are awfully impressive words. As a learned interpreter (Carpzov) remarks, in language suggested by a noble passage of Jerome—"Non loquentem, sed tonitrua detonantem Periclea audimus Paulum, et tremimus. Horrenda expectatio judicii, irarum sævities, æterna mortis calamitas, infelix in viventis Dei manus lapsus (verba quot, tot fulmina), manent hos, qui veri cognitionem assecuti, data opera peccant."

the knowledge of the truth, *sin*." The word *sin* here is plainly used in a somewhat peculiar sense. It is descriptive not of sin generally, but of a particular kind of sin,—apostasy from the faith and profession of the truth, once known and professed. "The angels that sinned" are the apostate angels. The apostasy described is not so much an act of apostasy as a state of apostasy. It is not, 'If we have sinned, if we have apostatized;' but, 'If we *sin*, if we apostatize, if we continue in apostasy.'

They are described as not only habitually sinning, or as continuing in a state of apostasy, but as doing this *wilfully*; i.e., obstinately, determinedly, in opposition to all attempts to reclaim them. The contrast implied in the use of the word "wilfully" does not seem so much between sins committed in ignorance and sins committed knowingly, as between a temporary abandonment of the faith and profession of the Gospel, under the influence of fear, or some similar motive, and a determined, persevering, final apostasy. The character here described, then, is that of a man who has at one time obtained such a knowledge of the meaning and evidence of the Gospel as to induce him to make an open profession of Christianity, but who has as openly abandoned its profession, and lives in a state of determined apostasy.

With regard to such a person, the Apostle declares that "there remains no more sacrifice for sins." The persons immediately referred to were Jews. When they became Christians, they gave up the legal sacrifices for sin; but then, in the one sacrifice of Christ they found what infinitely more than supplied the deficiency. But, renouncing the sacrifice of Christ, what are they to do? There is no salvation without pardon—no pardon without a sacrifice for sin. In apostatizing from the faith of Christ, they have renounced all dependence on His sacrifice: and there is no other. They may return to the legal sacrifices, but these "never could take away sin;" and now that the substance is come, of which they were but the shadow, they are no longer useful even for the subsidiary purpose they once served. Jesus is the High Priest promised in the ancient oracle. It is vain to look for another; and it is equally in vain to look for His appearing a second time to offer sacrifice. To the apostate, then, "there remaineth no more sacrifice for sins."

The Apostle's assertion is not, 'If a person apostatize, there is no hope of his obtaining pardon through the one sacrifice of Christ;' but it is, 'If a person persevere in apostasy, putting away from him the one sacrifice of Christ, there is not, there cannot be, for him any other sacrifice for sin.' The apostate must perish, not because the sacrifice of Christ is not of efficacy enough to expiate even his guilt, but because, continuing in his apostasy, he will have nothing to do with that sacrifice which is the only available sacrifice for sin.

Instead of another sacrifice for sin remaining for the apostate, so that, though he give up Christ, he may yet be saved, there remains for him nothing "but a certain fearful looking for of judgment and fiery indignation, which shall devour the adversaries." The word "judgment" here, as in many other places, is equivalent to 'punishment,' to which the sinner is doomed or adjudged: James ii. 13; 2 Pet. ii. 4. When it is said that "there remains" for the apostate "a fearful looking for" of this punishment, the meaning does not seem to be that every apostate is haunted by a dreadful anticipation of coming destruction; for, though this has been the case with some apostates, it is by no means characteristic of all apostates: the meaning is, the apostate has nothing to expect but a fearful punishment.[1] He has no reason to hope for expiation and pardon, but he has reason to fear condemnation and punishment.

The epithet *certain* here, does not denote either an assured expectation, or the certainty of the punishment. It is used in the same way as in the expressions, 'a *certain* man,' 'a *certain* place,' 'a *certain* occurrence.' It is intended to suggest the idea that the punishment to be expected by the apostate is a punishment of undefined, undefinable magnitude—something that is inexpressible, inconceivable. We cannot exactly say what it is; we can only say that a certain awful punishment awaits him, the nature and limits of which cannot be fully understood by any created being. As a sinner, he is exposed to the wrath of God. He obstinately refuses to avail himself of the only "covert from this" fearful "storm," and therefore he must meet it in all its terrors. It must break on his unsheltered head. And "who knows the power of His anger?" The extent of infinite power must be measured, the depths of infinite wisdom must be

---

[1] Equivalent to ἐκδοχή κρίσεως φοβερᾶς.

fathomed, ere that awful question can be resolved. We can only say, " According to His fear, so is His wrath." The most dreadful conception comes infinitely short of the more dreadful reality. We can only say of it, 'It is a certain fearful punishment which the apostate has to expect.'

This punishment is further described as " fiery indignation." There remains for the apostate, *indignation* or wrath, even the wrath of God. God is angry with him for all his sins, and especially for the sin of apostasy ; and this " wrath of God abideth on him." He is exposed to the fearful effects of God's moral disapprobation and judicial displeasure ; and having renounced the sacrifice of Christ, he has nothing to save him from these. The displeasure of God is termed " fiery indignation," or 'indignation of fire,' to represent in a striking manner its resistless, tormenting, destroying efficacy.

It will prove its power in " devouring the adversaries." " The adversaries" here, are, I apprehend, primarily the unbelieving Jews. The Apostle does not say here, as he does elsewhere, " those that believe not,"—" those who obey not the Gospel of Christ;" but, " *the adversaries.*" The appellation is peculiarly descriptive. The unbelieving Jews were actuated by a principle of the most hostile opposition to Christ and Christianity : " Who both killed the Lord Jesus and their own prophets, and have persecuted us ; and they please not God, and are contrary to all men."[1] The " fiery indignation" of God is to " devour" these adversaries, and along with them the apostates from the faith of Christ.

It is not improbable that here, as in the passage just quoted from the Epistle to the Thessalonians, there is a reference to the awful judgments which were about to befall the unbelieving Jews, and in which the apostates were to have their full share ; but the ultimate reference seems to be to the great " day of wrath and revelation of the judgment of God," when " the Lord Jesus shall be revealed from heaven, with His mighty angels, in flaming fire, taking vengeance on them that know not God, and obey not the Gospel of our Lord Jesus Christ," who " shall be punished with everlasting destruction from the presence of the Lord, and from the glory of His power." Such was the punishment which awaited the apostate of the primitive age, and mate-

[1] 1 Thess. ii. 15.

rially the same is the punishment which awaits the apostate of every succeeding age.

In the verses which follow we have at once an illustration of the certainty and severity of the doom which awaits the apostate, and a vindication of the justice of that doom. Vers. 28, 29. "He that despised Moses' law died without mercy under two or three witnesses: of how much sorer punishment, suppose ye, shall he be thought worthy, who hath trodden under foot the Son of God, and hath counted the blood of the covenant, wherewith he was sanctified, an unholy thing, and hath done despite unto the Spirit of grace?"

The general sentiment obviously is—'If their punishment shall exceed in severity that of the despiser of Moses' law as much as their crime exceeds his in heinousness—and strict justice requires and secures this,—then it will be severe indeed.' Let us proceed now to examine these dreadful words somewhat more minutely.

The person with whom the apostate is compared, is "the despiser[1] of Moses' law." In every violation of a law there is an implied contempt of the law and the lawgiver. But "the despiser of Moses' law" is plainly not every violator of that law; since for many of its violations there were expiatory sacrifices. "The despiser," or *annuller,* "of Moses' law," is the person who acts by the law of Moses the part which the apostate does by the Gospel of Christ, who renounces its authority, who determinedly and obstinately refuses to comply with its requisitions. I cannot help thinking that the Apostle has probably a peculiar reference to the person who, having violated the law of Moses, refuses to have recourse to the appointed expiations. But whatever there may be in this, "the despiser of Moses' law" is the person who treats Moses as if he were an impostor, and refuses, obstinately refuses, to submit to his law as of divine authority.

Now, such a person under the Mosaic economy, whether a native Jew or a sojourner in the Holy Land, was doomed to death. He "died without mercy under[2] two or three witnesses;" *i.e.,* when the crime was satisfactorily proved, he was capitally

---

[1] ἀθετήσας.

[2] ἐπί,—expressive of the condition on which their condemnation and punishment depend; = the Heb. עַל־פִּי: Deut. xvii. 6, xix. 15.

punished; and it was particularly enjoined, that in such cases no pardon nor commutation of punishment should be allowed. The highest punishment man can inflict on man was in such cases uniformly to be inflicted. The best illustration of this statement of the Apostle is to be found in the law to which he refers. " If thy brother, the son of thy mother, or thy son, or thy daughter, or the wife of thy bosom, or thy friend, which is as thine own soul, entice thee secretly, saying, Let us go and serve other gods, which thou hast not known, thou, nor thy fathers; namely, of the gods of the people which are round about you, nigh unto thee, or far off from thee, from the one end of the earth even unto the other end of the earth; thou shalt not consent unto him, nor hearken unto him; neither shall thine eye pity him, neither shalt thou spare, neither shalt thou conceal him: but thou shalt surely kill him; thine hand shall be first upon him to put him to death, and afterwards the hand of all the people."—" If there be found among you, within any of thy gates which the Lord thy God giveth thee, man or woman, that hath wrought wickedness in the sight of the Lord thy God, in transgressing His covenant, and hath gone and served other gods, and worshipped them, either the sun, or moon, or any of the host of heaven, which I have not commanded; and it be told thee, and thou hast heard of it, and inquired diligently, and, behold, it be true, and the thing certain, that such abomination is wrought in Israel; then shalt thou bring forth that man or that woman, which have committed that wicked thing, unto thy gates, even that man or that woman, and shalt stone them with stones, till they die. At the mouth of two witnesses, or three witnesses, shall he that is worthy of death be put to death; but at the mouth of one witness he shall not be put to death. The hands of the witnesses shall be first upon him to put him to death, and afterward the hands of all the people: so thou shalt put the evil away from among you."[1] The justice of this law would be very readily admitted by those to whom the Apostle refers, and must be evident to every person who acknowledges the divine legation of Moses. These, then, are the principles which lie at the foundation of the Apostle's argument, that " the despiser of Moses' law" was doomed to certain death, and that it was just that he should be thus doomed.

[1] Deut. xiii. 6-9, xvii. 2-7.

He now goes on to describe the conduct of the apostate in such language as to make it plain that he is far more deeply criminal than " the despiser of the law of Moses," and thus to prepare the way for the conclusion to which he wishes to bring his readers, that he shall most certainly be far more severely punished. The apostate is one who has " trodden under foot the Son of God." The general idea is—' He has treated with the greatest conceivable contempt a personage of the highest conceivable dignity.' "The despiser of Moses' law" trampled under foot Moses as a divine messenger—the servant of God; but the apostate " tramples under foot" Jesus, who is a divine Person— " the Son of God." " Trampling under foot the Son of God" may be considered as referring generally to the dishonour done to Jesus Christ by apostasy. It is a declaration that He is an impostor,—a declaration that His Gospel is "a cunningly devised fable." But I cannot help thinking that there is a peculiar reference to the dishonour done to Christ Jesus as the great sacrifice for sin by the apostate. The sacrifice He offered was Himself. Now the apostate, in declaring that in his estimation Jesus Christ had offered no sacrifice for sin, as it were tramples on that sacred body, by the offering of which " once for all" Christ Jesus made expiation for the sins of His people. Instead of treating His sacrifice as it ought to be treated—as something of ineffable value, inconceivable efficacy—he treads it under foot as vile and valueless.

He "accounts the blood of the covenant, wherewith he was sanctified, an unholy thing." " The blood of the covenant" is obviously the blood of Christ; and it receives this name, because by the shedding of this blood the New Covenant was ratified, as the Old Covenant was by the shedding of the blood of animal sacrifices.

Interpreters have differed as to the reference of the clause, " by which he was sanctified,"—some referring it to Christ, and others to the apostate. Those who refer it to Christ explain it in this way,—' By His own blood Jesus Christ was consecrated to His office as an intercessory Priest.' Those who refer it to the apostate consider the Apostle as stating, that in some sense or other he had been sanctified by the blood of Christ. I cannot say that I am satisfied with either of these modes of interpretation. I do not think that Scripture warrants us to say that any man who finally apostatizes is sanctified by the blood of Christ in any sense, except that the legal obstacles in the way of human salvation generally were removed by the atonement He made; and though I have no doubt that by His bloodshedding our Lord was separated, set apart, sanctified, consecrated, and fitted for the performance of the functions of an interceding High Priest, I cannot distinctly apprehend the bearing which such a statement has on the Apostle's object, which is obviously to place in a strong light the aggravations of the sin of the apostate. I apprehend the word is used impersonally, and that its true meaning is, 'by which there is sanctification.' It is just equivalent to—' the sanctifying blood of the covenant.' The word "sanctify," as I have had occasion fully to show in the course of this exposition, is used in a somewhat peculiar sense in the Epistle to the Hebrews. It signifies, when used in reference to men, to do what is necessary and sufficient to secure them, who are viewed as unclean, favourable access to the holy Divinity. When the blood of Jesus Christ, by which the New Covenant is ratified, is called sanctifying blood, the meaning is, that that blood shed expiates sin—renders it just and honourable in God to pardon sin, and save the sinner; and that this blood sprinkled (*i.e.*, in plain words, the truth about this blood understood and believed), " purges the conscience from dead works," removes the jealousies of guilt, and enables us to serve God with a true heart. This is the peculiar excellence of the blood of Christ. It, and it alone, thus sanctifies.[1]

Now the apostate accounts this " blood of the covenant, by which," and by which alone, " there is sanctification, an unholy thing;" *i.e.*, a common thing, not a sacred thing,—and not only an unconsecrated thing, but a polluted thing. The apostate, instead of accounting the blood of Christ, by which the New Covenant is ratified, possessed of sanctifying virtue, looks upon it as a common, vile, polluted thing,—the blood not only of a mere man, but the blood of an impostor, who richly deserved the punishment he met with,—blood which not merely had no tendency to sanctify, but blood which polluted and rendered doubly hateful to God all who were foolish enough to place their

[1] It was with great satisfaction I found Professor Moses Stuart had come to the same conclusion as to the meaning of this phrase, translating —" the blood of the covenant, by which expiation has been made."

hopes of expiation and pardon on its having been shed in their room, and for their salvation.

The apostate is still further described as "doing despite to the Spirit of grace." "The Spirit of grace" is a Hebraism for 'the gracious, the kind, the benignant Spirit.' It has been supposed that this phrase is borrowed from Zech. xii. 10. But "the spirit of grace" there being joined with "the spirit of supplication," seems descriptive, not of the Holy Spirit personally, but of the temper He forms—'a grateful, prayerful temper.' By "the gracious Spirit," I understand that divine Person who, along with the Father and the Son, exists in the unity of the Godhead; and He is termed "the Spirit of grace," or "the gracious Spirit," to bring before our minds the benignant object of all His operations in the scheme of mercy. This benignant Spirit the apostate is represented as "doing despite to,"—as treating with indignity and insult. That Holy Spirit dwelt in "the man Christ Jesus." By that Holy Spirit numerous and most striking attestations were given to the truth of His doctrine. "God bare witness by gifts of the Holy Ghost, according to His own will." When a man in the primitive age apostatized, he necessarily joined with the scribes and Pharisees in ascribing to diabolical agency what had been effected by the influence of the Holy Ghost; than which, certainly, a greater indignity, or more atrocious insult, could not be offered to that divine Person. There can be little doubt that the person described here belongs to the class described in the 6th chapter, who are said to have been "made partakers of the Holy Ghost;" *i.e.*, to have been themselves in the possession of the supernatural gifts of the Spirit, as well as the subjects of His common operations. And certainly for such persons to ascribe the benignant operations of the Holy Ghost on themselves to infernal agency, was the most outrageous and malicious indignity of which human nature is capable.

Such, then, is the crime of the apostate. He treats with the greatest conceivable indignity two divine Persons—the Son and the Spirit of God; he "tramples under foot" Him whom angels adore; he counts polluted and polluting that which is the sole source of sanctification; he repays benignity with insult—the benignity of a divine Person with the most despiteful insult. His punishment, then, must be inconceivably severe, and absolutely certain.

This sentiment is stated by the Apostle far more energetically in the heart-appalling question that follows, than it could have been by any direct assertion : " Of how much sorer punishment, suppose ye, shall he be counted worthy? If he that despised," etc. In one point of view the despiser of the law and the apostate from the Gospel seem to stand on a level. They both wilfully renounce a sufficiently accredited divine revelation; but the aggravations attending the apostate's crime are numerous and great. " The despiser of Moses' law" despised indeed a holy man—a divine messenger; but the apostate despises the Son and Spirit of God, and acts towards them in a far more malicious and insulting manner than the contemner of Moses' law did towards that legislator. If the one deserved death, does not the other deserve damnation—destruction, " everlasting destruction, from the presence of the Lord, and from the glory of His power?" And if the punishment of " the despiser of Moses' law" was absolutely certain, can the punishment of the contemner and despiser of God's Son and Spirit be in any degree doubtful? The justice of God requires that the punishment of the apostate be awfully severe, and indubitably certain.

In the two verses which follow we have a further illustration of the awful severity and the absolute certainty of the punishment of the apostate, from the circumstance, that the declaration that a God of infinite power will punish them is made by a God of infinite veracity. Ver. 30. " For we know Him that hath said, Vengeance belongeth unto Me, I will recompense, saith the Lord. And again, The Lord shall judge His people." The quotations are made from the prophetic song of Moses,— " To Me belongeth vengeance and recompense; their foot shall slide in due time: for the day of their calamity is at hand, and the things that shall come upon them make haste. For the Lord shall judge His people, and repent Himself for His servants, when He seeth that their power is gone, and there is none shut up, or left,"[1]—and refer to the punishments which God would inflict on the wicked Israelites at their latter end. The meaning of the words is plainly,—' I *Myself* will punish them, and the punishment shall bear the impress of My omnipotence.'

The appositeness of the second quotation may not at first

---

[1] Deut. xxxii. 35, 36.

sight appear so plainly. It may seem a promise rather than a threatening. It is indeed a promise, and not a threatening; and I apprehend, that both in the place where it originally occurs and in the passage before us, it is brought forward for the purpose of comforting the minds of those who continued stedfast in their attachment to their God,—assuring them that while He punished rebels and apostates, He would watch over their interests, and protect them from dangers which threatened to overwhelm them. In the prophetic writings generally, the punishment of the enemies of God and the deliverance of His people are closely connected. The same event is very often vengeance to the former and deliverance to the latter. This was the case with the fearful events which were impending over the impenitent and apostate Jews, and to which, in the whole of this passage, I think it highly probable that the Apostle has an immediate reference. The words admit, however, of another interpretation. The word *judge* is not unfrequently used as equivalent to 'punish,' or ' take vengeance:' Gen. xv. 14; 2 Chron. xx. 12; Ezek. vii. 3. In this case it is equivalent to—' Beware of supposing that the relation you think you stand in to God will protect you. "Judgment will begin at the house of God." "You only have I known of all the families of the earth; therefore will I punish you for your iniquities." Whoever escapes, you shall not escape:' Matt. xi. 21-25; Luke xii. 47, 48.

The words, "We know Him that hath said," are just a very emphatic manner of saying, ' We know His power to destroy: and we know also that "His word is quick and powerful, sharper than a two-edged sword." We know that "He is not a man, that He should lie; nor the son of man, that He should repent: hath He said, and shall He not do it? or hath He spoken, and shall He not make it good?"'

The same sentiment, as to the omnipotence of God to punish, is very strikingly repeated in the 31st verse. "It is a fearful thing to fall into the hands of the living God."[1] "Who knows the power of His wrath? According to His fear, so is His wrath." The scriptural description of the final punishment of the enemies of God is enough to make the ears of every one

---

[1] ἐμπεσεῖν εἰς τὰς χεῖρας is a Hebraistic mode of expression,—נָפַל בְּיַד. In classic Greek it would be—*i. ὑπὸ τὰς χεῖρας*. Ζῶντος, ' powerful, ever-living.'

that heareth it to tingle. Well may we say, with our Lord,—" Be not afraid of them that kill the body, and after that have no more that they can do: but I will forewarn you whom ye shall fear: Fear Him, which, after He hath killed, hath power to cast into hell; yea, I say unto you, Fear Him."[1] Such is the doom, the certain doom, of the man who lives and dies an apostate. Let none despair. It is not the act of apostasy, it is the state of apostasy, that is certainly damnable. Let all beware of being " high-minded." " Let them fear, lest a promise being left them, any man should seem to come short of it." Let them guard against every approach to apostasy. The grand preservative from apostasy is to grow in " the knowledge of our Lord and Saviour Jesus Christ;" and to " add to our faith virtue, knowledge, temperance, patience, godliness, brotherly-kindness, and charity."[2] It is in doing these things that we are assured that we shall " never fall," and that " so an entrance shall be ministered to us abundantly into the kingdom of our Lord and Saviour Jesus Christ."

To apprehend distinctly the meaning, to feel fully the force, of the exhortations contained in the paragraph which follows, it is necessary that the circumstances of those to whom they were originally addressed should be before the view of the mind.

This Epistle was written a few years before the final destruction of the Jewish civil and ecclesiastical polity by the Romans. This was a season of peculiar trial to the Christians in Judea. Christianity was now no longer a new thing. Its doctrines, though they had lost nothing of their truth and importance, no longer were possessed of the charm of novelty; and their miraculous attestations, though to a reflecting person equally satisfactory as ever, were from their very commonness less fitted than at first to arrest attention, and make a strong impression on the mind. The long-continued hardships to which the believing Hebrews were exposed from their unbelieving countrymen, were clearly fitted to shake the stability of their faith, and to damp the ardour of their zeal. Jesus Christ had plainly intimated to them, that ere that generation had passed away He would appear in a remarkable manner, for the punishment of His enemies, and the deliverance of His faithful followers. The greater part of that generation had passed away,

[1] Luke xii. 4, 5. [2] 2 Pet. i. 5-7.

and Jesus had not yet come, according to His promise. The scoffers were asking, with sarcastic scorn, "Where is the promise of His coming?" and "hope deferred" was sickening the hearts of those who were "looking for Him." The "perilous times" spoken of by our Lord had arrived. Multitudes of pretenders to Messiahship had made their appearance, and had " deceived many." Many of the followers of Jesus were offended— many apostatized, and hated and betrayed their brethren. "Iniquity abounded, and the love of many," who did not cast off the Christian name, " waxed cold."

In these circumstances, it was peculiarly necessary that the disciples of Christ should be fortified against the temptations to apostasy, and urged to perseverance in the faith and profession of the Gospel. This is the grand object of this Epistle, and every part of it is plainly intended and calculated to gain this object. The whole of the doctrinal part of the Epistle is occupied in showing the pre-eminent excellence of Christianity, by displaying the matchless glory of Christ; and the greater portion of the practical part of the Epistle is employed in stating and enforcing the exhortation to remain "stedfast and unmoveable" in their attachment to their Lord, in their belief of the doctrines, the observance of the ordinances, and the practice of the duties of their " most holy faith."

In the preceding context the Apostle has most impressively urged on their minds the peculiar advantages to which their new faith had raised them as to favourable and delightful intercourse with God, and the fearful consequences of apostasy, as irresistible arguments to "hold fast their profession;" and in the passage which lies before us for interpretation, in order to gain the same end, he calls on them to recollect their past experience in reference to Christianity,—to reflect on all they had suffered for it, and on all which it had done for them under their sufferings, —and to pause and ponder before, by apostasy, they rendered useless all the labours and sorrows they had endured, and blasted all the fair hopes which they had once so fondly cherished, and which had enabled them to bear, not only patiently, but joyfully, all the trials to which they had been exposed. Vers. 32-34. "But call to remembrance the former days, in which, after ye were illuminated, ye endured a great fight of afflictions; partly, whilst ye were made a gazing-stock both by reproaches and afflictions; and partly, whilst ye became companions of them that were so used. For ye had compassion of me in my bonds, and took joyfully the spoiling of your goods, knowing in yourselves that ye have in heaven a better and an enduring substance."

The period to which the Apostle wishes to recall their minds is that which immediately followed their illumination, or, in other words, their obtaining the knowledge of the truth. That state of ignorance and error in which they were previously, is figuratively represented as a state of darkness; and when, by the statement of Christian truth and its evidence, they were delivered from ignorance and error, they are said to have been enlightened.

On their being enlightened, they had to " endure a great fight of afflictions." It is not improbable that the Apostle refers to the severe and general persecution which followed the death of Stephen, and with which, as he had taken a very active part in it himself, he was intimately acquainted; and to that which took place not long afterwards by Herod, when "he slew James, the brother of John, with the sword." The variety and severity of the trials to which at that period Jewish believers were exposed, are very strikingly expressed in the phrase, "great fight of afflictions." It is not improbable that, in using the word *endure*, the Apostle meant to convey the idea, not only that they had been exposed to these varied and severe trials, but that they had worthily sustained them—they had *endured* the fight. They had persevered till the conflict was finished, and they had come off conquerors. That is plainly the meaning of the word when the Apostle James says, " Behold, we count them happy who endure."

In these afflictions they had been involved both personally and by their sympathy with their suffering brethren. They "endured a great fight of afflictions, partly, when they were made a gazing-stock,"—made public spectacles, as malefactors, who in the theatres were often made, in the presence of the assembled people, to fight with each other, or with wild beasts. This was literally the case with some of the Christians, though I do not know that any of the Hebrew Christians were thus treated. The idea is—'set up as objects of the malignant and scornful notice of the public.' This they were by the "reproaches" which were cast on them. These reproaches were of two kinds : false charges were brought against them, and their faith and hope were ridiculed—their character and conduct as Christians held up to scorn. By " afflictions," as distinguished from " reproaches," we are to understand sufferings in person, such as torture of various kinds. And as many of the Hebrew Christians had been " made gazing-stocks" by personally undergoing their trials, so also had they become so by avowing themselves "the companions of those who were so used." Genuine Christians feel towards one another as brethren; and when they see their Christian brethren suffering for the cause of Christ, they naturally, though not directly, attach themselves to, take part with, their suffering brethren, and thus come in for a share of the public scorn which is poured on them.

The Apostle particularly notices one instance in which they " became companions of those who were thus used:" " For ye had compassion of me in my bonds." Supposing these words to be the genuine reading, they seem to refer to the kind attention shown to Paul by some of the Hebrew Christians when in *bonds* at Jerusalem and Cesarea.[1] But, according to the best critics, the true reading is—" for ye had compassion on those who were bound," or " on the prisoners."[2] Those among the Hebrew Christians who were not themselves imprisoned, became companions with them by sympathizing with them, owning them as their brethren, and doing everything which lay in their power to alleviate their sufferings.

The Apostle, having noticed the sufferings to which they had been exposed in their reputation and persons, and by sympathy with their suffering brethren, now calls to their mind the sufferings they had sustained in their property, and the manner in which they had borne them. They were " spoiled of their goods,"—they were unjustly deprived of their property; and when they were so, instead of repining, or thinking of retaining their property by giving up their religion, they " took the spoiling of their goods joyfully." They were as it were glad that they had this means of showing their attachment to Christ

---

[1] Comp. Phil. i. 13, 16; Col. iv. 18.

[2] Besides the external evidence for δεσμίοις, there is internal evidence also. Συμπαθεῖν δεσμοῖς is a strange and unprecedented expression : μνημονεύειν τῶν δεσμῶν is quite another thing.

and His cause—they counted themselves honoured in being called on to make such a sacrifice.

This mode of feeling did not arise from stoical apathy, or from enthusiastic feeling: it arose from their persuasion that the religion which called on them to sacrifice their worldly property secured them in a far more valuable property. In some of the most ancient MSS. the words, "in heaven," are wanting. On the supposition that they do not form a part of the original text, the meaning is—"Ye took joyfully the spoiling of your goods, knowing that in yourselves you had a better and enduring substance;" *i.e.*, 'You cheerfully parted with your external property, because you knew that your most valuable and permanent property was within you. They could not take from you the love of God—the comforts of the Holy Ghost—the hope of eternal life. If they could have taken these from you—and these you would cast from you if you renounce Christianity—they would have made you poor indeed; but whatever else they might take from you, if they left you these, you knew that you were *rich*, rich for ever.'

If the words, "in heaven," be considered as belonging to the text, then the meaning is somewhat different. 'Ye took joyfully the spoiling of your goods, knowing in yourselves'—*i.e.*, being fully persuaded—'that whatever the world may think, this is the truth, that in heaven there is laid up for you[1] true and abiding substance.'[2] Worldly wealth scarcely deserves the name of *substance*: it is, like all things worldly, unsubstantial; and it is, like all things worldly, fading and shortlived. But celestial wealth is real substance, and permanent as real. "Moth and rust do not" there "corrupt: thieves do not" there "break through, nor steal." The man who is fully persuaded that he has in heaven this substance will not grieve very much at the loss of worldly substance in any circumstances; but when the giving up of the latter is required in order to the obtaining of the former, he will show that he counts it but as the dust in the balance, and will "joyfully take the spoiling of his goods."

---

[1] ἑαυτοῖς, which is the true reading, expresses peculiar property—'that as *your own* you have,' etc.

[2] The natural order of the words seems to be—κρείττονα ὕπαρξιν καὶ μένουσαν ἐν οὐρανοῖς; but μένουσαν, as expressing the chief idea, is placed behind. Their worldly substance had been found anything but μένουσα.

Such, then, are the things which the Apostle wishes the Hebrew Christians to "call to remembrance."

It is easy to see how the calling of these things to remembrance was calculated to serve his purpose—to guard them from apostasy, and establish them in the faith and profession of the Gospel. It is as if he had said, 'Why shrink from suffering for Christianity now? Were you not exposed to suffering from the beginning? When you first became Christians, did you not willingly undergo sufferings on account of it? And is not Christianity as worthy of being suffered for as ever? Is not Jesus the same yesterday, to-day, and for ever? Did not the faith and hope of Christianity formerly support you under your sufferings, and make you feel that they were but the light afflictions of a moment? and are they not as able to support you now as they were then? Has the substance in heaven become less real, or less enduring? and have you not as good evidence now as you had then that to the persevering Christian such treasure is laid up? Are you willing to lose all the benefit of the sacrifices you have made, and the sufferings you have sustained? and they will all go for nothing if you endure not to the end.' These are considerations all naturally suggested by the words of the Apostle, and all well calculated to induce them to "hold fast the profession of their faith without wavering."

Accordingly, he adds, ver. 35, "Cast not therefore away your confidence, which has great recompense of reward." The "confidence" of the Christian Hebrews is just a general name for the open, consistent, fearless adherence to Christianity amid all the difficulties they had been exposed to. This they were to hold fast, and not to cast away. If they shrunk from the contest, and became cowards, this was to cast it away. Instead of casting it away, they were to hold it fast—to continue "stedfast and unmoveable," in nothing moved by their adversaries; for it "has great recompense of reward;"—*i.e.*, a steady, uniform, persevering adherence to Christ will be abundantly rewarded. The sufferings, however great, "were not worthy to be compared with the glory which was to be revealed." Faithful is He who hath said, "Blessed are ye when men shall revile you, and persecute you, and shall say all manner of evil against you falsely, for My sake. Rejoice, and be exceeding glad; for great is your reward in heaven."

But then the reward can be obtained only by holding fast this confidence—by adhering steadily and perseveringly to Christ and His cause. It is "he who endures to the end that shall be saved." This is the sentiment contained in the 36th verse: "For ye have need of patience, that, after ye have done the will of God, ye might receive the promise."

The word "patience" properly signifies 'perseverance;'[1] and the phrase, "ye have need of perseverance," is just equivalent to—'ye must persevere,' "that, having done the will of God, ye may receive the promise." "The promise" here is the blessing promised; to receive the promise, is to obtain the promised blessing.[2] Now the only way of obtaining the promised blessing is to persevere in doing the will of God. It is by "adding to faith, virtue; and to virtue, knowledge; and to knowledge, temperance; and to temperance, patience; and to patience, godliness; and to godliness, brotherly-kindness; and to brotherly-kindness, charity;"—it is in doing these things that we are secured that "we shall never fall," and it is thus that there "will be ministered to us abundantly an entrance into the everlasting kingdom of our Lord and Saviour Jesus Christ."

The Apostle encourages the Christian Hebrews to persevere, from the consideration that their Lord's promise to appear in their behalf was inviolably faithful, and would soon be accomplished. Ver. 37. "For yet a little while, and He that shall come will come, and will not tarry."

In these words there is an allusion to words employed by the prophet Habakkuk; but it is a mere allusion.[3] "He that shall come," or 'He that is coming,' was an appellation given by the Jews to the Messiah. It is here used plainly in reference to some "promise of His coming." It cannot refer to His first coming in the flesh, for that was already past. It cannot refer to His second coming in the flesh, for that is even yet future,

---

[1] ὑπομονή: Luke xxi. 19; 1 Thess. i. 3; Matt. x. 22, xxiv. 13.

[2] Τὴν μεγάλην μισθαποδοσίαν, ver. 35; τὴν ὕπαρξιν ἐν οὐρανοῖς, ver. 34; ἐπαγγελία, res promissa, Heb. vi. 15, ix. 15, xi. 39.

[3] Habakkuk's words (ii. 3, 4), according to the LXX., are: ἐὰν ὑστερήσῃ, ὑπόμεινον αὐτόν, ὅτι ἐρχόμενος ἥξει καὶ οὐ μὴ χρονίσῃ. Ἐὰν ὑποστείληται, οὐκ εὐδοκεῖ ἡ ψυχή μου ἐν αὐτῷ, ὁ δὲ δίκαιος ἐκ πίστεώς μου ζήσεται. The writer uses the words of the prophet as the vehicle of his own ideas.

after the lapse of nearly eighteen centuries; whereas the coming here mentioned was a coming just at hand. But though these are the only comings of the Son of God in the flesh, they are by no means the only comings that are mentioned in Scripture. There are particularly two comings mentioned in the New Testament: His coming in the dispensation of the Holy Spirit; and His coming for the destruction of His Jewish enemies, and the deliverance of His persecuted people. The first is referred to in John xiv. 18, 19: "I will not leave you comfortless: I will come to you. Yet a little while, and the world seeth Me no more; but ye see Me: because I live, ye shall live also." The second, in Matt. xxiv. 27: "For as the lightning cometh out of the east, and shineth even unto the west; so shall also the coming of the Son of man be." It is to the last of these that there is a reference in the passage before us. Jesus Christ had promised, that when He came to execute vengeance on His enemies of the Jewish nation, His friends should not only be preserved from the calamity, but obtain deliverance from their persecutions: "When these things begin to come to pass, then look up, and lift up your heads; for your redemption draweth nigh."[1] This coming was to take place before that generation passed away. More than thirty years had already elapsed; and within eight or nine years—"a little while"—the prediction was accomplished. It is as if the Apostle had said, 'Hold out but a little longer, and the coming of the Lord, both as showing the fearful doom of His enemies and His faithfulness in reference to the promise made to His friends, will free you from your present temptations to apostasy.'

The Apostle concludes this paragraph by asserting at once the necessity of faith—continued faith—in order to salvation, and the certainty of apostasy leading to destruction. The words in the 38th verse are also an allusion to the words of Habakkuk, but they do not seem quoted in the way of argument: "Now, the just shall live by faith: but if any man draw back, My soul shall have no pleasure in him." The words, "The just by faith shall live," may either mean, 'The just or righteous man shall live by faith as the influencing principle of his conduct,'—as the Apostle says, "The life I live in the flesh, I live by the faith of the Son of God;" or

---

[1] Luke xxi. 28.

they may signify, "The man who is just by faith, shall live," *i.e.*, shall be saved, shall obtain eternal life. The passage is quoted and reasoned from by the Apostle in two passages: Rom. i. 16, 17, "For I am not ashamed of the Gospel of Christ: for it is the power of God unto salvation to every one that believeth; to the Jew first, and also to the Greek. For therein is the righteousness of God revealed from faith to faith: as it is written, The just shall live by faith." And Gal. iii. 11, "But that no man is justified by the law in the sight of God, it is evident: for, The just shall live by faith." In both these passages, the words are to be understood in the last of these senses; and though either of them will afford a suitable meaning in the place before us, I think it most likely that the Apostle uses them in the same way as in other places of his writings. It is the man justified by believing that is saved; and the man justified by believing is not the man who *has* believed merely, but the man who continues believing: that is the man who " shall live"—who obtains true, permanent happiness.

"But if any man draw back, My soul shall have no pleasure in him." The word, *any man*, is a supplement, and has been added to prevent any inference unfavourable to the perseverance of the saints from being drawn from this passage. It is not right, however, to add to the word of God, even to defend truth.[1] If the man "justified by faith" were to "draw back," God's "soul could have no pleasure in him." This is in no way inconsistent with the doctrine of the perseverance of the elect, which appears to us very plainly taught in Scripture. If God has "chosen them in Christ before the foundation of the world," and " predestinated them to the adoption of children to Himself"—if He has "called them according to His purpose," and if they are really "washed, and sanctified, and justified in the name of the Lord Jesus, and by the Spirit of our God"—if there is " an inheritance laid up in heaven for them," and if they are "kept to it by the power of God, through faith unto salvation"—if there be an inseparable connection between being foreknown and predestinated, and being called, and justified, and glorified,—then it is evident that they must "persevere" in faith and holiness "unto the end," and at last "receive the end of their faith, even the salvation of their souls." But it should never be forgotten that

[1] Bloomfield's long note here deserves to be consulted.

the Scripture doctrine of the perseverance of the elect is one thing, and the application of it to individuals quite another thing. No elect person can know that he is an elect person till he believe the Gospel; or that he shall "persevere unto the end," but while he is actually persevering in faith and holiness. The question is not, whether the elect shall persevere; that is a clearly revealed truth; but the question is, Am I among the number? This I cannot know but by believing, and persevering in believing, and in the necessary results of believing: adding to my faith virtue, knowledge, temperance, patience, godliness, brotherly-kindness, and charity. Yet it is perfectly consistent with this for me to believe that if I "draw back," God's "soul will have no pleasure" in me; and the faith of this is just one of the appropriate means to prevent my drawing back.

"But," says the Apostle, in the spirit of Christian charity, which "hopeth all things," on the principle that the Hebrew Christians were what they professed to be—ver. 39: "We are not of them who draw back to perdition"[1]—among those who, having apostatized, shall perish; "but of them who believe to the saving of the soul,"[2]—*i.e.*, who believe straightforward till the soul is saved—who continue to the end, and, continuing to the end, are saved. This passage, though containing some things peculiar to the state of the Hebrew Christians, is in its substance plainly applicable to Christians in all countries and in all ages.

The Apostle now, for the illustration and enforcement of his exhortation, brings forward a great variety of instances, from the history of former ages, in which *faith* had enabled individuals to perform very difficult duties, endure very severe trials, and obtain very important blessings. The principles of the Apostle's exhortation are plainly these: 'They who turn back, turn back unto perdition. It is only they who persevere in believing that obtain the salvation of the soul. Nothing but a persevering faith can enable a person, through a constant continuance in

---

[1] 'Ἡμεῖς οὐκ ἐσμὲν ὑποστολῆς εἰς ἀπώλειαν. Many interpreters supply υἱοί or τέκνα; but this is not necessary. We do not belong to the apostasy—the apostates doomed to destruction.

[2] 'Ἡμεῖς ἐσμὲν πίστεως εἰς περιποίησιν ψυχῆς. We belong to *the faith*—the believers, destined to obtain " the salvation that is in Christ with eternal glory." Kypke considers the phrase as = ἡμεῖς οὐκ ἐσμὲν (ἐξ) ἀ.—ἀλλ' (ἐκ) π., and considers οἱ ἐκ πίστεως, Gal. iii. 7; τὸν ἐκ π., Rom. iii. 26; οἱ ἐξ ἐριθείας, Rom. ii. 8, as parallel modes of expression.

well-doing, and a patient, humble submission to the will of God, to obtain that glory, honour, and immortality which the Gospel promises. Nothing but a persevering faith can do this; and a persevering faith can do it, as is plain from what it has done in former ages.'

The Apostle's illustration of the efficacy of faith in enabling the believer to perform duty, endure trial, and obtain blessings, is prefaced by a remark or two explicatory of the sense in which he employs the word *faith* in this discussion. Chap. xi. 1. "Now faith is the substance of things hoped for, the evidence of things not seen."

Faith is in the New Testament employed sometimes to signify the act or state of the mind which we call belief, and sometimes the object of the mind in this state or act—the thing believed. It is here obviously employed in the first sense, as equivalent to 'believing.' Now what, according to the Apostle, is faith, or believing? It is "the substance of things hoped for, the evidence of things not seen." I have always felt it difficult to attach distinct ideas to these English words. They have generally been considered as intended to express the following sentiment:—'Faith gives, as it were, a real subsistence in the mind to things hoped for; it makes evident things which are not seen—it gives a present existence to things future, a visible form to things unseen. A promise is made of future good—a revelation of something not discoverable by sense or reason. To the unbeliever the promised good, the revealed truths, are an unsubstantial vision—mere creatures of the imagination; to the believer they are substantial realities.' This is no doubt truth; but I cannot help thinking these ideas are rather put into the words than brought out of them.[1] Taking the English words in their ordinary meaning: Believing a promise respecting future good, is not the substance of that good; nor is believing a revelation with respect to things unseen, the evidence on which I believe. The act of faith or believing, the object of faith or truth in reference to what is future or unseen, and the ground of faith, or evidence, are obviously three completely distinct things; and without the greatest confusion of thought, one of them cannot be mistaken for any of the two other.

[1] Kuinoel says of this exegesis, "Arguta interpretatio nec a simplicitate commendabilis."

The word translated "substance" occurs only five times in the New Testament, and all these instances are in the writings of the Apostle Paul. In one case, Heb. i. 3, it is translated *person;* but that passage is plainly altogether inapplicable to the illustration of the phrase before us. In the other three places where it occurs—2 Cor. ix. 4, xi. 17; Heb. iii. 14—it is translated *confidence;* and that, too, is the reading in the margin in the present instance. I have little doubt that that word expresses the Apostle's idea. 'Faith, or believing, is a confidence respecting things hoped for.' The word translated "evidence" is derived from a verb which signifies 'to convince;' and its natural and most obvious meaning is, 'conviction.' It occurs only in one other place in the New Testament—2 Tim. iii. 16, where I think there is little doubt that its meaning is 'conviction.' "All Scripture is profitable for doctrine, for reproof,"—rather, ' for conviction,' *i.e.*, for teaching men what is true, and for showing them that it is true. This, I apprehend, is its meaning here : ' Faith is a conviction in reference to things not seen.' This, then, is the Apostle's account of faith : ' It is a confidence respecting things hoped for; it is a conviction respecting things not seen.' A promise is made respecting future good. I am satisfied that He who promises is both able and willing to perform His promise. I believe it; and in believing it, I have a confidence respecting the things which I hope for. A revelation is made respecting what is not evident either to my sense or my reason. I am satisfied that this revelation comes from One who cannot be deceived, and who cannot deceive. I believe it ; and in believing it, I have a conviction in reference to things which are not seen. Faith in reference to events which are past, is belief of testimony with regard to them ; faith in reference to events which are future, is belief of promises with regard to them.

This "confidence respecting things hoped for," founded on a divine promise—this " conviction respecting things unseen"—is the grand spring of dutiful exertion, and dutiful submission ; it is this, and this alone, that can induce a man to persevere in doing and suffering the will of God, till in due time the promised blessing is obtained. That it had been so in past ages, is the proposition which the Apostle is about to prove and illustrate by a numerous induction of particular instances ; and he introduces them by remarking generally, that by this faith the ancient saints had been enabled to do, and suffer, and obtain, so as to have their names, and services, and trials, and attainments honourably recorded in the Book of God. Ver. 2. "For by it the elders obtained a good report."

For is here obviously a mere connective particle, equivalent to *moreover*. The words do not contain in them any reason for what is stated in the previous verse. The word "elders" is used both in the Old and New Testament as a title of office; but here it is plainly equivalent to 'ancients,' and refers to the same persons who are called "the fathers"[1] in the first verse of the Epistle. By means of their faith these good men performed actions, sustained trials, and obtained blessings, of which we have an account in the Book of God. Thus on account of their faith they are favourably testified of by God, or have "obtained a good report." The reference does not seem to be chiefly, if at all, to the high opinion entertained of them by their descendants, but to the honourable record which God has given of them, and to which the Apostle is about more particularly to turn his attention.[2] We would have naturally expected that the Apostle should now immediately proceed to bring forward one of these ancients, as an illustration of the efficacy of faith in enabling men to do duty, sustain trial, and obtain blessings. But instead of this, he interposes an observation, the object of which seems to be, to illustrate by an example what he meant by faith being "a conviction in reference to things not seen."

Ver. 3. "Through faith we understand that the worlds were framed[3] by the word of God; so that things which are seen were not made of things which do appear." The particular manner of the creation of the world is an object of faith. It is one of the unseen things. We did not witness it. Reason might perhaps have discovered, what when discovered it can satisfactorily prove, that the world was created, and created by God; but how the world was created, whether out of nothing or out of pre-existent materials, reason could say nothing. God has given us a revelation on this subject, and our knowledge rises out of our belief of that revelation. It is because we be-

---

[1] πατέρες.

[2] Ebrard considers the words as = 'were testified to in reference to their faith,' *i.e.*, as being believers. This is probably the true exegesis.

[3] καταρτίζειν, parare, creare, = ποιεῖν. Ps. lxxiii. 16.

lieve what we find written in the first chapter of Genesis, that we know that "in the beginning" God created the universe by merely commanding it to be. The concluding clause of this verse is very obscure: "So that the things which are seen were not made of things that do appear."[1] This, then, is an illustration of what faith is, viewed as a "conviction in reference to things not seen." I know that God created the world out of nothing; but how do I know? I did not see it; but God has told me so in a well-accredited revelation, which I believe; and by believing it, or by faith, "I understand that the worlds were framed by the word of God."[2]

The Apostle now proceeds to give us an account of the efficacy of faith in enabling men to perform duties, endure trials, and obtain benefits, as exemplified in the experience of some of

---

[1] Many interpreters, following the Vulgate, Chrysostom, Theodoret, Theophylact, and Œcumenius, think that μὴ ἐκ φαινομένων stands for ἐκ μὴ φαινομένων. Chrysostom's words are, δῆλόν ἐστι ὅτι ἐξ οὐκ ὄντων τὰ ὄντα ἐποίησεν ὁ Θεός, ἐκ τῶν μὴ φαινομένων τὰ φαινόμενα, ἐκ τῶν μὴ ὑφεστώτων τὰ ὑφεστῶτα. In support of these views, they assert that such transpositions are common in the best writers, and that the Hebrews were in the habit of calling a thing not existing, לֹא נִמְצָא, οὐχ εὑρισκόμενον ; and they quote as a parallel passage, 2 Macc. vii. 28, οὐκ ἐξ ὄντων ἐποίησεν αὐτά (viz., the heaven and the earth, and all things in them). On the other hand, Beza, Schmid, Storr, Schulz, Böhme, Winer, and Kuinoel, consider this transposition as arbitrary, and think that the particle μὴ should be connected with γεγονέναι. The meaning in this case is, 'The world exists by the will of God; so that it is not formed of pre-existent matter, but called into being, when there was nothing but God.' We have the same sentiment, 2 Macc. vii. 28, ἀξιῶ σε, τέκνον, ἀναβλέψαντα εἰς τὸν οὐρανὸν καὶ τὴν γῆν, καὶ τὰ ἐν αὐτοῖς πάντα ἰδόντα, γνῶναι, ὅτι οὐκ ἐξ ὄντων ἐποίησεν αὐτὰ ὁ Θεός, καὶ τὸ τῶν ἀνθρώπων γένος οὕτως γεγένηται. Calvin, usually so judicious in his interpretations, for the sake of an ingenious notion, as Tholuck justly says, departs from the prevalent and correct explanation. He connects ἐκ with the verb, forces on τὰ βλεπόμενα the signification of 'mirror,' and translates, "fide intelligimus aptata esse secula verbo Dei, ut non apparentium (the τὰ ἀόρατα of Rom. i. 20) specula fierent."

[2] Rational as the doctrine is, I apprehend no man ever held it who did not owe it to revelation. Thales, Plato, Aristotle, and other eminent philosophers, indulged in visionary speculations about the creation of the world, very different indeed from the view which "He who made it, and revealed His work to Moses," has given. The opinions of the ancient philosophers may be reduced to two. They either thought that the world had existed from eternity, or that its materials were eternal, which the Divinity at some very remote period had put into order.

those ancients of whom God in His word has, on account of their faith, given a favourable testimony. The first individual in whose history the Apostle finds an illustration of the beneficial efficacy of believing is Abel. Ver. 4. "By faith Abel offered unto God a more excellent sacrifice than Cain, by which he obtained witness that he was righteous, God testifying of his gifts; and by it he, being dead, yet speaketh."

The history to which the Apostle refers is to be found Gen. iv. 1–5: "And Adam knew Eve his wife; and she conceived, and bare Cain, and said, I have gotten a man from the Lord. And she again bare his brother Abel. And Abel was a keeper of sheep, but Cain was a tiller of the ground. And in process of time it came to pass, that Cain brought of the fruit of the ground an offering unto the Lord. And Abel, he also brought of the firstlings of his flock, and of the fat thereof. And the Lord had respect unto Abel, and to his offering: but unto Cain, and to his offering, He had not respect. And Cain was very wroth, and his countenance fell." Both Cain and Abel offered sacrifice; but Abel offered a more excellent sacrifice. It has been supposed by many interpreters, that the word translated *more excellent*[1]—properly signifying, 'fuller, larger, more abundant'—refers to Abel's offering an expiatory sacrifice, in addition to the eucharistic sacrifice, which alone Cain presented. It has been thought by others that the Apostle's meaning is, that the sacrifice of Abel was in itself a more valuable one, consisting of animals, than that of Cain, which consisted of vegetables. We are rather disposed to think that the meaning is, generally, 'Abel's sacrifice was a better, a more valuable, a more availing sacrifice, than Cain's.' It better answered the end of a sacrifice, which is to be acceptable to God. How it was so, will appear by and by.

It was by faith that Abel offered a more acceptable sacrifice than Cain. Faith throughout the whole of this chapter is the belief of a divine revelation. It is plain, then, that a revelation had been made both to Cain and Abel respecting the duty of offering sacrifice, and the acceptable method of performing that duty. Though we have no particular account of the institution of sacrifice, the theory of its originating in express divine appointment is the only tenable one. The idea of expressing re-

[1] πλείονα.

ligious feelings, or of expiating sin, by shedding the blood of animals, could never have entered into the mind of man. We read that God clothed our first parents with the skins of animals; and by far the most probable account of this matter is, that these were the skins of animals which He had commanded them to offer in sacrifice.[1] We have already seen, in our illustrations of the ninth chapter, ver. 16, that all divine covenants, all merciful arrangements in reference to fallen man, have been ratified by sacrifice. The declaration of mercy contained in the first promise seems to have been accompanied with the institution of expiatory sacrifice. And expiatory sacrifice, when offered from a faith in the divine revelation in reference to it, was ac-

[1] "It is easy to be demonstrated," says Hallett, "that sacrifices owed their original to the will and appointment of God. The Apostle says, as Moses said before him, that Abel's sacrifice was acceptable to God. But it would not have been acceptable if it had not been of divine institution, according to that plain, obvious, and eternal maxim of all *true* religion, Christian, Mosaic, and natural, ' In vain do they worship God, teaching for doctrines the commandments of men,' Mark vii. 7. If there be any truth in this maxim, Abel would have worshipped God in vain, and God would have had no respect to his offering, if his sacrificing had been merely a commandment of his father Adam, or an invention of his own. The divine acceptance, therefore, is a demonstration of a divine institution."—
" Anything that has been answered to the argument for the divine institution of sacrifice, taken from this passage, is," as Dr M'Crie remarks, " extremely futile. The words of Episcopius are self-contradictory, and even ridiculous : ' Abel fide sola, nullo præcepto divino adductus, *i.e.*, rationis rectæ solius instinctu, Deum judicavit colendum esse rebus quas habebat in peculio suo optimis." *Instit. Theol.* lib. i. cap. viii. § 3. That must be fancy, not faith, which has a respect to no precept or word of God. Is it then the same thing to act from faith and from the dictates of right reason? This is not only glaringly untheological, but unphilosophical also. Nor is the attempt of the learned Spencer to elude the force of this argument more successful. He describes the faith of Abel to have been a firm persuasion, deeply fixed in his mind, as to the favourable disposition of God to men, which caused him to form his conduct by the rules of piety. He adds, that he and the rest of the patriarchs offered sacrifice ' from a certain pious simplicity of mind (ex pia quadam simplicitate).' But the Apostle does not speak of any general persuasion which influenced Abel's worship ; but he asserts that faith was specially exercised by him in the act of offering this sacrifice, and that it was this which rendered it more excellent than Cain's. As to this *pia simplicitas*, it is degrading to the patriarchs to impute it to them, although this is often done by persons who, boasting of their own superior light, have become ' vain in their imaginations.'"—PHILISTOR. *Christian Magazine for* 1803, vol. vii., pp. 407, 408.

ceptable to God, both as the appointed expression of conscious guilt and ill desert, and of the hope of mercy, and as an act of obedience to the divine will.

It would appear that this revelation was not believed by Cain, that he did not see and feel the need of expiatory sacrifice, and that his religion consisted merely in an acknowledgment of the Deity as the author of the benefits which he enjoyed. Abel, on the other hand, did believe the revelation. He readily acknowledges himself a sinner, and expresses his penitence and his hope of forgiveness in the way of God's appointment. Believing what God had said, he did what God had enjoined;—he brought the sacrifice God had appointed, and offered it in the way in which He had appointed it to be offered. What was the extent of Abel's knowledge of the nature and design of expiatory sacrifice, we cannot tell. All that we know, and all that is necessary for the Apostle's argument, is this: Abel, believing what God revealed, did what God commanded, and obtained evidence that God was pleased with him and his services; while, on the other hand, Cain, not believing what God had revealed, did not do what God had commanded, and instead of receiving evidence that God was pleased with him, had a clear demonstration that He was displeased with him.[1]

On account of this faith thus influencing his conduct, Abel "obtained witness that he was righteous." "The Lord had respect unto Abel and his offering." To be righteous, is just to be an object of the approbation of the Supreme Judge. How God manifested His approbation of Abel, and disapprobation of Cain, we cannot tell. It is not an improbable conjecture, that it was in a manner similar to that in which He testified His approbation of Elijah and his sacrifice, of Abram and his sacrifice, and of Aaron's sacrifice on his entering on the priest's office: Gen. xv. 17; Lev. ix. 24; 1 Kings xviii. 3. Abel's sacrifice was probably consumed by fire from heaven, while Cain's remained untouched. At the same time, though a probable conjecture, this is but a conjecture. It is enough that we know that he did receive a distinct testimony of the approbation of God. "God testifying of his gifts;" *i.e.*, 'God making it manifest that his gifts were acceptable to Him, while his brother's gifts were not acceptable.'

[1] δι' ης, *i.e.*, πίστεως, not θυσίας.

The concluding clause of the verse is somewhat obscure: "And by it he, being dead, yet speaketh;" *i.e.*, I apprehend, 'By or on account of his faith,' manifested in his sacrifice. Following a different reading from that adopted by our translators, some render the words, 'and on account of this, he is yet spoken of.' This, though a truth, is one which has no direct bearing on the Apostle's object. Besides, the reading followed by our translators is admitted by the best critics to be the genuine one.

But what are we to understand by these words, "On account of his faith," or, "by means of his faith, he, though dead, yet speaketh?" It has been common to suppose that this just means, that Abel still speaks to us by his example, as recorded in Scripture—still speaks to us of the importance and efficacy of faith. But this is not at all peculiar to Abel; it is equally true of all the persons who are mentioned in this chapter. Besides, in whatever the Apostle states in reference to these elders, he obviously alludes to what is testified of them in Scripture. I therefore cannot at all doubt that the Apostle refers to the subsequent part of Abel's history, as detailed in the fourth chapter of the Book of Genesis: "And He said, What hast thou done? the voice of thy brother's blood crieth unto Me from the ground."[1] And this conviction is strengthened by noticing the way in which the Apostle contrasts the blood of Christ—called by him "the blood of sprinkling"—with "the blood of Abel," chap. xii. 24. 'On account of his faith, manifested in his sacrifice, though dead, he yet spoke;'[2] *i.e.*, God manifested His regard to him by the punishment He inflicted on his murderer. The earth would not cover his blood. His blood was precious in God's sight; and He proved it to be so by not allowing him who shed it to escape unpunished. His faith, manifested by his sacrifice, drew down upon him, both while living and dead, proofs that he was the object of the divine favourable regards. Such

---

[1] Gen. iv. 10.
[2] From Philo it appears that the Jews were struck with the representation of Abel, though dead, speaking by his blood to God: ζῇ δὲ τὴν ἐν Θεῷ ζωὴν εὐδαίμονα, μαρτυρεῖ δὲ τὸ χρησθὲν λόγιον, ἐν ᾧ φωνῇ χρώμενος καὶ βοῶν—εὑρίσκεται. "He," *i.e.*, Abel, "lives in God a happy life; for the sacred Scripture gives testimony of him, in which he is found using a voice," *i.e.*, 'speaking and crying.'

is the first of the Apostle's illustrations of the importance and efficacy of faith.

The second example of the power of faith is that of Enoch. Ver. 5. "By faith Enoch was translated that he should not see death; and was not found, because God had translated him: for before his translation he had this testimony, that he pleased God."

To the illustration of this paragraph, two things are necessary. We must first attend to the Apostle's account of the high privilege which Enoch obtained—he "was translated;" and then to the Apostle's proof that it was "by faith" that he obtained this privilege.

The account we have of the strange transaction referred to, in Gen. v. 24, is in these words: "Enoch was not, for God took him."[1] The Apostle quotes from the Septuagint, and by his quotation sanctions the view that version gives of the words. Enoch, instead of dying like other men, was in some miraculous manner carried bodily to heaven; some change taking place, no doubt, on his body, and that of Elijah, similar to that which is to take place on the bodies of the saints that are found alive at the end of the world, to fit them for the celestial state; for we know that "flesh and blood cannot inherit the kingdom of God, neither can corruption inherit incorruption." This is all the information the Scriptures give us with respect to Enoch's translation; and it were worse than a waste of time to bring forward the baseless conjectures which men, anxious to be wise beyond what is written, have advanced on the subject.

Let us now attend to the Apostle's proof that it was "by faith" that Enoch obtained this distinguished privilege. That proof is brought forward in the following words: "For before his translation he had this testimony, that he pleased God." Ver. 6. "But without faith it is impossible to please Him: for he that cometh to God must believe that He is, and that He is a rewarder of them that diligently seek Him."

The words, "before his translation," etc., are obviously equivalent to—'for in the sacred history, before we read of his translation, we read of his being the object of the peculiar favour of God. His translation is there represented as the consequence of

---

[1] לָקַח, the same word used in reference to Elijah, 2 Kings ii. 3.

this peculiar favour of God; and this peculiar favour he could not have enjoyed, had he not been a believer, for to the enjoyment of this peculiar favour faith is absolutely necessary.' This is the Apostle's argument. Let us look at its various parts, that we may distinctly see that it is fairly drawn from the passage of Old Testament history from which it is deduced.

In our version of Genesis we read nothing of Enoch's pleasing God. We read, " Enoch walked with God," which is a literal version of the Hebrew text. The expression, " walked with God," has commonly been considered as descriptive of Enoch's character as a singularly pious man, who, realizing the divine presence, habitually thought and felt, spoke and acted, as under the eye of God. I am rather disposed to consider it as descriptive of Enoch's privilege: he was beloved of God, and, as an evidence of it, he was admitted to intimate and delightful intercourse with Him. He was a prophet, to whom God made communications of His will; and it is not at all unlikely that, as in the case of Moses, sensible proofs might be given to his cotemporaries that he was in a remarkable degree the object of the divine regard. I am induced to take this view of it, because I find the two most ancient versions of the Scriptures (the Syriac and Greek) rendering the phrase, " walked with God," " pleased God," not only here, but in Gen. vi. 9, where the same phrase again occurs in reference to Noah;[1] and the Apostle sanctions this interpretation by reasoning from it. This, then, is the first step in the Apostle's argument, to prove that " by faith Enoch was translated." The Scriptures testify that Enoch was the object of the divine peculiar regard previously to his translation, and represent that translation as an expression of this peculiar regard.

The second step is, Faith, or believing, is absolutely necessary in order to any man's being the object of the peculiar regard of Jehovah. " Without faith it is impossible to please God." These words admit of two different interpretations, according as you explain the reference of the phrase, " to please God." They may either signify, ' without believing the truth about God, it is impossible to enjoy His favour;' or, ' without believing the truth about God, it is impossible to possess that character, or to prosecute that course of conduct, which

---

[1] *Vide* Gen. xvii. 1, xxiv. 40; Ps. lvi. 13, cxvi. 9.

only can meet with His approbation.' Both are truths. The last is the view most commonly taken of the assertion here; but I am inclined to consider the first as probably expressing the Apostle's idea. The only way in which guilty men, who have forfeited God's favour, can regain it, is through the faith of the truth respecting Him. "By the deeds of the law no flesh living can be justified." If Enoch enjoyed the divine favour, it must have been through believing.

The Apostle confirms his assertion, that without believing, it is impossible to be well-pleasing to God, by adding, "for every one that cometh to God must believe that He is, and that He is the rewarder of them who diligently seek Him." "To come to God," is here plainly equivalent to—'to be the object of His kind regards.' No one can draw near to Him with acceptance, as to a Father and a Friend, who does not "believe that He is, and that He is the rewarder of them who diligently seek Him." To "believe that God is," is something more than to believe that there is a God. There are many who believe that there is a First Cause, whom they call God, whose notions of the character of God are not only greatly defective, but greatly erroneous. These persons believe that there exists a being whom they call God; but their faith is not the faith of the truth. There really exists no such being in the universe as the being they conceive of: he is a mere creature of their own minds. To "believe that God is," is to believe in the existence of such a Being as God's works and word declare Him to be: it is to believe the truth with regard to Him. No person can be the object of the complacency of God who does not credit the revelation He has made to him of Himself.

There is particularly one truth about God which must be believed by all who would approach to Him with acceptance, and that is, that "He is the rewarder of all who diligently seek Him;"—in other words, that He is merciful, and disposed to pardon and save all who seek Him,—that is, who in the way of His appointment, by believing His word and hoping in His mercy, seek their happiness in Him. The faith of the truth about God, as disposed to pity, pardon, and save all, even the most guilty of the children of men, who come to Him in the way of His appointment—that is the faith by which, in every age of the world, men have been justified. The degree of information respecting the details of the method of salvation has been very different in different ages; but the great truth, through the faith of which men are interested in that method of salvation, has never varied. It is, " that God is, and that He is the rewarder of them who diligently seek Him."

This, then, is the Apostle's argument, and it is plainly a good one: ' Enoch is a glorious illustration of the efficacy of faith in obtaining benefits. He obtained a most important benefit—translation to heaven without tasting of death; and it was through believing that he obtained this benefit. The Scriptures represent him as before his translation an object of the peculiar divine favour; and they represent his translation as a manifestation of this peculiar favour. But none but a believer can be an object of the divine peculiar favour. It is by faith, and faith alone, that a man can be justified.'

The concluding part of the 6th verse is valuable, as giving us a further illustration of the Apostle's description of faith in the first view. To believe the truth with regard to the character of God, is " conviction with regard to things unseen," " for no man hath seen God at any time ;" and to believe " that He is the rewarder of them who diligently seek Him," is " confidence respecting things hoped for." It is also useful for confuting two very absurd tenets which have been adopted by some men. There are men, even professed Christians, who maintain the innocence of error,—who say it is of no consequence what men believe, if they but live well. That is just equivalent to saying that it is of no consequence to " please God"—to be an object of His complacency and kind regard; for " without faith it is impossible to please God." There are others who affirm, that in serving God we ought to have no respect to the " recompense of reward." But the Apostle states it as forming a necessary part of that truth which must be believed in order to our pleasing God, " that He is the rewarder of those who diligently seek Him."

This passage has often been abused for the purpose of proving that the heathen, who have no written revelation, are not in such deplorable circumstances as the friends of missions represent them. They have the means of knowing that " God is, and that He is the rewarder of them who diligently seek Him ;" and if they believe this, they, like Enoch, will please

God, and though they should not, like him, be translated, yet when they die they will certainly go to heaven. That the heathen have to a certain extent the means of knowing that "God is," is plain from the first chapter of the Romans; but the Apostle, who asserts this truth, asserts also, that in consequence of the depravity of man's nature, these means are not improved, and therefore but increase their guilt and deepen their condemnation; and that, in fact, the heathen world "by wisdom knew not God," but, on the contrary, "did service to them who by nature are no gods." The views of every heathen are not only necessarily very defective, from the imperfection of the means of knowledge, but, as experience teaches, they are uniformly greatly erroneous. The god or gods in whose existence they believe, is not the true God. With regard to the second article of that faith which the Apostle represents as necessary to please God, "that He is the rewarder of them that diligently seek Him," that is what no man without an express revelation could ever discover. It is very consonant with reason to believe that God will make innocent and obedient creatures happy; but as to whether God will be reconciled to sinners, and make them ultimately happy, or in what way He is to be sought for this purpose, it is plain that unenlightened reason can give no information. The faith here spoken of must be founded on a supernatural revelation of the true character of God, and of His purposes of mercy towards a lost world. It was through the faith of the revelation made in his time on this subject, that Enoch was accepted of God; it is through the faith of the revelation now made to us, that we are to be accepted of God. It is not my purpose to enter into the general question of the salvability of the heathen; but I think it must be evident to every careful reader, that that doctrine receives no support from the passage before us. It would be a strange thing indeed, if in an Epistle, the great object of which is to show the supreme importance of the faith of the Gospel, we should meet with a declaration that men may be saved without knowing anything about the Gospel.

The third example of the efficacy of faith which he brings forward, is that afforded by the history of Noah. Ver. 7. "By faith[1] Noah, being warned of God of things not seen as yet,

---

[1] πίστει must be construed, not with χρηματισθείς, but with κατεσκεύασε: δι' ἧς must not be referred to κιβωτόν, but to πίστει.

moved with fear, prepared an ark to the saving of his house; by the which he condemned the world, and became heir of the righteousness which is by faith." Let us first shortly attend to the facts of the case; and then consider the illustration which they afford of the efficacy of faith in enabling to perform duties, to endure trials, and to obtain blessings.

The facts are these: "Noah was warned of God of things not seen as yet;" in consequence of this, he was "moved with fear," and built an ark; he obtained the salvation of his family; "he condemned the world, and he became an heir of the righteousness that is by faith."

The first fact is, "Noah was warned of God of things not seen as yet." The approaching deluge was the event of which Noah was warned. The circumstances of that event are termed "things not seen *as yet*;" because, though in their own nature sufficiently apprehensible by the senses, they were *then* unseen, because future, and because nothing in the appearance of nature indicated their approach. We have a particular account of the warning in Gen. vi. 12–18: "And God looked upon the earth, and, behold, it was corrupt: for all flesh had corrupted his way upon the earth. And God said unto Noah, The end of all flesh is come before Me; for the earth is filled with violence through them: and, behold, I will destroy them with the earth. Make thee an ark of gopher-wood: rooms shalt thou make in the ark, and shalt pitch it within and without with pitch. And this is the fashion which thou shalt make it of; The length of the ark shall be three hundred cubits, the breadth of it fifty cubits, and the height of it thirty cubits. A window shalt thou make to the ark, and in a cubit shalt thou finish it above; and the door of the ark shalt thou set in the side thereof; with lower, second, and third stories shalt thou make it. And, behold, I, even I, do bring a flood of waters upon the earth, to destroy all flesh, wherein is the breath of life, from under heaven; and every thing that is in the earth shall die. But with thee will I establish My covenant: and thou shalt come into the ark, thou, and thy sons, and thy wife, and thy sons' wives with thee."

The second fact refers to the influence which this warning had on the mind and conduct of Noah. He was "moved with fear," and he "prepared an ark." When it is said that Noah was "moved with fear," we are not to suppose that he was in any degree afraid that he or his family were to perish in the approaching deluge. He had precisely the same reason for expecting his deliverance, and that of his family, along with a small remnant of all species of living creatures, that he had for expecting the destruction of the rest of mankind and the animal tribes. It is easy, however, to see how Noah was "moved with fear." An evil of such tremendous magnitude, inflicted on account of sin, placed in a very striking light the irresistible power, the immaculate purity, the inflexible justice of God, and was fitted to fill the mind with reverence and godly fear. Besides, Noah knew that he and all his family were sinners, and deserved to perish along with the rest of their race; and he knew also, that though, if the ark was prepared, according to the divine appointment, all was safe; it was equally true, that if the ark was not prepared, he and they must perish in the general ruin. The very idea of this must have excited a salutary terror, and operated as a powerful motive to diligence in the building of the ark. When we consider the size of the ark,—especially when connected with the collection of the various animals, which from the history seems to have been Noah's work,—the undertaking, in any circumstances, must have been an arduous one; and when we consider the difficulties which must have arisen out of the state of sentiment and feeling of the great body of mankind, it may well be considered as one of the most extraordinary examples of difficult duty which the world has ever witnessed. The testimony of God on this subject is this—adding, after a particular detail of the commands laid on Noah,— "Thus did Noah; according to all that God commanded him, so did he."

The third fact stated by the Apostle is, that Noah thus obtained the deliverance of his family. He "built an ark to the saving of his house." "House," here, is plainly equivalent to 'family.' The words, "to the saving of his house," taken by themselves, may either signify what was the design of Noah in building the ark, or what was the result of his building the ark. In the first case, they are equivalent to—'he built an ark that his family might be saved;' in the second case, they are equivalent to—'he built an ark, and thus his family was saved.' Both are truths; but it is the last of these truths which serves the Apostle's object—the illustration of the efficacy of faith. By building the ark, Noah obtained the salvation of his family. "And all flesh died that moved upon the earth, both of fowl, and of cattle, and of beast, and of every creeping thing that creepeth upon the earth, and every man: all in whose nostrils was the breath of life, of all that was in the dry land, died. And every living substance was destroyed which was upon the face of the ground, both man, and cattle, and the creeping things, and the fowl of the heaven; and they were destroyed from the earth: and Noah only remained alive, and they that were with him in the ark."[1] When "all flesh" had died, "Noah remained alive, and they that were with him in the ark."

The next fact stated is, "He condemned the world." These words have generally been supposed to refer to that tacit condemnation which Noah, by his conduct, in obeying the divine commandment, and preparing for the coming deluge, as it were pronounced on an ungodly world.[2] But as it is said that "by faith" (for I apprehend there can be no doubt the reference is to faith in the relative "which," and not to the ark, as some have supposed; for it was by the same thing, whatever it was, that he "condemned the world" and "became the heir of the righteousness of faith;" and certainly it was not by the ark that he was justified) "he condemned the world," I am disposed to consider the words as referring to the same fact which Peter, in his second Epistle, ii. 5, refers to, when he calls Noah "a preacher of righteousness." I think we are warranted from the declaration here, as explained by that in the Epistle of Peter, to conclude, that the warning Noah received from God he publicly proclaimed,—remonstrated with the men of his age on their wickedness, called them to repentance, and denounced, on their continuing in sin, the awful sentence of a common and universal destruction.

The last fact stated is, that Noah "became," or *was*, "an heir of the righteousness which is by faith." "The righteousness by faith" is just the justification by believing; and to be

---

[1] Gen. vii. 21-23.
[2] The following passage from Ecclesiasticus has been referred to for illustration:—κατακρίνει δὲ δίκαιος καμὼν τοὺς ζῶντας ἀσεβεῖς, καὶ νεότης τελεσθεῖσα ταχέως πολυετὲς γῆρας ἀδίκου. "The dead just man condemns the living ungodly; and the finished youth swiftly condemns the protracted old age of the wicked."

"an heir of the righteousness of faith," is just to participate in the blessing of justification by believing—to be justified by believing. In this part of his statement, I apprehend the Apostle refers to two passages in the book of Genesis: the first, ch. vi. 8, "Noah found favour in the sight of the Lord;" and the second, ch. vi. 9, "Noah walked with God;" which, as the Apostle has explained it in the preceding context, is equivalent to—'Noah was well-pleasing to God,'—Noah was a justified person—a person treated by God as if he had been righteous, as an object of His peculiar favour; and, as the Apostle has shown, if he was so, it must have been through believing.

These are the facts of the case. Let us now see how they illustrate the efficacy of faith for enabling to perform duties, to endure trials, and to obtain blessings.

It has been supposed by some, that the Apostle means to say that it was *by faith* that Noah was " warned of God of things not seen as yet;"—that is, that the warning given to Noah was a proof of God's peculiar regard to Noah; and that this token of peculiar regard, like every other, was bestowed on him as a believer. But I rather think that the phrase, " by faith," is intended to refer to " moved by fear, prepared an ark;" the warning being considered as the revelation which was the subject of that faith through which Noah performed his difficult duties, endured his severe trials, and obtained the glorious reward. Had the warning not been believed, Noah would not have been " moved with fear"—he would not have " prepared an ark." He would have continued, like the unbelieving generation among whom he lived, careless and disobedient. But believing, as he did, the warning in all its extent, he could not but be " moved with fear"—he could not but set about "preparing the ark." Noah believed the whole testimony. It was a declaration of universal destruction, with the exception of himself and his family, and a declaration that even they could be saved only by the " preparing of an ark." Had Noah believed merely that " the end of all flesh was come before God," he would indeed have been filled with fear, but that fear would not have moved him to prepare an ark. It was the faith at once of the coming general destruction and the particular way of escape which produced the effect of his prosecuting the laborious and difficult work of preparing the ark.

As it was by faith that Noah prepared the ark, so it was by faith that he obtained the salvation of his family. That privilege was connected in inseparable union with a preceding duty, which preceding duty could not have been performed without faith. Had not the ark been prepared, Noah and his family could not have been saved; and had not Noah believed, the ark would not have been prepared. You see, then, how the salvation of Noah's family was the result of his faith.

It was by faith also that he " condemned the world." The revelation which he believed furnished him with the great subject of his condemnatory addresses; and it was the faith of this revelation that enabled him, in defiance of their scorn, to tell them the truth. He believed, and therefore spoke.

It was by faith also that " he became an heir of the righteousness which is by faith." This scarcely requires any illustration. The language of the Apostle is not in reality, what it is in appearance, tautological. When he says, Noah by faith " became heir of the righteousness which is by faith," he just means, that Noah by his own personal faith obtained an interest in that method of justification, in which no man can obtain an interest but by believing.[1]

This example of Noah is thus admirably fitted to serve the Apostle's purpose. Faith enabled Noah to perform very difficult duties. It enabled him to make the laborious preparations, which must have occupied many years, for the approaching deluge; it enabled him to do his duty, and to persevere in doing it, amid many difficulties and discouragements; it enabled him fearlessly, though alone, as " a preacher of righteousness," to pronounce the sentence of condemnation on a guilty world, though in doing so he must have exposed himself to cruel mockings, and very probably to imminent hazards. Faith enabled Noah to endure very severe trials. The conviction, that without building the ark he and his family must perish, and if it were prepared they were safe, rendered powerless the shafts of ridicule. He endured, as seeing what was yet invisible. Faith enabled him to obtain most important benefits,—the deliverance of his family, and a personal interest in the justification that is by believing.

---

[1] The phrase, ἡ κατὰ πίστ. δικ., is plainly the same thing as ἡ δικ. ἐκ πίστ., Rom. i. 17, ix. 30, x. 6; and διὰ πίστ., Rom. iii. 22, Phil. iii. 9; or simply δικ. πίστ., Rom. iv. 13.

The example is the more instructive, as it naturally, and almost necessarily, brings before the mind the fearfully destructive efficiency of unbelief. The world that perished had materially the same message delivered to them as that which Noah received. Had they repented, there is no reason to doubt that the fearful infliction would not have taken place. Noah believed, and feared, and obeyed, and was saved. They disbelieved, and mocked, and were disobedient, and perished.

Faith and unbelief are the same things still. The believer, like Noah, has been "warned of God of things not seen as yet." He has heard that "all have sinned," and that God cannot "clear the guilty," and "the wicked must be turned into hell;" and he has heard also, that "God hath set forth His Son a propitiation through His blood," and that "whosoever believeth shall not perish, but have everlasting life;" and that by the believer seeking "glory, honour, and immortality," eternal life shall assuredly be obtained. Like Noah, he believes the divine warning; he is filled with fear at the display which these truths give of the power, and holiness, and justice of God; he sees that everlasting destruction is his inevitable portion, unless he avail himself of the only way of escape, and that, availing himself of this way of escape, he is secure of everlasting happiness; and believing this, he "flees for refuge to the hope set before him,"—and he continues fleeing for refuge; and in the way of God's appointment, the way of faith and holiness, he seeks perseveringly, and he obtains assuredly, "the end of his believing, even the salvation of his soul." He believes the whole of the divine testimony. If he believed only the first part of it, he would despair; if he believed only the last part of it, he would presume. But believing both, he both fears and hopes; and under the combined influence of fear and hope, he performs duty, endures trials, and ultimately obtains the promised blessing.

The unbeliever, like the ungodly world in the days of Noah, hears the divine testimony, but will not receive it. Hell excites no fears—heaven no desires. He continues in impenitence and disobedience, till down comes the thunderbolt. He is conveyed into the regions of hopeless punishment, and learns, too late, how criminal and dangerous it is, under the influence of "an evil heart of unbelief," to "depart from the living God."

The fourth example of the efficacy of faith is derived from the history of Abraham, the father of the Hebrew nation. Vers. 8-10. "By faith Abraham, when he was called[1] to go out into a place which he should after receive for an inheritance, obeyed; and he went out, not knowing whither he went. By faith he sojourned in the land of promise, as in a strange country, dwelling in tabernacles with Isaac and Jacob, the heirs with him of the same promise: for he looked for a city which hath foundations, whose builder and maker is God."

Of the facts referred to in the 8th verse, we have an account in the beginning of the 12th chapter of the book of Genesis. "Now the Lord had said unto Abram, Get thee out of thy country, and from thy kindred, and from thy father's house, unto a land that I will show thee: and I will make of thee a great nation, and I will bless thee, and make thy name great; and thou shalt be a blessing: and I will bless them that bless thee, and curse him that curseth thee: and in thee shall all families of the earth be blessed. So Abram departed, as the Lord had spoken unto him; and Lot went with him: and Abram was seventy and five years old when he departed out of Haran."[2]

Though in the Mosaic history the account of this call is not given till after the account of the death of Terah in Haran, yet it is plain from the speech of Stephen that it took place in Mesopotamia, previously to his leaving that country along with his father. The call consisted of two parts,—a command and a promise. The command was, "Get thee out of thy country, and from thy kindred, and from thy father's house, unto a land that I will show thee." The promise was partly implicit,—"I will give thee this land for an inheritance;" and partly explicit, —"I will make of thee a great nation, and I will bless thee, and make thy name great; and thou shalt be a blessing: and I will bless them that bless thee, and curse him that curseth thee: and in thee shall all the families of the earth be blessed."

---

[1] Theodoret supposes that $\varkappa\alpha\lambda o\acute{u}\mu\varepsilon\nu o\varsigma$ $\;$ Ἀβραάμ refers to the change of the patriarch's name from Abram to Abraham. Some MSS. and versions read ὁ $\varkappa\alpha\lambda o\acute{u}\mu\varepsilon\nu o\varsigma$; but the whole context shows that the reference is to what is usually termed "the call" of Abraham,—his being divinely commanded to leave his native country, and go into a land to be pointed out to him.

[2] Gen. xii. 1-4.

Abraham believed that both the command and the promise came from God; and therefore he obeyed the command, and expected the fulfilment of the promise. His faith was "confidence in reference to things hoped for;" it was "conviction in reference to things not seen as yet." Had Abraham not believed that the call came from God, or had he not believed that God was at once able and disposed to perform His promises, he would have disregarded the call, and continued in Mesopotamia; but because he believed, he obeyed. It was his faith which led him to break asunder those very strong bands which bind men to their country and their kindred, and to undertake a journey of unknown length, and difficulty, and danger,—towards a country of which he knew nothing, but that God had said to him, "I will show it thee." "He went forth, not knowing whither he went." He proceeded in the direction which the divine call pointed out; and he went onward till the same divine call directed him to stop.

This certainly was a very remarkable manifestation of the power of faith in enabling a man to perform a difficult duty. It is difficult for us to form a distinct conception of it, as no case strictly analogous can occur among us. But let us suppose a person, previous to the discovery of America, leaving the shores of Europe, and committing himself and his family to the mercy of the waves, in consequence of a command of God, and a promise that they should be conducted to a country where he should become the founder of a great nation, and the source of blessings to many nations; and we have something like what actually took place in the case of Abraham.

The object for which this instance of the power of faith is brought forward is obvious, and it is well fitted to serve that object. Nothing but faith could have enabled Abraham to act as he did. Faith made what would otherwise have been impossible, easy. God was calling the Hebrew Christians to break through bands as strong as those which bound Abraham to Mesopotamia, in abandoning Judaism, and to take a course in a determined attachment to Christianity, the consequences of which were as apparently hazardous, and as completely unknown to them and beyond their control, as the circumstances of Abraham's journey from Mesopotamia to Canaan. Nothing could enable them to do this but faith—a full persuasion that the command to embrace Jesus of Nazareth as "the end of the law for righteousness," and the promise of eternal life as the gift of God to all who did so, equally came forth from God. And while nothing could enable them to do this but such a faith, such a faith would make these otherwise impracticable duties easy. This would prevent them from "turning back to perdition," and would enable them to "press onward to the mark, for the prize of the high calling of God in Christ Jesus."

And it is equally true now as it was then. Nothing but the faith of the Gospel can induce a man to abandon the world and commence a pilgrimage towards heaven. And wherever there is the faith of the Gospel, there will be such an abandonment—there will be the commencement and the prosecution of such a pilgrimage. If Abraham had continued in Mesopotamia, or stopped short of Canaan, it would have been a proof that he did not believe the divine testimony; and whatever men may profess, if they continue to love the world, and become "weary in well-doing," it is clear evidence that they have not believed the Gospel.

We have another instance of the power of faith in enabling to persevere in a course of duty, while the blessing promised is not immediately conferred, brought before our minds in the next verse. This, too, is taken from the history of Abraham. Ver. 9. "By faith he sojourned in the land[1] of promise, as in a strange country, dwelling in tabernacles with Isaac and Jacob, the heirs with him of the same promise."

When Abraham came into the land of Canaan, the promise which was implied in what was said to him at his call in Mesopotamia, was given him in the most explicit language: "The Lord appeared unto Abram, and said, Unto thy seed will I give this land."[2] Hence that country received the appellation, "the land of promise," or the promised land. But that promise was not immediately, was not soon, fulfilled. Abraham did not obtain possession of it, nor did his posterity, till nearly five centuries after. To use the language of Stephen, "God gave him no inheritance in it, no, not so much as to set his foot on: yet

---

[1] εἰς γῆν for ἐν γῇ. Such a use of εἰς with a noun of place is not unfrequent. Bretschneider's Lex. εἰς, 5, c.

[2] Gen. xii. 7.

He promised that He would give it to him for a possession, and to his seed after him, when as yet he had no child."[1] Had Abraham not been a persevering believer—had he not continued to "account Him faithful who had promised"—he would not have continued in Canaan in such circumstances, a pilgrim and sojourner, dwelling in tents, and having no certain or abiding dwelling-place. He would have returned to the country from which he had come out, and where his relations had possessions and fixed places of abode; or he would have gone into some other country, where, with the property he had, he might have procured for himself an inheritance. But because Abraham believed that in due time the promise would be fulfilled, he preferred dwelling in a tent in Canaan to dwelling in a palace anywhere else. He goes into Egypt during the time of famine; but it is to sojourn, not to settle. He sends Eliezer to obtain a wife for Isaac into Mesopotamia, and takes an oath of him, that even in the case of his not succeeding in getting one of his kinswomen as a wife to Isaac, he was not to take Isaac back again to the land of his ancestors. He continued, along with Isaac and Jacob—to whom as well as to Abraham the promises were made, and who are therefore called "heirs with him of the same promise,"—to live in Canaan, though not put in possession of it. Though the promise was long in being fulfilled, he did not doubt but it would be in due time fulfilled; and therefore he determined that he and his posterity should continue in the land to which the promise referred.

It is equally easy here, as in the former case, to see the object the Apostle had in view in bringing forward this particular exemplification of the power of faith, and to see how well fitted it is for gaining that end. Nothing but continued faith could have enabled Abraham to continue a pilgrim and a sojourner in Canaan, waiting for the fulfilment of the promise. Continued faith did enable Abraham to do so. Nothing but continued faith could enable the Christian Hebrews to continue "stedfast and unmoveable" in the profession and practice of Christianity during that season of privation and suffering, of undefined length, which might intervene before the full accomplishment of the promises which had been made to them. Per-

---

[1] Acts vii. 5.

severing faith would enable them to do this. He who continues believing will "endure to the end," and "be saved."

The words which follow in the 10th verse seem to contain the reason why Abraham continued to sojourn in the land of promise. Ver. 10. "For he looked for a city which hath foundations, whose builder and maker is God."

These words have been supposed by some very learned interpreters to refer to the literal Jerusalem, the metropolis of the Holy Land, when it became the possession of the descendants of Abraham. They consider the Apostle as saying, 'The reason why Abraham continued to live in Canaan, though he had no inheritance there, though he and his family had to live in moveable tents, was, that he expected that in due time, in that country, a stable city would be erected for them by the remarkable providence of God—that the whole territory should be peopled by his descendants, not as wandering tribes, but as the inhabitants of towns and cities, having Jerusalem built on the rocky mountains as its metropolis.' This is ingenious, but it is not satisfactory. We have no reason to believe that any revelation was made to Abraham as to the building of Jerusalem. The "city which has foundations" seems plainly the same city mentioned in the subsequent context as a city prepared for them by God, in the better, the heavenly country and the description, "whose builder and maker is God," which seems nearly equivalent in meaning to the expression respecting the true tabernacle, "which, it is said, God pitched, not man," seems to exclude the workmanship of man, and points it out to us as not a literal but a figurative expression, indicating not an earthly, but a heavenly city. The Apostle's assertion then is, that Abraham "looked for a city which has foundations, whose builder and maker was God." What does it mean?

The land of promise is in the Scriptures the emblem of the heavenly inheritance, and the earthly Jerusalem of the residence of the saints there. They are represented as dwelling in a glorious city, with Jehovah in the midst of them as their King. To denote the stability, the immutability, and the eternity of this state of happiness, the heavenly city is said to "have foundations." It is not a collection of tents or tabernacles, which have no foundations, and which are easily removed, but it is a city built on the everlasting hills of Paradise.

It is not unlikely that Psalm lxxxvii. 1 was in the Apostle's mind: "His foundation is in the holy mountains." The travelling tent, pitched in the evening and struck in the morning, finely contrasts with the "city which has foundations"—firmly builded. And to denote its divine origin and transcendent excellence, it is termed a city "whose builder and maker is God." It is thus opposed to all earthly cities, which are built by man's hands, just as the Apostle distinguishes the heavenly sanctuary from the earthly by describing it as being "made without hands," and as he distinguishes the resurrection body from the "earthly house of this tabernacle," as "a house not made with hands, eternal in the heavens."

According to the Apostle, then, Abraham expected true, permanent happiness from God in a future state. This expectation must have been founded on a revelation made to him, and believed by him. Our Lord teaches us that the promise of immortality and the resurrection is implied in the promise, "I will be a God to thee;" and there is nothing improbable in the supposition, that the patriarchs may have had clearer revelations of a future state made to them than any that are recorded in Scripture. If we admit the inspiration of this Epistle, it is plain, however we may explain it, that Abraham did cherish an expectation of permanent and perfect happiness in a future world.

All that remains to be explained, is the connection in which the words in the 10th verse stand to the preceding statement. If the word *for* be understood in its most usual sense, as expressing the reason of a previous assertion, then the meaning is—'Abraham's expectation of permanent, perfect happiness in heaven, enabled him patiently to submit to all the inconvenience of a state of pilgrimage in Canaan during the period which was to elapse before that land became the inheritance of his posterity.' If the word *for* be understood, as it often must, as merely connective, as equivalent to 'moreover,' then the meaning is—'Abraham's expectation that God would in His own time fulfil the promise, that Canaan was to be the inheritance of his posterity, induced him to continue in that country, though but a pilgrim and sojourner. But Abraham had higher expectations than this. He not only expected for his posterity a secure settlement in Canaan, but he expected for himself an everlasting abode in heaven.' It matters very little in which of these two ways the connection is explained.[1]

The great practical truth intended to be taught us by this passage of Scripture is, that it is the faith of the Gospel, producing the expectation of eternal life, that can alone enable a person cheerfully to submit to all the privations and sufferings connected with the Christian life, and induce him, " by a patient continuance in well-doing, to seek," so as to obtain, " glory, honour, and immortality."

The design of the paragraph which follows, is to show, from the history of Abraham, that faith is not only efficacious in enabling men to perform difficult duties and to endure severe trials, but also to obtain important blessings. Vers. 11, 12. "Through faith also Sara herself received strength to conceive seed, and was delivered of a child when she was past age, because she judged Him faithful who had promised. Therefore sprang there even of one, and him as good as dead, so many as the stars of the sky in multitude, and as the sand which is by the sea-shore innumerable." The substance of this statement is—' Through believing, Abraham and Sarah, though arrived at a time of life when, according to the ordinary course of nature, it was not to be expected that they would have any children, became the founders of a family numerous as the stars of heaven, or as the sand along the sea-shore.' This blessing was conferred on them as *believers*. It was as the gracious reward of their faith that they obtained this high honour.

Some learned interpreters have supposed that it is Abraham's faith alone that is spoken of in this paragraph, and that the Apostle's intention is to say, ' As the reward of Abraham's faith, Sarah became fruitful, and brought him a son, from whom sprang innumerable descendants.' The words, however, certainly seem

---

[1] Wakefield's note on these verses does credit to his taste. "Orationem magis exquisitæ venustatis nusquam reperies. Παροικεῖν est *hospitari pro tempore*; κατοικεῖν, *fixam domum habere*. In *terra* igitur ista vivebant, ut *hospites*; in *tabernaculis* vero *semper*: certam domum incolebant in *aliena* terra; *hanc* mox relicturi, *illam*, dum viverent, nunquam. Et eleganter opponuntur *tabernacula mobilia*, in terræ superficie posita, ἐπίγεια, atque huc illuc pro re nata transferenda, civitati *fundamentis stabilitæ*: Isa. xxxviii. 12, LXX. Τεχνίτης vero is est qui *excogitat* formam ædificii; δημιουργός, qui struit ædificium. Hinc nostri reddere debuerant, ut poterant satis simpliciter: whose *contriver* and builder is God."

more naturally to refer to Sarah's faith. The facts of the case seem to have been these :—Jehovah appeared to Abraham, and promised that he should have a son by his wife Sarah. The promise was afterwards repeated in the hearing of Sarah, who laughed at it within herself as a thing incredible, considering the advanced age of herself and her husband; and afterwards, through fear, she denied that she laughed; so that she was in the first instance guilty both of unbelief and of falsehood. But when she found that the hidden reasonings of her heart had been detected by the divine Messenger—when she heard Him put the silencing question, "Is anything too hard for the Lord?" and received from Him new assurances that she certainly would become a mother,—she perceived that the promise was the word of Him who was able to do as He had said, however inconsistent with the ordinary course of nature; and she no longer laughed at the promise, but believed it, reckoning that He who had promised was faithful. As the gracious reward of her faith, Sarah obtained strength to lay the foundation of a race or family; for so the words may be, and so we apprehend they ought to have been rendered.[1] The meaning of the whole verse is—' To Sarah the believer God gave the high honour of being the mother of His peculiar people.'

The connective particle *therefore* seems to me equivalent to —' for this cause ;' *i.e.*, Because of faith, through means of believing, " there sprang of one, and him as good as dead,"—or in reference to these things, dead,—" so many as the stars of the sky in multitude, and as the sand which is by the sea-shore innumerable." It is not necessary to enter into a minute examination of these words. The general sentiment is, plainly, ' Abraham and Sarah, through believing, obtained a high honour, an important privilege,—the honour and privilege of being the founders of the holy nation,—an honour and privilege, the attainment of which

---

[1] καταβολή signifies 'foundation,' ch. iv. 3, ix. 26 ; σπέρμα signifies 'a family—offspring,' ch. ii. 16, ver. 18 *inf*. The Latins says, " fundare domum" or " familiam." Euripides, Herc. Fur. 1261, uses the verb καταβάλλομαι in this sense. This is the exegesis of Ernesti, C. F. Schmid, Cramer, Böhme, and Kuinoel. It is greatly preferable to scarcely decent interpretations of many critics. The manner in which some critics contrive to introduce discussions of an indelicate kind into works of Scripture interpretation, a fault by no means uncommon, is exceedingly revolting to every rightly constituted mind. " A lewd interpreter is never just."

at the time it was promised to them was highly improbable—was all but impossible, which nothing but faith in God could have led them to expect, which without faith in God they would never have obtained.'

It is not difficult to see how this statement was calculated to gain the Apostle's object. God had made promises to the Christian Hebrews, the fulfilment of which seemed to involve as great difficulties at least as the fulfilment of the promise made to Abraham. The language of Abraham's example to them was, "Fear not, only believe." All the blessings and honours included in the salvation that is in Christ with eternal glory—all these will assuredly be yours, if ye continue to "count Him faithful who has promised." Whatever difficulties, whatever apparent impossibilities, lie in the way, like Abraham, "be strong in faith, and give glory to God;" be fully persuaded that " what He has promised He is able to perform ;" be fully persuaded that "He cannot deny Himself;" "against hope, believe in hope,"—*i.e.*, confidently expect what but for the divine promise it would have been folly, it would have been presumption, to have expected. Abraham did so, and his hope did not make him ashamed. "Go ye and do likewise," and your hope shall not make you ashamed nor confounded, world without end.

But let us never forget that it was God's testimony and promise which Abraham believed, and not a figment of his own imagination. Let us take heed that it is God's testimony and promise that we believe—let us take heed that we really *believe* it—let us take care to cherish no hope but what that testimony and promise warrant ; and then it is impossible for us to believe too firmly, or to hope too confidently.

The importance of *persevering* faith is plainly an idea which the Apostle wished to impress on the minds of those to whom he was writing; and to gain this object, he turns their attention to the instructive fact, that the ancient saints of whom he had been speaking continued believers as long as they continued in this world. They lived believing, and they died believing. Vers. 13-16. "These all died in faith, not having received the promises, but having seen them afar off, and were persuaded of them, and embraced them, and confessed that they were strangers and pilgrims on the earth. For they that say such things declare plainly that they seek a country. And truly, if they had been mindful of that country from whence they came out, they might have had opportunity to have returned: but now they desire a better country, that is, an heavenly: wherefore God is not ashamed to be called their God; for He hath prepared for them a city."

The expression, "all these," does not refer to the whole of the ancient saints mentioned in the previous context, for Enoch never died at all; and though Abel and Noah died, and died in faith, yet from the 15th verse it is plain that the expression refers only to the whole of the persons last mentioned as sojourners in the land of Canaan, Abraham and Sarah, Isaac and Jacob. "They all died *in faith;*" *i.e.*, they all died believers—they all died expecting the fulfilment of the divine promises. They had lived in this faith, and they died in it. They had not indeed "received the promises," *i.e.*, the promised blessings. They had not received the inheritance of Canaan—they had not received the blessings connected with the coming of that illustrious descendant of Abraham, " in whom all the nations of the earth were to be blessed;" but they saw these blessings " afar off," *i.e.*, they knew that at a future period—with regard to some of them a distant period—the promise would certainly be fulfilled. They " were persuaded of them." These words are not to be found in the most valuable MSS., or in any of the ancient versions or commentators, and are probably a comparatively modern interpolation. They add nothing to the sense. They merely give the meaning of the previous figurative expression, they " saw them afar off,"[1] and they " embraced them." They were not only persuaded of the truth and certainty of the promises, but also of the goodness of the things promised. The blessings promised were the objects of their desire, esteem, and affection; and in consequence of this—in consequence of their placing their chief affection on objects which they knew they were never to enjoy in this world—they " confessed that they were strangers and pilgrims on the earth." Abraham did so when he wished to purchase, not an inheritance for himself living, but a sepulchre

---

[1] The ἐπαγγελίαι, the promised blessings, are represented as coasts which the seafaring man descries at a distance. Virgil has a similar expression:

" Quum procul obscuros colles humilemque videmus Italiam."—*Æn.* iii. 522, 523. THOLUCK.

for himself and his family when dead: "I am a stranger and a sojourner with you: give me a possession of a burying-place with you, that I may bury my dead out of my sight."[1] Jacob made the same confession to Pharaoh. He represents his own life and the life of his fathers as a pilgrimage: "And Jacob said unto Pharaoh, The days of the years of my pilgrimage are an hundred and thirty years: few and evil have the days of the years of my life been, and have not attained unto the days of the years of the life of my fathers, in the days of their pilgrimage."[2] This confession meant more than that they had not yet obtained the earthly inheritance. Long after Israel had entered into Canaan we find David saying, "Hear my prayer, O Lord, and give ear unto my cry; hold not Thy peace at my tears: for I am a stranger with Thee, and a sojourner, as all my fathers were." "I am a stranger in the earth; hide not Thy commandments from me."[3] We find him using this expression not only for himself, but for the whole congregation of Israel: "For we are strangers before Thee, and sojourners, as were all our fathers: our days on the earth are as a shadow, and there is none abiding."[4]

That the confession, that "they were strangers and sojourners," implied more than that they had not obtained that inheritance which they yet firmly believed their posterity would obtain, is plain from what follows: Ver. 14. "For they that say such things declare plainly that they seek a country."

They who confess that they are "pilgrims and strangers on the earth," and do so as long as they continue on the earth, by doing so, plainly[5] intimate that they are seeking a country which is not on earth.

The word rendered "country" is very expressive. It is exactly rendered by a word lately borrowed from the German, and scarcely yet fully naturalized in our language, *fatherland*— a country where a man's father dwells, which he possesses as his own, and in which his children have a right to dwell with him. Thus it is exactly opposed to a strange or foreign land. That it was not their earthly fatherland that they were seeking,

---

[1] Gen. xxiii. 4.   [2] Gen. xlvii. 9.
[3] Ps. xxxix. 12, cxix. 19.   [4] 1 Chron. xxix. 15.
[5] ἐμφανίζουσιν—'they did not conceal it.' This is the word used by the LXX., Isa. iii. 9, to render לֹא כִחֵדוּ.

is plain. Abraham at God's command had renounced that; "and indeed," ver. 15, "if they had been mindful of that country from whence they came out, they might have had opportunity to have returned."

The country of Terah, their father, where their natural relations had possessions, was Chaldea; and if it had been it that they were seeking, they might easily have returned to it. From the call of Abraham to the death of Jacob was a space of 200 years. During this period they might easily have returned to Chaldea. The distance was no obstacle. There does not seem to have been any external obstruction. But they gave clear evidence that they were not disposed to return. Abraham takes an oath of his servant that he will not endeavour to induce Isaac to return to that land. Jacob indeed went thither; but there he would not stay, and through innumerable dangers returned to Canaan. 'No,' says the Apostle; 'they were indeed seeking a country, but it was a better country, even a heavenly one.' They looked for true happiness in a future state. They expected the complete fulfilment of the promise, "I will be thy God," in heaven.

"Wherefore," or *for this cause,* "God is not ashamed to be called their God; for He hath prepared for them a city." God had "prepared for them a city;" *i.e.,* in plain terms, 'God had secured for them immutable, eternal happiness in heaven;' and because He had done so, He "was not ashamed to be called their God." The idea here, I apprehend, is not the condescension on the part of God in taking the name of the God of the patriarch, but the inconceivable glory and blessedness of that final state which He has prepared for them. It is a glory and happiness worthy of God to bestow on those who are the objects of His peculiar love. In preparing *such* a city for them, and in bringing them to it, He fully answers all the expectations which His calling Himself their God, and calling them His people, could awaken in their minds. When "brought home to glory," every one of His people will be disposed to say, 'Now I understand what is meant by the promise, "I will be thy God." He has done all that He said; He has done more than it ever could have entered into my mind to conceive. He has no reason to be ashamed when he calls Himself *my God.*'

These remarks of the Apostle (vers. 13–16), though in some

measure a digression, are well fitted to gain his great object. It is as if he had said, 'The grand ultimate object of the faith and hope of the patriarchs was not Canaan, nor the blessings of the external economy to be established there; it was substantially the very same object which Christianity more clearly holds out to our faith and hope—spiritual, eternal happiness in the enjoyment of God in heaven.' Religion is materially the same thing in all countries and ages. Are we in possession of it?

Another very striking illustration of the efficacy of faith in enabling to sustain a very severe trial, to perform a very difficult duty, and to obtain a very important blessing, is contained in the paragraph which follows, vers. 17–19. The passage of Old Testament history referred to is one of the most interesting in the sacred volume. " And it came to pass after these things, that God did tempt Abraham, and said unto him, Abraham. And he said, Behold, here I am. And He said, Take now thy son, thine only son Isaac, whom thou lovest, and get thee into the land of Moriah; and offer him there for a burnt-offering upon one of the mountains which I will tell thee of. And Abraham rose up early in the morning, and saddled his ass, and took two of his young men with him, and Isaac his son, and clave the wood for the burnt-offering, and rose up, and went unto the place of which God had told him. Then on the third day Abraham lifted up his eyes, and saw the place afar off. And Abraham said unto his young men, Abide ye here with the ass; and I and the lad will go yonder and worship, and come again to you. And Abraham took the wood of the burnt-offering, and laid it upon Isaac his son; and he took the fire in his hand, and a knife; and they went both of them together. And Isaac spake unto Abraham his father, and said, My father: and he said, Here am I, my son. And he said, Behold the fire and the wood; but where is the lamb for a burnt-offering? And Abraham said, My son, God will provide Himself a lamb for a burnt-offering: so they went both of them together. And they came to the place which God had told him of; and Abraham built an altar there, and laid the wood in order, and bound Isaac his son, and laid him on the altar upon the wood. And Abraham stretched forth his hand, and took the knife to slay his son. And the Angel of the Lord called unto him out of heaven, and said, Abraham, Abraham. And he said, Here am I. And He said, Lay not thine hand upon the lad, neither do thou anything unto him: for now I know that thou fearest God, seeing thou hast not withheld thy son, thine only son, from Me. And Abraham lifted up his eyes, and looked, and behold behind him a ram caught in a thicket by his horns: and Abraham went and took the ram, and offered him up for a burnt-offering in the stead of his son. And Abraham called the name of that place Jehovah-jireh: as it is said to this day, In the mount of the Lord it shall be seen. And the Angel of the Lord called unto Abraham out of heaven the second time, and said, By Myself have I sworn, saith the Lord; for because thou hast done this thing, and hast not withheld thy son, thine only son: that in blessing I will bless thee, and in multiplying I will multiply thy seed as the stars of the heaven, and as the sand which is upon the sea-shore; and thy seed shall possess the gate of his enemies: and in thy seed shall all the nations of the earth be blessed; because thou hast obeyed My voice."[1] Such is the inspired narrative.

Let us now attend to the Apostle's inspired annotations. "By faith Abraham, when he was tried, offered up Isaac: and he that had received the promises offered up his only begotten son, of whom it was said, That in Isaac shall thy seed be called: accounting that God was able to raise him up, even from the dead; from whence also he received him in a figure."

The whole of the Apostle's statements are reducible to the following propositions:—Abraham sustained a very severe trial;

[1] Gen. xxii. 1-18.—The audacity of the German neological interpreters is amusingly displayed in the manner they dispose of this narrative. "Cananæi, inter quos Abrahamus degebat, homines et imprimis infantes immolare solebant. Die quodam Patriarcha, cui persuasum esset hostias humanas Deo abominabiles esse, audierat vicinos deo litasse hostiis humanis. Ea quæ vigilans cogitarat, somnium ipsi ita reddebat ut Gen. xxii. legimus, et persuasionem ipsius, Deum ejus modi sacrificia detestari, graviter confirmabat. Somnium narrabat domesticis. Narratio ore propagata, quæ in somniis evenerant, vere evenisse tradebat, et ita literis consignabatur."—GREVERUS, in Comm. Misc. Syntag., Oldenburg, 1794, p. 94. Whatever Abraham did, there is no doubt this interpreter dreamed, when he wrote this; and unless men are themselves under the influence of the πνεῦμα κατανύξεως, Rom. xi. 8, they will but laugh at such dreamers and such dreams.

Abraham performed a very difficult duty; Abraham obtained a very important blessing; and it was through believing that he did all this. It was his faith which enabled him thus to suffer, thus to act, and thus to obtain.

Abraham sustained a very severe trial. "He was *tried.*" In these words the Apostle obviously refers to the first verse of the 22d chapter of Genesis. The words used, both in Genesis and in the passage before us, signify, either 'to put to trial,' or 'to tempt,' *i.e.*, to solicit to sin; and in order to know which of these two senses it bears in any particular passage, it is necessary to inquire what is the character of the agent who occasions the trial or temptation, and the objects which he has in view. Wherever God is represented as tempting men—as in the case before us—the word is to be understood in the sense of trial. "Let no man," says the Apostle James, "say, when he is tempted"—*i.e.*, plainly, to commit sin—"that he is tempted of God: for God cannot be tempted of evil, neither tempteth He any man." He never deceives any man's judgment; He never corrupts any man's affections; He never does anything that can make Him chargeable with the blame of men's sins. In the case before us, Abraham was not solicited to sin; but a trial was made of the reality and of the strength of his principles of faith and obedience.

When we speak of God's trying men, we are not to suppose that He needs to discover by experiment what is their real character. He knows what is in them before the trial, He knows beforehand what will be the effect of the trial; but He thus makes men's characters known to themselves and to their fellow-men, for ends worthy of His own infinite wisdom, righteousness, and kindness. It also deserves to be noticed that the means which God employs to prove His people are fitted to improve them. The means He employs to discover the good that is in them are calculated to increase and perfect it; the means He employs to discover the evil that is in them are calculated to lessen and destroy it. The means of Abraham's trial was the command recorded in the 2d verse of the 22d chapter of Genesis. The commandment was given apparently in such a manner as left Abraham no room to doubt that it was the commandment of Jehovah. Without this, there had been no sufficient ground for faith, or for the trial of faith.

This trial of faith was perhaps as severe as ever was experienced. He is commanded to do a thing for which no reason could be assigned but the will of Him who gave the command. He is commanded to do what was most abhorrent to natural, and to innocent, praiseworthy, natural feeling. He must not only consent to the death of a son, but he must with his own hand put him to death; and he must do this, not while his mind is warm and agitated by the divine communication, but after an interval of some days, during the whole of which the revolting deed, in all its horrors, must be before his mind. And then such a son!—the son of his old age—a son just at that time of life when the opening faculties and affections made him an object of peculiar fond regard to a father—a son, too, we have reason to believe, of the most amiable dispositions and most engaging manners. He is commanded to do what is, apparently, equally inconsistent with the divine command and the divine promise. The sacredness of human life was a principle very distinctly stated in the revelation made to man after the deluge: " I will require the life of man of the hand of his brother. Whosoever sheddeth man's blood, by man shall his blood be shed." The apparent incongruity between such a statute and a command to put to death a human being who had been guilty of no crime, was well fitted to try the reality and strength of Abraham's faith. Besides, God had promised to Abraham a numerous posterity, through whom the most important blessings were to be communicated to mankind at large; and it had been distinctly stated to him, that "in Isaac his seed should be called;" *i.e.*, that the posterity in reference to whom these glorious predictions had been given forth, were to be the descendants of Isaac. Isaac had yet no children; and his death at this period, in any circumstances, seemed to lay the gravestone on Abraham's hopes, rendering the accomplishment of them altogether impossible. It is quite natural to suppose also that such thoughts as the following would suggest themselves to his mind:—' How will Sarah bear this awful bereavement? Isaac's death in any circumstances would probably bring down her grey hairs in sorrow to the grave. How will it be possible for me to inform her of this awful mandate, or, more dreadful still, of that awful mandate having been executed? What effect will this apparently most unnatural action have on the minds of the surrounding inhabitants, who know not Jehovah? Must they not account me a monster, and my Divinity a demon?'

Such was the trial to which Abraham was exposed. But he sustained the trial. He yielded obedience to the apparently unreasonable and hard command. He performed the difficult and all but impracticable duty. He "offered his son," says the Apostle.[1] We know that he did not actually slay his son and burn his body; but he laid him on the altar, his hand was lifted up to inflict the fatal blow, and the sacrificial pile was prepared and ready to be lighted up. The sacrifice on the part of Abraham was essentially offered up. Whatever inward workings of natural affection there may have been, however strange and unaccountable the command may have appeared to him, Abraham seems never for a moment to have hesitated. He rises early in the morning which succeeded the night when the divine communication was made to him, makes the necessary preparations, commences his journey, and loses no time in reaching the spot which he believed destined for the fearful sacrifice; and even there, there is no trace of hesitation, or even reluctance to execute the will of Jehovah in the immolation of a child inconceivably dear to him. Never was a human being, perhaps, called to a more difficult duty; and never, perhaps, was any duty performed in a spirit of more perfect submission of mind and heart to the will of God.

But Abraham is represented as not only sustaining a very severe trial, and performing a very difficult duty, but as obtaining a very important blessing. He receives his son from the dead as "in a figure."[2] It seems to me not probable that the

---

[1] προσενήνοχεν, 'showed himself ready to offer:' John viii. 27, xiv. 17; Acts xxi. 13. The word, like our English word *offer*, has a general meaning, as well as the particular meaning of *present in sacrifice*. It is well rendered by C. F. Schmid, "adduxit eum instar victimæ." As Salvian says, "quantum ad defunctionem cordis pertinet, immolavit."—*De guberu. Dei*, lib. i.

[2] ὅθεν may be rendered either *unde* or *quare*: 'whence'—that is, ἐκ νεκρῶν—or 'for which reason,' διὰ πίστιν, manifested in his readiness to obey. In the first sense it occurs, Matt. xiv. 7; Acts xxvi. 19, = ἐξ οὗ; in the second, Heb. ii. 17, iii. 1, vii. 25, viii. 3, ix. 18. The words, αὐτὸν καὶ ἐν παραβολῇ ἐκομίσατο, are among the δυσνόητα, 2 Pet. iii. 16. They admit, and as a matter of course they have received, a great variety of interpretation. Most consider the words, ἐν παραβολῇ, as meaning, 'in a similitude,'

Apostle, in showing the influence of faith, not only in enabling men to sustain trials and perform duties, but also to obtain benefits, would neglect to avail himself of the very striking illustration afforded by this very remarkable event. In Abraham's estimation, and in his own, Isaac was as it were already dead, and God as it were restored him from the dead. Isaac's restoration to Abraham in these circumstances must have been felt as a greater blessing than his bestowal at first, especially when connected, as it was, with a most gracious declaration of the divine approbation, and a renewal of the "exceeding great and precious promises" which had been formerly made to him.

Now the Apostle's assertion is, that it was *by faith*, or through believing, that Abraham sustained this trial, performed this duty, and obtained this benefit. Let us inquire into the nature and extent of this influence of faith.

It was faith which enabled him to sustain the trial. Had he not believed that God is infinitely wise, and powerful, and faithful, and good; and had he not believed that the command to offer up his son came from God, as well as the promise that in him should his seed be called,—had he not believed this, it is obvious that he could not have sustained the trial to which he was exposed; and it is equally obvious that a sufficiently

'as it were;' but they explain this similitude variously. Some refer it to his having received Isaac ἐκ τῆς νεκρᾶς μήτρας Σάρρας,—from a mother as good as dead. But the words seem to refer to something subsequent to his offering Isaac—the reward of his offering him. Others consider it as saying that he received Isaac as a type of his great descendant, who was to be really offered, and really to rise from the dead. We should need a new revelation to assure us that this is the meaning. Others, as an image or type of the resurrection of the dead generally. This is equally unsupported; it is entirely arbitrary. Others have considered ἐν παραβολῇ as = 'in circumstances of great danger,'—as if it were παρ' ἐλπίδα; but this is not satisfactorily supported, though I find, to my surprise, Tholuck adopting this view. Others consider ἐν παραβολῇ as equivalent to—'with an oracular declaration,' and suppose the reference to be to the declaration made by God to Abraham, Gen. xxii. 12, 16-18; and consider the use of the word παραβολή as applied to Balaam's oracles, Num. xxiii. 7, 18, xxiv. 3, 15, 20, as supporting this view of it. This is ingenious, but too ingenious to be satisfactory,—*arguta*, not *simplex*. By far the simplest and most satisfactory interpretation adopted, is that which considers the words as = 'he received him *as it were*,' quodammodo—not actually, but ἐν παραβολῇ, ἐν ὁμοιώματι—'from the dead.'

firm faith in these truths was quite adequate to produce the effects which we know were produced.

It was this which enabled him to perform a duty so peculiarly difficult. Had he been weak in faith, he would have doubted whether two revelations, apparently inconsistent, could come from the same God, or, if they did, whether such a God ought to be trusted to or obeyed. But being strong in faith, he reasoned in this way : 'This is plainly God's command. I have satisfactory evidence of that ; and therefore it ought to be immediately and implicitly obeyed. I know Him to be infinitely wise and righteous, and what He commands must be right. Obedience to this command does indeed seem to throw obstacles in the way of the fulfilment of a number of promises which God has made to me. I am quite sure God has made these promises. I am quite sure that He will perform them. How He is to perform them, I cannot tell. That is His province, not mine. It is His to promise, and mine to believe—His to command, and mine to obey—His to bestow blessings, and mine to receive them ; but I am persuaded that, sooner than let these promises fail of accomplishment, God will reanimate the ashes of my Isaac, and that in him, though offered up as a burnt-offering, my seed shall yet be called.' He was persuaded "that God was able even to raise him from the dead." You thus see how it was through believing that Abraham performed this very difficult duty.

It is equally plain that it was through believing that Abraham obtained the great blessing of receiving his beloved Isaac, as "in a figure," from the dead. This important favour was conferred on Abraham as the gracious reward of his believing. It was indeed the reward of his submission and obedience ; but that submission and obedience were the result of his believing.

The bearing which this statement has on the Apostle's object is direct and obvious. The Christian Hebrews were exposed to severe trials, called to difficult duties, and they had promises made to them which, if they "consulted with flesh and blood," they must have supposed were not very likely ever to be performed. How are these trials to be endured, these duties to be performed, these benefits to be obtained ? Look to Abraham. Are your trials more severe than his ? are your duties more difficult than his ? are the blessings you look for less likely to be conferred on you than the blessings which were promised to him, and which in due time were all performed to him? How did he sustain the trial? how did he perform the duty? how did he obtain the blessing? By believing. "Go ye and do likewise." Without faith, any trial becomes insupportable, any duty becomes impracticable. With faith, no trial is insupportable, no duty is impracticable; nay, every trial, every duty, is easy. Of such infinite importance is it that we believe, and persevere in believing. A very natural practical reflection from what has been said is, that Christians should not be afraid of trials, nor backward to submit to them, when God calls them to it. Abraham's trial, though as severe a one as any saint ever met with, was meant in kindness, and in effect was conducive both to his spiritual improvement and to his true happiness. Who would not willingly endure Abraham's trial to obtain Abraham's reward? Trials are necessary to the saint in the present state. There is a 'need be' that we be "in heaviness through manifold trials." Yet ought Christians "to count it all joy when they are brought into manifold trials, knowing that the trying of faith worketh patience," or rather perseverance. "Tribulation worketh patience; patience, experience; and experience, hope." "No chastisement for the present is joyous, but grievous; but it yieldeth the peaceable fruits of righteousness to those who are exercised thereby." "The trial of our faith, which is more precious than that of gold, will be found to glory and honour at the coming of our Lord Jesus Christ." Let us never forget, however, that, in order to our trials being useful to us, they must be endured in faith. "Our afflictions will work out for us a far more exceeding and an eternal weight of glory, if"—but only if—"we look not at the things which are seen and temporal, but at the things which are unseen and eternal." No spiritual child of Abraham need expect an exemption from trials—from severe trials. These are not to be courted, but neither are they to be sinfully shunned. They are to be submitted to in a humble dependence on Him who supported and strengthened Abraham, and who says to all His people in their trials, "My grace is sufficient for you; My strength shall be made perfect in weakness." A firm faith in this will carry us through the severest trials triumphantly; and "we shall be made more than conquerors through Him that loves us."

We have three new witnesses brought forward to the importance of faith, in the 20th, 21st, and 22d verses—Isaac, Jacob, and Joseph. "By faith Isaac blessed Jacob and Esau concerning things to come. By faith Jacob, when he was a dying, blessed both the sons of Joseph; and worshipped, leaning upon the top of his staff. By faith Joseph, when he died, made mention of the departing of the children of Israel; and gave commandment concerning his bones."

The general principle contained in these statements seems to be this: Faith enabled Isaac, and Jacob, and Joseph to do what otherwise they could not have done—to pronounce prophetic benedictions on their posterity, which in succeeding ages were accurately accomplished. Now, fully to apprehend the meaning and design of the Apostle's statements, it will be necessary that we first attend to the facts to which he refers—to what Isaac and Jacob did; then show how it was through believing that they did what they did; and, lastly, point out the manner in which this illustrates the importance of faith, and serves the Apostle's object—the placing in a clear point of light the necessity of the Hebrew Christians persevering in the faith of the Gospel, notwithstanding all the temptations to apostasy to which they were exposed.

The facts to which the Apostle refers in the 20th verse are recorded in the 27th chapter of the book of Genesis. "And it came to pass, that when Isaac was old, and his eyes were dim, so that he could not see, he called Esau his eldest son, and said unto him, My son. And he said unto him, Behold, here am I. And he said, Behold now, I am old, I know not the day of my death. Now therefore take, I pray thee, thy weapons, thy quiver and thy bow, and go out to the field, and take me some venison; and make me savoury meat, such as I love, and bring it to me, that I may eat; that my soul may bless thee before I die. And Rebekah heard when Isaac spake to Esau his son. And Esau went to the field to hunt for venison, and to bring it. And Rebekah spake unto Jacob her son, saying, Behold, I heard thy father speak unto Esau thy brother, saying, Bring me venison, and make me savoury meat, that I may eat, and bless thee before the Lord before my death. Now therefore, my son, obey my voice, according to that which I command thee. Go now to the flock, and fetch me from thence two good kids of the goats; and I will make them savoury meat for thy father, such as he loveth. And thou shalt bring it to thy father, that he may eat, and that he may bless thee before his death. And Jacob said to Rebekah his mother, Behold, Esau my brother is a hairy man, and I am a smooth man: my father peradventure will feel me, and I shall seem to him as a deceiver; and I shall bring a curse upon me, and not a blessing. And his mother said unto him, Upon me be thy curse, my son; only obey my voice, and go fetch me them. And he went, and fetched, and brought them to his mother: and his mother made savoury meat, such as his father loved. And Rebekah took goodly raiment of her eldest son Esau, which were with her in the house, and put them upon Jacob her younger son. And she put the skins of the kids of the goats upon his hands, and upon the smooth of his neck. And she gave the savoury meat and the bread, which she had prepared, into the hand of her son Jacob. And he came unto his father, and said, My father. And he said, Here am I; who art thou, my son? And Jacob said unto his father, I am Esau thy first-born; I have done according as thou badest me: arise, I pray thee, sit and eat of my venison, that thy soul may bless me. And Isaac said unto his son, How is it that thou hast found it so quickly, my son? And he said, Because the Lord thy God brought it to me. And Isaac said unto Jacob, Come near, I pray thee, that I may feel thee, my son, whether thou be my very son Esau or not. And Jacob went near unto Isaac his father; and he felt him, and said, The voice is Jacob's voice, but the hands are the hands of Esau. And he discerned him not, because his hands were hairy, as his brother Esau's hands. So he blessed him. And he said, Art thou my very son Esau? And he said, I am. And he said, Bring it near to me, and I will eat of my son's venison, that my soul may bless thee. And he brought it near to him, and he did eat: and he brought him wine, and he drank. And his father Isaac said unto him, Come near now, and kiss me, my son. And he came near, and kissed him: and he smelled the smell of his raiment, and blessed him, and said, See, the smell of my son is as the smell of a field which the Lord hath blessed: therefore God give thee of the dew of heaven, and the fatness of the earth, and plenty of corn and wine: let people serve thee, and nations bow down to thee: be lord over thy brethren, and let thy mother's sons bow down to thee : cursed be every one that curseth thee, and blessed be he that blesseth thee. And it came to pass, as soon as Isaac had made an end of blessing Jacob, and Jacob was yet scarce gone out from the presence of Isaac his father, that Esau his brother came in from his hunting. And he also had made savoury meat, and brought it unto his father, and said unto his father, Let my father arise, and eat of his son's venison, that thy soul may bless me. And Isaac his father said unto him, Who art thou ? And he said, I am thy son, thy first-born, Esau. And Isaac trembled very exceedingly, and said, Who ? where is he that hath taken venison, and brought it me, and I have eaten of all before thou camest, and have blessed him ? yea, and he shall be blessed. And when Esau heard the words of his father, he cried with a great and exceeding bitter cry, and said unto his father, Bless me, even me also, O my father ! And he said, Thy brother came with subtilty, and hath taken away thy blessing. And he said, Is not he rightly named Jacob ? for he hath supplanted me these two times : he took away my birthright ; and, behold, now he hath taken away my blessing. And he said, Hast thou not reserved a blessing for me ? And Isaac answered and said unto Esau, Behold, I have made him thy lord, and all his brethren have I given to him for servants ; and with corn and wine have I sustained him : and what shall I do now unto thee, my son ? And Esau said unto his father, Hast thou but one blessing, my father ? bless me, even me also, O my father ! And Esau lifted up his voice, and wept. And Isaac his father answered and said unto him, Behold, thy dwelling shall be the fatness of the earth, and of the dew of heaven from above ; and by thy sword shalt thou live, and shalt serve thy brother ; and it shall come to pass, when thou shalt have the dominion, that thou shalt break his yoke from off thy neck."[1] Thus " Isaac blessed Jacob and Esau concerning things to come ;" *i.e.*, he pronounced a prophetic benediction[2]—for that is the import of the original word —first on Jacob, and then on Esau, in reference to events which were to take place in future ages. The blessing pronounced on Jacob runs in these terms (vers. 28, 29) : " God give thee of the dew of heaven, and the fatness of the earth, and plenty of corn and wine : let people serve thee, and nations bow down to thee :

[1] Gen. xxvii. 1–40.   [2] εὐλογεῖν.

be lord over thy brethren, and let thy mother's sons bow down to thee: cursed be every one that curseth thee, and blessed be he that blesseth thee." The blessing pronounced on Esau runs thus: "Behold, thy dwelling shall be the fatness of the earth, and of the dew of heaven from above; and by thy sword shalt thou live, and shalt serve thy brother; and it shall come to pass, when thou shalt have the dominion, that thou shalt break his yoke from off thy neck." Both these prophetic benedictions respecting "things to come" were in due time fully and minutely realized. Such are the facts of the case as to Isaac.

Now the question naturally occurs, How was it *by faith* that Isaac pronounced these benedictions? The answer to that question is: A revelation was made to the mind of Isaac by God respecting the events which were to occur to his descendants in future times. Isaac firmly believed this revelation; and it was his faith in this revelation that led him to utter these prophetic benedictions. In ordinary circumstances, no wise man will be very minute or very confident in his statements respecting future events. But we see Isaac, believing the divine revelation, speaking with perfect confidence and with great minuteness " concerning things to come;" and we see also the event justifying the confidence with which he spoke. Though the events were, some of them, of a very improbable kind,—such as that the children of one who was but a stranger and sojourner, having no property but a burying-place, were to be numerous and powerful nations,—yet Isaac, believing that the revelation came from God, and having no doubt respecting the power and the faithfulness of the Revealer, unhesitatingly uttered the prediction.

There is indeed a difficulty connected with this subject, that is likely to suggest itself to the reflecting mind, arising out of the circumstance, that Isaac conceived that he was pronouncing a benediction on Esau when he uttered Jacob's blessing. The difficulty is more apparent than real. The revelation made to Isaac's mind was, that the events to which that benediction refers were to take place respecting the posterity of the individual who was now before him. That was Jacob, though Isaac supposed him Esau. And that this was the truth, is plain from the fact, that when Isaac discovered his mistake, he does not say, 'The blessing was originally intended for Esau, and therefore will be his, though through my mistake it was pronounced over his brother;' but he says, "I have blessed him, and he shall be blessed;"—plainly intimating two things: that in the revelation made to him, the reference was to the person before him; and that in uttering it, he merely declared the will and determination of Him "whose counsel shall stand, and who will do all His pleasure." The whole transaction is a striking proof of what the Apostle says, "The prophecy of old time came not by the will of man, but holy men spake as they were moved by the Holy Ghost." Isaac had too firm a faith in the unalterableness of the divine determinations to suppose for a moment that his private affection could transfer the superior blessing from his younger to his elder son.

The next inquiry that suggests itself is, How does this statement, that "by faith Isaac blessed Jacob and Esau concerning things to come," subserve the Apostle's object—the impressing on the minds of the Hebrew Christians the importance and necessity of their persevering in faith in order to their performing their duties, enduring their trials, and obtaining their inheritance as Christians? It plainly illustrates this general principle: 'Faith can enable a man to do what nothing else could enable him to do. What but faith in a divine revelation could have enabled Isaac, or any man, to utter predictions referring to distant ages, which predictions were in due time accurately fulfilled?' The Hebrew Christians were called on to act, and suffer, and expect, in a way which nothing but faith could enable them to do. They were required to "deny themselves, take up their cross, and follow Christ;" they were required to "forsake father, and mother, and houses, and lands;" they were required to "cut off right hands, and to pluck out right eyes;" and they were called on, amid all this, to cherish an unsuspecting dependence on the divine peculiar kindness, and an unclouded hope of glory, honour, and immortality. To do all this, was really, in a moral sense, as far out of their power as the prediction of future events, in a physical sense, was out of the power of Isaac. But as a faith in the revelation made to Isaac enabled him to do what otherwise he could not have done, so a faith in the revelation made to them would enable them to do what otherwise they could not have done. If they, knowing who and what Jesus Christ is—knowing His power, and His wisdom, and His faithfulness—firmly believed what He has said, that "whosoever believeth in Him shall not perish, but have everlasting life;" that whosoever denies Him shall be denied by Him, and whosoever confesses Him shall be confessed by Him, in the presence of His Father and the holy angels; that "it is the Father's good pleasure to give His people the kingdom,"—if they firmly believed this revelation, they would be enabled to do things as far exceeding the unassisted powers of man as predicting future events is—they would be brought under "the powers of the world to come," and be enabled to act, and to suffer, and to hope as "seeing the God that is invisible," and the world that is "unseen and eternal."

And as Isaac could not possibly have without faith prophetically blessed his children "concerning things to come," so neither could they without faith persevere in doing and suffering the will of God, and in looking for the mercy of God unto eternal life. Such, so far as I have been able to apprehend, is the force of the fact stated in the 20th verse, as affording an illustration of the importance of faith, and suggesting a motive to the Hebrew Christians to persevere in believing.

The next facts brought forward are quite of the same kind:—"By faith Jacob, when he was a dying, blessed both the sons of Joseph; and worshipped, leaning upon the top of his staff." "Jacob, when a dying," or drawing near death—when on his deathbed—like his father Isaac, under the influence of the Spirit of prediction, uttered prophetic benedictions respecting his posterity.

It is the ingenious conjecture of a learned interpreter, that the words, "of Joseph," did not originally belong to this verse, but were introduced by an early transcriber from the beginning of the next verse; and that the statement made by the inspired writer is, "Jacob, when dying, blessed each of his children." This certainly agrees with what we know to be the fact. He pronounced prophetic benedictions on all his children, which in the future history of their descendants were remarkably realized. He called his sons to him, and said, "Gather yourselves together, that I may tell you what shall befall you in the last days." You have a record of these prophetic benedictions in the 49th chapter of Genesis. And these were given "when a dying," in the strictest sense of the word; for "when he had made an end of commanding his sons, he gathered up his feet into the bed, and yielded up the ghost, and was gathered to his people."

At the same time, this, though an ingenious conjecture, is but a conjecture. The fact, as it is stated by the Apostle, agrees also with the history; and the mere circumstance of our thinking it more likely that he should refer to the blessing of all his children than to the blessing of Joseph's children, is no sufficient reason, in opposition to the uniform testimony of MSS. and versions, to conclude that there has been a change in the text. Considering, then, the present reading as correct, the facts referred to are these, recorded in the 48th chapter of Genesis. When Joseph heard that his father was sick, he went to visit him, along with his sons Manasseh and Ephraim. The history of their benediction cannot be so well told as in the words of the inspired historian:—" And Israel beheld Joseph's sons, and said, Who are these? And Joseph said unto his father, They are my sons, whom God hath given me in this place. And he said, Bring them, I pray thee, unto me, and I will bless them. (Now the eyes of Israel were dim for age, so that he could not see.) And he brought them near unto him; and he kissed them, and embraced them. And Israel said unto Joseph, I had not thought to see thy face; and, lo, God hath showed me also thy seed. And Joseph brought them out from between his knees, and he bowed himself with his face to the earth. And Joseph took them both, Ephraim in his right hand toward Israel's left hand, and Manasseh in his left hand toward Israel's right hand, and brought them near unto him. And Israel stretched out his right hand, and laid it upon Ephraim's head, who was the younger, and his left hand upon Manasseh's head, guiding his hands wittingly; for Manasseh was the first-born. And he blessed Joseph, and said, God, before whom my fathers Abraham and Isaac did walk, the God which fed me all my life long unto this day, the Angel which redeemed me from all evil, bless the lads; and let my name be named on them, and the name of my fathers Abraham and Isaac; and let them grow into a multitude in the midst of the earth. And when Joseph saw that his father laid his right hand upon the head of Ephraim, it displeased him: and he held up his father's hand, to remove it from Ephraim's head unto Manasseh's head. And Joseph said unto his father, Not so, my father: for this is the first-born; put thy right hand upon his head. And his father refused, and said, I know it, my son, I know it: he also shall become a people, and he also shall be great; but truly his younger brother shall be greater than he, and his seed shall become a multitude of nations. And he blessed them that day, saying, In thee shall Israel bless, saying, God make thee as Ephraim, and as Manasseh. And he set Ephraim before Manasseh."[1]

The words which the Apostle adds regarding Jacob, "and worshipped, leaning on the top of his staff," have by some been supposed merely to describe the circumstances in which the benediction of Ephraim and Manasseh was given. But we apprehend they refer to a different fact altogether, in which the power of faith was illustriously displayed. The fact referred to is recorded in the 47th chapter of Genesis. "And the time drew nigh that Israel must die: and he called his son Joseph, and said unto him, If now I have found grace in thy sight, put, I pray thee, thy hand under my thigh, and deal kindly and truly with me; bury me not, I pray thee, in Egypt: but I will lie with my fathers; and thou shalt carry me out of Egypt, and bury me in their burying-place. And he said, I will do as thou hast said. And he said, Swear unto me. And he sware unto him. And Israel bowed himself upon the bed's head."[2]

To remove the appearance of discrepancy which exists between the words of Moses and of Paul, it is but necessary to remark, that the word translated, to *bow himself*, often signifies 'to worship,' as bowing a person's self is an ordinary token or sign of religious worship; and that the word rendered "bed" by our translators in Genesis, and "staff" here, is a word which, according to the manner in which it is pointed, has the one or other of these significations.[3] The question is between the accuracy of the Masoretic punctuation, and the version of the LXX. and the Apostle's quotation.

[1] Gen. xlviii. 8-20.   [2] Gen. xlvii. 29-31.
[3] Great respect is due to the Masoretic punctuation, as generally the record of the ancient interpretation of the Hebrew Scriptures; but, as Mr Stuart justly remarks, "that the present vowel-points of the Hebrew do not in *every* case give the most probable sense of the original, will not appear strange to any one who reflects that they were introduced after the fifth century of our present era. All enlightened critics of the present day disclaim the idea that they are authoritative."

The reference does not seem to me to be so much to the fact taken by itself, as in connection with the other facts with which it is related in the sacred narrative. The words were intended to bring the whole scene before the mind, and in this way are equivalent to—'Jacob, when dying, by faith expressed an earnest desire to be buried in the land of promise; and on receiving satisfactory assurance that this wish would be complied with, testified his firm confidence in the promise—a belief in which excited this desire—by worshipping, bending over his staff, which was necessary to support his now enfeebled frame.'[1]

These are the facts: now let us see how it was *by faith* that Jacob did these things. The whole of the illustrations respecting Isaac's benediction of his sons, are plainly equally applicable to Jacob's benediction of his sons or grandsons. A revelation was made to Jacob's mind respecting their future fortunes; he believed it; and his faith in this revelation enabled him to do what otherwise he could not have done—predict what was to happen to his descendants through a long series of generations. With regard to the second fact: it plainly was Jacob's faith in the promise that Canaan was to be the inheritance of his posterity, and in the other promises connected with this, that led him to wish to be buried there, and not in the land of Egypt. The ordering that he should take enfeoffment of it, as it were, by his dead body, was a very strong expression of his full persuasion that in due time his posterity should, according to the

---

[1] The fact is mentioned not only as a picturesque one, bringing the whole scene before the mind of the reader, but as intimating that even in the last extremity of human feebleness Jacob "continued strong in faith, giving glory to God." It is scarcely credible how much absurdity has been taught about this act of worship. Some of the Fathers, Schoetgen says, have "pie magis quam docte" written on this subject: really we cannot help thinking their piety and learning on the subject much on a level. Hear the drivelling nonsense which flows from the pen of one of them :—" Jacob Patriarcha, filiis suis benedicturus, nonne, paullulum se attollens e lecto, in quo recubabat, καὶ ἐπὶ τὸ ἄκρον τῆς ῥάβδου αὐτοῦ ἐπιστηριχθείς, et in summo sive extremo baculi, *qui crucem pretiosam significabat,* innixus, ἐν τῷ σταυροῦν τὰς χεῖρας αὐτοῦ, οὕτως εὐλόγει αὐτούς, manus crucis in modum componendo, sic ipsis fausta et felicia precabatur?"—GRIGENTIUS SEPURENENSIS, *in disputatione cum Herbano Judæo.* A likely method indeed this to convert the Jews! Others insist that there was a cross on the top of the staff, and that the patriarch worshipped it. Surely men were given up to "strong delusions," who could believe this.

divine promise, possess it as an inheritance; and the pious expression of his satisfaction at obtaining security that this would be done, was a very becoming manner of testifying his full confidence in the divine promise.

The manner in which the first of these facts is calculated to serve the Apostle's purpose has been already explained. The manner in which the last of them does so may be thus stated: 'Faith enabled Jacob, when dying in Egypt, at a distance from Canaan, when all his family were in Egypt, and when there was nothing that looked like their returning to Canaan, firmly to expect, and to give clear evidence of his expecting, the fulfilment of the promise respecting that land being the inheritance of his posterity. Nothing but *faith* could have enabled him to do so. Faith, and nothing but faith, can enable you, amid events which seem to make the fulfilment of the promises made to you all but an impossibility, firmly to expect their accomplishment, and exhibit satisfactory evidence that you hold fast that confidence which has great recompense of reward.'

The next fact brought forward refers to Joseph, and is nearly of the same kind as those which we have just been illustrating. Ver. 22. "By faith Joseph, when he died"[1]—*i.e.*, when on his deathbed—"made mention of the departing of the children of Israel; and gave commandment concerning his bones." There are two facts stated here respecting Joseph. Of both we have the record in the 50th chapter of Genesis: "And Joseph said unto his brethren, I die; and God will surely visit you, and bring you out of this land unto the land which He sware to Abraham, to Isaac, and to Jacob. And Joseph took an oath of the children of Israel, saying, God will surely visit you, and ye shall carry up my bones from hence."[2] Joseph predicted the exodus of the children of Israel. He believed the promises made to Abraham, Isaac, and Jacob, that Canaan should be the possession of their posterity; he believed the promise made to Jacob immediately before he came into Egypt,—"And He said, I am God, the God of thy father: fear not to go down into Egypt; for I will there make of thee a great nation. I will go down with thee into Egypt; and I will also surely bring thee up again: and Joseph shall put his hand upon thine eyes;"[3]

---

[1] τελευτῶν: the complete expression, τελ. βίου.
[2] Gen. l. 24, 25.   [3] Gen. xlvi. 3, 4.

—and it is not at all unlikely that a direct revelation had been made to himself on the subject. As a proof of his faith in the divine promises, "he gave commandment concerning his bones;" —he took an oath of his brethren, that they should convey his remains to the land of promise.

We have already, by anticipation, said all that is necessary to show how these things were done by faith, and how their being done by faith is an illustration of the importance of faith, and in this way well fitted to serve the Apostle's purpose, as a motive to the Hebrew Christians to believe, and to persevere in believing—to live believing, and to die believing. Many of these displays of faith which have come under our review, have been given towards the close of life, or in the article of death. It is a question of deep interest to us all, Have we a faith which will support us amid the frailties of age, amid the debilities or the agonies of dissolving nature? We all profess faith now: the hour which is to try whether we possess it or not is fast approaching. The reality and the strength of our faith must by and by—God only knows how soon—be put to a severe trial. Ah! how many, who thought they had faith in health, find they have none in sickness; and how many, who thought their faith strong, find then that it is indeed but "as a grain of mustard-seed!" Let us now, by seeking clear, distinct, extended views of Christian truth and its evidence, "lay up a good foundation for the time to come, that we may lay hold on eternal life." Nothing but the faith of the Gospel can enable a rationally thinking man to enter with composure and delight into the unseen world. It is the faith of the Gospel, and that alone, which can enable the expiring mortal to exult in the dissolution of "the earthly house of this tabernacle," and say, "O death, where is thy sting? O grave, where is thy victory?"

In the paragraph which follows, we have a further illustration of the importance of faith, drawn first from the conduct of Moses' parents, and then from the conduct of Moses himself. The illustration drawn from the conduct of Moses' parents is contained in the 23d verse: "By faith Moses, when he was born, was hid three months of his parents,[1] because they saw he

[1] Πατέρες is used for both parents, as Euripides uses βασιλεῦσι for Admetus and his queen.

was a proper child; and they were not afraid of the king's commandment." Here, as in the preceding illustrations, I shall first attend to what Moses' parents did; then show how they did it by faith; and then point out the bearing of this illustration on the Apostle's great object—the fortifying of the believing Hebrews against the temptations to apostasy to which they were exposed.

The facts, as we learn from the 2d chapter of Exodus, were these:—Some time before the birth of Moses, the king of Egypt, alarmed at the rapid multiplication of the Israelites, issued an edict that every male child born among them should be put to death. On Moses being born, his parents, Amram and Jochebed, instead of complying with this atrocious enactment, concealed him for three months; and while they showed by concealing him that in one sense they were afraid of the king's commandment—as they knew, if they were discovered, that both his life and theirs would have been sacrificed to the tyrant's resentment,—yet they were not so afraid of the king's commandment as to purchase security, as it is to be feared too many did, by becoming to a certain degree accessory to the murder of their children. The remarkable beauty of the child, which is noticed by Stephen, and particularly described by Josephus, is here represented as having had its influence over the minds of his parents, in rendering them solicitous for his preservation: "They saw that he was a *proper*"[1]—rather, beautiful—"child."

But, though not insensible to the force of such natural principles, their conduct is chiefly to be traced to a higher principle. It was by faith that they did all this. A considerable number of good expositors consider this as just equivalent to—' In the exercise of trust in God, they acted in this way. They knew that, in endeavouring to protect their infant child, they were but doing their duty; and they, trusting in the divine righteousness and benignity, expected that they would be protected in the discharge of this duty.' This is, however, to depart from the meaning which the Apostle has given to the word "faith," as "confidence respecting things hoped for, conviction respecting things unseen," founded on an express revelation of the divine

---

[1] A child not maimed or sickly, but who looked well and likely to live: = the Heb. רְאִי טוֹב, 1 Sam. xvi. 12; ἀγαθὸς τῇ ὁράσει, LXX. Stephen represents him as ἀστεῖος τῷ Θεῷ, Acts vii. 20.

will. I have no doubt that the word has here the same meaning as in the other parts of the chapter, and that the Apostle's statement is, that it was Moses' parents believing a divine revelation that enabled them to act as they did. But the question naturally occurs, What revelation of the divine will did they believe? It is highly probable, not only that they were acquainted with the divine, frequently repeated, promises respecting the numerous posterity of Abraham, Isaac, and Jacob, and their possession of Canaan as an inheritance, and with the divine oracle respecting their deliverance in the fourth generation from that country in which they were to suffer so many hardships; but I cannot help thinking that there is a reference to a more particular revelation, made to the parents of Moses themselves. We have no account of any such revelation being made in the book of Exodus; but we know that many events, and many events of importance, took place which are not recorded in Scripture. We know that, at the time this Epistle was written, it was the common faith of the Jews that such a revelation had been made. Josephus, in his "Antiquities of the Jews," Book ii. chap. v., expressly states, that a divine communication was made to Amram during the pregnancy of Jochebed, that the child about to be born was to be the deliverer of his nation from Egyptian tyranny. There is nothing in Scripture inconsistent with this. Though we have no account in Scripture of an express revelation made as to sacrifice, we conclude, from its being said that it was "by faith Abel offered a more excellent sacrifice than Cain," that such a revelation was made; and on the same principle, I cannot help considering the Apostle as here giving sanction to the commonly received belief of the Jews on this subject, and stating that it was the faith of Moses' parents in this revelation that led them to act as they did, in preserving their infant's life at the risk of their own.

In this view of the matter, everything is plain. Had Amram and Jochebed not believed the divine declaration, it is probable that they would have acted as many others did, and, fearing the king's commandment, have secured their own lives by allowing the birth of their infant son to be known, which would have led to his destruction; but believing that the declaration came from God, and believing His power and faithfulness, they took a course which to the eye of sense seemed full of hazard, but which, through their believing, they knew to be the path of security as well as of duty.

The bearing of this on the Apostle's object is direct and obvious. The Hebrew Christians were required to follow a course full of difficulties and hazards; but if, like Amram and Jochebed, they believed that it was a course prescribed by God, and prescribed, too, as the means of the accomplishment of "exceeding great and precious promises," their faith would raise them above the influence of fear, and make what seemed at first impossible, not only practicable, but easy.

Though it is not particularly mentioned, there can scarcely be any doubt that it was under the divine direction that Moses' parents not only concealed him for three months, but at the expiration of this period had recourse to the plan which they adopted, by preparing for the infant deliverer of Israel a little ark of bulrushes, and laying him among the flags by the side of the Nile. The Jewish historian already referred to expressly says, that in doing so, they determined rather to entrust the care of the child to God than to depend on their own concealment of him, whereby both themselves and the child should be in imminent danger; but they believed that God would in some way for certain procure the safety of the child, in order to secure the truth of His own predictions. Whether we consider the conduct of the parents of Moses as the consequence of a belief in a second express revelation, or of such believing reasonings on the former revelation, it is a very striking demonstration of the power of faith. When constrained by the necessity of circumstances, or called by an express declaration of the divine will, they place their infant—peculiarly dear to them from the hazards they had already run for him, and the important interests which were bound up in his life—in circumstances of apparently great danger, assuredly believing that "He was faithful who had promised," and that Moses was as safe in the ark of bulrushes on the banks of the Nile, as he could have been in his mother's bosom, in some peaceful cottage far removed beyond the power of the cruel Egyptian king.

If the first part of the history strikingly illustrates the power of faith in enabling men to sustain severe trials and perform difficult duties, the sequel of it equally illustrates its power in enabling them to obtain important benefits. The expectations of

Amram and Jochebed, founded on their faith in a divine revelation, were not disappointed. Moses' life was preserved, and he was brought into the circumstances most favourable for his being trained up for the important work to which he was destined. The faith of Amram and Jochebed was richly rewarded, when they saw their son enjoying all the advantages of the most accomplished education which Egypt could supply, and, through the wonderful providence of Jehovah, that power which had meditated his destruction, employed for his welfare, and, in being so employed, preparing the means of its own overthrow.

The history of Moses' infancy, as an illustration of the faith of his parents, is thus admirably fitted to serve the Apostle's object. It illustrates his general principle: 'Persevering faith will do what nothing else can : it will enable you to do and suffer all the will of God, and, after having done so, to receive the promise.' You may be called to trials and duties as difficult and severe as those of Amram or Jochebed,—you may be called to what will expose your life, and what may be dearer to you than your life, to extreme danger ; but a faith in the Gospel will prevent you from shrinking from the task assigned you—will support you while engaged in it, while He in whom you believe will render even these difficulties and hazards the very means of securing for you the great end of your faith, and the great object of your hope—the salvation of your souls.

We are now to direct our attention to the still more remarkable display of the importance of faith afforded by the conduct of Moses himself. Ver. 24. "By faith Moses, when he was come to years, refused to be called the son of Pharaoh's daughter ; 25. Choosing rather to suffer affliction with the people of God, than to enjoy the pleasures of sin for a season ; 26. Esteeming the reproach of Christ greater riches than the treasures in Egypt : for he had respect unto the recompense of the reward."[1] We shall first attend to the account of Moses' conduct, and then show how his conduct was influenced by his

---

[1] In some codd. the following words are inserted between verse 23 and verse 24 : πίστει μέγας γενόμενος Μωϋσῆς ἀνεῖλεν τὸν Αἰγύπτιον, κατανοῶν τὴν ταπείνωσιν τῶν ἀδελφῶν αὐτοῦ. Mill considers the words as genuine ; but they are not by any means sufficiently supported. The repetition of πίστει M. μ. γ. is very unlike the concinnity of the writer of the Epistle to the Hebrews. It seems to have been added by some transcriber from Acts vii. 24.

faith. We shall first inquire what he did, and then show that it was by faith that he did it.

"When he came to years, he refused to be called the son of Pharaoh's daughter;" he "chose rather to suffer affliction with the people of God, than to enjoy the pleasures of sin for a season;" and he "esteemed the reproach of Christ greater riches than the treasures of Egypt." The phrase, "when he was come to years," literally signifies, 'when he became great;' and, taken by itself, might refer to that elevated station in society to which Moses was raised in the Egyptian court. It seems, however, plainly contrasted with the phrase, "when he was born," in the 23d verse, and is just equivalent to, 'when he arrived at maturity.'[1] "He refused to be called the son of Pharaoh's daughter." On Moses being found by this princess in the ark of bulrushes on the banks of the Nile, moved with compassion, she seems to have resolved immediately to take charge of the infant; and accordingly the charge she gave to his mother, who providentially became his nurse, was, "Take this child, and nurse it for me, and I will give you your wages." It might very probably then be her intention to educate him as her slave, or for some of the ordinary professions; but, on his being brought back by his mother, she was so much delighted with the beautiful child, that she resolved to adopt him as her own,—"he became her son;" and as a memorial of the remarkable circumstances of his coming under her protection, she called him Moses, which in the Egyptian language, signifies 'out of the water.' It has been supposed by some that the king of Egypt had no other child than the daughter mentioned in the book of Exodus; that she had no children; and that Moses, as her adopted son, might be considered as the heir apparent to the Egyptian crown. This appears not very probable; at any rate, it is not certain. It is obvious, however, that the adopted son of the daughter of the king of Egypt, then one of the richest, most populous, and civilised nations in the world, must have occupied a very dignified station in society, and possessed in no ordinary measure worldly wealth and honours. During childhood and youth he bare the name of "the son of Pharaoh's daughter," and enjoyed the secular advantages which were connected with so honourable a title.

[1] וַיִּגְדַּל is used in the same way, Exod. ii. 11.

But "when he was come to years"—arrived at mature age—" he refused to be called the son of Pharaoh's daughter." It is quite possible that the Apostle may refer to some particular fact in Moses' history, known when he wrote, but now forgotten. There may have been some public occasion on which the continued enjoyment of the honours connected with this title by Moses might be suspended on his doing something which would have amounted to a renunciation of the religion of his forefathers, and which led him openly to renounce the dignified situation he had so long occupied. This may have been the case, but the words before us do not warrant us to say that it was so. They merely intimate that he voluntarily renounced the honours and advantages connected with the title of "the son of Pharaoh's daughter." He saw his kinsmen enslaved and oppressed; he knew that by renouncing all connection with them, he might retain that situation of ease, and affluence, and honour which he possessed; he saw that, if he identified himself with them, he must renounce his wealth and his dignities; and he unhesitatingly made his choice. He gave up the name of an Egyptian prince and took in its room that of an Israelitish bondman.

When he was grown, he went out to his brethren, and looked on their burdens; and burning with indignation at the unjust treatment which one of them received from an Egyptian, executed summary vengeance on the oppressor. That act was a renouncing for ever of the name of "the son of Pharaoh's daughter." " He chose rather to suffer affliction with the people of God, than to enjoy the pleasures of sin for a season." By " the people of God" we are to understand the Israelites, now in Egypt. They were " chosen out of all the families of the earth" to be the depositaries of the true religion, to enjoy peculiar privileges, and to serve important purposes in the development of the grand scheme of divine mercy for the salvation of mankind. The number of genuine saints among them at the period referred to seems to have been small; but almost all the saints on the earth were to be found among them, and as a people —as the descendants of Abraham, Isaac, and Jacob—they were in covenant with God. This "people of God" were, at the period referred to, " suffering affliction." Of these afflictions we have an account in Exod. i. 13, 14, and ii. 23: " And the Egyptians made the children of Israel to serve with rigour. And they made their lives bitter with hard bondage, in mortar, and in brick, and in all manner of service in the field: all their service, wherein they made them serve, was with rigour." "And it came to pass, in process of time, that the king of Egypt died: and the children of Israel sighed by reason of the bondage, and they cried; and their cry came up unto God, by reason of the bondage." Moses was originally one of this people, and in the perils of his childhood shared in their afflictions. By the remarkable care of Providence, he had been for a season separated from them, and placed in circumstances of security and ease. But when he arrived at mature age, he voluntarily preferred casting in his lot with the afflicted people of God to the continued enjoyment of the honours and pleasures of the Egyptian court. These are termed "the pleasures of sin." Many of the pleasures of a court life are usually in their own nature sinful pleasures. But here, I apprehend, the idea intended to be conveyed is this: The pleasures of the Egyptian court, even such of them as were innocent in themselves—and we have no reason to think that Moses ever indulged in any other—were sinful pleasures in his case. He could not continue to enjoy them without in effect renouncing his connection with the people of God, and his interest in those blessings which were secured to them by the divine covenant. If he continued to enjoy them, he could not have discharged the duties of that office to which he was destined, as the deliverer of the people of God, and must have been implicated in the guilt of their Egyptian oppressors. The sinful pleasures which Moses renounced are termed "pleasures for *a season;*" *i.e.*, temporary—liable to innumerable interruptions in this life, and unavoidably ending with it. He chose rather to endure for a season the afflictions of the people of God, than to enjoy for a season the pleasures of an ungodly world.

The same general truth is represented in a different way in the next clause: "He esteemed the reproach of Christ greater riches than all the treasures of Egypt." I believe every attentive reader of the Bible has felt some difficulty in satisfactorily explaining to himself this passage. He to whom the appellation "Messiah, Christ, or Anointed" belongs, did not appear in our world till more than 1500 years after the days of Moses. The Son of God indeed existed from eternity, but He did not become the Christ till He assumed human nature. The great

Deliverer had indeed been promised, but He had not been promised under the name of the Messiah.

"The reproach of Christ" is a phrase of which, when taken by itself, the most natural meaning is, 'the reproach which Christ Himself suffered;' and if we depart from this primary sense, the next meaning which the words suggest is, 'reproach endured on account of Christ.' It does not seem possible to make sense of the passage, adopting either of these meanings. I shall very shortly state what appear to me the only two probable interpretations which have been given of the passage, leaving my readers to make their choice between them. I cannot say either of them is entirely satisfactory to my own mind.

The word "Christ" is by some interpreters considered as referring not to our Lord Jesus Christ, the anointed—*i.e.*, the divinely chosen and designated—Deliverer, but to the Israelitish people, the divinely chosen and designated people. There can be no doubt that the patriarchs of that people are termed God's christs, or anointed ones, Ps. cv. 15; and in Hab. iii. 13, it seems highly probable that the Israelitish people are termed God's anointed: "*with* Thine anointed;" rather, 'to save Thine anointed,' or 'for the salvation of Thine anointed.' In this case "the reproach of Christ" is nearly synonymous with the "afflictions of the people of God," just as "the treasures of Egypt" correspond with "the pleasures of sin for a season."

The second mode of interpretation goes on the principle, that "the reproach of Christ" is equivalent to—'reproach similar to that which Christ sustained;' just as in 2 Cor. i. 5 the phrase, "sufferings of Christ," is equivalent to—'sufferings similar to those which Christ endured.' In the first case the meaning is, 'Moses willingly took part in the contempt and reproach to which the oppressed Israelites were exposed;' in the second, the meaning is, 'Moses, the deliverer of Israel, willingly submitted to reproaches similar to those which were heaped on Jesus Christ, the Saviour of man.' It does not matter much which of the two modes of interpretation you adopt. In both cases the words express a truth, and an appropriate truth. At the same time, I confess that I lean to the first mode of interpretation.[1]

[1] I think it not improbable that there is a particular reference to "circumcision," the mark of belonging to the χριστὸς λαός, or χριστοῦ λ.,—that

Moses' voluntary preference of the abject state of the Israelites to the elevated station he held in Pharaoh's court, is very emphatically described as his "esteeming their reproach greater riches than all the treasures of Egypt." The idea intended to be conveyed, we apprehend, is this—he counted it more his interest to be poor and reproached with the Israel of God, than to be wealthy and honoured with the ungodly Egyptians.

Such was the estimate Moses formed, and his conduct corresponded with it. He took a decided part with them, the consequence of which was that he was obliged to abandon all the comforts of a courtly life, to flee into the deserts of Arabia, and remain there in obscurity for a considerable number of years; and on his return to Egypt, for the purpose of delivering his countrymen, he identified himself with them, and exposed himself to great difficulties and dangers by doing so. Now what was it that induced Moses to think and act in this way? What made him "refuse to be called the son of Pharaoh's daughter?" What led him to "choose rather to suffer affliction with the people of God, than to enjoy the pleasures of sin for a season?" What made him "esteem the reproach of Christ greater riches than the treasures in Egypt?" It was faith, says the Apostle. "By faith Moses, when he was come to years, refused to be called the son of Pharaoh's daughter; choosing rather to suffer affliction with the people of God, than to enjoy the pleasures of sin for a season; esteeming the reproach of Christ greater riches than the treasures in Egypt: for he had respect unto the recompense of the reward." Now there are here two questions: What did Moses believe? and how did his belief influence his judgment, his choice, and his conduct?

It is not very easy to say what was the extent of Moses' belief, for we do not know exactly the extent of the revelation made to him. It is not improbable that revelations were made to the patriarchal Church of which we have no record; but in speaking of Moses' faith, we must confine ourselves to what we know from Old Testament history was made known to him,

---

σημεῖον having a peculiar reference to the Messiah. This distinction excited contempt and ridicule among foreigners. How the Roman poets laugh at the *Verpi!* Mart. vii. 82; Catullus xlv.; Juvenal xiv. 104. On the other hand, the præputium, uncircumcision, is termed in Scripture "the reproach of Egypt," ὀνειδισμὸν Αἰγύπτου, Josh. v. 9.

or to what, from the statements in the passage before us, we have ground to conclude was made known to him. Moses, then, like his parents, believed the promises made to Abraham, Isaac, and Jacob, as to Israel being God's peculiar people, as to their ultimately being a numerous and prosperous nation, and as to Canaan being their inheritance. He believed also the prediction of their deliverance from the land in which they were for a long term of years to endure severe oppression, and that God would judge, or punish, their oppressors. He believed, I doubt not, the divine intimation given to his parents respecting his being the deliverer of Israel; and if, as is not improbable, a similar revelation was made directly to himself, he believed that.

Still further, it seems plain from the passage before us, that Moses believed a revelation which had been made respecting a future state of rewards in another world : " *he had respect*," we are told, " *to the recompense of the reward.*" This is one of the passages which lead me to think that plainer revelations of a future state were made to the patriarchs than any that are recorded in the Old Testament Scriptures. " The recompense of reward" cannot refer to the possession of Canaan, for Moses was never to enter into that country. The meaning seems to be this—'Moses expected that all the sacrifices he made in the cause of God and His people would be far more than compensated in a future state;' and this expectation could only be grounded on a corresponding revelation. Such was the faith of Moses.

Now it is not difficult to perceive how this faith led Moses to judge as he judged, to choose as he chose, to act as he acted. If Moses really believed that Israel was the peculiar people of God, whom He had promised to protect, and bless, and deliver; and if he believed that Jehovah was infinitely powerful, and wise, and faithful; was it not the natural and the necessary consequence of this, that he should seek to identify himself with them ? If he really believed that Jehovah would certainly punish their Egyptian oppressors, and that the time of righteous retribution was fast approaching, was not the natural consequence of this to renounce all connection with them, and to consider the highest and most honourable situation among them as the very reverse of desirable ? If he really believed that God had appointed him to be the agent in effecting the deliverance of Israel, was not this sufficient to make him leave the court of Pharaoh, and interfere for the protection and defence of his oppressed brethren? And if he really believed that in a future world Jehovah would abundantly recompense him for all the sacrifices, and losses, and sufferings to which he might be exposed, was it not natural for him to prefer affliction with the Israelites to ease and pleasure with the Egyptians, and to count it his true interest to be poor and despised with the former, rather than affluent and honoured with the latter? In all this there is no mystery. It is the rational account of Moses' conduct: it is impossible to account for it in any other way. Had Moses had no faith on these subjects, or an opposite faith, his judgment, and choice, and conduct would have been different. He would have gladly been "called the son of Pharaoh's daughter;" he would have chosen rather to enjoy "the pleasures of sin for a season," than to "suffer affliction with the people of God;" he would have accounted "the treasures of Egypt" greater riches than "the reproach of Christ;" for, not believing, he could not have "had respect to the recompense of reward."

None of the exemplifications of the importance of believing, brought forward by the Apostle, is better fitted to serve his purpose than that which we have been considering. The Hebrew Christians were called on to part with an honour which they were accustomed to value above all other dignities. They were excommunicated by their unbelieving brethren, and denied the name of true children of Abraham. Their unbelieving countrymen were enjoying wealth and honour. The little flock they were called on to join were suffering affliction and reproach. Like Moses, they were called on to make great sacrifices, submit to great privations, endure severe sufferings. Now, how is this to be done? 'Look at Moses. Believe as Moses believed, and you will find it easy to judge, and choose, and act as Moses did. If you believe what Christ has plainly revealed, that "it is His Father's good pleasure to give" His little flock, after passing through much tribulation, "the kingdom;" if you are persuaded that, according to His declaration, "wrath is coming to the uttermost" on their oppressors, you will not hesitate to separate yourselves completely from your unbelieving countrymen in a religious point of view, at whatever expense,—you will "come out from among them, and be separate,"—you will at all hazards connect yourselves with the suffering people of God, fully persuaded that " faithful is He who hath promised." " Every one that hath forsaken houses, or brethren, or sisters, or father, or mother, or wife, or children, or lands, for My name's sake, shall receive an hundred-fold, and shall inherit everlasting life."[1]

The practical bearing of the passage is not confined to the Hebrew converts, or to the Christians of the primitive age. In every country, and in every age, Jesus proclaims, "If any man would be My disciple, he must deny himself, he must take up the cross and follow Me." No man can do this but by believing. Believing, every man may, must do this. The power of the present world can only be put down by "the power of the world to come;" and as it is through *sense* that the first power operates on our minds, it is through *faith* alone that the second power can operate on our minds. Some find it impossible to make the sacrifices Christianity requires, because they have no faith. Multitudes find it difficult to make them, for they have little faith. If we have faith, we shall find such sacrifices practicable; if we have strong faith, we will find them easy. They must be made; otherwise our Christianity is but a name, our faith is but a pretence, and our hope a delusion.

The verses which follow bring before our mind other illustrations of the importance and efficacy of faith, derived from the history of Moses. The first of these is contained in the 27th verse. "By faith he forsook Egypt, not fearing the wrath of the king: for he endured, as seeing Him who is invisible." Here we shall follow the general plan we have adopted in reference to these illustrations:—Attend first to the facts, and then to the Apostle's account of these facts; inquire first what Moses did, and then show how it was by faith that he did what he did.

Now, what did Moses do? "He left Egypt;" he "did not fear the wrath of the king;" and " he endured." Moses twice left Egypt—once as a solitary fugitive, and once as the leader of the hosts of the Israelitish people. It has been a question among expositors, to which of these events does the Apostle refer. This appears to us a question of no very difficult solution. Whether it was by faith that Moses left Egypt when he fled

[1] Matt. xix. 29.

into Midian, is a point not very easily determined; but certainly, when he left Egypt on that occasion, it could not have been said that he "did not fear the wrath of the king;" for fear of the king was obviously the principal cause of his flight. When Moses found that his slaughter of the Egyptian was known, he "feared." And "when Pharaoh heard of it, he sought to slay Moses;" "and Moses," we are told, "fled from the face of Pharaoh, and dwelt in Midian." It plainly, then, cannot be to this leaving of Egypt that the Apostle refers: it must be to his second leaving of Egypt. Now, as this was the closing act of a long, closely connected series of events, there can be little doubt that it is in this point of view that the Apostle considered it; and therefore, in order to bring the illustration fully before the mind, we must take a hurried view of these antecedent events.

Moses left the land of Midian, where he was comfortably settled, and for forty years had enjoyed the advantages of the tranquillity of the pastoral life; returned to Egypt for the purpose of effecting the deliverance of his countrymen from servitude, and leading them towards Palestine, their promised inheritance; and, after a long struggle with the unbelief of his countrymen, and the obstinacy of the Egyptian king, which was overcome by a series of the most wonderful miracles, ultimately succeeded in his hazardous and apparently hopeless enterprise.

In thus "forsaking Egypt," he "did not fear the wrath of the king." The king was very much enraged at Moses, and no doubt wished above all things to destroy him, and seemed to have it completely in his power to realize his wish. But Moses discovered no fear. He prosecuted his object till he gained it, unterrified by all Pharaoh's threats; and having left Egypt, though followed by Pharaoh and his embattled hosts, yet still he remained unmoved. "Fear not," said he to the terrified Israelites,—" fear ye not, stand still, and see the salvation of God."

It is also stated that Moses "endured." The word, we apprehend, is expressive of Moses' firm, determined perseverance in the course of conduct which he had adopted, notwithstanding all the difficulties he met with in it, from the unbelief of his countrymen, and from the policy and power of the Egyptian king. The whole statement in reference to Moses' conduct is this: Neither the terrors of the wrath of the king of Egypt, nor the disgust which the ingratitude, and unbelief, and waywardness of his countrymen were calculated to produce, prevented him from prosecuting the great object which he had in view till he brought it to a prosperous issue. Such was the conduct of Moses.

Now, to what are we to attribute it? The Apostle's answer is, To his faith. "By faith he forsook Egypt, not fearing the wrath of the king: for he endured, as seeing Him who is invisible." And here, as formerly, there are two questions which call for resolution: What did Moses believe? and how did his faith influence his conduct? The answer to these two questions will be most satisfactorily given, not in a separate, but in a combined form.

Moses believed the revelations made to him respecting the deliverance of the children of Israel, the part he was to act in that deliverance, and the assistance Jehovah would afford him in accomplishing it. What these revelations were, you will find by consulting the book of Exodus. "Now Moses kept the flock of Jethro his father-in-law, the priest of Midian: and he led the flock to the back-side of the desert, and came to the mountain of God, even to Horeb. And the Angel of the Lord appeared unto him in a flame of fire out of the midst of a bush; and he looked, and, behold, the bush burned with fire, and the bush was not consumed. And Moses said, I will now turn aside, and see this great sight, why the bush is not burnt. And when the Lord saw that he turned aside to see, God called unto him out of the midst of the bush, and said, Moses, Moses. And he said, Here am I. And He said, Draw not nigh hither: put off thy shoes from off thy feet; for the place whereon thou standest is holy ground. Moreover He said, I am the God of thy father, the God of Abraham, the God of Isaac, and the God of Jacob. And Moses hid his face; for he was afraid to look upon God. And the Lord said, I have surely seen the affliction of My people which are in Egypt, and have heard their cry by reason of their taskmasters; for I know their sorrows. And I am come down to deliver them out of the hand of the Egyptians, and to bring them up out of that land unto a good land and a large, unto a land flowing with milk and

honey; unto the place of the Canaanites, and the Hittites, and
the Amorites, and the Perizzites, and the Hivites, and the
Jebusites. Now therefore, behold, the cry of the children of
Israel is come unto Me: and I have also seen the oppression
wherewith the Egyptians oppress them. Come now therefore,
and I will send thee unto Pharaoh, that thou mayest bring forth
My people, the children of Israel, out of Egypt." "And they shall
hearken to thy voice: and thou shalt come, thou and the elders
of Israel, unto the king of Egypt, and ye shall say unto him,
The Lord God of the Hebrews hath met with us: and now let
us go, we beseech thee, three days' journey into the wilderness,
that we may sacrifice to the Lord our God. And I am sure
that the king of Egypt will not let you go, no, not by a mighty
hand. And I will stretch out My hand, and smite Egypt with
all My wonders which I will do in the midst thereof: and after
that he will let you go."[1] Had Moses not believed that this revelation came from God, or had he not believed that Jehovah
was at once powerful and faithful, able and disposed to do what
He had said, Moses would have remained in Midian, where he
seems to have been very comfortably settled; but, firmly believing
that this revelation did come from God, and that He was both
able and willing to do what He had said, Moses could not but leave
Midian, and deliver the message with which he was entrusted,
both to his kinsmen and to the Egyptian king. The reception he
at first met with from the Israelites was powerfully calculated,
both in itself and as a begun fulfilment of the divine oracle, to
encourage him. On the message being delivered, and the signs
performed, "the people believed; and when they heard that the
Lord had visited the children of Israel, and that He had looked
upon their affliction, they bowed their heads and worshipped."[2]
But subsequent events were in their own nature fitted to dis-
courage him; and indeed, had it not been for his faith, would
certainly have induced him to abandon his enterprise in despair.
When he delivered his message to Pharaoh, he met with a direct
and most insolent refusal. "Thus saith the Lord," said Moses,
"the God of Israel, Let My people go, that they may hold a feast
to Me in the wilderness." Pharaoh's impious reply was, "Who
is the Lord, that I should obey His voice to let Israel go? I
know not the Lord, neither will I let Israel go." Instead of

---

[1] Exod. iii. 1-10, 18-20. [2] Exod. iv. 31.

procuring Israel's release, this interference brought on them a double weight of oppression, which drew forth from them cutting reproaches against Moses, and even imprecations of divine vengeance on him. And here Moses' faith seems to have begun to fail him; for he "returned unto the Lord, and said, Lord, wherefore hast Thou so evil-entreated this people? why is it that Thou hast sent me? For since I came to Pharaoh to speak in Thy name, he hath done evil to this people; neither hast Thou delivered Thy people at all."[1] A new revelation was made to him for the strengthening of his faith. "Then the Lord said unto Moses, Now shalt thou see what I will do to Pharaoh: for with a strong hand shall he let them go, and with a strong hand shall he drive them out of his land. And God spake unto Moses, and said unto him, I am the Lord: and I appeared unto Abraham, unto Isaac, and unto Jacob, by the name of God Almighty; but by My name Jehovah was I not known to them. And I have also established My covenant with them, to give them the land of Canaan, the land of their pilgrimage, wherein they were strangers. And I have also heard the groaning of the children of Israel, whom the Egyptians keep in bondage; and I have remembered My covenant. Wherefore say unto the children of Israel, I am the Lord, and I will bring you out from under the burdens of the Egyptians, and I will rid you out of their bondage; and I will redeem you with a stretched-out arm, and with great judgments. And I will take you to Me for a people, and I will be to you a God; and ye shall know that I am the Lord your God, which bringeth you out from under the burdens of the Egyptians. And I will bring you in unto the land, concerning the which I did swear to give it to Abraham, to Isaac, and to Jacob; and I will give it you for an heritage: I am the Lord."[2] And though after this the people of Israel "hearkened not to him for anguish of spirit and cruel bondage;" and though Pharaoh continued obstinate, amid all the miraculous judgments inflicted on him and his people; yet Moses, believing the divine declarations, persevered. Had he not believed, he must have soon given up the undertaking as hopeless; but believing, he found even in Pharaoh's obstinacy, which had been predicted, encouragement to persevere. The state of exasperation into which Pharaoh was thrown by such repeated and dreadful

[1] Exod. v. 22, 23. [2] Exod. vi. 1-8.

calamities, was well fitted to fill with terror such an unprotected individual as Moses; but believing that "God was for him," he "did not fear what man could do to him." At last, overwhelmed by the fearful infliction of the sudden death, in one night, of all the first-born in the land of Egypt, Pharaoh gave an extorted consent to the departure of the Israelites out of Egypt; and Moses, at their head, "forsook Egypt." The undertaking in which Moses thus engaged, was one which nothing but faith could have induced any rational man to enter on. The endless difficulties of conducting such a prodigious multitude of men, women, children, and cattle, through waste solitudes, or the territories of hostile tribes, towards a country already in the possession of numerous and powerful nations, must have appeared altogether insurmountable. But Moses, by faith, entered on this apparently desperate enterprise, because he believed that Jehovah had promised, and that He was both able and willing to perform His promise, " to bring them in unto the land, concerning which He had sworn to give it to Abraham, to Isaac, and to Jacob."

He persevered in the course prescribed to him " as one who saw Him who is invisible." These words admit of two modes of interpretation: Either, 'his faith had the same effect on him as if the unseen Deity, with every conceivable emblem of His power, and wisdom, and faithfulness, had become an object of bodily vision;' or, 'he endured as one who saw'—*i.e.*, by the eye of faith, the only way in which He can be seen—'the invisible Divinity.' Either mode of interpretation gives a good sense, but we apprehend the latter is the Apostle's meaning. The expression naturally leads the mind back to the declaration in the first verse. His faith was "confidence respecting things hoped for, conviction in reference to things not seen." Without such faith, Moses could not have done, and suffered, and obtained as he did; with such faith, the discharge of the duties enjoined on him, though very difficult—the enduring of the trials assigned him, though very severe—the attainment of the blessings, though very valuable and apparently unattainable, became natural and easy.

The bearing of this illustration on the Apostle's great object is direct and obvious : ' What faith did for Moses, faith can do for you ; what nothing but faith could do for Moses, nothing but faith can do for you.' The Hebrew Christians were placed in circumstances somewhat analogous to those of Moses. They were required to "come out and be separate" from their unbelieving countrymen. The difficulties that lay in the way of renouncing Judaism were, though of another nature, scarcely less formidable than those which lay in the way of Moses leaving Egypt; and, like him, in abandoning Judaism they had to commence a course of indefinitely long and severe labour and trial, previously to their obtaining a permanently secure and happy settlement in the heavenly Canaan. What could enable them to make such sacrifices, to put forth such exertions, to submit to such privations, to encounter such opposition, and to persevere in doing so, amid all those circumstances which had an obvious tendency to damp their ardour and shake their resolution? Faith, and nothing but faith.

In the word of the truth of the Gospel it had been distinctly stated to them that Jesus Christ was the divine Deliverer promised to the fathers—that "His blood cleanses from all sin" —that "all power in heaven and on earth" belongs to Him— that "whosoever believeth in Him shall not perish, but have everlasting life"—that, to be His disciples, men must "deny themselves, take up their cross, and follow Him"—that "He will never leave and never forsake His people"—that "His grace shall be made sufficient for them," and that He "will perfect His strength in their weakness"—that He will "make all things work together for their good"—that He "will confess before His Father and the holy angels" those who "confess Him before men," and "deny before His Father and the holy angels" those who "deny Him before men"—and that "to him who overcometh He will give to sit with Him on His throne, even as He also hath overcome, and is set down with His Father on His throne."

Now, if these truths were not believed, it could not be expected that they would "forsake father, and mother, and sisters, and brothers, and houses, and lands, for Christ's sake and the Gospel's,"—it could not be expected that they should enter on and prosecute a course of conduct directly opposed to all the strongest inclinations of unchanged human nature.

But if they really did believe these truths—if by the eye of faith they habitually contemplated the invisible God, the unseen Saviour, and the great realities of the eternal world,—would not the fear of God extinguish all other fear—the love of the Saviour neutralize the power of all opposing affections—the majestic glories of eternity make all earth-born glory grow dim or disappear, shrink to a thing of nought,—nay, would not the very afflictions and trials they met with, when viewed as a verification of the declarations of the Saviour, operate as a confirmation of their faith, that He whose declaration, that "in the world they should have tribulation," had been fulfilled, would be found equally true to the other connected declaration, "In Me ye shall have peace?" Under the influence of an enlightened faith, the very circumstances which to the unstable prove the occasion of apostasy, are found, as evidences of the faithfulness of the Saviour, and the truth of His declarations, the means of attaching the Christian the more closely to the cause of his Lord and Saviour.

The duties and difficulties, the trials and privations of Christians, are substantially the same in all countries and in all ages; and nothing can enable them to conduct themselves properly in reference to these but faith. Looking away from what is seen and temporal to the God who is invisible, the Saviour who is unseen, the world which is eternal,—that, and that alone, will enable us to brave dangers before which the stoutest heart, unsupported by the faith of the Gospel, must quail, and make the feeblest of us "more than conquerors" over the most powerful of our spiritual foes. Believing "the exceeding great and precious promises" of God, and the power and faithfulness of Him who has given them, the Christian remains "stedfast and unmoveable" amid all the storms of temptation which threaten to shake his attachment to Christ and His cause. Isa. xl. 28-31.

We come now to the last of these displays of the importance of faith, drawn from the history of Moses.

Ver. 28. "Through faith he kept the passover, and the sprinkling of blood, lest he that destroyed the first-born should touch them." Let us here, as in former cases, attend first to the facts, and then to the Apostle's account of the facts; or, in other words, inquire first what Moses did, and then show that it was by faith that he did what he did. The facts are—"Moses kept the passover, and the sprinkling of blood;" and he did so, "*in order that* the destroyer *might not*"—or, "*so that* the destroyer *did not*—touch them;" for the words will admit either rendering.

The phrase rendered, "kept[1] the passover," taken by itself, may either signify—'*instituted*,' or '*observed* the passover.' In one of the old English versions it is rendered—"he ordained the passover, and the sprinkling of blood." It was not so much Moses, however, as Jehovah, that ordained these religious observances. The phrase here employed is the same as that used by our Lord, when He says, Matt. xxvi. 18, "I will *keep* the passover at thy house with My disciples." "Keep" is perhaps not the best word which might have been employed: it suits very well with the word "passover," but it does not suit so well with the phrase, "sprinkling of blood." "Observe" applies equally well to both. 'Moses observed the passover, and the sprinkling of blood.' The facts referred to are narrated at large in the 12th chapter of the book of Exodus. The following is a brief summary of them:—A short time before the departure of Israel from Egypt, Moses gave warning both to Pharaoh and to the Israelites, that at midnight on the fourteenth day of the month Abib, all the first-born both of man and of beast were, by a miraculous visitation of Heaven, suddenly to die. He predicted also that this dreadful infliction of divine wrath would not only make the Egyptians consent to the departure of the children of Israel, but make them anxiously urge their departure. And, as a means of protecting the first-born of the children of Israel from the general desolation, he commanded every family to set apart a male lamb or kid of the first year, on the tenth day of the month; and on the fourteenth day of the month this lamb or kid was to be slain, in the evening; its blood was to be sprinkled, by means of a bunch of hyssop, on the doorposts and lintels of their house; and the flesh, having been roasted, was to be eaten with unleavened bread and bitter herbs; while, with girt loins, and sandals on their feet, and staff in hand, they stood ready to commence their march from Egypt towards the land of promise. The event exactly corresponded with Moses' prediction; and he and the children of Israel, according to the divine appointment, "observed the passover, and the sprinkling of blood." That is, they sacrificed the lambs and kids, and prepared all their carcases, according to the divine ap-

---

[1] πεποίηκε.

pointment, and with their blood sprinkled the door-posts and lintels of their dwellings.

This service received the name of "the passover," because, while Jehovah visited in wrath every house of the Egyptians, He passed over the houses of the Israelites, and did not suffer the destroyer to come into their houses to smite them. This fact is referred to in the concluding part of the verse. Moses "observed the passover, and the sprinkling of blood, lest he who destroyed the first-born should touch them."

The appellation, "destroyer[1] of the first-born," seems to be descriptive of some angelic agent employed by Jehovah in the execution of this awful judgment. No doubt Jehovah Himself must be considered as the grand primary agent; for "can there be evil in a city," or land, "and He has not done it?" but in the words, "The Lord will pass over the door, and will not suffer the destroyer to come in unto it to smite you," Jehovah and the destroyer are plainly distinguished from each other. Some interpreters would explain this by saying, that the ancient Jews were accustomed to ascribe all remarkable phenomena to the agency of invisible beings; and that all that is meant, is just that, by some means or other, the first-born of man and beast in Egypt suddenly died. It appears to us the far more rational mode of interpretation to consider the words as bearing their plain meaning, and as intended to teach us that one of those "angels who excel in strength" was employed by Him, whose will they do, and to the voice of whose word they dutifully listen, to execute the richly deserved, though awfully severe, judgment which He had denounced against the Egyptians.[2]

For this destroyer "not to touch" the Israelites, is obviously equivalent to—'not to injure, hurt, or destroy them.' The phraseology very probably is intended to suggest the idea of the perfect ease with which this angelic agent performed his dreadful office. His *touch* was fatal.

The words, "Moses observed the passover, and the sprinkling of blood, lest he who destroyed the first-born should touch them," may either be understood as expressing the *object* which Moses had in view in observing the passover and the sprinkling of

[1] מַשְׁחִית of the Hebrew.
[2] 2 Kings xix. 35; 1 Chron. xxi. 12, 15; 2 Chron. xxxii. 21; Ecclus. xlviii. 21; Isa. xxxvii. 36.

blood, or the *event* of his doing so. In the first case they are equivalent to—' Moses observed the passover, and the sprinkling of blood, in order that the destroyer of the first-born might not touch them.' In the second case they are equivalent to—' Moses observed the passover, and the sprinkling of blood, so that he who destroyed the first-born did not touch them.' Both are truths, and both are truths which directly bear on the Apostle's object. If I were required to choose between the two interpretations, I would probably prefer the second; as in this case the facts brought forward are a proof not only of faith enabling a man to do what otherwise he could not have done, but also of its enabling a man to attain what otherwise he could not have attained. So much, then, for the facts stated by the Apostle in this verse: "Moses observed the passover, and the sprinkling of blood."

Let us now inquire into the account which the Apostle gives of these facts. The following questions naturally present themselves to the mind: What made Moses observe the passover, and the sprinkling of blood? How came he to know that the children of Israel were to depart from Egypt on the fourteenth day of the month Abib? How came he to know that the proximate cause of their leaving Egypt was to be the sudden and simultaneous death of the first-born both of man and beast throughout that country? How came he to consider the sacrifice of a lamb or kid, the eating of it roasted, and the sprinkling of its blood on the door-posts and lintels, as a preservative for the Israelites from the destruction which walked in darkness?

The only satisfactory answer to all these questions is that given by the Apostle. It was by faith Moses did these things. Divine revelations were given him on these subjects; and he believed these revelations, and he acted accordingly. Without such revelations, or without a faith in these revelations, he could not have done as he did; with such revelations, and with a faith in them, he could not but act as he did. The deliverance of Israel from Egypt could not have been foreseen by human sagacity. It was, at the time Moses intimated that it would take place on a certain day, less probable than when he first entered on his enterprise. Even supposing the event to be of a kind which human sagacity could have predicted as at no great distance, could human sagacity have enabled him to fix the precise day? could it have enabled him to say what was to be the immediate cause of effecting so unlikely an event? and even supposing him possessed of all necessary information on these points, would it ever have entered into his mind to have encumbered the Israelites, on the very eve of their departure, with such an operose religious ceremony as the passover and the sprinkling of blood, or to have considered such rites as in any degree calculated to protect the Israelites from a calamity so general that not one family in Egypt was free from it? The only satisfactory account—and it is a satisfactory one—is this: By faith Moses did all this. God revealed to Moses that Israel was to be delivered on the fourteenth day of the month Abib—that the universal destruction of the first-born among the Egyptians was to be the proximate cause of their deliverance—that the appointed way of securing the Israelites from the general calamity was the passover and the sprinkling of blood; and Moses believed these revelations, and, believing them, spoke and acted accordingly.

Such appears to me to be the meaning of the declaration in the text, "By faith Moses kept the passover, and the sprinkling of blood, lest he that destroyed the first-born should touch them." I am aware that many excellent men have attached a very different meaning to these words. Misapprehending the design of the Apostle in the whole of this discussion,—supposing that it is his object to prove the doctrine of justification by faith in Christ Jesus, instead of to illustrate the importance and power of faith in a divine revelation,—they have considered the statement in the text as equivalent to—'Moses observed the passover and the sprinkling of blood by faith, looking through these rites as emblems of the atoning sacrifice of Jesus Christ, and the manner of that sacrifice becoming effectual for the salvation of the individual sinning.' That sacrifice, and especially the sacrifice of the passover, was a divinely intended emblem of the manner in which our guilt was to be expiated, and our salvation obtained, by the obedience to the death of the incarnate Son of God, is most clearly taught in the Holy Scriptures. But how far Moses and the other Old Testament saints were aware of this emblematical reference, is another question, and one by no means so easily resolved. What were the precise views entertained by the true Israel respecting the offices of the Messiah and the work of redemption—respecting the import and reference of expiatory sacrifice, is indeed among the most curious and intricate questions in theology. We know that they were saved, as we are, through the atonement; and we know also that they were saved by faith. We know, to use the language of a great writer, that "the cross of Christ, considered as the meritorious basis of acceptance, the only real satisfaction for sin, is the centre round which all the purposes of mercy to fallen men have continued to revolve. Fixed and determined in the counsel of God, it operated as the grand consideration in the divine mind on which salvation was awarded to believers in the earliest ages, as it will continue to operate in the same manner to the latest boundaries of time."[1] We know, too, that it was through believing that in every age the individual sinner obtained a personal interest in the blessings secured by that atonement; but that faith must have corresponded to the revelation made. We have no evidence that any revelation was made to them of the precise manner in which the salvation of a sinner is to be made compatible with the perfections of God, the honour of His law, and the great ends of His moral administration. In offering sacrifice, the believing Israelite recognised his guilt, his just exposure to destruction, and his exclusive reliance on divine mercy. "The way into the holiest was not made manifest" to them. I do not know if the circumstances of the ancient Church have ever been more accurately—they cannot be more beautifully—described, than in the words of the author whom I have just quoted:—" Exposed to dangers from which they knew of no definite mode of escape, and placed on the confines of an eternity feebly and faintly illumined, they had no other resource besides an implicit confidence in mysterious mercy."

But apart from these general considerations altogether, I apprehend that in the object of the Apostle, which we have endeavoured to bring distinctly out in the course of these lectures, we have the most satisfactory evidence that the faith by which Moses observed the passover and the sprinkling of blood, was just the belief of the revelations which were made to him on these subjects.

[1] Robert Hall.

It only remains that we very shortly show the bearing which this statement has on the Apostle's great object, which is the importance, and necessity, and sufficiency of believing, and continuing to believe, in order to the discharge of the duties enjoined on the Christian, the sustaining of the trials allotted to him, the attainment of the blessings promised to him. Christians are called on sometimes to perform duties which must appear unreasonable and absurd to an unbelieving world, and for which they themselves can assign no reason but the will of Him who has appointed them. A Christian in a heathen country strictly observing the Lord's day, to the apparent material disadvantage of his worldly interests, is a case in point. How is he to be enabled to persevere in the performance of this duty, amid the temptations to neglect it to which he is exposed? Look to Moses and the children of Israel observing the passover and the sprinkling of blood. The Egyptians, no doubt, thought it a very strange and unaccountable thing for the Israelites to be, all of them, bedaubing the entrances of their houses with blood; and the Israelites themselves could give no reason but one for it—God had commanded it. Yet believing this, they observed the appointed rite. In like manner, faith in the divine origin of the Christian Sabbath, and in the threatenings and promises in reference to it, will induce a Christian, even amid very strong temptations to act otherwise, to remember the Sabbath day to keep it holy. A similar case in point might be taken from a small body of Christians in a heathen country observing the Lord's Supper. But further, Christians are called on also to expect very important ends by very strange means. They are called on to expect a complete change of state and character by means of the death of God's Son on a cross, and by means of their understanding and believing the truth respecting this death. This seems as irrational an expectation as that of obtaining security from the destroyer of the first-born by observing the passover and the sprinkling of blood. A firm faith that God had established a connection between these two things, led Moses and the Israelites to perform the commanded rites as the means of obtaining the promised security; and a belief that " God so loved the world as to give His only-begotten Son, that whosoever believeth in Him shall not perish, but have everlasting life," will enable the Christian to hold fast this confidence, that, believing the truth as it is in Jesus, he shall have peace with God, and victory over the world, and eternal life, through the blood of the Lamb.

The next illustration of the power of faith which the Apostle, following down the course of Israelitish history, brings forward, is that furnished by that people passing in safety through the Arabian Gulf, while their Egyptian pursuers, in attempting to follow them, were overwhelmed by its waters. Ver. 29. " By faith they passed through the Red Sea as by dry land; which the Egyptians assaying to do were drowned."

The facts of the case are narrated at large in the 14th chapter of the book of Exodus. " And the Lord spake unto Moses, saying, Speak unto the children of Israel, that they turn and encamp before Pi-hahiroth, between Migdol and the sea, over against Baal-zephon: before it shall ye encamp by the sea. For Pharaoh will say of the children of Israel, They are entangled in the land, the wilderness hath shut them in. And I will harden Pharaoh's heart, that he shall follow after them; and I will be honoured upon Pharaoh, and upon all his host; that the Egyptians may know that I am the Lord. And they did so. And it was told the king of Egypt that the people fled: and the heart of Pharaoh and of his servants was turned against the people, and they said, Why have we done this, that we have let Israel go from serving us? And he made ready his chariot, and took his people with him. And he took six hundred chosen chariots, and all the chariots of Egypt, and captains over every one of them. And the Lord hardened the heart of Pharaoh king of Egypt, and he pursued after the children of Israel: and the children of Israel went out with an high hand. But the Egyptians pursued after them (all the horses and chariots of Pharaoh, and his horsemen, and his army), and overtook them encamping by the sea, beside Pi-hahiroth, before Baal-zephon. And when Pharaoh drew nigh, the children of Israel lifted up their eyes, and, behold, the Egyptians marched after them; and they were sore afraid: and the children of Israel cried out unto the Lord. And they said unto Moses, Because there were no graves in Egypt, hast thou taken us away to die in the wilderness? wherefore hast thou dealt thus with us, to carry us forth out of Egypt? Is not this the word that we did tell thee in Egypt, saying, Let us alone, that we may serve the Egyptians?

for it had been better for us to serve the Egyptians, than that we should die in the wilderness. And Moses said unto the people, Fear ye not, stand still, and see the salvation of the Lord, which He will show to you to-day: for the Egyptians whom ye have seen to-day, ye shall see them again no more for ever. The Lord shall fight for you, and ye shall hold your peace. And the Lord said unto Moses, Wherefore criest thou unto Me? speak unto the children of Israel, that they go forward: but lift thou up thy rod, and stretch out thine hand over the sea, and divide it; and the children of Israel shall go on dry ground through the midst of the sea. And I, behold, I will harden the hearts of the Egyptians, and they shall follow them: and I will get Me honour upon Pharaoh, and upon all his host, upon his chariots, and upon his horsemen. And the Egyptians shall know that I am the Lord, when I have gotten Me honour upon Pharaoh, upon his chariots, and upon his horsemen. And the angel of God, which went before the camp of Israel, removed, and went behind them; and the pillar of the cloud went from before their face, and stood behind them. And it came between the camp of the Egyptians and the camp of Israel; and it was a cloud and darkness to them, but it gave light by night to these: so that the one came not near the other all the night. And Moses stretched out his hand over the sea; and the Lord caused the sea to go back by a strong east wind all that night, and made the sea dry land, and the waters were divided. And the children of Israel went into the midst of the sea upon the dry ground: and the waters were a wall unto them on their right hand, and on their left. And the Egyptians pursued, and went in after them to the midst of the sea, even all Pharaoh's horses, his chariots, and his horsemen. And it came to pass, that, in the morning-watch, the Lord looked unto the host of the Egyptians through the pillar of fire, and of the cloud, and troubled the host of the Egyptians, and took off their chariot-wheels, that they drave them heavily: so that the Egyptians said, Let us flee from the face of Israel; for the Lord fighteth for them against the Egyptians. And the Lord said unto Moses, Stretch out thine hand over the sea, that the waters may come again upon the Egyptians, upon their chariots, and upon their horsemen. And Moses stretched forth his hand over the sea, and the sea returned to his strength when the morning appeared; and the Egyptians fled against it; and the Lord overthrew the Egyptians in the midst of the sea. And the waters returned, and covered the chariots, and the horsemen, and all the host of Pharaoh that came into the sea after them: there remained not so much as one of them. But the children of Israel walked upon dry land in the midst of the sea; and the waters were a wall unto them on their right hand, and on their left. Thus the Lord saved Israel that day out of the hand of the Egyptians; and Israel saw the Egyptians dead upon the sea-shore. And Israel saw that great work which the Lord did upon the Egyptians; and the people feared the Lord, and believed the Lord, and His servant Moses." Such is the inspired historian's narrative: now for the inspired Apostle's commentary.

"By faith they"—*i.e.*, Moses and the Israelitish people—"passed through the Red Sea as by dry land." A revelation had been made to them, that they should safely pass along that strange pathway, which, by the arm of Jehovah, had been opened up for them through the waters of the Arabian Gulf. Had no revelation been made to them,—in which case there could have been no faith, there being nothing to believe,—or had the revelation not been believed by the Israelites, they durst not have ventured into the fearful chasm, but in all probability would have sought, by unqualified submission, to appease the fury of the tyrant from whose grasp they had escaped, as the more probable way of saving their lives. But believing the divine declaration, and no doubt having their faith strengthened by the miraculous division of the waters as they approached them (for it was natural for them to reason in this way: 'He who has divided the waters can keep them divided;—He has performed one part of His wonderful prediction; He will perform the other also. He cannot have done this great wonder to lure us to our doom, but to open a way for us to secure deliverance'), they entered the dried-up channel, and proceeded along that untrodden path, till they safely arrived on the opposite shore. Faith thus enabled the Israelites to do what otherwise they could not have done—obey the command of God, to attempt a passage of this arm of the sea through the midst of its waters. It enabled the Israelites also to obtain what otherwise they could not have obtained—a safe passage, and complete security from their Egyptian pursuers.

The question has often been put, Was the faith by which the Israelites passed through the Red Sea *saving faith*? I have no doubt that a number of the Israelites, as well as Moses, were believers of the comparatively dim revelation of that scheme of mercy of which we have the completed revelation, and through that faith obtained eternal life. I have as little doubt, however, that by far the greater part of them were in this sense of the word unbelievers; and, in consequence of their unbelief of this revelation, never entered into the heavenly rest, even as, on account of their unbelief of another revelation, they never entered into the rest of God in Canaan. It is equally obvious, I think, that the faith of the revelation made to Moses respecting the Israelites obtaining a safe passage through the Red Sea, was not what we ordinarily term saving faith; and there is nothing to make us think that the Israelites, in believing that revelation, understood that it had a typical reference, and in consequence believed that God would deliver them from spiritual dangers, of which the waves of the Arabian Gulf, furiously agitated by tempest, afforded but an imperfect emblem.

The Apostle's object is to show the power of real faith in God, whatever be its object. The nature and extent of that efficacy will depend on the nature and extent of the revelation believed. A faith in a revelation respecting the safe passage of the Red Sea enabled the Israelites fearlessly to entrust themselves in the strangely formed valley between two mountainous ridges of tumultuous waves, and to reach in safety the opposite shore. A faith in the revelation of salvation from guilt and depravity, and death and hell, will enable the Christian to perform all the duties, and endure all the difficulties, that are involved in obtaining complete possession of this salvation, and will in due time bring him into the enjoyment of all its blessings, in all their perfection.

A subject often receives much illustration by contrast. This mode of illustration is adopted here. The power of faith, in enabling the Israelites to pass through the Red Sea safely, is illustrated by the helpless, hopeless destruction of the infatuated Egyptians, who attempted to follow them. The Egyptians had no faith on this subject—they could have none. No revelation had been made to them; and even if the revelation had been made to them which was made to the Israelites, it is doubtful if they would have believed it. And if they had believed it, it would not have led them to follow the Israelites, but, on the contrary, would have prevented them. The same revelation, though equally firmly believed, will produce different effects on different individuals. A revelation that the Israelites were to be safely led through the Red Sea, though believed by an Egyptian, could be no ground of expectation that *he* was to be led safely through the Red Sea also. The revelation of a free and a full salvation to the guiltiest of the human race, believing in Jesus, though believed by a fallen angel, could be no ground of expectation that *he* was to be a partaker of this salvation.

The Egyptians, led not by faith in a divine revelation, but by their furious passions, followed the Israelites into the Red Sea. It was night, and, to the Egyptians, dark night. The chasm in the waters of the gulf was probably of very considerable width, extending very likely for some miles. The Egyptians were probably neither aware of the great miracle which had been wrought for Israel, nor of the extreme danger in which they had involved themselves. In darkness they were pursuing Israel. Where Israel went, they supposed they might follow; and it does not seem that they discovered their real circumstances till in the morning they found themselves in the midst of the sea. Then they said, "Let us flee from the face of Israel; for the Lord fighteth for them against the Egyptians."[1] But it was too late. Now had arrived the hour when much-enduring, long-despised divine forbearance was to be avenged for all the insults offered to it. It is difficult to say whether the historical or the poetical account of the fearful catastrophe is most picturesque and affecting. We have the first in Exod. xiv. 26–28: "And the Lord said unto Moses, Stretch out thine hand over the sea, that the waters may come again upon the Egyptians, upon their chariots, and upon their horsemen. And Moses stretched forth his hand over the sea, and the sea returned to his strength when the morning appeared; and the Egyptians fled against it; and the Lord overthrew the Egyptians in the midst of the sea. And the waters returned, and covered the chariots, and the horsemen, and all the host of

[1] Exod. xiv. 25.

Pharaoh that came into the sea after them: there remained not so much as one of them." We have the second in chap. xv. 4-11: "Pharaoh's chariots and his host hath He cast into the sea: his chosen captains also are drowned in the Red Sea. The depths have covered them: they sank into the bottom as a stone. Thy right hand, O Lord, is become glorious in power: Thy right hand, O Lord, hath dashed in pieces the enemy. And in the greatness of Thine excellency Thou hast overthrown them that rose up against Thee: Thou sentest forth Thy wrath, which consumed them as stubble. And with the blast of Thy nostrils the waters were gathered together, the floods stood upright as an heap, and the depths were congealed in the heart of the sea. The enemy said, I will pursue, I will overtake, I will divide the spoil; my lust shall be satisfied upon them; I will draw my sword, my hand shall destroy them. Thou didst blow with Thy wind, the sea covered them; they sank as lead in the mighty waters. Who is like unto Thee, O Lord, among the gods? who is like Thee, glorious in holiness, fearful in praises, doing wonders?"

The general truth taught by the ineffectual and ruinous attempt of the Egyptians is this: that they who attempt to do without faith, what believers successfully do by faith—those who attempt to obtain without faith, what believers succeed in obtaining by faith—will assuredly be disappointed. The believer obtains peace with God; but all the unbeliever's attempts to obtain solid peace will end in disappointment. Men are sanctified through the belief of the truth; but all attempts to make a person's self holy without believing, will assuredly end in disappointment. By believing, a man will make a consistent profession of Christianity amid all the temptations to which he may be exposed: a man who enters on a profession of Christianity without faith, is sure, sooner or later, to manifest its hollowness. Every persevering believer will certainly obtain the salvation of his soul as the end of his believing; but every man who is seeking genuine and permanent happiness without believing, will find himself at last, like the Egyptians, engulphed in the depths of destruction, when he hoped as a conqueror to set his foot on the shore of the celestial country.

The bearing of this illustration on the Apostle's object is direct and obvious. The Hebrew Christians were exposed to numerous and severe afflictions in the maintenance of their Christian profession, and submission to these was absolutely necessary in order to their progress towards the heavenly promised land. Faith alone could enable them—faith would assuredly enable them—to enter on and pass through these trials, however severe. Without faith, in the mere prospect of them, they may very probably return to spiritual Egypt; or, if they presumptuously plunge in, like the Egyptians, they are likely to be overwhelmed by them. Nothing but faith, persevering faith, can enable the Christian to pass safely through all the trials and dangers of the wilderness, uphold him amid the waves of the Red Sea of affliction and the swellings of the Jordan of death, and give him a sure and everlasting resting-place in the Canaan above.

The next illustration of the importance of faith, is that taken from the miraculous overthrow of the walls of Jericho. Ver. 30. "By faith the walls of Jericho fell down, after they were compassed about seven days."

The facts of this case are narrated at large in the book of Joshua: "And it came to pass, when Joshua was by Jericho, that he lifted up his eyes and looked, and, behold, there stood a man over against him, with his sword drawn in his hand: and Joshua went unto him, and said unto him, Art thou for us, or for our adversaries? And he said, Nay; but as captain of the host of the Lord am I now come. And Joshua fell on his face to the earth, and did worship, and said unto him, What saith my lord unto his servant? And the captain of the Lord's host said unto Joshua, Loose thy shoe from off thy foot; for the place whereon thou standest is holy. And Joshua did so. Now Jericho was straitly shut up because of the children of Israel: none went out, and none came in. And the Lord said unto Joshua, See, I have given into thine hand Jericho, and the king thereof, and the mighty men of valour. And ye shall compass the city, all ye men of war, and go round about the city once. Thus shalt thou do six days. And seven priests shall bear before the ark seven trumpets of rams' horns; and the seventh day ye shall compass the city seven times, and the priests shall blow with the trumpets. And it shall come to pass, that when they make a long blast with the ram's horn, and when ye hear the sound of the trumpet, all the people shall shout with a great shout; and the wall of the city shall fall down flat, and the people shall ascend up, every man straight before him. And Joshua the son of Nun called the priests, and said unto them, Take up the ark of the covenant, and let seven priests bear seven trumpets of rams' horns before the ark of the Lord. And he said unto the people, Pass on, and compass the city, and let him that is armed pass on before the ark of the Lord. And it came to pass, when Joshua had spoken unto the people, that the seven priests, bearing the seven trumpets of rams' horns, passed on before the Lord, and blew with the trumpets; and the ark of the covenant of the Lord followed them. And the armed men went before the priests that blew with the trumpets, and the rere-ward came after the ark, the priests going on, and blowing with the trumpets. And Joshua had commanded the people, saying, Ye shall not shout, nor make any noise with your voice, neither shall any word proceed out of your mouth, until the day I bid you shout; then shall ye shout. So the ark of the Lord compassed the city, going about it once: and they came into the camp, and lodged in the camp. And Joshua rose early in the morning, and the priests took up the ark of the Lord. And seven priests, bearing seven trumpets of rams' horns before the ark of the Lord, went on continually, and blew with the trumpets: and the armed men went before them; but the rere-ward came after the ark of the Lord, the priests going on, and blowing with the trumpets. And the second day they compassed the city once, and returned into the camp: so they did six days. And it came to pass on the seventh day, that they rose early, about the dawning of the day, and compassed the city after the same manner seven times: only on that day they compassed the city seven times. And it came to pass at the seventh time, when the priests blew with the trumpets, Joshua said unto the people, Shout; for the Lord hath given you the city. And the city shall be accursed, even it, and all that are therein, to the Lord: only Rahab the harlot shall live, she and all that are with her in the house, because she hid the messengers that we sent. And ye, in anywise keep yourselves from the accursed thing, lest ye make yourselves accursed, when ye take of the accursed thing, and make the camp of Israel a curse, and trouble it. But all the silver, and gold, and vessels of brass and iron, are consecrated unto the Lord: they shall come into the treasury of the Lord. So the people shouted when the priests blew with the trumpets: and it came to pass, when the people heard the sound of the trumpet, and the people shouted with a great shout, that the wall fell down flat, so that the people went up into the city, every man straight before him, and they took the city."[1]

The destruction of the walls of Jericho was obviously miraculous—produced immediately by the power of God. It may be asked, Then how was it "by faith?" Whose faith is referred to, and how did this faith influence the event? The faith referred to is plainly the faith of Joshua, believing the divine oracle uttered to him, and the faith of the people of Israel, believing the same oracle as reported to them by Joshua. How, then, faith influenced the event, is easily explained. The oracle distinctly declared that the manifestation of the divine power in a particular way was connected with certain actions to be performed by the children of Israel. They believed the oracle; because they believed the oracle, they performed the actions; and according to the oracle, the miraculous event took place. Suppose no oracle delivered, or suppose the oracle not to be believed—suppose Joshua or the people of Israel to have considered the appearance of the glorious personage, styling

[1] Joshua v. 13-15, vi. 1-20.—The comment of a rationalist interpreter is worth recording, if but to prove what fearful στρεβλωταί of the divine word these men are: "Historia *procul dubio*" (the confidence of men believing without evidence is generally proportioned to their confidence in disbelieving in the face of evidence. Neological interpreters do wonderful feats in both ways) "hæc est. Jussit Josua milites suos per septem dies urbem circuire, et ab omni in eam impetu abstinere; quo facto cum incolæ ita securi essent, Josua milites suos septimo die *in urbis eam partem, quæ minus munita esset*" (where did he find out that?) "irruere jussit, et mœnia urbis inter tubarum clangorem et clamores horridos oppugnare, idque tanta cum vehementia actum putamus, ut mœnia cadere sponte viderentur. In qua quidem historia si vel maxime nonnulla sint poetice adumbrata, nihil tamen ejus gravitati derogatur. Nam ad πίστιν nihil refert, utrum hæc miraculosa ratione, an ordine rerum antea ignoto gesta sint."—DINDORF.

"To laugh were want of goodness and of grace,
But to be grave exceeds all power of face."

But ridicule and scorn are not the appropriate feelings. We "do well to be angry" at such unfair treatment of an ancient, still more an inspired writer; and our hearts should dissolve in pity for men who, endowed with strong intellects and extensive learning, and applying both to the study of the Scriptures for a lifetime, arrive only at such results as these.

himself "the captain of the Lord's host," to have been a mere delusion of the fancy: their conduct is altogether unaccountable. They are before one of the most strongly defended cities in the land of Canaan. They dig no trenches to preserve themselves safe. They stand not in battle-array to meet any sally on them by the garrison. They lay no formal siege, set no battering engines, raise no shouts to intimidate the inhabitants. But in solemn silence, in sacred procession, the whole armed men, following the ark and the priests, encircled the city once every day for six days. On the seventh day the strange procession compassed the devoted city six times in accustomed portentous silence, till at last, at a signal given by Joshua, the priests blew a united blast on their unmusical trumpets, and the people raised one shout of anticipated triumph, and by the power of God the walls of Jericho fell flat, and they marched at once on all sides into the heart of the city. On the supposition of the revelation being made and believed, all is natural. Joshua and the people of Israel could not have acted differently.

The general truth here is the same as that involved in the former instance. Faith, persevering faith, enabled Joshua and the Israelites to do what otherwise they could not have done, and by doing so, to obtain what otherwise they could not have obtained; and the bearing of this on the Apostle's object is not difficult to perceive or explain.

The Hebrew Christians were engaged in a cause, the success of which, in the estimation of human reason, was even more hopeless than the capture of Jericho by the Israelites. The final triumph of the religion of Jesus over Judaism and paganism, false philosophy and worldly power, which had been distinctly predicted, seemed very unlikely. The means—the only means they were warranted to employ, appeared very ill fitted to gain their object. The preaching of the Gospel, the prayers of the Church, the holy conversation of believers, and their patience under manifold and severe afflictions,—what Milton happily styles "the unresistible might of weakness,"—these were to be the means by which the powers of darkness were to be shaken, and the walls of adamant and iron, reaching even up to heaven, within which superstition had entrenched herself, levelled with the ground. "The Captain of the Lord's host" had uttered the following oracle:—" All power in heaven and earth is given unto Me. Go ye therefore, and teach all nations: and, lo, I am with you alway, even unto the end of the world." This believed, was quite enough to induce them to commence and continue, amid all discouragements, the use of the appointed means, till the promised end was gained. Nothing else could have induced them to do so.

And it is equally true still, that faith—that nothing else but faith—can carry forward the Christian Church in its predicted triumph over the world and hell. What is the reason that there has been so little missionary effort in the Christian Church, in comparison of what there ought to have been? and why has that little effort been so languid, interrupted, and ineffectual? What but the want of a sufficiently implicit persevering faith in the promises, leading to a correspondingly implicit and persevering obedience to the commandments, of the great "Captain of our salvation?"

Nor is it difficult to perceive that this has a bearing on the transactions of the inward life of every Christian. Every individual Christian, in "working out his own salvation," has to contend with the same enemies, as in doing his part in the great work of the propagation of Christianity throughout the world. The Apostle's words, Eph. vi. 12, which in their primary meaning refer to the difficulties of the apostolic ministry, are true when used in reference to every Christian. They have to "wrestle with flesh and blood;" but not only with flesh and blood, but " with principalities and powers, with the rulers of the darkness of this world, with spiritual wickedness in high places." Barriers more difficult to be broken down than the walls of Jericho, seem to stand between them and holiness and heaven. How are these enemies to be overcome? how are these barriers to be removed? Faith can do it; nothing but faith can do it. Let all the allurements and all the terrors of the world be laid before the Christian, and use their combined influence to draw him away from truth, and holiness, and God; and let, through means of believing, the awful and the delightful realities of the eternal world be brought before his mind, and "this will be the victory, even our faith" overcoming the world. O how false, and hollow, and worthless, and absurd, and detestable seem all the promises and all the threats of " the prince of this world," when by the ear of faith we hear the Prince of the universe proclaim, "Be of good cheer, I have overcome the world,"—"I am the First, and the Last, and the Living One,"—"Be faithful to death, and I will give you a crown of life,"—"To him that overcometh, will I give to eat of the hidden manna, and will give him a white stone, and in the stone a new name written, which no man knoweth saving he that receiveth it!" Then the Christian feels that greater indeed is "He who is in him, than he who is in the world." Difficulties vanish; great mountains become a plain; there is no propensity so strong but he finds it now possible to resist, almost delightful to mortify; and just in the degree in which he believes, can he "do all things through Christ strengthening him."

The last of those Scripture illustrations of the power of faith which the Apostle unfolds particularly, is drawn from the history of Rahab the Canaanitess. Ver. 31. "By faith the harlot Rahab perished not with them that believed not, when she had received the spies with peace." Here, as on former occasions, let us look first at the facts, and then at the Apostle's account of the facts: first to what Rahab did and obtained; and then to the influence of her faith in leading her to act as she acted, and in enabling her to attain what she attained.

The discreditable appellation given to Rahab in our version has appeared to some learned men not warranted by the original term. They consider it as properly signifying 'a hostess or innkeeper;' or, understanding the word in a figurative sense, interpret it as equivalent to 'idolater.'[1] I rather think our translators, in common with by far the greater part of other interpreters, have accurately expressed the truth; and that in the conversion of Rahab (for I apprehend we have good evidence of her spiritual conversion) we are furnished with a beautiful display of the sovereignty of divine grace, and the power of divine influence, through the faith of the truth, to elevate the most degraded, and purify the most depraved, forms of human character.

The facts stated in reference to Rahab are two. She "received the spies[2] in peace;" and she "perished not with them

---

[1] The word cannot be derived regularly from זון, 'to feed.' It comes obviously from זנה, 'to commit whoredom;' and though idolatry was spiritual whoredom in the Israelitish people, yet I do not know that an individual Jewish idolater is termed a whoremonger or adulterer, far less a Gentile who did not belong to the nation married to Jehovah.

[2] κατασκόπους. James calls them ἀγγέλους, ii. 25.

who believed not." When Joshua, previously to Israel's passing the Jordan, sent from Shittim two men as spies to Jericho, to bring him intelligence of the state of matters among the Canaanites, they were hospitably entertained by Rahab, to whose house they were providentially directed; and when sought for by order of the king of Jericho, they were concealed by her at the peril of her own life, and through her dexterity obtained a secure retreat. As a reward for this important service, when all the inhabitants of Jericho were put to the sword, Rahab and her family were preserved alive, and obtained a place among the peculiar people of God,—Rahab marrying Salmon, the prince of Judah, and thus becoming one of the ancestors of the Messiah. Such are the facts: now for the Apostle's account of these facts.

How came Rahab to act as she acted?—how came she to obtain what she obtained? It was by believing, says the Apostle. Had Rahab acted on the ordinary principles of human nature, she would immediately, on discovering who the Israelitish spies were, and what was their errand, have given information to the authorities of the city, that they might be apprehended; at any rate, when search was made for them, she never would have exposed her own life to imminent peril in order to save them. What was that principle which exceeded in force the love of country and the fear of death? It was faith. Hear Rahab's own confession of her belief: "And she said unto the men, I know that the Lord hath given you the land, and that your terror is fallen upon us, and that all the inhabitants of the land faint because of you. For we have heard how the Lord dried up the water of the Red Sea for you, when ye came out of Egypt; and what ye did unto the two kings of the Amorites, that were on the other side Jordan, Sihon and Og, whom ye utterly destroyed. And as soon as we had heard these things, our hearts did melt, neither did there remain any more courage in any man, because of you; for the Lord your God, He is God in heaven above, and in earth beneath."[1] Had Rahab not heard these things in reference to Jehovah as the God of Israel, or had she, like many of her countrymen, heard but not believed them, she could not have acted as she did; but having heard and believed them, she could not but act as she did. It

[1] Joshua ii. 9-11.

deserves notice that no direct revelation was made to Rahab, but she had credible evidence of the reality of the revelations which Jehovah had made of His power and regard for Israel, which laid a foundation for firm belief. The efficacy of faith as an operative principle does not depend on the divine revelation which is the subject of faith being made directly to the individual, but on the individual's being fully persuaded, on sufficient evidence, that such a revelation has been made.

But how was it by faith that Rahab perished not with her unbelieving countrymen? The answer is obvious : her deliverance was the reward of her treatment of the spies, which originated in her faith. Had she not believed, she would not have been delivered ; had she remained an unbeliever, she must have perished among the unbelievers.

We are not to suppose that the whole conduct of Rahab in reference to the spies receives the approbation of the inspired writer, while he represents that conduct as an illustration of the power of faith. Rahab's falsehood cannot be justified, and is a proof that, if strong in faith in one way, she was weak in faith in another. All that the Apostle says—and we have seen how completely he is borne out by the history in what he says—is, 'Faith enabled Rahab to do what otherwise she could not have done, and to attain what otherwise she could not have attained.'

This illustration of the power, the necessity, the sufficiency of faith, was peculiarly fitted to come home to the business and bosom of the Hebrew Christians. They, like Rahab, were called on to do violence to their patriotic feelings, to separate themselves from their unbelieving kindred and country, and to follow a course which exposed them not only to "the spoiling of their goods," but to imminent hazard of their lives. Nothing but faith could enable them to act properly in these circumstances. If they really believed Jesus Christ to be the true Messiah, their Saviour and Lord—if they really believed His declarations, and promises, and threatenings : "He that loveth father, or mother, or sister, or brother, or houses, or lands, more than Me, is not worthy of Me ;" "He that loseth his life shall find it ; he that saveth his life shall lose it ;" "He that continueth to the end shall be saved ;"—if they really believed this, they would readily do all and suffer all that was required of them—they would submit to privations, expose themselves to dangers, and make sacrifices, from which otherwise they would have shrunk with terror; they would be content to have "their name cast out as evil" by their countrymen; and in this "patient continuance in well-doing," growing out of their believing, they would in due time attain to complete deliverance—"to glory, honour, and immortality." While, on the other hand, if they did not believe, they must fall before their temptations, and perish among their unbelieving countrymen.

And is not the illustration replete with instruction to professors of Christianity in every country and in every age? The terms of discipleship have never varied. "If any man will be My disciple, let him deny himself, take up his cross, and follow Me." All who would live godly must make sacrifices, and expose themselves to hazards. Faith, and nothing but faith, can enable persons cheerfully to make such sacrifices, to expose themselves to such dangers. Faith can do it; and, in the deliverance from the destruction which awaits the unbelievers, will in due time obtain for them a rich recompense for all they have hazarded and all they have lost in the cause of Christ.

Instead of prosecuting the course which he had begun, of particularly detailing the facts in which the power of faith manifested itself in the doings, and sufferings, and attainments of the Old Testament worthies, the Apostle, perceiving that this would have extended the Epistle beyond due limits, contents himself with barely enumerating the names of a number more of these believers, and in general terms describing the effects of their faith; intimating at the same time that there were many more besides those whom he mentions, who, in their actions and sufferings, in their lives and in their deaths, gave striking evidence to the power of believing in endowing man as it were with a supernatural strength, both for action and endurance. Vers. 32–38. "And what shall I more say? for the time would fail me to tell of Gedeon, and of Barak, and of Samson, and of Jephthae; of David also, and Samuel, and of the prophets: who through faith subdued kingdoms, wrought righteousness, obtained promises, stopped the mouths of lions, quenched the violence of fire, escaped the edge of the sword, out of weakness were made strong, waxed valiant in fight, turned to flight the armies of the aliens. Women received their dead raised to life again: and others were tortured, not accepting deliverance;

that they might obtain a better resurrection. And others had trial of cruel mockings and scourgings, yea, moreover of bonds and imprisonment: they were stoned, they were sawn asunder, were tempted, were slain with the sword: they wandered about in sheep-skins and goat-skins; being destitute, afflicted, tormented (of whom the world was not worthy): they wandered in deserts, and in mountains, and in dens and caves of the earth."

This is a very beautiful paragraph. It divides itself into two parts. Generally, it is an illustration of the power of faith; but the power of faith is viewed in two aspects—its power to enable men to do what otherwise they could not have done, and its power to enable men to suffer what otherwise they could not have suffered. We have an illustration of the first from the beginning of the 32d to the end of the first clause of the 35th verse; we have an illustration of the second from the beginning of the second clause of the 35th verse to the end of the 38th verse.

Let us examine, then, the Apostle's illustration of the power of faith to enable men to do what otherwise they could not have done. "And what shall I more say?" or, 'Why should I recite examples any longer? The point is already fully proved, clearly illustrated. Besides, time would fail me to recount all the examples recorded in Old Testament history of the power of faith. It would swell the Epistle to an inconvenient size.' He therefore contents himself with referring to a number of other illustrious individuals, who by faith had "obtained a good report;" and by turning to the Old Testament they could easily verify his reference, and see that in their actions the power of faith was not less strikingly manifested than in those which had been more particularly detailed.

The first person mentioned is Gideon. At a time when the worship of Baal prevailed to such an extent in Israel that the opposer of it was considered as a criminal worthy of death, Gideon cut down the grove dedicated to that idol, and overthrew his altar. What enabled Gideon to do this? It was faith. A revelation was made to him; he believed the revelation, and acted accordingly. "And it came to pass the same night, that the Lord said unto him, Take thy father's young bullock, even the second bullock of seven years old, and throw down the altar of Baal that thy father hath, and cut down the grove that is by it; and build an altar unto the Lord thy God upon the top of this rock, in the ordered place, and take the second bullock, and offer a burnt sacrifice with the wood of the grove which thou shalt cut down. Then Gideon took ten men of his servants, and did as the Lord had said unto him: and so it was, because he feared his father's household, and the men of the city, that he could not do it by day, that he did it by night."[1] Gideon, after collecting an army of thirty-two thousand men to fight against the Midianites and Amalekites, who at that time oppressed Israel, made proclamation, that every individual who was afraid of the approaching combat was at liberty to retire, and thus reduced his troops to ten thousand. He then subjected them to a very strange kind of trial, by bringing them to a pool of water and making them drink; dismissing such of them as lay down to drink, and retaining only such as, in a bending posture, lapped the water with their hands. His army was thus reduced to three hundred men; and these three hundred men he armed in a very extraordinary manner—with trumpets and with empty pitchers, and with lamps in these pitchers. By these most unlikely means Gideon obtained a complete victory, and delivered Israel out of the hands of their enemies.

Now how are we to account for Gideon's conduct, and for Gideon's success? There is but one way. He did all this "by faith." A divine revelation was given him; he believed, and acted accordingly. He used the means appointed by God, though in themselves utterly unfit for gaining the end; and it was to him according to his faith. Without such a revelation as he had, and without faith in that revelation, he could not have acted as he did; with such a revelation, and with faith in such a revelation, he could not but act as he did.

Barak is the next person mentioned as affording in his history an illustration of the power of faith. He, at a period when the Israelites were completely subjected to the oppressive yoke of Jabin, king of Canaan, raised a small band of ten thousand men, and at their head attacked Sisera, the commander of Jabin's numerous and well-appointed army, and completely discomfited him.

What was it that enabled Barak to undertake, and what was

[1] Judges vi. 25–27.

it that enabled him to succeed in, so apparently hopeless an enterprise? It was faith. A divine revelation was made to him through the medium of Deborah the prophetess; he believed it, and acted accordingly. Had no revelation been made, or had he disbelieved it, the attempt would never have been made.

The next illustration of the power of faith is taken from the very singular history of Samson. Samson performed many wonders. He tore a lion to pieces, as if it had been a kid; he burst asunder the strongest cords with which he could be bound, and, single-handed, slew a thousand of his enemies; he carried off the gates of Gaza and their posts on his shoulders; and he overturned the pillars by which the stately temple of Dagon was supported.

Now how did Samson do all these things? By faith. We are generally told, previously to any of his extraordinary feats, "The Spirit of the Lord came upon him." That is, I apprehend, a revelation was made to his mind that the divine power was to be put forth in connection with some exertion of his, so that he was to be enabled to do something far exceeding his natural powers. He believed this, and acted accordingly; and found that it was to him according to his faith.

Jephthah is next mentioned as an exemplification of the power of faith. At the time when the children of Israel were oppressed by the Ammonites, Jephthah, a man of low birth, with very inadequate means, effected their deliverance. How was this accomplished? It was through his believing. "The Spirit of the Lord came upon him;" *i.e.*, a revelation was made to him that he was to be the deliverer of Israel. He believed it, and acted accordingly.

David is next mentioned; but it were tedious to bring before you all the illustrations of the power of faith furnished by his eventful history. It is not improbable that the Apostle particularly refers to his victorious combat with the Philistian giant. David, a young man, unarmed but with a sling and a few pebbles, entered the lists with the veteran and well-accoutred gigantic champion of the Philistines, and gained the victory. These are the facts. What is the only rational account of them? David had received a divine revelation. This is plain from the confident manner in which he speaks: "This day will the Lord deliver thee into mine hand: and I will smite thee, and take thine head from thee; and I will give the carcases of the host of the Philistines this day unto the fowls of the air, and to the wild beasts of the earth; that all the earth may know that there is a God in Israel. And all this assembly shall know that the Lord saveth not with sword and spear: for the battle is the Lord's, and He will give you into our hands."[1] He believed it, and this accounts satisfactorily both for his conduct and for his success. Other instances of the power of faith will readily occur to the mind of every person intimately acquainted with David's history.

Samuel is the last of the ancients mentioned by name as exemplifying the power of faith. We cannot say certainly to what the inspired writer refers. It is possible that he refers to his anointing David to be king over Israel, notwithstanding the extreme danger to which this exposed him. A divine revelation was made to him; he believed it, and acted accordingly. His anointing Saul was another proof of the power of faith. But the event to which we are disposed to think it most probable, from its miraculous character, that the Apostle refers, is that recorded in 1 Sam. xii. 16–18: "Now therefore stand and see this great thing, which the Lord will do before your eyes. Is it not wheat-harvest to-day? I will call unto the Lord, and He shall send thunder and rain; that ye may perceive and see that your wickedness is great, which ye have done in the sight of the Lord, in asking you a king. So Samuel called unto the Lord; and the Lord sent thunder and rain that day: and all the people greatly feared the Lord and Samuel." A revelation was made to Samuel that the divine power was to be put forth in connection with certain words which he spoke. He believed that revelation; he spoke the words, and the event followed.

"The prophets" are then brought forward as exemplifying the power of faith. Appropriate instances will readily occur to every person familiarly acquainted with Old Testament history. Nathan reproving David; Micaiah denouncing Ahab's overthrow; Elijah fed by ravens—miraculously increasing the meal and the oil of the widow of Zarephath, and raising from the dead her son—bringing down fire from heaven to consume the sacrifice on Mount Carmel—withholding and bestowing rain by

---
[1] 1 Sam. xvii. 46, 47.

his prayers; Elisha performing similar wonders; Isaiah predicting Hezekiah's lengthened life, and the sudden destruction of the Assyrian army. These, and multitudes of other similar events in the history of the prophets, attest the power of faith. They are events of which no rational account can be given on any principle but this: A revelation of the divine will was made to them; they believed it, and this produced its appropriate effect. They were enabled to do what otherwise they could not have done.

The Apostle goes on to particularize some of the wonderful works which these men did, under the influence of faith, in the 33d and following verses.

The question has sometimes been put, Were all the persons here mentioned true saints? The question is rather a curious than a useful one. My answer to it is, Really I do not know. I am sure that some of them were; I hope all of them were. But all that is of importance for us to know is this, that all of them believed some divine revelation made to them, and that their faith of that revelation enabled them to do what otherwise they would not have been able to do. Their being brought forward here as illustrations of the power of faith, in no degree sanctions any pieces of their conduct which are inconsistent with the principles of truth and righteousness. Gideon's making an ephod out of the spoils of the Midianites; Jephthah's immolating his daughter, or devoting her to perpetual celibacy—for it seems difficult to determine which of these he did; Samson's taking a Philistian wife, and keeping company with a harlot; David's complicated sin in the matter of Uriah the Hittite;—none of these receive any sanction from the statement of the plain, well-supported fact, that all of these men, in consequence of their believing, were enabled to do things which otherwise they could not have done. These sins were proofs, not of faith, but of unbelief. In every one of them they acted without a divine revelation, or in opposition to a divine revelation. In reading Scripture history, let us recollect that the faults of good men are recorded to serve as beacons, not as guide-posts; that in copying any mere human character we must be cautious. There is but one *all*-perfect pattern. HE is "all fair; there is no spot in Him." He has "set us an example;" let us "follow *His* steps."

The paragraph from vers. 33–38 naturally divides itself into two parts: the first, illustrative of the power of faith to enable men to accomplish successfully the most difficult enterprises; the second, illustrative of its power to enable men to sustain patiently the most severe trials. Let us examine these two divisions of the paragraph in their order.

The first reaches from the beginning of the 33d verse to the end of the first clause of the 35th verse. "Who" (*i.e.*, the ancient worthies referred to in the preceding verses) "through faith subdued kingdoms, wrought righteousness, obtained promises, stopped the mouths of lions, quenched the violence of fire, escaped the edge of the sword, out of weakness were made strong, waxed valiant in fight, turned to flight the armies of the aliens. Women received their dead raised to life again."[1]

They "subdued kingdoms." This refers, I apprehend, to Joshua and David. Joshua subdued the kingdoms in Canaan, and David subdued those which were around that country—such as Moab, Ammon, Edom, and Syria; and they both subdued these kingdoms through believing. God had clearly revealed, not merely that it was His purpose that these kingdoms should be subdued, but also that Joshua and David were to be instruments of their subjugation. They believed this divine revelation; their faith manifested itself by corresponding exertions; and God, according to His promise, and in reward of their faith, crowned their exertions with success.

They "wrought righteousness." To "work righteousness," sometimes means in Scripture, to 'live a holy life;' as in such passages as these:—"Lord, who shall abide in Thy tabernacle? who shall dwell in Thy holy hill? He that walketh uprightly, and worketh righteousness." "But in every nation he that feareth God, and worketh righteousness, is accepted with Him."[2] There can be no doubt that many of the persons re-

---

[1] This is a very admirable passage. Most justly does Carpzov remark, " Demosthenico artificio exempla cumulat eorum, qui sola fide constantiam servarunt, qui calamitates, pericula, ignes, vincula, cruciatus, ludibria, scuticas, lapides, gladiorum mucrones, mortem ipsam, magno animo pertulerunt. Hic omnes notæ, in dicendo æstus, vis et fulmen in eloquendo, ἀσύνδετα, delectus vocum, αὔξησις καὶ δείνωσις, πεῦσις καὶ ἐρώτησις, κλίμακες, ἀθροισμοί, σφοδρὸν καὶ ἐνθουσιαστικὸν πάθος, comparent."

[2] Ps. xv. 1, 2; Acts x. 35.

ferred to did live holy lives, and that their living holy lives was owing to their believing the truth with regard to the divine character and will; and that the enabling an entirely depraved being, such as all men naturally are, habitually to live a holy life, is one of the most remarkable exemplifications of the power of faith. Yet I apprehend the general scope of the passage leads us to interpret the phrase, "wrought righteousness," in a more restricted sense, as equivalent to—'carried the laws of justice into execution, executed judgment.' I think it not improbable that the Apostle had in his eye Phinehas and Elijah, who both of them, through believing, executed judgment—inflicted merited punishment on notorious offenders—in circumstances in which, had they not been believers, they durst not have done it. The particulars of the two cases may be read —the first, in Num. xxv. 7; and the second, 1 Kings xviii. 40. Or the phrase may signify, ' procured justice for the oppressed;' as many of the judges did, by executing righteous judgment on the oppressors.

They "received promises." The word "promise" in the New Testament is often used to signify the thing promised. " The promise of the Father," is that which the Father has promised ; " the promise of the Spirit," is the Spirit who is promised —the promised Spirit; to " inherit the promises," is to enjoy the promised blessings. In the same way, in the passage before us, to " receive promises," is to obtain the blessings promised. Through believing, these elders who have " obtained a good report," obtained possession of the blessings promised to them. It was promised to Joshua that he should conquer Canaan; and through believing he obtained the conquest of Canaan. It was promised to Gideon that he should defeat the Midianites; and through believing he obtained their complete discomfiture. It was promised to David that he should be king over Israel; and through believing he obtained the kingdom. Great difficulties seemed to be in the way of these good men obtaining the blessings promised. Without believing, they could not have obtained them ; by believing, they did obtain them.

There is no inconsistency between the declaration here, that these " received promises," and the declaration in the 39th verse, that they " did not receive the promise." They received the accomplishment of many particular promises made to them, but they did not receive the accomplishment of the promise—the promise of the Messiah, or of the "salvation with eternal glory" which is in Him.

They "stopped the mouths of lions." This has by some been referred to what Samson and David did when, unarmed, they each of them slew a lion. But the words seem rather to describe what took place in the case of Daniel, when cast into the den of lions for his fidelity to his God. God sent His angel to shut the lions' mouths, that they did not hurt him. And this was done by faith; for it is expressly stated, that this was done "because he believed in his God."

They "quenched the violence of fire." Some have supposed that the reference here is to Aaron running, under a divine impulse, in consequence of a revelation made by Moses, into the midst of the congregation at the time a plague was destroying the Israelites by thousands, and, by making an atonement for them, arresting its fatal progress. But these interpreters seem to have confounded two separate events—the destruction of the 250 men of the company of Korah by fire from heaven, the violence of which was not quenched; and the plague, which does not seem to have been fire from heaven, that on the succeeding day destroyed 14,700 of the people, on account of their impious murmurings. The reference is probably to what happened to the three young Israelites in Babylon, who refused to yield obedience to the edict of Nebuchadnezzar, requiring all to worship the colossal image which he had erected in the plain of Dura. They were cast into "a burning fiery furnace, seven times heated,"— in which they were not only preserved alive, but walked up and down in the midst of the flames; and on being taken out, it was found that the violence of the fire had indeed been quenched—that it had had no power over their bodies—that "not even the hair of their heads was singed, nor their coats changed, nor had the smell of fire passed upon them." It was by faith that the violence of the fire was quenched. A revelation had been made to their minds that God would preserve them alive in the fiery furnace. They believed it; and, believing it, they permitted themselves to be cast into it, and found that it was to them according to their faith. "Our God, whom we serve," said they, "is able to deliver us from the burning fiery furnace; and He will deliver us out of thine hand, O king. But if not,"—that is, even if it were otherwise, though no such deliverance awaited us,—"be it known unto thee, O king, that we will not serve thy gods, nor worship the golden image which thou hast set up."[1]

They "escaped the edge of the sword." To "escape from the edge of the sword," may be considered as a general phrase: 'to obtain deliverance in circumstances of extreme danger.' And in this case it is applicable to many incidents recorded in the Old Testament, of persons, through the faith of a divine revelation, obtaining such deliverances; as in the case of David when in Keilah, where, but for a divine revelation and faith in it, he must have fallen by the sword of Saul. You have the story at length in the 23d chapter of 1st Samuel. It is not unlikely, however, that there is a direct reference to the cases of Moses and Elijah. We find Moses saying, Exod. xviii. 4,—"The God of my father was mine help, and delivered me from the sword of Pharaoh." The flight of Moses from Egypt into Midian was probably the result of a divine revelation made to him, and believed by him. Elijah's life was in extreme danger when Jezebel threatened to slay him with the sword, as he had done the priests of Baal. But he "escaped the edge of the sword." He fled into the wilderness; and though we have no particular account of this being the result of a divine revelation, yet, as Elijah seems to have taken few steps of importance without direct divine instruction, it is highly probable that it was. This seems to us a more probably just interpretation of the phrase, "by faith they escaped the edge of the sword," than considering it as equivalent to—'God protected them because they believed in Him.'

"Out of weakness they were made strong." When weak, through faith they became strong. This may refer to such instances as Barak, and Gideon, and Jephthah, who in consequence of believing the divine revelation made to them, and acting on it, from weak, helpless individuals, became powerful leaders of mighty armies. But as the word "weakness" properly refers to bodily sickness or disease, the reference most probably is to the case of Hezekiah, who in consequence of his faith recovered from a mortal disease. You have the particulars of this case in 2 Kings xx., and in Isa. xxxviii. A revelation was made to Hezekiah by the prophet Isaiah, confirmed by a miraculous

[1] Dan. iii. 17, 18.

sign. Hezekiah believed it; it was to him according to his faith—"out of weakness he became strong."

They "waxed," or were made,[1] "valiant"—that is, strong—"in fight," or battle. In the case of many of the heroes mentioned above, their faith of the divine promise of success gave them a kind of preternatural courage and strength in battle—enabled them to achieve exploits to which otherwise they would have found themselves entirely unequal.

"Turned to flight[2] the armies of the aliens." Of this we have many examples in Old Testament history. Let two or three serve as a specimen. Josh. x. 1–10. Here we have "armies of the aliens;" here we have a divine revelation; Joshua believing it; and in consequence of his faith, "turning these armies of the aliens to flight." 2 Sam. v. 17–25. Here, too, we have "armies of the aliens;" a divine revelation made; David believing it; and in consequence of believing it, "turning these armies to flight." 2 Chron. xx. 1–26.

"Women received their dead raised to life again." The reference seems here plainly to the restoration to life of the Sareptan and Shunammite widows' sons by Elijah and Elisha: 1 Kings xvii. 22–24; 2 Kings iv. 36. It was "by faith" that these strange events were brought about. A revelation, made to the minds of the prophets and believed by them, led them to speak the word or do the action which by divine appointment was connected with the putting forth of the divine power to work the miracle. Such is the illustration of the power of faith to enable men successfully to accomplish the most arduous enterprises; and the conclusion to be drawn from it plainly is, There is no enterprise so difficult, but faith in a divine revelation promising success can enable a man cheerfully to undertake, steadily to prosecute, and prosperously to finish it.

The second division of the paragraph is an illustration of the power of faith to enable men patiently to endure the severest trials—to continue stedfast in their duty to God notwithstanding their being exposed to extreme suffering.

Ver. 35. "Others were tortured, not accepting deliverance; that they might obtain a better resurrection." "Others,"—*i.e.*,

---

[1] ἐγενήθησαν.

[2] ἔκλιναν is well rendered, "turned to flight." Thus Homer, Il. E. 37: Τρῶας ἔκλιναν Δαναοί.

another set of believers, persons different from those whose wonderful achievements and attainments have just been mentioned. The word translated "tortured," properly signifies to stretch upon an instrument called τύμπανον (the shape of which is not certainly known at present), for the purpose of giving the body an attitude of peculiar exposure to the power of cudgels or rods. It involves the idea of double suffering, from being stretched on this instrument of torture and beaten; and, as used here, it plainly signifies tortured to death in this way.[1] Perhaps the word may, without impropriety, be considered as signifying torturing to death in any way. There can be little doubt that, under the idolatrous kings of Israel and Judah, numbers of individuals were put to death for their steady attachment to the pure worship of Jehovah; but it is scarcely possible, I think, carefully to read the history of the persecutions under Antiochus Epiphanes without coming to the conclusion that it is to them the inspired writer directly refers.

There is no doubt, says the judicious Dr Owen, that the Apostle here refers to the story that is recorded in the sixth and seventh chapters of the second book of the Maccabees. For the words are a summary of the things and sayings that are ascribed to Eleazar, who was beaten to death when he had been persuaded or allured to accept deliverance by transgressing the law. And the same may be said of the mother and her seven sons, whose story and torments are there also recorded. The words of Josephus are—"They every day underwent great miseries and bitter torments; for they were whipped with rods, and their bodies were torn to pieces, and were crucified while they were still alive and breathed."[2] When they were thus tortured they would not accept of deliverance; *i.e.*, on the condition of their denying Jehovah and violating His law. When Eleazar was offered the means of escaping punishment, he replied, "It becometh not our age to dissemble. For the present time I should

---

[1] To this mode of torture Prudentius seems to refer in the 14th Hymn of his Peristephanon:

"Tundatur tergum crebris ictibus,
 Plumboque cervix verberata extuberet.
      *   *   *   *
 Pulsatur ergo martyr, illa grandine,
 Postquam inter ictus hymnum dixit plumbeos."

[2] Antiq. ix. 5.

be delivered from the punishment of men, yet should I not escape the hand of the Almighty, alive and dead."[1] When the youngest of the seven sons of the Jewish mother was assured by Antiochus, with an oath, "that he would make him both a rich and a happy man if he would turn from the laws of his fathers, and that also he would take him for a friend, and trust him with affairs," he obstinately refused; and when the king urged the mother to counsel the young man to save his life, her reply was, "I will counsel my son;" and turning to her son, she said, "Fear not this tormentor, but, being worthy of thy brethren, take thy death, that I may receive thee again in mercy with thy brethren."

The reason of their constancy amid tortures is given—"that they might obtain a better resurrection." The reference of the word "better" is not at once seen by an English reader. The first clause of the verse, literally rendered, is, "Women received their dead by *a resurrection*." These tortured saints refused deliverance that they might obtain a resurrection, and a better resurrection than that which restored these dead persons to a life in this world—even the resurrection to life eternal. It deserves notice that the hope of the resurrection is expressly stated by those who were tortured to death, and who would not accept of proffered deliverance, as the reason of their continuing constant unto death. "It is good," said one of those noble martyrs, when mangled, and tormented, and ready to die—"It is good, being put to death by men, to look for hope from God, to be raised up again by Him." "My brethren," said the youngest of them, "are dead under God's covenant of everlasting life;" and the mother bore all her sufferings with a good courage, because of the hope which she had in the Lord.

Ver. 36. "Others had trial of cruel mockings and scourgings, yea, moreover of bonds and imprisonment." "Mockings" refer to the scorn, derision, and buffetings which the victims of persecution experienced. "Scourgings" refer to another mode of inflicting stripes than that referred to in the former verse. Micaiah and Jeremiah are instances of persons who were tried by "bonds and imprisonment," and who stood the trial—remained "stedfast and unmoveable."

---

[1] Afterwards, too, he said, Δυνάμενος ἀπολυθῆναι τοῦ θανάτου, σκληρὰς ὑποφέρω κατὰ τὸ σῶμα ἀλγηδόνας μαστιγούμενος, κατὰ ψυχὴν δὲ ἡδέως διὰ τὸν αὐτοῦ (ΤΟΥ ΚΥΡΙΟΥ) φόβον ταῦτα πάσχω. 2 Macc. vi. 30.

Ver. 37. "They were stoned, they were sawn asunder, were tempted, were slain with the sword." Sawing asunder was a most cruel method of inflicting death, in use in very early times —2 Sam. xii. 31—and still employed, it is said, in the Burman Empire. Tradition teaches that Isaiah the prophet was put to death in this horrible manner by Manasseh. The instances mentioned in this verse are not recorded in the Old Testament, but were doubtless all of them realities, and often repeated under the dreadful persecution of Antiochus Epiphanes.

The phrase, "they were tempted," has occasioned much difficulty to interpreters.[1] It does seem strange that a word expressive of suffering in general should be introduced in the midst of words descriptive of particular kinds of suffering. The word does not seem used in its general sense of trial, but of temptations to forsake their religion, presented to them in the midst of their sufferings, of which we have already had an instance. This seems to have been a common practice. Not only life, but wealth and honour, were frequently proffered in the midst of tortures most agonizing to the human frame, in order to tempt the martyrs to forsake their religion. Such temptations, in such circumstances, were among the severest trials of faith; and to enable them to rise above them, was one of faith's noblest triumphs.

Others of these ancient believers, who were not deprived of life, were yet exposed to numerous and great inconveniences. They had to abandon their own habitations, and, destitute of the ordinary accommodations of human civilised society, lived in the wilderness like wild beasts. "They wandered about in sheep-skins and in goat-skins, in deserts, and in mountains, and in dens and caves of the earth, destitute, afflicted, and tormented."[2] These

---

[1] Some consider it as an interpolation, inserted by mistake, in consequence of the preceding word being twice written. Others suppose that the original reading was—ἐπυρώθησαν, ἐπυράσθησαν, ἐπρήσθησαν—all signifying, 'they were burned;' or ἐπηρώθησαν, 'they were mutilated;' or ἐπράσθησαν, 'they were sold as slaves;' or ἐσπειράσθησαν, or ἐσπειράθησαν, 'they were tortured and killed by being tied to the spokes of wheels put in motion;' or ἐπάρθησαν, 'they were transfixed.' But all this is conjecture, and the best critics keep the word in the text.

[2] Mountains, waste places, and caves, are spoken of in Scripture as the usual places of refuge in times of affliction: Matt. xxiv. 16; 1 Sam. xxii.; 2 Sam. xxiv.; Judges vi. 2; 1 Sam. xiii. 6; Isa. ii. 19.

words need no explanation; and the best commentary on them is just the history of the persecutions which the people of God, in various ages, have undergone. It is a striking fact, that these words are just as descriptive of what the Christian Church has undergone since the Apostle wrote, as they were of what the Jewish Church had undergone before he wrote.

The parenthesis in the beginning of the 38th verse is peculiarly beautiful: " Of whom the world was not worthy." Their persecutors thought them not worthy of the world; but the truth was, the world was not worthy of them. The world could not bear a comparison with them in respect of worth. They were of a character far elevated above the rest of the world. " To tell the great, the mighty, the wealthy, the rulers of the world, that they are not worthy of the society of the poor, destitute, despised wanderers whom they hunt and persecute as the offscouring of all things, fills them with indignation. There is not an informer or apparitor but would think himself disparaged by it. But they may esteem it as they please. We know that this testimony is true, and the world shall one day confess it to be so."

The great truth which the Apostle means to bring before the mind by these statements is: 'Faith can enable men to endure the severest sufferings. It was faith that enabled these holy confessors to suffer all this patiently, cheerfully, perseveringly. Nothing but faith could have done this.' The application to the Hebrews is plain and obvious: 'You have much to do, you have much to suffer, as Christians. Faith can—nothing but faith can—enable you to do and suffer it all.' The truth is one of importance to *us* as well as to *them*.

The Apostle concludes his historical illustrations of the importance of faith in the remarkable words, vers. 39, 40, " And these all, having obtained a good report through faith, received not the promise: God having provided some better thing for us, that they without us should not be made perfect."

The words, "*all these*," have by some interpreters been considered as referring only to the whole of those who are represented as having suffered under the influence of faith; and they have supposed that they are here spoken of in contrast with those who *acted* under the influence of faith. The latter class, by faith, obtained promises; the former, though they have obtained a good report through faith, received not the promise.

While Gideon, and Barak, and Jephthah, and Samson, and David, and Samuel, by their heroic deeds, performed under the influence of faith, obtained possession of blessings that had been promised to them, those who, when exposed to the fierce persecutions of the Syro-Macedonian king, through faith endured tortures of the most exquisite kind, died without obtaining such blessings. On carefully looking at the passage, however, it must appear that the statement of such a contrast could in no way serve the Apostle's purpose; and the contrast stated is not between two different classes of the ancient worthies—between the working believers and the suffering believers, but between believers under the ancient economy and believers under the new economy. All those persons to whose history the Apostle in the preceding part of the chapter has referred, as an illustration of the power of faith,—all those whose names are honourably recorded in the book of God, either expressly on account of their faith, or on account of achievements which originated in faith,—" all these received not the promise."

These words, taken by themselves, may either signify, 'had not the promise *made* to them,' or, 'had not the promise *fulfilled* to them.' Those interpreters who take the first view of these words explain them thus: 'Those ancient believers had a number of promises made to them; but there was one promise, which by way of eminence may be called *the* promise—the promise of the resurrection and of an immortal life of happiness,—that promise was not given to them—they obtained it not. " Life and immortality have been brought to light by the Gospel." This better thing has been provided for us.' This is, however, by no means satisfactory; for it is quite evident, from the statements made in the preceding part of this chapter, that the promise, "I am the Lord thy God," included the promise of the resurrection and immortal happiness, and was understood by these ancients to include this promise. The promise, no doubt, is more fully unfolded, and expressed in much plainer terms, under the new than it was under the old economy; but the promise of eternal life, though forming no part of the law, was yet given to the people of God both before the law and under the law. To "receive the promise," must be understood as signifying, to receive the promised blessing, just as to "inherit the promises" is to possess the promised blessings.

But what is the promised blessing which none of these Old Testament worthies, though renowned for their faith, received? The great blessing promised to the ancient Church was the Messiah, and salvation, in all the extent of that word, through Him. It was promised to them that "the seed of the woman should bruise the head of the serpent;" that "in Abraham's seed all the families of the earth should be blessed;" that to them "a Son should be born, a Child given, whose name should be Wonderful, Counsellor, the Mighty God;" that Israel should be "saved in the Lord with an everlasting salvation." Now, this blessing, which is indeed a congeries of blessings, these ancient believers did not receive while they lived. They died before the Messiah became incarnate, and suffered, and died, and rose again; and of course they could not enjoy those blessings which originate in that fuller and clearer revelation of the truth respecting the salvation of the Messiah, and that correspondingly enlarged communication of divine influence which were the natural consequences of that great event. On their death, indeed, they entered into a state free from sin, and fear, and suffering; but still they "received not the promise." They waited in heaven, some of them for some thousands of years, expecting the revelation of the mystery of mercy; but till that took place they could not have the full knowledge and enjoyment of the promised blessing. We have no reason to think that the departed spirits of good men knew more of the plan of redemption than the angels did, who had to learn from the dispensations of God to the Church this "manifold wisdom of God." On the finishing of the great work given to the incarnate Son to do, and on His taking possession of His mediatorial throne, a prodigious accession must have been made to the happiness of the spirits of the ancient believers. But even yet they have not fully received the promise. The promise of a glorious resurrection, and an immortal restored life in their glorified bodies, remains yet unperformed. This is not matter of enjoyment, but of expectation. Their "flesh rests in hope," and their spirits, looking forward to the glorious consummation, breathe out the words, "How long, O Lord, how long!" Thus did all these ancient worthies, though celebrated for their faith, not receive the promised blessing.

One would have naturally expected a declaration of an

opposite kind: 'All these, having obtained a good report through faith, did receive the promise. After all the difficulties and trials, labours and sufferings, to which they were exposed, they at last obtained in the promised blessing a rich recompense for them all.' And this might have been justly enough said; for all true believers under the former economy did, immediately on death, obtain blessings which more than compensated for all their toils and sorrows; and further, such a statement would have been well fitted to support the Christian Hebrews amid their trials. But the statement contained in the text is equally true—that these excellent men, notwithstanding their faith, were not immediately, nor soon, put in possession of the great blessing promised to them. And its statement was well fitted also to prevent the Christian Hebrews from casting away their confidence, and to induce them to persevere, though the promised blessing might be long in being conferred on them.

Some have supposed that the intended practical application of the Apostle's remark may be thus expressed:—' These ancient believers persevered in their attachment to Jehovah and His cause in life and in death, though the great object of their faith, and hope, and desire, was not bestowed on them. How much stronger is the obligation, how much greater the encouragement, to perseverance in your case, who have received the promise! How easy it is to continue to believe in a well attested past fact, in comparison with continuing to believe in a future event, which is in itself very improbable, and for which they had no ground of expectation but the divine promise! How much more are your circumstances calculated to facilitate perseverance than theirs!'

There is force in this arguing; but we do not think that it is the argument suggested by the Apostle's train of thought. It is quite plain that he represents the enjoyment of the promised blessing as yet future, even with regard to the Christian Hebrews: "Ye have need of patience, that, after ye have endured the will of God, ye may obtain the promise."[1] It is as if he had said, 'Let not the fact, that the great object of your expectation is something yet future—something which you are never to enjoy in this world—something which, in all its extent, you are not to enjoy till the time of the consummation of all things,—

[1] Heb. x. 36.

let not this prevent you from persevering. All these elders, who through faith obtained a good report, and are now entered on the inheritance of the promised blessing,—all these, during the whole of their lives on earth, and many of them for ages after their death, did not obtain the promised blessing.'

That this is the practical bearing of the passage, will, I trust, become more apparent as we proceed with the illustration of the 40th verse, which is certainly one of the most difficult in the whole Epistle :—" God having provided some better thing for us, that they without us should not be made perfect."

" God has provided some better thing for *us*." There can be no doubt that the pronoun *us* refers to saints under the Christian economy. For them God has " provided some better thing." The question naturally occurs, Better than what? And the answer ordinarily returned is, Better than what the saints under the Old Testament economy enjoyed. *They* did not receive the promise, *i.e.*, the promised blessing: *we* have received it. The Messiah is come, and we are blessed with heavenly and spiritual blessings in Him. " Blessed," says our Lord, " are the eyes which see the things which ye see; for verily I say unto you, that many prophets and righteous men have desired to see the things which ye see, and have not seen them, and to hear the things which ye hear, and have not heard them." " The mystery which was kept secret from former ages and generations, is now made manifest." The true atonement for sin has been made, and clearly revealed. " The way into the holiest has been made manifest." The influence of the Holy Spirit has been more copiously dispensed. Life and immortality have been illuminated by the Gospel. A rational, spiritual, and easy system of worship, has taken the place of the complicated, and burdensome, and carnal ordinances of the law. The Church has passed from a state of minority, subjected to tutors and governors—a state of pupillage, into a state of mature sonship. All this is truth, and important truth ; but still I doubt if it is the truth here stated. The promise here spoken of does not seem to be directly and principally the promise of the Messiah, or of the blessings of His reign to be enjoyed in this world ; but " the promise of eternal inheritance,"—a promise, the full accomplishment of which the saints under the new economy do not obtain in the present state, any more than the saints under the ancient economy,—a promise, the full accomplishment of which they are to obtain after a patient enduring of the will of God. These "better things" which God has provided for us, or foreseen concerning us, are to be enjoyed when we and our elder brethren are together perfected.

The answer to the question, What is the reference of the word "better" in the clause before us?—with what are the things provided for Christians by God compared?—which we would be disposed to give is this: The comparison is not between what the saints under the old economy enjoyed and what saints under the New Testament economy enjoy on earth, but between what the saints under the new economy enjoy on earth, and what they are ultimately to enjoy in heaven. 'God has provided something better for us than anything we can attain in the present state, just as He had provided something better for them than anything they could attain in the present state. The ultimate object of their faith and hope lay beyond death and the grave, and so does ours.'

The good things provided for us by God are thus described by the inspired writers:—"We know that when the earthly house of our tabernacle is destroyed, we shall have a building of God, a house not made with hands, eternal in the heavens." When we are "absent from the body," we shall be "present with the Lord." "We know that them who sleep in Jesus, God will bring with Him." "When He who is our life shall appear, we shall appear with Him in glory." "When He shall appear, we shall be like Him; for we shall see Him as He is." "We look for the Saviour from heaven, who shall change these vile bodies, and fashion them like unto His own glorious body." "And so shall we be for ever with the Lord." "For this mortal shall put on immortality, and this corruptible shall put on incorruption; and then shall be brought to pass that saying, Death is swallowed up in victory." These are the things provided for Christians by God, inconceivably better than anything they can enjoy here below.

But it may be said, 'These things are not provided *exclusively* for Christians; they are equally provided for the ancient believers. We readily admit this; but we do not think that there is anything in the Apostle's language that would lead us to consider the good things spoken of as the exclusive possession of

Christians. Indeed, the Apostle does not seem to be here pointing out a contrast, but a resemblance, in the circumstances of Old Testament and New Testament believers: 'Old Testament believers did not obtain the promise in the present state, and neither do New Testament believers; for God has provided for them better things than any bestowed on them here below. We, as well as our elder brethren, must die in faith as well as live in faith. We must live believing, and die believing.'

It now only remains that we turn our attention to the concluding clause of the sentence, "that they without us should not be made perfect." Some connect the words with the first clause, considering the second as a parenthesis; thus: "All these, having obtained a good report through faith, received not the promise, that they might not without us be perfected." We consider them as equally connected with both clauses. Their meaning, I apprehend, would be brought out somewhat more distinctly by a very slight change in their order, which the original certainly warrants, if it does not demand: "that they, not without us, might be made perfect." God has so arranged matters, that the complete accomplishment of the promise, both to the Old Testament and New Testament believers, shall take place together; they shall be made perfect, but not without us; we and they shall attain perfection together.

The Old Testament saints died without receiving the promised blessing; but their faith was not therefore of no avail. In due season they shall be perfected; *i.e.*, the promise, in its full extent, shall be performed to them. And as God has provided for us, too, "better things" than any we enjoy here below, when they are perfected we shall be perfected along with them.

To "be made perfect," is, I apprehend, just the same thing as to "receive the promise," or to enjoy the "better things" provided for us. This exactly accords with the representations in other parts of Scripture. The whole body of the saved are together to be introduced into the full possession of the "salvation that is in Christ Jesus with eternal glory." There is to be "a gathering together unto the Lord Jesus at His coming." They are to be presented "a glorious Church," perfect and complete, "without spot, or wrinkle, or any such thing." As one assembly, they are to be invited to enter into "the kingdom prepared for them from the foundation of the world." They are to be "caught up together to meet the Lord in the air; and so are they to be for ever with the Lord."

Such views were well fitted to encourage the Christian Hebrews to persevere in believing,—to live by faith, to die in faith. 'The ancient believers lived and died without obtaining the great promised blessing, and so must you; but the promised blessing, in all its extent, will in due time be conferred on you both. They shall be perfected, and so shall you.'

Such is the interpretation of this very difficult passage which appears to me most probable. It is an interpretation which gives meaning and coherence to every part of the statement; the meaning given is in accordance with the doctrine of the Scriptures generally, and bears directly on the particular object which the Apostle has in view, the impressing on the mind of the Hebrews the importance of persevering faith.

At the same time, as in a number of points it is not the common mode of interpretation, it may be proper to state, in as few words as possible, how this passage is ordinarily explained. "The ancient worthies persevered in their faith, although the Messiah was known to them only by promise. We are under greater obligations than they to persevere; for God has fulfilled His promise respecting the Messiah, and thus placed us in a condition better adapted to perseverance than theirs. So much is our condition preferable to theirs, that we may even say, Without the blessing we enjoy, their happiness could not be completed." This is excellent sense, but I cannot bring it out of the Apostle's words.

The particular use to be made of the great truth which we think taught in them, that the great object of our hope, as well as that of the ancient believers, is yet future, is abundantly obvious; and the Apostle has in another of his Epistles very clearly pointed it out. If "our life is hid with Christ in God," and if we are not to appear in glory till we appear along with Him, ought we not supremely to "seek the things which are above, where Christ sitteth at God's right hand,"—"set our affections on the things above, and not on the things which are on the earth,"—"mortify our members which are on the earth," —"mortify the flesh, with its affections and lusts?" Habitually "looking for and hasting to the coming of our Lord Jesus," which is to be the gathering together of all His chosen people, may we all of us in that day find mercy of the Lord; and along with the venerable assembly of patriarchs and prophets, the goodly fellowship of the ancient believers, with the glorious company of the apostles, with the noble army of the martyrs, and the holy catholic Church of God throughout all the earth, obtain the " salvation that is in Christ with eternal glory."

The words which follow, in ch. xii. 1, 2,—" Wherefore, seeing we also are compassed about with so great a cloud of witnesses, let us lay aside every weight, and the sin which doth so easily beset us, and let us run with patience the race that is set before us, looking unto Jesus, the Author and Finisher of our faith; who, for the joy that was set before Him, endured the cross, despising the shame, and is set down at the right hand of the throne of God,"—contain the practical improvement of the Apostle's long and eloquent historical proof and illustration of the power of persevering faith, to enable men to do whatever God commands, however difficult,—to endure whatever God appoints, however severe,—and to obtain whatever God promises, however great and glorious, strange, and apparently unattainable. They are substantially an exhortation to the Hebrew Christians to a steady, active, persevering discharge of Christian duty, notwithstanding all the privations and sufferings, dangers and difficulties, to which this might expose them. Fully to apprehend their meaning and feel their force, it will be necessary that we attend in succession to the principle on which the exhortation proceeds, to the duty which it enjoins, to the means which it prescribes for facilitating its performance, and to the manner in which it requires this duty to be performed.

The principle on which the exhortation is founded is, " We are surrounded by a great cloud of witnesses;" the duty enjoined is, " running perseveringly the race set before us;" the means prescribed for facilitating the performance of this duty are, " the laying aside every weight, and especially the laying aside the sin that does most easily beset us;" and the manner in which this duty is to be performed is, " looking to Jesus, the Author and Finisher of our faith, who, for the joy that was set before Him, endured the cross, despising the shame, and is set down at the right hand of the throne of God."

The paragraph is highly rhetorical; and its meaning will

be but imperfectly understood—its force and beauty will be utterly lost to us—if we do not distinctly apprehend, and steadily keep in view, those historical facts or ancient customs from which the inspired writer borrows his imagery, and in allusion to which he fashions his language.

Some learned interpreters have considered the imagery and language as borrowed from the march of the Israelites through the deserts of Arabia towards the promised land; and that the divinely recorded experience of the faithful under the Old Testament dispensation, guiding the steps and cheering the hearts of Christians in their journeyings through the wilderness of this world towards the heavenly Canaan, is here represented under the emblem of that cloud of glory which marshalled the way for the hosts of Israel through untrodden paths to the good land promised to their fathers. The suggestion is ingenious, but not at all satisfactory. It applies only to the first clause of the paragraph; and even in reference to it, the analogy does not hold, for the cloud of glory did not encompass the camp of Israel—it went before them; and valuable as the recorded experience of the saints undoubtedly is, it could very imperfectly serve to the spiritual Israel the purpose which the cloud of glory served to Israel after the flesh. It is to the word and Spirit of the great God our Saviour, and not to the experience of men, however holy, that we look primarily for direction and consolation amid the perplexities and sorrows of our pilgrimage.

The reference is not to Jewish history, but to Grecian custom; and the Hebrew Christians are not here represented as journeying through a "waste, howling wilderness" towards a fertile country, but as engaged in running a race, the gaining of which would crown them with rich rewards and unfading honours. The allusion is here, as in many other parts of the Apostle's writings,[1] to those public agonistic or gymnastic games, which among the Greeks had less the character of a frivolous amusement than that of a grave civil institution, or a solemn religious ceremony. The most imposing form of this singular custom was perhaps that presented at Olympia, a town of Elis, where games were celebrated in honour of Jupiter once every five years. An almost incredible multitude, from all the

---

[1] *E.g.*, 1 Cor. ix. 24; Phil. iii. 12; 1 Tim. vi. 12; 2 Tim. iv. 7, 8.

states of Greece and from the surrounding countries, attended these games as spectators. The noblest of the Grecian youths appeared as competitors. In the race, to which there is an allusion in the paragraph before us, a course was marked out for the candidates for public fame, and a tribunal erected at the end of the course, on which sat the judges—men who had themselves in former years been successful competitors for Olympic honours. The victors in the morning contests did not receive their prizes till the evening, but, after their exertions, joined the band of spectators, and looked on while others prosecuted the same arduous labours which they had brought to an honourable termination. By keeping these few facts in your memory, the meaning and force of the Apostle's language will be much more readily and distinctly perceived.

The first thing to which our attention is to be directed, is the principle on which the Apostle's exhortation proceeds, "We are surrounded with a great cloud of witnesses." He takes this for granted, as already proved. The words are a brief summary of what he had stated at length in the preceding chapter, expressed in language suited to the figurative view which he is giving of the character and duty of the Hebrew Christians. The *witnesses* here referred to are plainly the worthies under the former dispensations, mentioned or referred to in the preceding context.

The word "witness" has two meanings: 'a person who gives testimony,' and 'a spectator.' The word is applicable to the elders, who for their faith are honourably mentioned in Scripture, in the first of these senses. Their recorded achievements, and sufferings, and attainments, attest in the most satisfactory way the power of faith, its necessity, and its sufficiency for all the purposes of duty and trial. And had it been simply said, 'Seeing we have so many witnesses to the power and importance of persevering faith, let us persevere in believing,' we should at once have said, this is the meaning of the expression. But when we look at the whole passage in its connection, we cannot help seeing that the word is used here in its second sense. These venerable men are represented as the spectators of the exertions of the Christian Hebrews.

These witnesses are represented as surrounding the Christian racers, as, in the course appointed for them, they "run that they may obtain." It has been supposed by many that these words teach us that the departed spirits of holy men are acquainted with what is going on in the Church below, and take a deep interest in the labours and trials of those who, after their example, are through persevering faith seeking for the full possession of the promised blessings. It may be so, it not improbably is so; but the words do not teach any such doctrine. They obviously, as I have already said, are just a summary of the statements contained in the 11th chapter; and certainly there is no such statement made there, as that "the spirits of the just made perfect" are spectators of the labours and trials of their younger brethren still on the earth.

The whole paragraph is figurative; and, in accordance with the principal figure—that which represents the Hebrew Christians as racers—the ancient worthies whose actions are recorded in Scripture are represented as spectators; their deeds, and sufferings, and triumphs, as recorded in Scripture, being calculated to have the same influence on the minds of the believing Hebrews, as the interested countenances and encouraging plaudits of the surrounding crowd had on the minds of the Grecian combatants. The solitary Christian, in the exercise of faith, finds that, under the influence of that divine principle, he is not solitary. The inspired history is converted as it were into a glorious amphitheatre, from which, while he treads the arena, or courses along the stadium, a countless host of venerable countenances beam encouragement, and ten thousand times ten thousand friendly voices seem to proclaim, 'So run that ye may obtain: we once struggled as you now struggle, and you shall conquer as we have conquered. Onward! onward!'

The Apostle speaks of a *cloud* of such witnesses. The word is expressive of their great number. It is common, I apprehend, in all languages to describe a vast assembly under the figure of a cloud.[1] We find instances of this use of the phrase both in the Old and New Testament. "Who are these"—says the prophet Isaiah, referring to the prodigious numbers of converts in the latter days, when, to use another figure, "nations shall

---

[1] Virgil, Æn. vii. 793, speaks of "nimbus peditum." Livy, xxxv. 49, speaks of "peditum equitumque nimbus." Herodian viii. 105 : νέφος τοσοῦτο ἀνθρώπων. Euripides, Phœniss. 1321 : νέφος πολεμίων. Homer, Il. ψ. 133 : νέφος πεζῶν. Diodorus Siculus, iii. 28 : νεφέλη, i.q. νέφος ἀκρίδων.

be born in one day,"—"Who are these that fly as a cloud, and as the doves to their windows?"[1] And Ezekiel, speaking of Gog and Magog, whose number is to be as the sand of the sea, says, "Thou shalt be like a cloud to cover the land."[2] And the Apostle Paul, in the Epistle to the Thessalonians, speaking of the joyful events of the time of the consummation of all things to the people of Christ, says, they who have been raised, and they who have been changed, shall be "caught up together in *clouds*," not 'in *the* clouds,'—*i.e.*, in prodigious numbers,—"to meet the Lord in the air." The number of the holy men who, in consequence of their experience being recorded to us in the Bible, are as it were present with us, cheering and encouraging us, is very great. The Apostle particularizes a great many, and then says, "But what shall I say more?"—or, 'why should I go on to multiply examples?'—" for the time would fail me," etc.

The peculiar mode of the Apostle's statement deserves notice. It is not, ' *Ye* are surrounded,' but " *we* ;" not, ' Do *ye* run,' but " let *us* run." He here speaks " according to the wisdom given to him,"[3] and admonishes Christian teachers, that their duties and those of their hearers are substantially the same ; that they need the motives they urge on others ; and that they are then most likely to be successful in impressing truth on others, when they show that they feel strongly their own individual interest in it.

The particle *also* is in our version unfortunately placed. As it stands, it conveys the idea—' The ancient worthies were surrounded with a cloud of witnesses, and so are we ;' which certainly is not what he intends to communicate. The particle, unless it is simply an expletive, which is not unfrequently the case, ought either to be connected with the particle which precedes it, and the two rendered, ' And therefore ;' or with the succeeding clause, " let us run the race that is set before us." ' They ran the race set before them ; let us also run the race set before us.'

The force of the connective particle " wherefore," or ' therefore,' is sufficiently plain. ' Since such a multitude of great and good men, by the recorded triumphs of their persevering faith,

---

[1] Isa. lx. 8.   [2] Ezek. xxxviii. 9, 16.

[3] We prefer this view to Carpzov's, who says, " More rhetorum, facundus scriptor ac θεόπνυστος, ἡμεῖς scripsit, ut 2 Cor. ix. 4, ἡμεῖς, ἵνα μὴ λέγωμεν ὑμεῖς."

cheer us on as if they were spectators of our labours and trials, *let us run the race set before us.*'

These words bring before our mind the second point to which we proposed to turn your attention—the duty which the Apostle enjoins. The language is figurative, but it is not obscure. The whole of Christian duty is represented as a race— a race set before them, which they must run, and "run with patience." The principal ideas suggested by this figurative view of Christian duty are the following: It is active, laborious, regulated, progressive, persevering exertion.

The duties of the Christian are of a kind that call for the *vigorous* exertion of all the faculties of his nature, both intellectual and active. The Christian life is a race, in which the powers of movement require to be fully put forth. Christianity does not consist, as too many seem to think it does, in abstract or mystical speculation, enthusiastic feeling, and specious talk. It no doubt does interest the understanding and the heart; but it proves the hold it has of both by unlocking the sources of activity which they contain, and making them flow forth abundantly in useful exertion. It leads the man to "deny ungodliness and worldly lusts, and to live soberly, and righteously, and godly;" "to do justly, to love mercy, to walk humbly with his God."

Christianity is *laborious* as well as active exertion. The angels never tire in their race, but it is otherwise with even the most thoroughly sanctified of the children of God in the present state. In their but imperfectly renewed natures, as well as in external circumstances, they have numerous causes which tend to check the rapidity and regularity of their movement. "Without are fightings, within fears." They are in danger of stumbling and falling; their attention is in danger of being called off by surrounding objects; and through continued exertion they are apt to become "weary and faint in their minds." To represent the Christian life as an unvaried scene of pleasurable employment, is equally to contradict the declarations of Scripture and the lessons of experience. There is pleasure, higher pleasure than aught that the world can afford, even in the most laborious parts of Christian duty, if performed under the influence of Christian principle; but there is toil and difficulty also. It is no easy matter to "flesh and blood" to deny self, to take up the cross, to follow Christ, to cut off the right hand, to pluck out the right eye, to "mortify our members which are on the earth," to "crucify the flesh, with its affections and lusts."

Christian duty, still further, is *regulated* exertion. A man may make active and laborious exertion by running up and down in various directions, but this is not to run a race. The racer must keep to the course prescribed; he must "run the race set before him," else his exertions, however active and laborious, will serve no good purpose. Christian duty must be regulated by the law of Christ. It consists not merely in doing, but in doing what Christ has commanded; not merely in suffering, but in suffering what Christ has appointed.

Progression is another idea suggested by the figurative representation here given of Christian duty. A man may be very active and laborious without moving from the spot where he stands, but this is not a race. The Christian must make progress; he must grow in knowledge, and faith, and humility, and usefulness, and universal holiness; he must, to use the language of one Apostle in reference to himself, "forget the things which are behind, and reach forth towards those which are before, and press toward the mark"—or along the prescribed course—"for the prize of the high calling of God in Christ Jesus;" or, to borrow the language of another Apostle in prescribing the duty of Christians, he must "add to his faith virtue, and to virtue knowledge, and to knowledge temperance, and to temperance patience, and to patience godliness, and to godliness brotherly-kindness, and to brotherly-kindness charity."

Finally, Christian duty is here represented as *persevering* exertion. This idea is suggested by the very term *race*; for no race is won in which the runner does not continue running till he reach the goal. But it is still more distinctly brought out in the exhortation, "Run with patience the race set before you."

Patience[1] properly signifies that temper which enables us to bear long-continued privation or suffering without murmuring, and to maintain a quiet, contented mind, while promised and expected blessings are long in being bestowed on us. This is a most valuable temper, but it is not exactly the temper which best suits the running of a race. That requires *ardour* rather than

[1] ὑπομονή.

patience. The truth is, the word here, and in many other passages of the New Testament, rendered "patience," properly signifies 'perseverance.' To "run with patience" is to run perseveringly, to persevere in running, just as "the patience of hope" is persevering hope. Christian duty is not to be thought of as having any limit but the limits of life. We must "be faithful to the death" if we would "obtain the crown of life;" we must "endure to the end" if we would "be saved." It is in continuing to "add to our faith virtue, knowledge, temperance, patience, godliness, brotherly-kindness, and charity," that we are assured "we shall never fall, but *so* an entrance shall be ministered to us abundantly into the everlasting kingdom of our Lord and Saviour Jesus Christ."

From these remarks, the meaning of the Apostle's exhortation to the Hebrew Christians, "Run with patience the race set before you," appears to be—'Persevere in the active discharge of all the duties enjoined on you as Christians, notwithstanding all the difficulties and dangers to which this may expose you. Hold fast the faith of Christ, and live under its influence. Let neither the allurements nor the terrors of the world induce you to turn from your course, or to slacken your pace. Beware of yielding to the influence of spiritual languor; but, trusting in the Lord, renew your strength; run, and be not weary; walk, and be not faint.'

The third topic to which these words call our attention, is the means which the Apostle prescribes for facilitating compliance with the exhortation, to persevere in running the race set before the Hebrew Christians. They must "lay aside every weight,[1] and the sin that did most easily beset them."

The language in the first of these clauses is figurative, and is borrowed from the practice of the Olympic racers laying aside all superfluous clothing, and disencumbering themselves of everything which could impede their movements as they pressed toward the mark for the prize. The meaning is, that Christians should immediately abandon and most carefully avoid everything, either in opinion, or disposition, or conduct, which tends to prevent the ready, persevering discharge of the duties enjoined on them. For the persevering performance of Christian duty, everything

---

[1] ὄγκος is properly "swelling;"—everything that increased the size and weight of the body, and was an encumbrance to free motion.

in itself sinful must be abandoned and avoided.[1] Christians are sometimes apt to think that they scarcely stand in need of being exhorted to abstain from what is obviously criminal; but such a thought springs from their not being sufficiently aware of the power of "sin that dwells in them,"—from their not believing with sufficient firmness that "in them, that is, in their flesh, dwells no good thing." He who knows them better than they do themselves has thought it proper to give to them such exhortations as the following:—"Take heed to yourselves, lest at any time your hearts be overcharged with surfeiting, and drunkenness, and cares of this life."[2] "Let us cast off the works of darkness, and let us put on the armour of light." "Let us walk honestly, as in the day; not in rioting and drunkenness, not in chambering and wantonness, not in strife and envying." "Put off, concerning the former conversation, the old man, which is corrupt according to the deceitful lusts.—Wherefore, putting away lying, speak every man truth with his neighbour: for we are members one of another.—Let him that stole steal no more: but rather let him labour, working with his hands the thing which is good, that he may have to give to him that needeth. Let no corrupt communication proceed out of your mouth, but that which is good to the use of edifying, that it may minister grace unto the hearers.—Let all bitterness, and wrath, and anger, and clamour, and evil-speaking, be put away from you, with all malice." "Mortify therefore your members which are upon the earth; fornication, uncleanness, inordinate affection, evil concupiscence, and covetousness, which is idolatry."[3] False views, depraved dispositions, immoral actions, have obviously a direct and powerful influence in impeding the Christian in his Christian race. His principal danger is perhaps, however, from another kind of weight—the indulging in an undue degree, affections, and the prosecuting with an undue degree of intensity, pursuits which are not in

---

[1] Chrysostom explains ὄγκον as = τὸν ὕπνον, τὴν ὀλιγωρίαν, τοὺς λογισμοὺς τοὺς εὐτελεῖς, πάντα τὰ ἀνθρώπινα. "Sleep, negligence, low and abject thoughts, all human business."—Theophylact's exposition is: τὸ βάρος τῶν γηίνων πραγμάτων, καὶ τῶν ἐπ' αὐτοῖς φροντίδων. "The weight of worldly businesses, and anxious thoughts about them."

[2] Luke xxi. 34.

[3] Rom. xiii. 12, 13; Eph. iv. 22, 25, 28, 29, 31; Col. iii. 5.

themselves sinful; nay, which may be not only innocent, but praiseworthy. It is our duty to love father and mother, sister and brother; but if we love them more than Christ, we are unfit for the Christian course. It is our duty to be "diligent in business;" but if we embark in worldly pursuits, however just and honourable, with an undue ardour—if we devote to them too many of our thoughts, and too much of our time, we are subjecting ourselves to a load under which we shall move heavily, if we move at all, in the spiritual race. Indeed, every earthly inclination—every earthly pursuit, however innocent in itself, when it interferes with the cultivation of Christian dispositions and the practice of Christian duties, becomes a weight which must be laid aside. There are certain habits in reference to religion itself which form great encumbrances to the persevering discharge of Christian duty. A fondness for what is curious and new in religion—a disposition to "intrude into things not seen," because not revealed—a giving heed to doctrines which minister questions rather than godly edifying—a turning aside unto vain janglings,—this appears to me one of the weights which Christians of the present as well as of the apostolic age need to lay aside, if they would so run as to obtain. The great enemy of our souls does not care much what it is that keeps us from prosecuting our Christian course, if we are but kept from prosecuting it; and when he can so far delude us as to make us believe that we are prosecuting that course when we are either standing still or proceeding in another direction, he considers his object as gained in the best possible way.

There is one general principle which may be laid down on this subject. Whatever tends to bring us more under the influence of present, sensible objects, is a weight which must impede our progress towards heaven. Hence the necessity of guarding against the love of the world in all its varied forms, so strongly stated by our Lord and His Apostles: "Take heed, and beware of covetousness." "Love not the world, neither the things of the world." The language of the Apostle in the clause before us, places in a very forcible point of view the extreme folly of Christians allowing themselves to be unduly attached to worldly pursuits. An Olympic racer binding himself with a heavy load, which greatly retarded his progress, rendered doubtful his success, and could be of no use to him when he reached the goal, is but a feeble figure of the incongruous folly of a worldly-minded professor of Christianity.

But in order to their running the Christian race, they must not only "lay aside every weight," but also, or especially, " the sin that does so easily beset them." This sin, whatever it is, is considered as the burden or encumbrance of which it was especially desirable that they should get and keep rid. Interpreters have found much difficulty in fixing the precise import of the word which is rendered in our translation by the circumlocution, "*which so easily besets.*"[1] It occurs nowhere else in the New Testament, and it occurs in no classical Greek author. Etymology, analogy, and the context, are therefore the only means we have of ascertaining its signification. Some expositors render it ' perilous, full of danger,' and consider it as referring to the peculiarly hazardous nature of the sin of apostasy, into which the Hebrew Christians were in peculiar danger of falling. The hazards connected with that sin are strikingly depicted in the beginning of the 6th and the end of the 10th chapter. Others, rendering the word 'the well-surrounded sin,'[2] consider the Apostle as referring to the frequent occurrence of this sin at this period, according to our Lord's prophecy, that " when iniquity abounded, the love of many should wax cold," and guarding them against committing the well-patronized sin—following the multitude in deserting the Saviour.

Upon the whole, we are disposed to prefer the sense given by our translators to both of these. It equally suits the etymology of the word,—which may with as much regard to the analogy of the language be rendered, *which readily surrounds*, as *which is well surrounded;* the epithet is very descriptive of the sin to which, we apprehend, he refers; and in this case there is an allusion—which is not the case in either of the other modes of interpretation—to the leading figure of the paragraph. This sin is compared to a loose garment which readily comes round the limbs of the racer, and, entangling him, diminishes his speed, retards him in his course. So much for the meaning of the word. Now for its reference.

Many good divines have supposed that there is no reference

[1] εὐπερίστατον.
[2] Sin in this case is to be considered as personified—as a θαυματαποιός, who has crowds of worshippers and admirers around him.

to any particular sin; but that it is a caution to the Hebrew Christians individually to be particularly on their guard against that sin to which, from constitution or circumstances, they are peculiarly liable. That there is in every individual a predominant tendency to some one form of immoral disposition or habit, is more than I am prepared to admit. At the same time, there can be no doubt that, from the constitution of the body or of the mind, and from the circumstances in which individuals are placed, there are certain sins into which they may more readily fall than others. The young are in most danger from the love of pleasure; the middle-aged, from the love of influence and power; the old, from the love of money. One has a tendency to be parsimonious, another to be profuse. Riches and poverty have their respective temptations; and even the desirable middle lot is not without them; and a great deal of practical religious wisdom consists in carefully marking these tendencies and temptations, and guarding against them. While I have no doubt that this general truth is very fairly deducible from the passage before us, I apprehend that the Apostle refers to that sin to which, from the peculiar circumstances in which they were placed, the Hebrew Christians were especially liable.

What that sin was, it is not difficult to discover. It is the sin, to guard them against which is the great object of the whole of the Epistle—the yielding to the "evil heart of unbelief, in departing from the living God." Their former prejudices in favour of Judaism, the privations and sufferings to which their profession of Christianity exposed them, the numerous instances of those who "went back and walked no more with Jesus,"—all these powerfully operated, along with those depraved principles which are common to human nature in all circumstances, to shake the constancy of their faith. While they ought to watch against everything which might impede their progress, it was peculiarly their duty to guard against what would assuredly prevent them from ever reaching the goal, by turning them aside from the course altogether.

We, my brethren, are not exposed to the same temptations as the Hebrew Christians to *open* apostasy; but that inward apostasy from Christ which consists in unbelieving thoughts and feelings, is a sin that easily besets Christians in all countries and ages, and is indeed the bitter and abundant source of all their sins and all their sorrows. We live by faith—we walk by faith—we run by faith—we fight by faith. Without faith we cannot run at all; and if our faith wax feeble, our pace will be slackened. There is no prayer the Christian needs to put up more frequently than, "Lord, increase my faith; help my unbelief." Whatever darkens our views or shakes our confidence with respect to any of the great principles of our Christian faith, cuts the very sinews of dutiful exertion, so that it becomes very difficult, or rather altogether impossible, to persevere in running "the race that is set before us."

It only remains now that we turn our attention to the manner in which the Apostle calls on the Hebrew Christians to perform the duty enjoined on them. They are to persevere in running the race set before them, "looking to Jesus, the Author and Finisher of their faith; who, for the joy that was set before Him, endured the cross, despising the shame, and is set down at the right hand of the throne of God."

The first thing to be done here, is to inquire into the meaning of the appellation here given to our Lord, "The Author and Finisher of our faith." You will notice that the word *our* is a supplement. The Apostle's expression is, "the Author and Finisher of faith," or rather, "of the faith." The ordinary meanings of faith are two—'believing,' and 'what is believed.' Understanding the word in its first sense, Jesus may be considered as "the Author and Finisher of faith," as He by His Spirit enables men first to believe, preserves them believers, and increases their faith, till that, like every other part of the Christian character, is made perfect in heaven. Understanding the word in its second sense, Jesus Christ is "the Author and Finisher of the faith," *i.e.*, of the Christian religion. He is the Introducer and Perfecter of it. He is at once its Author and its subject—"the Alpha and Omega, the beginning and the ending, "the *all in all* of it. Both of these modes of interpretation bring out a good meaning, but neither seems to bring out a meaning particularly appropriate to the Apostle's object.

I cannot help thinking that *the faith* here is a general name for 'the faithful,' or believers; just as the *circumcision* is for the circumcised, the *uncircumcision* for the uncircumcised, the *captivity* for the captives; or, to refer to analogous modes of expression from later times, the *League*, in French history, for the

Leaguers; or, to come nearer home, *Dissent* for Dissenters, *the Secession* for the Seceders. The word translated *author* occurs in application to our Lord in three other passages of Scripture: "The *Prince* of life, Acts iii. 15;" "A *Prince* and a Saviour," Acts v. 31; "The *Captain* of salvation," Heb. ii. 10. The proper signification is 'leader'—one who goes before and conducts others, and who thus by example shows them how to proceed. This, we apprehend, is its meaning here: 'Jesus, the Leader, and as the Leader, the Exemplar, of the faith.'[1] Jesus, who has run the race before us, and "set us an example, that we should follow His steps."

The word rendered *finisher* or *perfecter*, is, I apprehend, equivalent to—'rewarder.' The Apostle never loses sight of the principal figure, the Olympic stadium; and Jesus is here represented as one who, Himself having gained the highest honours of the race on a former occasion, sits now on an exalted throne, near the goal, as judge of the competitors, and with garlands in His hand to crown the victors.[2] He is the Rewarder of the faithful, or believers. "Be faithful to death," says He, "and I will give thee a crown of life." "To him that overcometh will I give to sit with Me on My throne, even as I also overcame, and am set down with My Father on His throne."

The words that follow seem to me illustrations of these two appellations here given to our Lord. He is the Leader and Exemplar of the faithful; for "He endured the cross, despising the shame," and He did this "for the joy that was set before Him." The Man Christ Jesus lived a life of faith when here below; He "looked not at the things which were seen and temporal, but at the things unseen and eternal." He believed that His own exaltation and the salvation of His people would certainly be the result of His doing and suffering the will of God; and therefore He "endured the cross." He patiently and perseveringly did and suffered all the will of God. "He became obedient to death, even the death of the cross." And He "de-

---

[1] ἀρχηγοὶ τῆς κακίας, 1 Macc. ix. 61, are "examples of wickedness." Lachish is represented by Mic. i. 13 as ἀρχηγὸς ἁμαρτίας, "the exemplar of sin." Cicero calls Cato (de Fin. iv. 16), "Omnium virtutum auctor"—the example, or pattern, of every virtue.

[2] τελειωτὴς was the name of the βραβεύς, who judged the competitors and conferred the prizes.

spised the shame;" *i.e.*, the ignominy to which He was exposed, never in the slightest degree induced Him to shrink from the discharge of duty,—not that He did not count ignominy an evil, for "reproach broke His heart,"—but that no evil could shake His determination to "finish the work which the Father had given Him to do."

As our Leader and Exemplar He thus acted, "*for* the joy which was set before Him." This clause admits of two different interpretations, according to the meaning you affix to the particle *for*. The proper signification is, *instead of*; but it is not unfrequently used to signify *on account of*. If we understand it in the first way, the meaning is, that Jesus, our Leader and Exemplar, voluntarily gave up a state of glory and enjoyment in order to endure the cross, and despise the shame. "Being in the form of God, He emptied Himself, and took on Him the form of a servant." In this case, the exhortation, to "look to Jesus" as our Exemplar, is nearly parallel to that in Phil. ii. 5, "Let this mind be in you, which was also in Christ Jesus," etc. The only objection to this mode of interpretation is, that the epithet, "set before Him," does not seem so well to suit our Lord's pre-existent glories, as His mediatorial honours laid before Him, held up to Him as the reward of His mediatorial labours.

If we understand the particle *for* in the second way, as equivalent to—'for the sake of,' the meaning is, that the anticipated glories of that state to which Jesus was to be raised on His finishing the work given Him to do, animated Him to a persevering performance of the duties and endurance of the evils connected with its performance. This is a true and scriptural sentiment also. Our Lord believed the promises made to Him: He believed that He was to "be exalted, and extolled, and made very high"—that He was to "see of the travail of His soul, and be satisfied"—that "His soul should not be left in the separate state, nor His body see corruption"—that "God would show Him the path of life;" and, believing this, He "did not fail, nor was He discouraged;"—He persevered, amid inconceivable difficulties and sufferings, till He could say, "It is finished."

We are disposed to prefer the latter mode of interpretation, as it presents Jesus as an example of the very duty which the

Apostle is here enjoining on the Hebrews—the persevering, under the influence of faith, in doing the will of God, notwithstanding all the dangers and difficulties in which this may involve us. Such is the Apostle's illustration of the appellation, "the Leader or Exemplar of the faithful.' As the *Finisher*, the *Perfecter*, the Rewarder of the faithful, " He is set down on the right hand of the throne of God ;" *i.e.*, He is exalted to a state of the highest honour and authority. "All power in heaven and in earth" is given to Him, and therefore He is able abundantly to reward those who continue faithful to the death; and His being so gloriously rewarded, is satisfactory evidence that in due time they shall be rewarded also.

Now, in running with perseverance the race that is set before them, Christians are to "look to Jesus Christ" as their Leader and Exemplar, their Perfecter and Rewarder ; *i.e.*, they are habitually to make the truth respecting Him in these characters the subject of their believing contemplation. It is as if he had said, 'The record of the labours, and sufferings, and triumphs of Old Testament believers, may and ought to be a source of instruction, motive, and encouragement to you amid your difficulties and trials; but the record of the unparalleled labours, and sufferings, and glories of your Lord and Saviour is the grand source of instruction, motive, and encouragement.' A firm habitual faith of what Christ has done for them, and of what He will do for them, is at once necessary and sufficient to make Christians, in opposition to every conceivable difficulty and temptation, persevere in running "the race set before them." If they " become weary and faint in their minds," it is because they do not " consider Him." If they neglect their duty, it is because they forget their Saviour. How infinitely important, then, is the knowledge of the truth in reference to *our Lord!* All our comfort, all our holiness, depends on this. Let us, with the Apostle, count all things loss for this excellent knowledge. Let those who are destitute of it seek above all things to obtain it. " It is more precious than rubies ; and all the things that can be desired are not to be compared to it." Seek, then, this wisdom ; and with all your seeking, seek this understanding; and let those who know the Lord follow on to know Him.

In the paragraph which follows, the Apostle's object plainly is, to guard the Hebrew Christians against the temptations to apostasy which naturally arose out of that state of suffering in which their profession of Christianity involved them. And the first consideration which he brings forward for this purpose, is derived from the sufferings to which the Son of God patiently submitted, while working out the salvation of His people. Ver. 3. " For consider Him that endured such contradiction of sinners against Himself, lest ye be wearied and faint in your minds."

The connective particle translated *for*, is here, as in many other places, equivalent to 'moreover.' The Hebrew Christians were in danger of " becoming weary and faint in their minds." The language is figurative, but not obscure. Scripture is generally the best interpreter of Scripture; and a passage in the book of Revelation, ch. ii. 2, throws much light on that now before us. " I know," says our Lord to the church of Ephesus, " thy works, and thy labour, and thy patience" — rather, thy perseverance. — " Thou hast borne, and hast patience" — or rather, hast persevered — " and for My name's sake hast laboured, and not fainted." To faint and be weary, is just the reverse of persevering labour and suffering for the name of Christ.¹ It is, under the depressing and discouraging influence of severe and long-continued trials, to abandon, either partially or totally, the duties which rise out of the Christian profession. Severe and long-continued privations and sufferings on account of our connection with Christ, try the reality and the strength of our attachment to Him.

To such privations and sufferings the Hebrew Christians were exposed; and that they might not yield to their influence, the Apostle turns their minds to the multiplied, severe, and long-continued sufferings of our Lord, and His patient and persevering endurance of them. He was exposed to worse sufferings than they were, and yet He never became weary or faint in His mind. This is the great truth he brings forward as a preventive and antidote to spiritual weariness and faintness.

Jesus Christ was exposed to " the contradiction of sinners

---

¹ Some connect ταις ψυχαις υμων with καμνετε. It is better to connect with εκλυομενοι. Καμνω is often used in reference to mental fatigue, without any qualifying phrase, which is not the case with εκλυομαι. At ver. 5 indeed it is used simply; but then the full expression had been employed immediately before.

against Himself." The word rendered *contradiction*, in its strict sense, refers to contumelious language; but it is here, as in other places, used as equivalent to 'opposition,'—ill usage generally.[1] Jesus Christ was opposed, by words and actions, on the part of "sinners," *i.e.*, by the wicked Jews who were His cotemporaries. The whole of our Lord's history is a commentary on these words. They ridiculed Him as a low-born, low-bred, fanatical madman; they branded Him as " a glutton and wine-bibber"—" a friend of publicans and sinners"—an impostor—a seditious person—an impious usurper of divine honours—a person in league with apostate spirits; and their conduct corresponded with their language. They laid snares for His life; and after, through the treachery of one of His disciples, He was put into their hands, they treated Him with the most contumelious scorn and barbarous cruelty.[2]

The Apostle not only states that our Lord was exposed to this opposition from sinful men, but that He *endured* it. That expression not merely intimates that He suffered this, but it describes how He suffered it. He " endured this contradiction :" He patiently bore it; He did not " become weary or faint in His mind." His purpose of " finishing the work given Him to do" was never shaken. He *endured*—endured to the end.

The Apostle's exhortation, " Consider[3] Him that endured such contradiction of sinners against Himself," contains more in it than a careless reader is apt to suppose; and everything contained in it is calculated to serve his purpose, to prevent the Christian Hebrews from yielding to the dispiriting influence of the calamities to which they were exposed. " Consider Him who endured," etc. 'Recollect His relation to God and His relation to you. Remember that He was the only-begotten and well-beloved Son of God,—the brightness of His glory, and the express image of His person. If *He* suffered, should *you*,

---

[1] It is = the Heb. רִיב, Hos. iv. 4, and סָרַר, Isa. lxv. 2, LXX. *Vide* John xix. 12; Tit. ii. 9.

[2] The expression is ἀντιλογία εἰς αὐτόν. In some codd., for αὐτόν we read αὐτούς. This is obviously a gloss, arising from supposing that εἰς αὐτόν was superfluous, and that εἰς αὐτούς expressed the idea—' in opposition to their own true interests.' The genuineness of the text. recep. is undoubted.

[3] ἀναλογίσασθε, cogitate, instituta comparatione.

creatures, sinners, wonder that you suffer, or murmur when you suffer? Remember that He is your Lord and Teacher; and is it not enough that the disciple should be as his teacher, and the servant as his lord? Remember that all His sufferings were for you; and will you shrink to suffer for Him? Consider not only Him who suffered, but what He suffered. Consider Him who endured such contradiction of sinners against Himself. Think how numerous, how varied, how severe, how complicated, how uninterrupted, how long-continued, were His sufferings. What are your sufferings in comparison of His? And then consider not only what He suffered: think of the temper in which He suffered,—how meek in reference to men—how submissive in reference to God! and by this consideration learn not to allow your sufferings to produce, on the one hand, resentment towards men, nor, on the other, discontent towards God. And especially, let the thought, that He *endured* all this—that notwithstanding all this, He stood steadily to His purpose of saving you, at whatever price—excite in you an invincible resolution also to *endure*,—to suffer no affliction to shake your attachment to Him; but, as every reproach, and insult, and injury but made Him the more set His face as a flint, let your afflictions but rouse into more energetic vigour all the principles of Christian obedience; and knowing that He suffered for you, and what He suffered for you, and how He suffered for you,—and knowing how well He deserves that you suffer for Him, and has, in suffering for you, set you an example, that ye should follow His steps,—instead of being weary and faint in your minds, let tribulation work perseverance, and perseverance experience, and experience hope.' Such, and so powerful, is the first consideration which the Apostle brings forward to counteract the influence of affliction on the minds of the Christian Hebrews to produce a partial or total abandonment of Christian duty.

The second consideration is drawn from the fact, that the sufferings to which they had yet been exposed were by no means so severe as they might have been—so severe as they might yet be—so severe as the sufferings not only of Christ, but of many confessors in former ages, had been. Ver. 4. " Ye have not yet resisted unto blood, striving against sin."

The Hebrew Christians were engaged in a contest. They were " striving against sin." " Sin" has, by some very good interpreters, been considered as equivalent to 'sinners,' referring to their unbelieving countrymen. We think it more natural to consider the words as figurative. Sin is personified, and is represented as the combatant with which the Hebrew Christians were contending. The various afflictions to which they were exposed in consequence of their attachment to the cause of Christ, may be viewed as the means which sin employs in order to subdue them, or as the evils to which they are exposed in the prosecution of their warfare.

Now, in " striving against sin"—in resisting the attempts made to induce them to apostatize—they had sustained temporal loss in a variety of forms. They had lost the good opinion of their countrymen. Their " names had been cast out as evil." They had been reviled and calumniated. They had, some of them, been " spoiled of their goods." They had " endured a great fight of afflictions," having been made " a gazingstock by reproaches and afflictions." Some of them had even fallen as martyrs, such as Stephen, and James the brother of John. But at the period when this Epistle was written, none of them were called to lay down their life for the cause of truth and righteousness. The force of the Apostle's admonition may be thus expressed:—'Your sufferings, though numerous and severe, are not such as to excuse weariness or faintness of mind. You have not yet been called to part with life.[1] Many believers under a former dispensation were called on to make this sacrifice, and they cheerfully made it. When tortured even to death, they refused deliverance on the condition of apostasy; and will you abandon the cause of truth before you are exposed to such a trial? Jesus, the great Leader and Rewarder of the faithful, resisted to blood. He would not abandon your cause, though it should cost Him His life; and will ye abandon His cause, merely because it exposes you to reproach and poverty?'

The words seem also to intimate, that not yet called on to resist to blood in their combat with sin, it was quite possible that they might soon. And in this view of the matter, there is an appeal made to the principle of honourable shame. When they became Christians, they were told plainly at what hazard they

---

[1] $\mu\acute{\epsilon}\chi\rho\iota$ $\alpha\H{\iota}\mu\alpha\tau\sigma\varsigma$ = $\mu\acute{\epsilon}\chi\rho\iota$ $\phi\acute{o}\nu\sigma\upsilon$ sive $\theta\alpha\nu\acute{\alpha}\tau\sigma\upsilon$, 2 Mac. xiii. 14. $A\H{\iota}\mu\alpha$, like the Heb. דם, often signifies a violent death: 2 Sam. iii. 28; Matt. xxiii. 30, xxvii. 24.

became so: they were not inveigled into the profession of that religion by false representations of ease and worldly comfort. They were told, that if they would live godly in Christ Jesus, they must lay their account with suffering persecution; and that losing even their life for Christ's sake was by no means an impossible or an improbable event. 'Now what sort of soldiers are you, if the minor hardships of warfare so dispirit you as to make you think of abandoning your standard before you have received a wound, in a cause of which you are not worthy to be defenders if you are not ready to shed the last drop of your blood?' The Christian soldier should be thankful when his trials are not extreme ones. To use Dr Owen's words, whatever befalls us on this side blood is to be looked on as a fruit of divine tenderness and mercy. In taking on them the profession of the Gospel, the Christian Hebrews had engaged to bear the cross in all the extent of that expression. They were not yet called on to redeem their pledge in all its extent; but that very circumstance rendered their conduct the more blameable and shameful, if they refused to give what was much less than they had promised. It is of great importance, if we would remain faithful in times of trial, that we habitually keep in mind the worst evils we can be exposed to. This will preserve us from being shaken or surprised by the less evils which may befall us, and make us feel that, instead of murmuring that the burden laid on us is so heavy, we have reason to be thankful that it is not heavier.

The third consideration brought forward in the following verses is founded on the nature and design of the afflictive dispensations to which they were exposed. Their afflictions were not, as their enemies insisted, and as their unbelieving hearts were but too apt to suspect, intimations that they were the objects of the divine displeasure,—tokens that God disapproved of their connecting themselves with Jesus of Nazareth and His followers,—but were indeed tokens of His parental love, and means used by Him for disciplining them for that higher state of being, and that nobler order of enjoyment, which Jesus had died on earth to procure for them, and gone to heaven to prepare for them. This is the subject of the Apostle from the 5th down to the 13th verse.

The words in the beginning of the fifth verse ought, we apprehend, to be read interrogatively: "And have ye forgotten the exhortation which speaketh unto you as unto children? My son, despise not thou the chastening of the Lord, nor faint when thou art rebuked of Him: for whom the Lord loveth He chasteneth, and scourgeth every son whom He receiveth." The afflictions which befell the primitive Christians in consequence of their attachment, were to many of them stumblingblocks. With their Jewish prejudices, this was the very reverse of what they expected. The peculiar people of God, the followers of Messiah, were, in their estimation, entitled to anticipate a very different lot. This mode of thinking naturally led them to entertain doubts that they had done wrong in embracing Christianity; that, instead of being the favourites of Heaven, they were the objects of divine displeasure; and that the best thing they could do was to revert to their old creed, by means of which they would obtain security from the evils which so severely pressed on them.

The Apostle meets this tendency to apostasy by showing them the true nature and design of the afflictive dispensations to which they were exposed. And he does so by appealing to those Scriptures which they admitted to be " given by inspiration of God," and which were " profitable for doctrine, for reproof, for correction, and for instruction in righteousness." It is as if he had said, ' Surely these afflictions could never have made you weary and faint in your minds if you had understood and habitually remembered the words of God in the Old Testament Scriptures, in which, as a wise and kind Father, He represents affliction as a necessary discipline for the spiritual improvement of His children.'

There are two very important general remarks which are naturally suggested by the manner in which the Apostle introduces this quotation. The first is, that the Old Testament Scriptures are intended for our instruction as well as for the instruction of those to whom they were originally addressed. The exhortation contained in the book of Proverbs speaks to the Christians of the primitive age. "Whatsoever things were written aforetime, were written for our learning." There is need of wisdom in drawing from the Old Testament Scriptures the instruction they are intended to give *us;* but, directly or indirectly, every part of these holy writings is intended to instruct us.

The second general remark is, that the true way of being

preserved from going wrong, is to look at everything in the light of the Holy Scriptures. Afflictions, which, when considered by themselves, may be considered as a temptation to apostasy, when viewed in the light of God's word, will be found to be an argument to stedfastness. If, in consequence of their afflictions, the Hebrew Christians were in danger of " becoming weary and faint in their minds," it was because they had forgotten the scriptural view of the nature and design of afflictions, and of their duty under afflictions.

The passage quoted is from the book of Proverbs, ch. iii. 12 : " For whom the Lord loveth He correcteth, even as a father the son in whom he delighteth." The quotation is made from the LXX., the version in common use at the time the Epistle was written. Though not a literal rendering of the Hebrew text, it yet gives its meaning with sufficient accuracy; and this is one out of very many instances in which it is evident that the writers of the New Testament, in quoting the Old, frequently quote in a general way, keeping close to the meaning, though by no means to the words.

The view given of the nature of affliction is contained in the 6th verse, as connected with the address, *My son*. " Whom the Lord loveth He chasteneth, and He scourgeth every son whom He receiveth." The general truth is, Affliction, in some form or other, is allotted by God to every individual whom He regards with peculiar favour, as the necessary means of promoting their spiritual improvement; and is therefore to be considered as a proof of His parental love. The doctrine is not, that in every case affliction is a proof of God's fatherly love to the individual afflicted; but, that every child of God may expect affliction, and that to him affliction is a proof of his heavenly Father's kind regard.

The exhortation founded on this view of the nature and design of affliction is, " Despise not thou the chastening of the Lord, neither faint when thou art rebuked of Him." The Hebrew Christians were not to despise the chastisements of the Lord; they were not to count them of little value. ' Instead of spurning them from you, regard them as important blessings. They are chastisements,—discipline, intended, calculated, necessary for your real welfare; they are not the strokes of an enemy, but the rod of a Father; they are the chastisement of the Lord, the greatest, the wisest, the best of beings, who can do nothing without a reason, nothing without a good reason—nothing in caprice, nothing in cruelty. Treat them not, then, as common, valueless things.'

And while you thus regard them, "faint not when you are rebuked of Him." To faint when we are rebuked of God, is, under the influence of despondency, to sink into a state of criminal inaction—to become unfit for the discharge of our active duties. Now Christians should not thus faint under afflictions; for they are the rebukes of a Father—of One who loves them, and who rebukes them, not to depress, but to excite them. Let our afflictions rouse our spiritual energies. The thought that we need rebuke, and that He who rebukes is infinitely wise and good, should equally prevent us from sinking into a state of desponding, helpless inactivity. In this case we directly contradict the design of God in these dispensations, which is to quicken and animate us.

The words which follow are the Apostle's amplification of the argument against apostasy contained in the words of the inspired Israelitish sage, and his application of it to the circumstances of those to whom the Epistle was addressed. Vers. 7-11. "If ye endure chastening, God dealeth with you as with sons: for what son is he whom the father chasteneth not? But if ye be without chastisement, whereof all are partakers, then are ye bastards, and not sons. Furthermore, we have had fathers of our flesh which corrected us, and we gave them reverence: shall we not much rather be in subjection unto the Father of spirits, and live? For they verily for a few days chastened us after their own pleasure; but He for our profit, that we might be partakers of His holiness. Now, no chastening for the present seemeth to be joyous, but grievous: nevertheless afterward it yieldeth the peaceable fruit of righteousness unto them which are exercised thereby." The substance of his statements may be summed up in the following propositions:—Afflictions are so far from being proofs that those who are visited with them are objects of the divine displeasure, that an entire freedom from them would be a ground of doubt whether the individual was an object of the divine peculiar favour. The character of Him from whom these afflictions come, and the design for which they are sent, should induce us dutifully to receive, and patiently to bear them. The consequences of these afflictions, when thus endured, are so advantageous, that they more than compensate the pain they occasion to us during their continuance.—To the consideration of these truths, peculiarly suited to the circumstances of the believing Hebrews, but full of interest to Christians in all countries and in all ages, let us now turn our attention.

The first of these principles is contained in the 7th and 8th verses. "If ye endure chastening, God dealeth with you as with sons: for what son is he whom the father chasteneth not? But if ye be without chastisement, whereof all are partakers, then are ye bastards, and not sons."

The words, "if[1] ye *endure* chastening," have by many good interpreters been considered as equivalent to—'if ye patiently and perseveringly submit to the afflictions laid on you.' There is no doubt that the phrase, taken by itself, may signify this; but it seems plain, from its being opposed, not to impatient suffering, but to exemption from suffering, that the Apostle's intention is to express merely the fact of being afflicted, not to describe the manner in which the affliction is received. 'If ye meet with affliction, God deals with you as with *children*.' We cannot conclude that when we meet with affliction, therefore we are the children of God—the objects of His peculiar favour; for affliction is the common lot of man; in that respect, "one event happens to the righteous and the wicked;"—but neither can we conclude that we are His enemies, the objects of His judicial displeasure. The Apostle's sentiment is, 'Afflictions, however severe, are no proofs that we are not God's children.'

"For what son is there whom the father chastens not?" This question presents in a very lively manner, the reason, along with the proof that afflictions are not necessarily wrathful inflictions, why we are not to conclude from our afflictions merely that

[1] There is a various reading here worth noticing. A number of good MSS., and some of the ancient versions and Fathers, read, instead of ε παιδείαν, εἰς παιδείαν, and connect it with what goes before—παραδέχεται εἰς παιδείαν. Ὑπομένετε. The ordinary reading is, however, preferable. Παιδεύειν is not exactly = μαστιγοῦν or κολάζειν : the word signifies, in its primitive sense, 'to educate;'—this is its classic signification. It then came to signify, 'correction,' as a part of education—'discipline.' In Greek the allusion to the paternal relation is retained, which is not the case in our word 'chastisement.'

we are not the children of God. Every son among men stands in need of chastisement in some form or degree; and every wise and kind father will inflict chastisement when he sees it to be necessary for the good of his son. The most endearing of all the relations in which God is pleased to reveal Himself to His people, that of a Father, thus leads them to expect afflictions. There is none of them but stand in need of discipline; and He who condescends to call them children, and Himself their Father, means all that these words convey, and certainly loves them too well to withhold those chastisements which in His infinite wisdom He sees to be absolutely necessary and most fitted for promoting their spiritual improvement.[1]

But this is not all. Not only is it true that affliction is no proof that we are not the children of God, but the want of affliction would be a ground of doubt whether the individual exempted was a member of God's spiritual family. "But if ye be without chastisement, whereof *all*"—*i.e.*, all the children—"are partakers, then are ye bastards, and not sons."

The allusion here, is either to spurious children whom an adulterous wife attempts to impose on her husband, and whom he refuses to take care of as his children; or to illegitimate offspring, who usually—though certainly most criminally—are almost entirely neglected, so far as parental superintendence and discipline are concerned, by their father. 'If ye were free of affliction, that, instead of being a proof of your being the objects of God's peculiar regard, would be the very reverse.'

The words do not necessarily imply that any human being is a stranger to affliction. They only assert that, were any human being in these circumstances, it would be a proof, not of his being an object of the divine peculiar favour, but of his being an outcast of His family. They, however, suggest the

---

[1] There is a remarkable passage in Seneca, which almost tempts one to believe that he had seen the passage before us. After representing a good man as "progenies Dei," he goes on to say: "Parens ille magnificus, virtutum non lenis exactor, sicut severi patres, progeniem durius educat. Itaque quum videris bonos viros acceptosque diis laborare, sudare, per arduum ascendere, malos autem lascivire et voluptatibus fluere : cogita filiorum nos modestia delectari, vernularum licentia ;—illos disciplina tristiore contineri, horum ali audaciam : idem tibi de Deo liqueat. Bonum virum in deliciis non habet, non molliter educat, experitur, indurat, sibi illum praeparat."—SENECA, *de providentia*, cap. i. *ad fin.*

truth—and, I apprehend, were intended to suggest the truth—that a life of comparative freedom from afflictions, being unfriendly, in the present state, to our religious and moral improvement, is by no means to be considered by itself as an indication of the peculiar regard of God. In all ages, the remarkable prosperity of individuals obviously and decidedly irreligious has attracted attention. Not that the irreligious are uniformly, or usually, remarkably prosperous—the reverse is the truth,—but that they are occasionally so; and where it is so, their prosperity, instead of being a blessing to them, is a curse: just as the illegitimate child, deprived of the advantage of parental discipline, and left in many cases to the unrestrained influence of his appetites and passions, finds his liberty his ruin. "Wherefore do the wicked live, become old, yea, are mighty in power? Their seed is established in their sight with them, and their offspring before their eyes. Their houses are safe from fear, neither is the rod of God upon them. Their bull gendereth, and faileth not; their cow calveth, and casteth not her calf. They send forth their little ones like a flock, and their children dance. They take the timbrel and harp, and rejoice at the sound of the organ. They spend their days in wealth, and in a moment go down to the grave. Therefore they say unto God, Depart from us; for we desire not the knowledge of Thy ways. What is the Almighty, that we should serve Him? and what profit should we have, if we pray unto Him?" "For I was envious at the foolish, when I saw the prosperity of the wicked. For there are no bands in their death; but their strength is firm. They are not in trouble as other men; neither are they plagued like other men. Therefore pride compasseth them about as a chain; violence covereth them as a garment. Their eyes stand out with fatness: they have more than heart could wish. They are corrupt, and speak wickedly concerning oppression: they speak loftily. They set their mouth against the heavens; and their tongue walketh through the earth."[1]

Remarkable prosperity should produce gratitude, but it should not produce exultation. On the contrary, it should excite fear and caution, lest we should be among those whose portion is in the present state, and whose prosperity will destroy them.

[1] Job. xxi. 7-15; Ps. lxxiii. 3-9.

The statement contained in these two verses seems a deduction from the quotation from the book of Proverbs. God chastens whom He loves; He scourges His sons. Of course, "when ye endure chastening, God deals with you as with sons." He chastens *all* whom He loves; "He scourges *every* son whom He receives." It follows, "If ye be without chastisement, of which all the children are made partakers, then are ye bastards, and not sons."

The second proposition to which we were to give our attention is, The character of Him from whom these afflictions come, and the purpose which they are intended to answer, should induce us dutifully to receive and patiently to bear them. This is contained in the 9th and 10th verses.

There is a very striking contrast between our human and divine fathers. "We have had fathers of our flesh"—*i.e.*, we have had natural parents; they chastened us—they had a right to do so from their relation, and they did so; they restrained us—they "corrected us;" and we did not rebel against them—"we gave them reverence." Now, if it was reasonable and right in us to submit to *their* chastisement, must it not be much more obviously reasonable and right to submit to the chastisement of the Father of our spirits? *i.e.*, as I apprehend, not so much the Creator of our immortal minds, who "breathed into our nostrils the breath of life," and thus made us "living souls," which is true, but our spiritual Father, as opposed to our natural fathers,—He to whom we are indebted for spiritual and eternal life. "Shall we not much rather be in subjection to Him?"

To be in subjection to our spiritual Father is a phrase of extensive import. It denotes " an acquiescence in His sovereign right to do what He will with us as His own; a renunciation of self-will; an acknowledgment of His righteousness and wisdom in all His dealings with us; a sense of His care and love, with a due apprehension of the end of His chastisements; a diligent application of ourselves unto His mind and will, or to what He calls us to in an especial manner at that season; a keeping of our souls by persevering faith from weariness and despondency; a full resignation of ourselves to His will, as to the matter, manner, times, and continuance of our afflictions;"[1]—in one word, a

[1] Owen.

"lying passive in His hand, and having no will but His." This is to be subject to "the Father of our spirits."[1] And surely, if our natural relation to our earthly parents, and the favours they are the instruments of conferring on us, make it fitting that we should submit to them, surely the spiritual relation in which we stand to our heavenly Father, and the infinitely more valuable and numerous blessings of which He is the Author, make it proper that we should be subject to Him.

A strong additional motive to this subjection is contained in the concluding clause—"*and live.*" To *live,* here, is equivalent to—'to be happy.' Subjection to "the Father of our spirits," when He chastens us, is the only way, and the sure way, to true happiness. There is an inward satisfaction in a childlike submission to divine chastisement—a conscious union of mind and will with God, fellowship with "the Father of our spirits"—which is far superior to any earthly pleasure; and it is in a patient suffering, as well as in a persevering doing, of the will of God, that His children in due time arrive at "glory, honour, and immortality," and receive, in its most perfect form, "eternal life."

A further argument for submission to the chastisements of our spiritual Father is derived from His object in these chastisements, as contrasted with the object which our natural fathers had in their chastisements. "For they verily for a few days chastened us after their own pleasure; but He for our profit, that we may be made partakers of His holiness." Our earthly fathers restrained us and corrected us "for a few days,"[2] —a short season—the season of infancy, childhood, and early youth; and they did so "after their own pleasure,"[3] or as it seemed good to them.

There are many parents who, in inflicting chastisement, are guided just by the impulse of the moment, and have no direct reference to the ultimate welfare of the child; and even the

---

[1] As Num. xvi. 22, xxvii. 16, אֱלֹהֵי הָרוּחֹת לְכָל־בָּשָׂר, ὁ Θεὸς τῶν πνευμάτων καὶ πάσης σαρκός. Proclus terms the Demiurgus τῶν ψυχῶν Πατήρ. Plat. Theol. lib. vi. cap. iii.

[2] πρός joined to nouns of time is = *ad*, or *per:* Gal. ii. 5; Luke viii. 13; John v. 35; 2 Cor. vii. 8. *Their* chastisement has a reference to our brief sojourn on earth—at best, ὁ ἤ.; *His*, to our everlasting state.

[3] κατὰ τὸ δοκοῦν, *pro arbitrio suo.* In many cases parents act on the principle, "Sic volo, sic jubeo, stat pro ratione voluntas."

wisest and kindest human parent, in chastising his child, may not only mistake as to the kind and measure of chastisement that is best fitted for promoting his child's moral improvement, but may be to a very considerable degree arbitrary in his corrections—more influenced by natural irritation than by a reasonable wish to do his child good.

But our heavenly Father never chastises His children except "for their profit." His object is uniformly their real advantage; and the form, the degree, the duration of the affliction, is all ordered by infinite wisdom so as best to gain this object. He "does not afflict willingly," *i.e.*, arbitrarily, nor grieve without cause. All the afflictions of His people are intended and are requisite for promoting their highest interest. Kind, wise intention does not always in an earthly parent secure the employment of the best means to realize that intention; but in God they are always united in the highest degree.

> "Parents may err, but He is wise,
> Nor lifts the rod in vain."

The concluding words are commonly considered as stating in what the "profit" of God's children, which is His object in their afflictions, consists. It consists in their becoming "partakers of His holiness." The holiness of God consists in His mind and will being in perfect accordance with truth and righteousness. And to become "partakers of His holiness," is just to have the mind brought to His mind, the will brought to His will: to think as He thinks—to will as He wills—to find enjoyment in that in which He finds enjoyment. This is man's profit. This is the perfection of his nature, both as to holiness and happiness. This is *to live*—to live the life of angels, to live the life of God; to partake of His holiness is to "enter into *His* joy." And this is the design of God in all the afflictions of His people—experimentally to convince them of the vanity of the creature, and the absolute necessity and sufficiency of God in order to true happiness.

I am not quite sure but this clause is to be considered as opposed to the clause, "for a few days," and ought, as it may be rendered, "*till*[1] we become partakers of His holiness."

---

[1] There is no doubt this is a signification of the preposition εἰς: Gal. iii. 24, εἰς Χριστόν, until Christ. *Vide* note on εἰς τὸν καιρὸν τὸν ἐνεστηκότα, sup. ch. ix. 9.

God's chastening will never entirely cease till its end be gained. So long as we are here below, we need chastening, and we shall receive it. The great transforming process, in which chastisement holds an important place, will go on till it is completed in our being made "partakers of His holiness"—till we have no mind different from the mind of God, no will different from the will of God—till, according to our measure, we be holy as He is holy, and perfect as He is perfect. And then, the end of chastisement being gained, it will cease for ever; and as the mature, the fully grown, the thoroughly educated children of God, we shall live for ever in our Father's house above, in the eternal enjoyment of that happiness which He has secured for us by the obedience to the death of His own Son, and for which He has prepared us by the influence of His Spirit and the discipline of His providence. Oh! who would not submit patiently, thankfully, to discipline, necessary, fitted, intended, certain—if endured in a childlike spirit—to produce so glorious a result?

We proceed now to the illustration of the third of these propositions :—The consequences of these afflictions, when dutifully sustained, are so advantageous, that they more than compensate the pain which they occasion during their continuance. This is plainly stated in the 11th verse : "Now, no chastening for the present seemeth to be joyous, but grievous : nevertheless afterward it yieldeth the peaceable fruit of righteousness unto them which are exercised thereby."

One of the excellences of Christian morality is its suitableness to the essential principles of our nature. There is nothing impracticably rigid in its principles. It makes war with nothing in human nature but with its depravity. It proves itself the work of Him who at once is intimately acquainted with, and who tenderly pities, the innocent weakness of humanity—one who "knows our frame, and remembers that we are dust." The principles of Christian morality in reference to affliction are striking illustrations of these remarks. Fortitude, and patience, and resignation under affliction are required, but not apathy to affliction. The stoical philosophy, the purest of all the ethical systems of the Grecian schools, required its followers to account pain no evil, and to be equally joyful in the deepest adversity and in the highest prosperity. It has been justly observed, this is either *absurdity*, or it is a mere play upon words.

The Apostle admits that it is of the very nature of affliction to produce pain and sorrow. "No chastisement"—*i.e.,* no affliction—"for the present"—*i.e.,* while it continues—"*seemeth to be.*" These words are not intended to intimate that the pain produced by affliction is merely apparent, not real; they suggest the idea—'Afflictions are thought and felt by those who bear them to be not joyous, but grievous.' They produce painful, not pleasurable emotions; they are intended to do so; they cannot serve the purpose for which they are sent without doing so. There is a necessity not only that we be occasionally and "for a season in manifold tribulations" or trials, but "in heaviness," through means of these manifold tribulations or trials.

There are men who seem to think it a point of mental courage and hardihood, when visited with affliction, to keep off a sense of it. They count it pusillanimity to mourn or be affected with sorrow on account of them. This is neither natural nor Christian. Reason and revelation equally condemn all such attempts, as calculated to counteract the great design of affliction. There is no pusillanimity in acknowledging that we feel the strokes of an almighty arm. It is the truest wisdom of a creature to humble itself "under the mighty hand of God." If we are among His people, He will mercifully compel us to acknowledge that His chastisement is not a thing to be despised or made light of. He will—O how easily can He do it?—continue or increase our affliction, or bring upon us other afflictions, till He break the fierceness and tame the pride of our spirits, and bring us like obedient children to be subject to "the Father of our spirits."

But while the Apostle admits that the afflictions of Christians are, during their continuance, "not joyous, but grievous," he at the same time teaches, that "afterwards they yield the peaceable fruit of righteousness to them who are exercised by them." Let us first attend to the phraseology, which is somewhat peculiar; and then, shortly illustrate the important and encouraging sentiment which it conveys.

The language is obviously figurative. "The peaceable fruit of righteousness." The phrase, "fruit of righteousness," taken by itself, most naturally signifies, 'the effects of righteousness —the fruits which righteousness, whatever that word signifies, produces.' But here you will notice that it is chastisement or affliction that is represented as producing the fruit. Whatever is meant by the "fruit of righteousness," is plainly represented as the effect of affliction. The phrase, "fruit of righteousness," seems to be a phrase of the same kind as "the first fruits of the Spirit;" *i.e.*, the influences of the Spirit tranquillizing, and purifying, and blessing the soul, which are the commencement of the celestial blessedness. The "fruit of righteousness" is not some effect of righteousness, but it is righteousness itself considered as the effect of affliction. Chastisement produces fruit, and that fruit is righteousness. *Righteousness* is here, I apprehend, to be understood as just equivalent to a frame of mind and a course of conduct corresponding to what is right; it is the same thing as becoming "partakers of God's holiness."

This fruit is termed "peaceable fruit." *Peace*, according to the Hebrew idiom, is equivalent to happiness or prosperity. "The peaceable fruit" is just equivalent to—'the salutary, useful, happy fruit.' Affliction produces the happy result of promoting spiritual improvement, making men more holy.

And it produces this happy result "to those who are exercised with it." The expression, "exercised with it," is a word borrowed from the gymnastic games. It describes those persons who, divested of the greater part or the whole of their clothing, were trained by a variety of hardships and exercises for the race or combat. The Apostle's idea seems to be this, that afflictive dispensations of Providence, when viewed and treated as divinely appointed means of disciplining men for the service of God, promote the spiritual improvement of those who are visited with them, which is a most salutary result, and more than compensates the pain which they occasion while they continue.

These salutary fruits are produced *afterwards*. The salutary effect may not be immediately produced.[1] Like the production of fruit, it may be gradual; but such will, in good time, be the result of all sanctified affliction.

Having thus explained the phraseology, and brought out the Apostle's meaning—namely, that afflictions, when viewed and treated as divinely appointed means for disciplining us for God's service, however painful while they continue, will ultimately pro-

[1] ὕστερον seems used in contrast with πρὸς ὀλ. ἡμ. above. '*Afterwards*, when the few days of life are gone by, the fruits of God's chastisement will be enjoyed.'

duce the salutary effect of bringing our minds, and hearts, and conduct into a completer correspondence with the perfect rule of righteousness, the divine will, in other words, will promote our spiritual improvement, let us briefly illustrate this principle.

And here let it be distinctly understood that it is not affliction taken by itself that is represented as producing this effect: it is affliction understood to be, and treated as, the chastisement of the Lord. The natural effect of affliction on an unsanctified mind, is either to irritate or depress; in either case, instead of promoting, it hinders spiritual improvement. That, however, arises entirely from the ignorance, and unbelief, and obstinacy of the person afflicted. And even with regard to Christians, it is true that it is just in the proportion as they regard and improve affliction as the chastisement of the Lord, that affliction will promote their spiritual interests.

Affliction, rightly considered, is calculated to impress on the mind the evil of sin generally, our own sinfulness, the vanity of the world, the importance of an interest in the divine favour, the value of a good conscience, the blessedness of a well-grounded hope of eternal life. In the time of ease and prosperity, the mind is naturally thoughtless and inconsiderate; the realities of the spiritual and eternal state are in some measure forgotten; the enjoyments of life supply, as it were, the place of the happiness which arises from a good conscience and peace with God. But sanctified affliction makes us see things as they really are; leads to serious self-inquiry; prevents us from saying, "Peace, peace, when there is no peace;" fixes the mind on the things which concern our everlasting interests, and excites an anxiety to remove everything which interferes with or endangers them. Prosperity not only produces inconsideration, but pride. It is said of the wicked, that "because their strength is firm, and they are not in trouble as other men, pride compasseth them about as a chain."[1] Even Christians are in danger of feeling in some measure this malignant influence of long-continued prosperity; they are in danger of being elated with, and glorying in, their enjoyment—of forgetting the Giver in the gift—of overestimating the value of such blessings, and underrating their dangers. In such cases afflictions are excellent and necessary correctives. They make us feel our own meanness, wretched-

[1] Ps. lxxiii. 4–6.

ness, frailty, and folly; they tend to wean the affections from the "things which are on the earth,"—to lead us to seek for happiness in growing conformity to the will of God,—in one word, to "look not at the things which are seen and temporal, but at the things which are unseen and eternal." It is in this way that "our afflictions work for us a far more exceeding and an eternal weight of glory;" it is in this way they improve our character, and increase our happiness; it is in this way they fit us for more actively doing and more patiently suffering the will of God; it is in this way they make death less dreadful and heaven more desirable, and thus prepare us for both.

In the 12th and 13th verses, the Apostle points out the use which the Christian Hebrews should make of the considerations which he had brought forward in reference to their afflictions. "Wherefore lift up the hands which hang down, and the feeble knees; and make straight paths for your feet, lest that which is lame be turned out of the way; but let it rather be healed."

In the first part of this sentence there is obviously a reference to Isa. xxxv. 3, "Strengthen ye the weak hands, and confirm the feeble knees;" and in the second part, to Prov. iii. 26, "For the Lord shall be thy confidence, and shall keep thy foot from being taken;" but it is merely an allusion. For the hands to hang down, and the knees to be feeble, are figurative expressions to denote a tendency to abandon the discharge of Christian duty. To "lift up the hands" and "the feeble knees" —to support them, as it were, by bandages bracing them—is a figurative expression for, 'Be active and persevering in the discharge of duty; rouse yourselves and each other to this activity and perseverance.' "Make straight paths for your feet;"[1]—*i.e.*, 'Proceed straight forwards in the discharge of Christian duty, notwithstanding all difficulties; beware of turning aside in any degree that may lead to abandonment of the right way altogether; proceed straight onwards;'—" lest that which is lame

---

[1] Καὶ τροχιὰς ὀρθὰς ποιήσατε τοῖς ποσὶν ὑμῶν. These words form a hexameter verse. It not rarely happens that writers in prose unconsciously express their ideas in what corresponds to the artificial rules of rhythm. T. ὀ. do not mean paths that have no windings in them, for it is no easy matter to make such paths straight; but the words denote smooth, in opposition to rough, and filled with obstructions and stumblingblocks. In this way the phrase occurs in the LXX., Prov. iv. 11, 12, xi. 5, xii. 15.

be turned out of the way." The word rendered, "turned out of the way," may with equal propriety be rendered, 'be dislocated :' 'Proceed straight onward; for if you go into bye-paths, the joints which are already lame may be dislocated, and you prevented from prosecuting the course altogether.' The meaning of that is, 'Beware of moving, even in a slight degree, from the path of duty; for that may end in final apostasy.' On the contrary, let what is lame "rather be healed"—let the feeble joint be bandaged and strengthened: *i.e.*, in plain words, 'By turning your minds to the truths which I have been pressing on your attention, let every disposition to halt in or abandon the onward way of well-doing be removed.'

The force of the connective particle is obvious. 'For these reasons,—since your great Leader endured such contradiction of sinners; since your sufferings are not so severe as those of many who have gone before you; since it is so far from being true that your sufferings are proofs that God does not love you, that an entire exemption from these sufferings would have given you ground to doubt if you belonged to His family; since these afflictions come from your spiritual Father, and are intended for your spiritual benefit; since, in one word, however painful at present, they certainly will, if rightly received by you, promote your spiritual improvement,—surely you ought not to abandon the cause of Christ. On the contrary, you should persevere with increasing determination and ardour, removing and disregarding all obstacles which obstruct your progress, and keeping straight forward, as the only way of reaching the mark for the prize of the high calling of God in Christ Jesus.'

The exhortation seems so expressed as to point out the duty of the Hebrew Christians not only to themselves, but to each other. We are to use the statements furnished us by the Apostle not only for our own special improvement, but also for that of our brethren. Let us all take care not to be the cause of stumbling to our brethren. The best way of doing this is by making "straight paths for our own feet." The fear of offending or making to stumble a brother, must not make us neglect our duty.

It seems universally agreed among expositors that the practical part of the Epistle to the Hebrews divides itself into two parts: the first consisting of a general exhortation to perseverance in the faith, profession, and practice of Christianity, notwithstanding all the difficulties and dangers in which this might involve them; and the second embracing a variety of particular exhortations suited to the circumstances of the Hebrew Christians at the time this Epistle was written.

There is not the same harmony of opinion as to where the first of these divisions terminates, and the second commences. In the judgment of some interpreters, the 13th verse of this chapter closes the first division, and the second opens at the 14th. It appears to me more probable that the first division reaches to the close of this chapter, and the second commences with the beginning of the following one. The comparative view of the two economies, the Mosaic and the Christian, and the impressive warning with which this chapter closes, form a most appropriate termination to the hortatory discourse commencing with the 19th verse of the tenth chapter, to " hold fast the profession of their hope without wavering," and seem plainly to mark the conclusion of one of the divisions of the Epistle.

This is not a mere question of arrangement—it has an important bearing on the interpretation of the passage which lies before us; as, on the supposition that it forms a part of the general exhortation to stedfastness, the particular duties here enjoined must be considered as urged with a peculiar reference to their circumstances, as exposed to temptations to apostasy, and under obligations to resist these temptations. The Apostle had placed before their minds the fearful consequences of apostasy; he had also presented them with abundant evidence, that persevering faith, as it was absolutely necessary, was completely sufficient, to enable them to perform all the duties enjoined on them, to undergo all the trials allotted to them, and to obtain all the blessings promised to them as Christians. He had shown them that the afflictions to which they were exposed on account of their Christian profession, instead of operating as temptations to apostasy, ought to be felt as motives to perseverance; and in the words which follow, he instructs them as to the course of conduct which in their circumstances they ought to follow, in order to their continuing " stedfast and unmoveable" in the faith, and profession, and practice of the religion of Christ.

Taking this general view of the paragraph, let us proceed to examine somewhat more minutely its various parts. Ver. 14.

"Follow peace with all men, and holiness, without which no man shall see the Lord."

It is the duty of Christians to be at peace among themselves, to be on their guard against all alienation of affection towards each other; and there can be no doubt that the maintenance of this brotherly-kindness is well fitted to promote stedfastness in the faith and profession of the Gospel. But in the words before us there seems to be a reference not so much to the peace which Christians should endeavour to maintain among themselves, as that which they should endeavour to preserve in reference to the world around them. They are to "follow peace with all men."

They live amidst men whose modes of thinking, and feeling, and acting are very different from—are in many points directly opposite to—theirs. They have been fairly warned, that "if they would live godly in this world, they must suffer persecution." They have been told that "if they were of the world, the world would love its own; but because they are not of the world, but Christ has chosen them out of the world, therefore the world hateth them." "In the world," says their Lord and Master, "ye shall have tribulation." But this, so far from making them reckless as to their behaviour towards the men of the world, ought to have the directly opposite effect. If the world persecute them, they must take care that this persecution has in no degree been provoked by their improper or imprudent behaviour. They must do everything that lies in their power, consistent with duty, to live in peace with their ungodly neighbours. They must carefully abstain from injuring them; they must endeavour to promote their happiness. They must do everything but sin in order to prevent a quarrel.

This is of great importance, both to themselves and to their unbelieving brethren. A mind harassed by those feelings which are almost inseparable from a state of discord, is not by any means in the fittest state for studying the doctrines, cherishing the feelings, enjoying the comforts, or performing the duties of Christianity; and, on the other hand, the probability of our being useful to our unbelieving brethren is greatly diminished when we cease to be on good terms with them. As far as lies in us, then, if it be possible, we are to "live peaceably with all men."

But while the Christian Hebrews were, by a harmless, kind, and useful behaviour towards their unbelieving neighbours, to cultivate peace with them, they were never to forget that there was something more valuable still—something which must not be sacrificed even to secure peace, *i.e.*, holiness. " Follow peace with all men, and holiness, without which no man shall see the Lord ;" *i.e.*, ' Endeavour to live at peace with all mankind, so far and no further than that is compatible with the holiness without which no man can see the Lord.'

The proper meaning of the word *holiness* is ' devotedness to God.' Christians " are not their own ; they are bought with a price ;"—they have been consecrated to God " by the washing of regeneration, and the renewing of the Holy Ghost." They have voluntarily devoted themselves to Him. Holiness is that temper of mind and that course of conduct which correspond to this state and character.

To " follow holiness," is to live like persons devoted to God, as the God and Father of our Lord and Saviour Jesus Christ ; to make it evident that we are His, and are determined to serve Him ; that to promote His interests and to advance His glory are our great objects in life.

Without this spiritual devotedness to God we shall never " see the Lord." By the Lord, I apprehend we are here to understand our Lord Jesus Christ ; and by seeing Him, we understand, the being with Him where He is, and beholding His glory—the enjoyment of the celestial happiness, the essence of which consists in more intimate knowledge of, more complete conformity to, more intimate fellowship with, Jesus Christ. Without sincere, habitual devotedness to God through Christ Jesus, we can never attain the heavenly happiness ; and that for two reasons: (1.) Such is the unalterable determination of God ; and (2.) this unalterable determination of God is not an arbitrary arrangement, but corresponds with the nature of things. A person not sanctified, not devoted to God, is entirely unfit for the celestial enjoyments. It is equally true that we must be like Him in order to our seeing Him as He is, and that the seeing Him as He is shall make us more and more like Him.

We must, then, at all events " follow holiness ;" at all hazards we must act the part of persons sincerely and entirely devoted to God. If, in consistency with this, we can live in peace with all men, it is so much the better; but if peace with men cannot be purchased but at the expense of devotedness to God, then we must—we must willingly—submit to the inconveniences arising from having men to be our enemies, knowing that it is infinitely better to have the whole world for our enemies and God for our friend, than to have the whole world for our friends and God for our enemy.

The whole exhortation seems to us equivalent to—'Beware of unnecessarily provoking the resentments of the men of the world. If possible, live at peace with them; but never act a part inconsistent with your character as persons devoted to God in order to secure yourselves from their persecutions: if you do, you will act a very unwise part, for you will shut yourselves out from the enjoyment of the celestial blessedness.'[1]

As a further means of preventing apostasy, the Apostle exhorts the Christian Hebrews to watch over each other with a holy jealousy. Vers. 15–17. "Looking diligently lest any man fail of the grace of God; lest any root of bitterness springing up trouble you, and thereby many be defiled; lest there be any fornicator, or profane person, as Esau, who for one morsel of meat sold his birthright. For ye know how that afterward, when he would have inherited the blessing, he was rejected: for he found no place of repentance, though he sought it carefully with tears."

The natural order in explaining such a passage as that now before us, is to attend, first, to the evils against which the Apostle exhorts the Hebrew Christians to guard; and then to the manner in which they are to guard against them. The evils to be guarded against are: "any man's failing of the grace of God"—"any root of bitterness which should trouble and defile them"—"any profane" or sensual "person" rising up among them, who should for present enjoyment sacrifice future happiness.

The Hebrew Christians are exhorted to guard against "any

---

[1] "'Follow peace with all men' (*i.e.*, Do not think it necessary to enter on hostile aggressions against any man, not even the heathen Romans), 'and holiness, without which no man shall see the Lord;' *i.e.*, but at the same time do not so mix yourselves up with them as to lose that purity, ἁγιασμόν, which is to Christians what ceremonial holiness was to the Jews."—STANLEY.

man's failing of the grace of God." Here two questions meet us: What is the grace of God? and what is it to fail of the grace of God?

The grace of God, in the language of systematic theology, is either *divine influence,* or the *effect* of divine influence. In the Scriptures, the grace of God is the divine kindness, or some effect of the divine kindness. In the passage before us, I apprehend, the grace of God, or this grace of God, refers to that effect of divine favour or kindness mentioned in the preceding verse: seeing the Lord—obtaining the celestial blessedness, which consists in the knowledge of, conformity to, and fellowship with, Christ. And to fail of this grace of God, is just to come short of heaven.

Now, the Hebrew Christians were to watch over each other, lest any of them should, by not following holiness, by not cultivating devotedness to God, fail of attaining that state of perfect holy happiness in the immediate presence of the Lord, which is the prize of our high calling.[1]

They were to watch particularly "lest any root of bitterness springing up should trouble them, and thereby many be defiled." The Apostle's language is figurative, and borrowed from a passage in Deuteronomy: "Lest there should be among you man, or woman, or family, or tribe, whose heart turneth away this day from the Lord our God, to go and serve the gods of these nations; lest there should be among you a root that beareth gall and wormwood."[2]

"A root that beareth gall and wormwood," is just another name for a secret apostate, a false-hearted professor of the true religion; or, as Moses expresses it, "a man or woman whose heart turneth away from the Lord our God." For such a root to "spring up," is for such individuals to manifest their apostatizing tendencies by their words or their conduct. When circumstances call these forth—as when persecution for the word's sake arises—then such persons trouble the Church. Their false doctrines and their irregular conduct trouble their

---

[1] This seems more satisfactory than interpreting χάρις Θεοῦ, 'religio Christiana;' and is certainly juster than the utterly untenable Arminian interpretation of this as well as Gal. v. 4, to lose finally the peculiar favour of God, once possessed.

[2] Deut. xxix. 18.

brethren, not only by producing grief and regret, but also in many cases by introducing strife and debate, and all the innumerable evils that rise out of them. And by this means "many are defiled." The "root of bitterness" has as it were a power of contaminating the plants in the neighbourhood of which it puts forth its bitter leaves and brings forth its poisonous fruits. A false-hearted professor, introducing false doctrines, or sinful practices, is very apt to find followers. " Evil communications corrupt good manners;" and "a little leaven," when allowed to ferment, will go far to "leaven the whole lump." " Profane and vain babblings increase unto more ungodliness."[1]

But they were to guard not only against speculative irreligion and error, to which I apprehend there is a direct reference in the words just explained, but also against practical ungodliness and immorality. They are to "look diligently, lest there be among them any fornicator, or profane person, like Esau, who for a morsel of bread sold his birthright." Esau is not in the Old Testament represented as a fornicator, but the Jewish interpreters with one consent accuse him of incontinence; and his marrying two Canaanitish wives against the will of his pious parents, certainly does not speak favourably either for his continence or piety.

It is strange that *fornicators* and *profane* persons should be in any way connected with a Christian church. They certainly have no business there. In a Christian church, where anything approximating to primitive discipline prevails, they will not be allowed to remain when they appear in their true colours. But it would appear that at a very early period such persons did find their way into the Christian Church; and it is deeply to be regretted that such persons are still to be found in her communion—persons who, while they make a profession of Christianity, are secretly the slaves of impurity, lightly regard the promises and threatenings of religion, and, where they think themselves safe, can speak contemptuously of its doctrines and laws. Esau was such a person; and he manifested

---

[1] " 'Lest any root,' etc.; 'lest there be any profane,' etc.: *i.e.*, lest any of you, for the sake of his temporary gratification, should go after heathen customs; lest any of you, for the sake of his temporary gratification in the sacrificial feast, fall into the sins by which these feasts are so often accompanied. 1 Cor. viii. 13, vi. 13."—STANLEY.

his character by relinquishing all claim and title to the privileges connected with primogeniture, for a trifling and temporary enjoyment. You have an account of the facts referred to in the 25th chapter of Genesis, vers. 29, etc.

The case of Esau is introduced not only for the purpose of the awfully impressive warning which follows, but also to suggest this thought to the Christian Hebrews: 'Beware of permitting sensual and profane men to find their way into, or to retain their place in, your society; for whenever the temptation occurs, they will act like Esau: they will openly apostatize; to avoid present suffering, or to obtain present enjoyment, they will make shipwreck of faith and a good conscience.' Such are the evils against which the Apostle exhorts the Hebrew Christians to guard.

The means which he recommends them to use for this purpose is to *look diligently*. The word rendered "looking diligently"[1] is the same which in 1 Pet. v. 2 is translated "taking the oversight," and from which the word usually employed to designate the rulers of the Church is taken—bishops, or overseers. A careful discharge of their official duties on the part of the elders, is one of the best safeguards of the Christian Church against the evils here referred to. But it seems plain that the Apostle is not here addressing the elders among the Hebrew Christians in particular, but the whole brotherhood; and of course he does not refer principally, if at all, to official superintendence, but to the common care and oversight which all the members of a Christian church should exercise in relation to each other. The relation in which the members of a Christian church stand to each other, gives rise, like every other relation established by God, to a set of corresponding duties; and this duty of mutual superintendence is one of the most important. Every member of such a society should consider himself as his "brother's keeper;" and recollecting that not only the best interests of the individual but of the society are concerned—that his own interests, and, what is of highest consideration, the interests of his Lord and Master, are concerned—every member of a Christian church should "look earnestly lest any" of his brethren "fail of the grace of God." If he discovers anything in his opinions, or temper, or language, or conduct which endangers his final salvation, he ought to attend to our Lord's rule,

[1] ἐπισκοποῦντες.

by first speaking to the individual by himself; then, if this does not serve the purpose, by speaking to him in the presence of one or two of the brethren; then, if this does not serve the purpose, by bringing the matter before the assembly appointed for that purpose, that is, according to our views of Church discipline, the assembly of the elders. In this way a constant watch should be kept "lest any man fail of the grace of God;" "lest any root of bitterness spring up;" "lest there be any profane" or sensual "person," who in the day of trial will abandon his profession.

I am afraid that a great deal of that impurity of Christian communion which is one of the worst characters of the Christianity of our times, and produces such deplorable results in many ways, is to be traced to a neglect of this mutual superintendence. I do not mean to exculpate those who are officially overseers; but it must be obvious that all their attempts, however honest, to secure purity of communion will be of but little avail, if they are not seconded by the brotherly oversight of the members themselves. This is a duty very plainly commanded in the passage before us; and this is by no means the only passage of Scripture where it is enjoined. See Heb. iii. 13; 1 Thess. v. 14; 1 Cor. xii. 24, 25.

The words in the 17th verse are obviously intended to strike terror into the minds of those who might be induced, like Esau, to sacrifice spiritual privileges for worldly advantages; and the general idea is, 'A time will come when you will bitterly, but in vain, regret your foolish choice and conduct.' Esau did so. When he found that, by the overruling providence of God, the blessings connected with primogeniture were given to Jacob, he earnestly sought to inherit the blessing; and when he was told it was impossible, he still sought, even with tears, to make his father repent, or change his mind. But in vain. He had despised and sold his birthright, and must take the consequences.[1]

---

[1] Schoetgen's note is excellent. "Vox μετάνοια h. l. non notat pœnitentiam in sensu theologico, sed quamcunque mentis et consilii immutationem. Isaacus benedixerat Jacobo. Esavus malebat, ut benedictionem retractaret; et id cum lacrimis quæsivit. Pœnitentiam vero male factorum et levitatis tunc nondum egerat, quia erat βέβηλος et Jacobo fratri mortem intentabat." The Jews, who are often wise beyond what is written, say he afterwards became a true penitent. We shall be glad to find it so. "Vox μετάνοια non pœnitentiam quasi Esavo denegatam, sed Isaaci retractationem frustra quæsitam, denotat."—HUTCHINSON, Not. ad Cyropædiam, lib. i.

In like manner, the profane and sensual professor of Christianity, who for present enjoyment gives up the promised inheritance in heaven, will one day regret, and vainly regret, his choice: Luke xiii. 25-28. He will "find no room for repentance;" *i.e.*, no means of altering the divine determination, that the man who prefers earth to heaven while here, must, when he leaves earth, go to hell and not to heaven. This passage, rightly interpreted, throws no obstacles in the way of a sinner who has made and long persisted in a foolish choice, making a wise one now. "*Now* is the accepted time; *now* is the day of salvation." If you wish to inherit the blessing, you may; but there is only one way in which you can—the way of faith, repentance, and obedience. Eternal life is yours if you choose it, not otherwise. Eternal life is the gift of God through Jesus Christ our Lord; and nothing but an obstinate refusal to receive it shall exclude any man who hears the Gospel from its enjoyment.

The words which follow, vers. 18-28, form the concluding paragraph of the general exhortation, to hold fast the faith and profession of Christianity, in opposition to all temptations to return to Judaism, grounded on the demonstration of the immeasurable superiority of the former to the latter, which had been presented to them in the doctrinal part of the Epistle. It opens with a very striking comparative view of the two economies, the *Mosaic* and the *Christian;* and the general sentiment intended to be conveyed is plainly this: 'From the Sinaitic dispensation —rigid in its requisitions, terrible in its sanctions, severe and unbending in its whole character—it is in vain to look for salvation; but the Christian economy, "full of grace and of truth," reveals a propitiated Divinity, and unites earth with heaven. How wise is it to seek security from the terrors of Sinai in the peace and serenity of Sion! How foolish to abandon the perpetual sunshine, the unfading verdure, the undisturbed tranquillity of Sion, for the murky clouds, and lurid lightnings, and angry thunders, and barren wastes of Sinai!' Let us proceed to examine somewhat more minutely this comparative view of the two economies.

Vers. 18-21. "For ye are not come unto the mount that might be touched, and that burned with fire, nor unto blackness, and darkness, and tempest, and the sound of a trumpet, and the voice of words; which voice they that heard entreated that the word should not be spoken to them any more: (for they could not endure that which was commanded, And if so much as a beast touch the mountain, it shall be stoned, or thrust through with a dart: and so terrible was the sight, that Moses said, I exceedingly fear and quake.)"

The particle *for* does not connect these words with what immediately precedes, but with the general design of the section. It is equivalent to—'moreover,' or, 'another reason for your holding fast your profession is to be found in the contrast existing between the law and the Gospel.' The general sentiment is, 'Ye are not under the law, which was a rigid and severe economy.'

That sentiment is, however, very rhetorically expressed. That economy was established at Sinai. The assembled congregation of Israel were there placed under that order of things. To be under that economy is here figuratively represented as being of the congregation of Israel at Sinai at the giving of the law; and the severe character of that economy is indicated by a most graphic description of the terrific natural and supernatural phenomena by which its establishment was accompanied. Instead of saying in simple words, 'Ye are not under the law, that severe and wrathful economy,' he says, 'Ye are not of the congregation of Israel who came to Mount Sinai, and from its cloud-capt summit received, amid clouds, and darkness, and thunder, and lightnings, a fiery law.'

There can be no doubt that the mountain here referred to is Mount Sinai in the desert of Arabia. It is termed "the mount which might be touched." Some interpreters have suspected that the negative particle has been omitted, and that the Apostle's expression originally was, 'the mount that might not be touched,' referring to the injunction quoted in a succeeding verse; but this is a conjecture which receives no support from any MS. or version. Others have connected this word, as well as the word "burned," with the clause, "with fire:" 'the mount which was touched and burned with fire'—*i.e.*, 'struck by lightning;' but this is a sense which the words do not naturally suggest.[1] The Apostle's meaning is, that they were not come to the material,

---

[1] In that case, ὄρει would have either preceded ψηλαφωμένῳ, or followed κεκαυμένῳ.

tangible mountain, Sinai,[1] but to the immaterial, spiritual mountain, Sion. Before examining particularly the phraseology in which the Apostle describes the awful solemnities which attended the giving of the law, it will serve a good purpose to bring before your mind the Mosaic history of these transactions. "In the third month, when the children of Israel were gone forth out of the land of Egypt, the same day came they into the wilderness of Sinai. For they were departed from Rephidim, and were come to the desert of Sinai, and had pitched in the wilderness; and there Israel camped before the mount. And Moses went up unto God, and the Lord called unto him out of the mountain, saying, Thus shalt thou say to the house of Jacob, and tell the children of Israel; Ye have seen what I did unto the Egyptians, and how I bare you on eagles' wings, and brought you unto Myself. Now therefore, if ye will obey My voice indeed, and keep My covenant, then ye shall be a peculiar treasure unto Me above all people: for all the earth is Mine. And ye shall be unto Me a kingdom of priests, and an holy nation. These are the words which thou shalt speak unto the children of Israel. And Moses came, and called for the elders of the people, and laid before their faces all these words which the Lord commanded him. And all the people answered together, and said, All that the Lord hath spoken we will do. And Moses returned the words of the people unto the Lord. And the Lord said unto Moses, Lo, I come unto thee in a thick cloud, that the people may hear when I speak with thee, and believe thee for ever. And Moses told the words of the people unto the Lord. And the Lord said unto Moses, Go unto the people, and sanctify them to-day and to-morrow, and let them wash their clothes, and be ready against the third day: for the third day the Lord will come down in the sight of all the people upon Mount Sinai. And thou shalt set bounds unto the people round about, saying, Take heed to yourselves, that ye go not up into the mount, or touch the border of it: whosoever toucheth the mount shall be surely put to death: there shall not an hand touch it, but he shall surely be stoned, or shot through; whether it be beast or man, it shall not live: when the trumpet soundeth long, they shall come up to the mount. And Moses went down from the mount unto the people, and sanctified the people; and

---

[1] αἰσθητός, ἐπίγειος, in contrast with πνευματικός, νοητός, οὐράνιος.

they washed their clothes. And he said unto the people, Be ready against the third day: come not at your wives. And it came to pass on the third day, in the morning, that there were thunders and lightnings, and a thick cloud upon the mount, and the voice of the trumpet exceeding loud; so that all the people that was in the camp trembled. And Moses brought forth the people out of the camp to meet with God; and they stood at the nether part of the mount. And Mount Sinai was altogether on a smoke, because the Lord descended upon it in fire; and the smoke thereof ascended as the smoke of a furnace, and the whole mount quaked greatly. And when the voice of the trumpet sounded long, and waxed louder and louder, Moses spake, and God answered him by a voice. And the Lord came down upon Mount Sinai, on the top of the mount: and the Lord called Moses up to the top of the mount; and Moses went up. And the Lord said unto Moses, Go down, charge the people, lest they break through unto the Lord to gaze, and many of them perish. And let the priests also, which come near to the Lord, sanctify themselves, lest the Lord break forth upon them. And Moses said unto the Lord, The people cannot come up to Mount Sinai: for Thou chargedst us, saying, Set bounds about the mount, and sanctify it. And the Lord said unto him, Away, get thee down, and thou shalt come up, thou, and Aaron with thee: but let not the priests and the people break through to come up unto the Lord, lest He break forth upon them. So Moses went down unto the people, and spake unto them. And God spake all these words, saying, I am the Lord thy God, which have brought thee out of the land of Egypt, out of the house of bondage. Thou shalt have no other gods before Me. Thou shalt not make unto thee any graven image, or any likeness of anything that is in heaven above, or that is in the earth beneath, or that is in the water under the earth: thou shalt not bow down thyself to them, nor serve them: for I the Lord thy God am a jealous God, visiting the iniquity of the fathers upon the children unto the third and fourth generation of them that hate Me; and showing mercy unto thousands of them that love Me, and keep My commandments. Thou shalt not take the name of the Lord thy God in vain: for the Lord will not hold him guiltless that taketh His name in vain. Remember the Sabbath day, to keep it holy.

Six days shalt thou labour, and do all thy work: but the seventh day is the Sabbath of the Lord thy God: in it thou shalt not do any work, thou, nor thy son, nor thy daughter, thy man-servant, nor thy maid-servant, nor thy cattle, nor thy stranger that is within thy gates: for in six days the Lord made heaven and earth, the sea, and all that in them is, and rested the seventh day: wherefore the Lord blessed the Sabbath day, and hallowed it. Honour thy father and thy mother; that thy days may be long upon the land which the Lord thy God giveth thee. Thou shalt not kill. Thou shalt not commit adultery. Thou shalt not steal. Thou shalt not bear false witness against thy neighbour. Thou shalt not covet thy neighbour's house, thou shalt not covet thy neighbour's wife, nor his man-servant, nor his maid-servant, nor his ox, nor his ass, nor anything that is thy neighbour's. And all the people saw the thunderings, and the lightnings, and the noise of the trumpet, and the mountain smoking: and, when the people saw it, they removed, and stood afar off. And they said unto Moses, Speak thou with us, and we will hear: but let not God speak with us, lest we die" "And ye came near, and stood under the mountain; and the mountain burned with fire unto the midst of heaven, with darkness, clouds, and thick darkness." "These words the Lord spake unto all your assembly in the mount, out of the midst of the fire, of the cloud, and of the thick darkness, with a great voice; and He added no more: and He wrote them in two tables of stone, and delivered them unto me. And it came to pass, when ye heard the voice out of the midst of the darkness (for the mountain did burn with fire), that ye came near unto me, even all the heads of your tribes, and your elders; and ye said, Behold, the Lord our God hath showed us His glory, and His greatness, and we have heard His voice out of the midst of the fire: we have seen this day that God doth talk with man, and he liveth. Now therefore why should we die? for this great fire will consume us: if we hear the voice of the Lord our God any more, then we shall die. For who is there of all flesh that hath heard the voice of the living God speaking out of the midst of the fire, as we have, and lived? Go thou near, and hear all that the Lord our God shall say; and speak thou unto us all that the Lord our God shall speak unto thee, and we will hear it, and do it. And the Lord heard the voice of your words, when ye spake unto me; and the Lord said unto me, I have heard the voice of the words of this people, which they have spoken unto thee: they have well said all that they have spoken. Oh that there were such an heart in them, that they would fear Me, and keep all My commandments always, that it might be well with them, and with their children for ever! Go say to them, Get you into your tents again. But as for thee, stand thou here by Me, and I will speak unto thee all the commandments, and the statutes, and the judgments, which thou shalt teach them, that they may do them in the land which I give them to possess it."[1]

With the facts of the case before us, we will find little difficulty in explaining the language used by the Apostle in reference to them. Indeed, the greater part of his description is borrowed from the Mosaic history. The words rendered, "that burned with fire," according to our translation, are a further description of Mount Sinai. They may with equal propriety be rendered, 'the burning fire:' 'Ye are not come to the material mountain of Sinai, nor to the burning fire,'—a prodigious, supernatural burning, which is called in Deuteronomy "the great fire of God," and which reached up to heaven, from the midst of which came forth the voice of Him who "is a consuming fire." The "blackness and darkness" describes the lurid, murky state of the atmosphere; the "tempest," the violent agitation of the clouds by sudden gusts of wind. "The sound of a trumpet" refers either to thunder, or to some supernaturally produced noise more resembling the piercing sound of a trumpet, and, from its unnatural sound, more terrific than thunder. "The voice of words" is the articulate voice pronouncing, from the midst of the unearthly fire, the law of the ten commandments; and so awfully impressive was that voice, that when it ceased, the Israelites earnestly requested Moses to intercede with God that they might hear it no more.[2]

The Apostle notices in a parenthesis, that the prohibition,

[1] Exod. xix. 1-xx. 19; Deut. iv. 11, v. 22-31.

[2] The description of Philo is very graphic, and strikingly resembles that of the inspired writer. Πάντα δ', ὡς εἰκός, τὰ περὶ τὸν τόπον ἐθαυματουργεῖτο, κτύποις βροντῶν μειζόνων ἢ ὥστε χωρεῖν ἀκοάς, ἀστραπῶν λάμψεσιν αὐγοειδεστάταις, ἀοράτου σάλπιγγος ἠχῇ πρὸς μήκιστον ἀποτεινούσῃ καθόδῳ νεφέλης, ἣ κίονος τρόπον τὴν μὲν βάσιν ἐπὶ γῆς ἠρήρειστο, τὸ δὲ ἄλλο σῶμα πρὸς αἰθέριον

under a very severe penalty, of even touching the mountain, greatly alarmed the people of Israel. "They could not endure that which was commanded." These words have by some been referred to what goes before, as if it had been meant to state, that the reason why the children of Israel desired to hear no more "the voice of words," was that they could not endure the laws which it had promulgated. But not only does what follows require that these words should be viewed in reference to it, but it is obvious from the history that it was not the *law*, but the manner of its promulgation, which alarmed them. "They could not endure that which was commanded;" *i.e.*, it affected them with intolerable terror. If even an irrational animal was to be put to death in a manner which marked it as unclean, something not to be touched, what might rational offenders expect as the punishment of their sin? and if the violation of a positive institution of this kind involved consequences so fearful, what must be the result of transgressing the moral requisitions of the great Lawgiver?

Another circumstance mentioned by the Apostle as strikingly illustrating the terrific character of the giving of the law, is that Moses was agitated with fear, even to trembling. "So terrible was the sight, that Moses said, I exceedingly fear and quake." The fact here referred to is not recorded in the Mosaic history. It is indeed said, Exod. xix. 16, that "all the people in the camp trembled"—a declaration including Moses. The fear mentioned by Moses, Deut. ix. 19,—"For I was afraid of the anger and hot displeasure wherewith the Lord was wroth against you to destroy you"—was on a different occasion. The particular fact to which the Apostle refers, like others mentioned by him in his writings, seems to have been preserved by tradition, of which, indeed, traces are to be found in the rabbinical writings.[1] Of the truth of the fact here asserted by an inspired writer, we can have no doubt. Moses, who had witnessed so

ὕψος ἀνέτεινε, πυρὸς οὐρανίου φορᾷ καπνῷ βαθεῖ τὰ ἐν κύκλῳ συσκιάζοντος. "All things, as was meet (in the presence of the Deity), were preternatural and prodigious: deafening peals of thunder, most vivid coruscations of lightning, the sound of an invisible trumpet issuing from a distant cloud, like a lofty pillar resting on the earth, and its head in the height of heaven, and a thick smoky cloud, produced by the force of celestial fire, darkening the surrounding atmosphere."

[1] *Vide* Capell. *in loc.*, et Wetstein, Gal. iii. 19.

many remarkable displays of the divine power and majesty—who above every other mere human being had been accustomed to intercourse with God,—even he was constrained, by the overwhelming terror of the scene, to exclaim, "I exceedingly fear and quake."[1]

The circumstances of the giving of the law were in accordance with its genius as a divine economy. The people of Israel in a "waste, howling wilderness," standing in speechless terror at the foot of a rugged mountain enveloped with black clouds, now agitated by tempest, and now partially illuminated by flashes of lightning; while from the midst of a devouring fire, towering above the summit of the mountain, and flaming up to heaven, an unearthly trumpet uttered its spirit-quelling notes, and the voice of Jehovah proclaimed the statutes of that all-perfect law, which forbids sin in all its forms and degrees, and requires the unreserved submission of the mind and heart, and the undeviating obedience of the whole life,—were a striking emblem of the situation of all under that dispensation which was then established—a dispensation of which the leading features were strongly marked in these circumstances.

The material mountain is an emblem of its earthly and sensible character: the clouds and darkness, of its obscurity; and the tempest and flaming fire, the fearful trumpet, and yet more awful voice, of the strictness of its precepts, and of the severity of its sanctions;—the holiness and the justice of Jehovah being plainly revealed, while but a very dim and imperfect manifestation was made of His grace and mercy.

The Apostle's statement, then, is equivalent to—'The law—the Mosaic economy—is a system, the leading characters of which, marked in the circumstances of its establishment, are externality, obscurity, and severity; and you as Christians are not under this economy.'

He then goes on to describe the Christian economy in the same highly rhetorical manner, under the emblem of a spiritual mountain and city, whose names are borrowed from the mountain and city dedicated to the divine service in the Holy Land—Sion and Jerusalem; where is the spiritual temple of

---

[1] The Apostle seems to refer to some well-founded tradition, as Stephen seems to do when he represents Moses as ἔντρομος γενόμενος at the burning bush, Acts vii. 32.

Jehovah, the Judge, the God of all; where "Jesus, the Mediator of the New Covenant," ministers; where the host of angels, and the congregation of the first-born redeemed from among men, hold their holy and joyful assembly. And the fact of the Hebrew Christians being under this economy is represented by their coming to this holy hill and city, and joining this august convocation.

If this idea is distinctly apprehended, it will at once put an end to the question, whether the passage before us refers to the state of the Christian Church on earth or in heaven. It is plainly a description of the whole economy—an economy which extends both to earth and to heaven, and which, beginning in time, will continue throughout eternity. The general sentiment is, 'In becoming Christians you have joined a holy and happy society, at the head of which is the Father of spirits, and next to Him Jesus, the Captain of our salvation, and under them the whole host of holy angels, and the whole family of redeemed men, whether on earth or in heaven.' Let us examine somewhat more minutely the particular expressions.

"Ye are come to Mount Sion, and to the city of the living God, the heavenly Jerusalem." The literal Mount Sion was a beautiful hill on the south-east side of Jerusalem, on one of the eminences of which stood the temple: Ps. xlviii. 2. The name is plainly here used figuratively. The Sion here spoken of is a spiritual mountain, as contrasted with the mountain which could be touched—the mountain which is spiritually[1] called Sion, on which the Lamb stands with the hundred forty and four thousand who have His Father's name written in their foreheads. The literal Jerusalem was the divinely appointed metropolis of the Holy Land, the seat of government and religion. Jerusalem's "foundations were in the holy mountains," and "as a city, was builded compact together." "Thither the tribes went up, the tribes of the Lord, unto the testimony of Israel, to give thanks to the name of the Lord. For there are thrones of judgment, the thrones of the house of David." Jerusalem, like Sion, is here used figuratively for the heavenly Jerusalem. As the people of Israel, pilgrims in a wilderness, without fixed dwelling-place, trembling at the foot of a precipitous mountain covered with clouds and darkness, are an em-

[1] πνευματικῶς, Rev. xi. 8.

blem of those under the law, the same people, dwelling safely in stable habitations, in the magnificent and delightfully situated city Jerusalem, enjoying all the advantages of a pure religion and a stable government, are an emblem of those who possess the privileges of the Gospel economy.

The emblem is highly significant. It marks the economy to which they belong, as one which brings them into close and delightful fellowship with God. They do not stand at the foot of the mountain, while Jehovah dwells on its summit amid the thick darkness and the devouring fire; but they come even to His seat, they dwell in His presence, they have constant access to Him. It marks, too, the permanence of that economy. They dwell not in tents, but in "a city which has foundations, whose builder and whose maker is God." These appear to me the leading ideas: 'Ye are brought into a state of permanent, favourable intercourse with Jehovah; ye are become citizens of heaven.' All that follows is an expansion of that idea.

By coming to Mount Sion and the New Jerusalem, they of course mingle with the inhabitants of this divine city. These are of two kinds: angelic and human. "Ye are come," says the Apostle, "to an innumerable company of angels." A careful reader of the original text will see that the following word, "the general assembly," does not refer to the first-born, but to the angels. The words, literally rendered, are, "Ye are come to myriads, the general assembly, of angels." Angels are unembodied spiritual intelligences, holding a higher place than man in the scale of being. Those of them who kept their first abode are described in Scripture under the names of seraphim and cherubim—'burning ones, powerful ones,'—" principalities and powers," "thrones and dominions." They dwell in God's presence; they "do His commandments, hearkening to the voice of His word." Vast numbers of these holy beings were on Mount Sinai at the giving of the law: Deut. xxxiii. 2. The law was given by the ministration of angels. But the Israelites did not come to them. They were at the bottom of the hill in darkness, while the angels surrounded Jehovah in the inaccessible light. "But," says the Apostle, "ye are come to myriads, to the general assembly, of angels." The word rendered "general assembly" properly signifies a solemn festal convocation, such as was held by the Greeks at their public religious games. The general idea is, 'You are brought into intimate relation with the whole host of holy unembodied spirits.' By the mediation of Jesus Christ, the Apostle informs us that it is the purpose of God, " in the dispensation of the fulness of times," which is just the Gospel economy, to " bring together into one" holy society " things on earth and things in heaven." Christians come to angels, not by sensible intercourse, but by spiritual relation. On our being reconciled to God, we are reconciled to all His holy creatures. They love us—we love them. We engage in substantially the same religious services ; we have the same joys. Even in the present state, they, though unperceived by us, minister to our welfare ; and in due time the barriers in the way of immediate intercourse will be removed, and, equal to the angels of God, we shall mingle with them in an unreserved interchange of thought and feeling.

But angels are not the only citizens of the New Jerusalem. We come to "the church of the first-born, whose names are written in heaven." The word rendered *church* is by no means of so definite a meaning as that English word is. It designates any assembly, whether sacred or civil. Here, I apprehend, it refers to the whole body of truly good men on earth, viewed as one great assembly. Many consider it as referring to the sacred assembly of the upper world ; but they are afterwards described as " the spirits of just men made perfect ;" and in the other places of Scripture where persons are described as having their " names written in heaven," or " in the book of life," they are always spoken of as being on earth. The people of God are termed " the first-born " in allusion to what is said of Israel : " Israel is My son, My first-born." It marks them as dedicated to the service of God, and the heirs of the " inheritance incorruptible, undefiled, and that fadeth not away." And by their names being written in heaven, or enrolled in the celestial album, we apprehend we are to understand that the persons referred to are genuine Christians—men who have not only been admitted to external communion, whose names are not merely enrolled in the books of the visible Church, but who have been admitted to fellowship by the Great Head of the Church, and their names inscribed in His book of life. The idea is, ' In becoming Christians ye become connected with the whole body of the faithful, an innumerable company out of many a kindred, people, and tongue. Every good man is your brother.'

But, what is greater and more glorious still, you come "to God the Judge of all." These words ought to be rendered, "to the Judge the God of all." Christians approach, they draw near, the Judge. The Israelites stood afar off, but the Christian draws near—draws near with boldness—to the Judge; for he knows that He is "God in Christ, reconciling the world unto Himself, not imputing their trespasses unto them." "The God of all;" *i.e.*, the God of all the citizens of Sion—He "of whom all the family in heaven and in earth are named." When it is said He is their God, it means, He acknowledges them with favour and approbation: Eph. iv. 6; Rom. iii. 29; Heb. viii. 10, xi. 16; Rev. xxi. 3, 7.[1]

They come also to "the spirits of just men made perfect;" *i.e.*, to the disembodied spirits of departed holy men, who, having finished their course, have obtained their reward. They who by the faith of the truth become the subjects of the new economy, "sit down with Abraham, and Isaac, and Jacob," and all the prophets, and Apostles, and martyrs, and confessors, "in the kingdom of their Father."

"One family, we dwell in Him;
One Church, above, beneath;
Though now divided by the stream—
The narrow stream of death."

We are bound together by the tie which binds us to one God and one Saviour. We think along with them; we feel along with them. They love us; we love them. It may be the intercourse on their side with us even here is more intimate than we are aware of; and yet a little while, and the whole family will be assembled in their Father's house, never more to go out for ever.

Still further, Christians "come to Jesus the Mediator of the New Covenant, and to the blood of sprinkling, which speaks better things than that of Abel." It may seem strange that Jesus and His atoning blood should be mentioned last; but it is easy to account for it; for it is by our coming to Him that we are led to the spiritual Sion, and introduced to Sion's God and

---

[1] Tholuck remarks: "I do not think that God is here mentioned as κριτής to enhance the idea of terror, but to point out God as the legislative Head—the fountain of that *law* which binds together the ' civitas cœlestis.' "

Sion's citizens. We have already explained at large the meaning of the phrases, "New Covenant," and "Mediator." Jesus is the person who, in the new and better economy, interposes between God and us, and does all that is necessary in order to our obtaining its advantages and blessings. We come not to the Aaronical priesthood, the mediator of the Old Covenant, but to "Jesus the Mediator of the New[1] Covenant," who is "such a Mediator and High Priest as becomes us ; holy, harmless, and undefiled, made higher than the heavens,"—"who being the brightness of the Father's glory, and the express image of His person, has by Himself purged our sins, and is set down on the right hand of the Majesty on high ; being made so much better than the angels, as He has obtained by inheritance a more excellent name than they,"—"worthy of more honour than Moses,"—having obtained a more excellent ministry than Aaron," —"a Priest for ever, after the order of Melchisedec."

The sentiment in the last clause might have been expressed thus: "Who hath sprinkled us with His own blood ;" but the Apostle prefers to speak of the blood of expiation separately. "The blood of sprinkling" is just the blood by the sprinkling of which the individual was so purified that he might lawfully approach unto God. "The blood of sprinkling" is just the obedience to the death of the Son of God. That blood shed expiates guilt, makes it a just thing in God to pardon sin ; that blood sprinkled on the conscience—*i.e.*, the truth in reference to this expiation understood and believed—removes the jealousies of guilt, produces love to God, and enables the sinner to worship with acceptance and delight. They have such an interest in His atonement as enables them to "draw near with boldness to the throne of grace."

That blood "speaks better things than *that of* Abel."[2] The language is figurative, but not obscure. Abel's blood cried for

---

[1] The Apostle uses νέας instead of καινῆς. The one word is more full of meaning than the other. It conveys the idea of freshness—perpetual freshness and vigour. What is καινή may become παλαιά ; but νέα and παλαιά are incongruous ideas.

[2] Griesbach considers the reading τὸ "Ἀβελ as equal to the T. R. In some MSS. τοῦ is found. 'Abel by his blood,' and 'the blood of Abel,' mean the same thing. The phrase, παρὰ τὸν "Ἀβελ, is just = ἢ τὸ αἷμα τοῦ "Ἀβελ λαλεῖ.

vengeance—for the infliction of punishment on the murderer; but the blood of Christ proclaims peace and salvation. The voice of Abel's blood drove Cain away from God; but the voice of Jesus' blood invites us, and, when sprinkled on the conscience, constrains us, to come near. It is a very unnatural interpretation to refer "the blood of Abel" to the blood of his sacrifice. His sacrifice, as *typical*, spoke the same things, though not so distinctly, as what is here termed "the blood of sprinkling." It spoke, though in enigmatical language, of atonement, and reconciliation, and pardon, and salvation.—Such is the contrast between the former and the latter dispensation. There, all is awful, terrible, and threatening; here, all is gracious, alluring, and animating. What folly to adhere to the former! what absolute madness to renounce the latter! It is impossible to conceive a more appropriate conclusion to the exhortation to perseverance than this comparative view, and the awfully impressive exhortation with which it is followed.

The words which follow—vers. 25-28—appear to me to be the conclusion of the body of the Epistle (the thirteenth chapter having much the appearance of a double postscript), and admirably comports with the place it holds. The Epistle commences with the declaration that the Gospel is the completed revelation of the divine will respecting the salvation of men,—a revelation made not by man or angel, but by the Only-begotten of God; and it closes with a solemn exhortation to beware of treating such a revelation in a manner unworthy of its character, as the ultimate manifestation of the mind of God, made by that Eternal Word of life who was in the beginning with the Father, and who has declared Him unto men. The first and the last paragraphs of the Epistle, properly so called, bind together as it were all the intervening statements, illustrations, and arguments. "God, who at sundry times spoke to the fathers by the prophets, hath in these last days spoken to us by His Son." "See, then, that ye refuse not Him that speaketh."[1]

The interpretation of the whole passage depends on the reference which we give to the phrase, *Him that speaketh.* By

---

[1] In reading such a passage as this, who does not feel the justice of the burning words of that accomplished scholar Burmann? "Quis unquam divinas illas, et ubertate et suavitate sermonis affluentes, beati Pauli Epistolas,—quis sacras ejus ad populum, vel ad Christianorum coetum, con-

some interpreters, the appellation has been considered as having a different reference each time it is used. They have supposed the Apostle's meaning to be, 'Beware of neglecting or despising the warning of him who now speaks to you,' *i.e.*, of the Apostle himself; 'for if they escaped not who neglected or despised him who spoke on earth'—*i.e.*, Moses, or, as some strangely think, Abel,—'how shall we escape if we neglect or despise Him who speaks from heaven?' *i.e.*, Jesus Christ. Others refer the phrases, " Him that speaketh," and " Him that speaketh from heaven," to Jesus Christ; and " him that spake on earth " to Moses. It appears to us far more simple and natural to consider the phrase, " Him that speaketh," as referring to the same person in all the three instances; and that the person referred to is *God*, as the Author of all revelation. " God, who at sundry times, and in divers manners, spake to the fathers by the prophets," and who " now in these last days speaks to us by His Son," who is " the brightness of His glory, and the express image of His person," and " who, having purged our sins by Himself, is set down on the right hand of the Majesty on high." " He who speaketh " is the general appellation; and " He that speaketh on earth " and "He that speaketh from heaven," or " He speaking on earth" and " He speaking from heaven," are not two different speakers, but the same speaker speaking in different circumstances.[1] These remarks, distinctly understood, will carry light throughout the whole paragraph.

When God is here termed " He that speaketh," the idea intended to be conveyed is, Christianity is a divine religion: the declarations of the Apostles are a revelation of the will of God. It is precisely the same sentiment which is more fully expressed in the beginning of the second chapter: 'A great salvation has been made known to us: it began to be spoken by the Lord; it has been confirmed by them who heard Him; and God has borne testimony, both by signs and wonders, and divers miracles,

ciones, sine ingente animi commotione legat? et in maximam admirationem traductus non exclamet. O eximiam dicendi vim! O uberrimum eloquentiæ flumen! O Deo ipso dignum et convenientem sermonem!"—*Orat. de eloquentia et poetica*, p. 25.

[1] Carpzov justly remarks : " In monte Sinai eadem φωνὴ ῥημάτων, idem terram concussit λόγος, qui cœlum suo tempore commovebit. Verba Haggæi ii. 7, laudata ad v. 26 et sumpta ibi de Deo Patre, hoc etiam loco suadent de Eo sumi, ne subjectum diversum subaudiatur."

and gifts of the Holy Ghost, according to His will.' Christ is to be considered as the Messenger of His Father. God spoke by Him. He was the Prophet of whom Jehovah spoke to Moses when He said, "I will put My words in His mouth, and He shall speak unto them all that I command Him. And it shall come to pass, that whosoever will not hearken unto My words, which He shall speak in My name, I will require it of Him." The " voice from the most excellent glory," proclaiming, "This is My beloved Son, hear ye *Him*," declared the words of Jesus the voice of God; and His declaration was, " The words which I speak are not Mine, but His that sent Me." And in the same manner, the doctrine of the Apostles was the voice of God; for, says our Lord, " He that heareth you, heareth Me; and he that heareth Me, heareth Him that sent Me." To "refuse Him that speaketh," then, is just not to attend to, not to believe, not to obey the Christian revelation, as the voice of God.

Against this sin the Apostle cautions the Hebrews: " See," then, " that ye refuse not Him that speaketh." ' Beware of inattention, unbelief, and disobedience in reference to the Christian revelation. Consider that it is a divine revelation—a divine revelation on the most important of all subjects—a divine revelation of the completest form—a divine revelation by the most exalted of messengers; and consider all this, see that ye neglect and despise it not.'

The exhortation is enforced by a fact and an argument. The fact is, " They who refused Him speaking on earth escaped not;" the argument is, "If they escaped not who refused Him speaking on earth, much more shall not they escape who refuse Him speaking from heaven." Let us attend to these in their order.

The fact is, "They who refused Him speaking on earth escaped not." God " speaking on earth" seems to me nearly equivalent to—' God making a revelation of His will by means of men; God speaking to the fathers by the prophets.' The phrase includes—it probably directly refers to—the revelation of the divine will by Moses; but I do not see any reason to limit it to that particular revelation. " They who refused God speaking on earth did not escape;" they met with " a just recompense of reward," and especially " they that despised Moses' law died without mercy." " With many of them," says the Apostle, " God was not well pleased"—the reason was, they refused Him speaking to them,—"and they were overthrown in the wilderness." The Old Testament history is full of illustrations of this statement, that "they who refused God speaking on earth did not escape." Many of them were punished in a most exemplary manner on earth, and such of them as died impenitent are suffering the vengeance of eternal fire.

The fact is in itself sufficiently alarming; but it lays a foundation for a still more alarming argument. "If they who refused Him speaking on earth did not escape, much more shall not we escape," says the Apostle, "if we turn away from Him speaking from heaven." As for God to speak on earth, is to speak—reveal His will, by the instrumentality of men; so, for God to speak from heaven, is to reveal His will by the instrumentality of a divine Person—His own Son,—one who, even when on earth, was in heaven, and who, in His glorified human nature, is now "at the right hand of the Majesty on high." The revelation referred to is the Christian revelation, the completion of which was given by our Lord after His ascension from earth to heaven. The Apostles had the mind of Christ. He came by them "preaching peace to them who were afar off," as well as "to them who were nigh." There is a double argument in the Apostle's words: 'If they were punished because they refused Him, we will be punished if we refuse Him,—if they were punished who refused Him speaking on earth, much more will we be punished if we refuse Him speaking from heaven.' The superior dignity of the Messenger, and the superior importance of the message, which the employment of such a Messenger necessarily implies, make it equitable, and that, under the government of a righteous God, makes it certain, that our punishment will be more severe than theirs. What must be the measure of the severity, if it corresponds to the value of the salvation rejected, and the dignity of the Saviour despised! Let us recollect that these awful words are not less applicable to us than to those to whom they were originally addressed. God speaks to us from heaven; for He speaks to us by His Son. In this precious book we have the voice of God in heaven; and His merciful exhortation is still, "After so long a time, To-day, if ye will hear My voice, harden not your hearts." "Now is the accepted time; now is the day of salvation."

We enjoy privileges of incalculable value, in having the Christian revelation,—of incalculable value, when we contrast our circumstances with the Jews under the law, and still more when we contrast them with those of the heathen nations. But if we "refuse Him who speaks," we will have reason to envy throughout eternity the comparatively tolerable doom of the disobedient Jew and the wicked heathen. "How can we escape, if we neglect so great salvation?"

It has sometimes occurred to me, that the Apostle, in the words now before us, carries forward the imagery of the preceding paragraph, and that he contrasts God speaking from the material mountain Sinai, and establishing a carnal and temporary economy, and God speaking from the spiritual mountain Sion, and establishing a spiritual and everlasting economy. This limits the reference of the words, "speaking on earth," to what took place at Sinai, and "speaking from heaven" to the revelation made by God through Jesus Christ, exalted to heaven, when the new economy was established. In this case the force of the argument is,—'If those who disobeyed Jehovah, speaking on earth respecting an earthly and temporary economy, were punished, surely much more will they be punished who disobey Him speaking from heaven, respecting a spiritual and everlasting order of things.' This view of the passage seems best to harmonize with what follows, in which the different effects of the voice of God on earth and the voice of God in heaven are very graphically described.

With regard to the voice of God on earth, it is said that it "shook the earth."[1] I cannot doubt that the language here was suggested by the fact, that at the giving of the law the mountain of Sinai and its neighbourhood were shaken by an earthquake. At the same time, as the material mountain is plainly emblematical of the external economy which was established then, the shaking of the earth is emblematical of the change which took place in the establishment of that economy. Shaking is emblematical of change; shaking the earth, of external change. A most important change took place at the giving of the law. The external state of the Jewish people was most materially altered,—high and important privileges were conferred on them; but great and glorious as was the change, it did

---

[1] Οὗ ἡ φωνὴ τὴν γῆν ἐσάλευσε τότε, is a complete elegiac verse.—CARPZ.

not extend to heaven. The *promise*—the economy which God, immediately after the fall, had established in reference to man's spiritual and eternal interests—remained unchanged. The economy established at Sinai, *viewed by itself*, was a temporal and temporary covenant with a worldly nation, referring to temporal promises, an earthly inheritance, a worldly sanctuary, a typical priesthood, and carnal ordinances.

The voice in heaven produces more extensive and more permanent effects. It shakes both earth and heaven—effects a change both on the external and spiritual circumstances of those who are under it; and it effects a permanent change, which is to admit of no radical essential change, for ever. The Apostle, according to the wisdom given to him, does not in plain direct terms assert the complete abolition of the Mosaic economy, and the establishment of a spiritual and perpetual order of things in its room; but he refers to an ancient oracle, in which the extent and nature of the change which was to take place on the coming of the Messiah are described; and thus in the least offensive manner introduces an important doctrine, to the reception of which the prejudices of the Jews opposed very powerful obstacles.

" But now He hath promised." The word *now* does not denote the period when the promise was made, but the period to which the promise refers, which was *now*, opposed to *then*, when the law was established. It is equivalent to—' But with regard to the present period, which is the commencement of a new order of things, He has promised, saying.' This use of the word *now* in the Apostle's writings is common: Rom. iii. 21, xvi. 26. The passage referred to is Hag. ii. 7, " And I will shake all nations, and the Desire of all nations shall come: and I will fill this house with glory, saith the Lord of hosts;"—a passage admitted by the Jews to refer to the coming of the Messiah.

" To shake heaven and earth," is in Scripture often expressive of a very great change. Here, however, the meaning is obviously more definite; it is a shaking heaven and earth as contrasted with a shaking earth only. Some interpreters consider these words as referring to events yet future,—the changes which will usher in the consummation of all things; but it is plain the Apostle considers the shaking as past, and as having produced its effect in the establishment of " a kingdom which cannot be moved." Some interpreters would refer these words to the miraculous changes, both in the visible heavens and in the earth, by which the commencement of the Christian dispensation was distinguished; others, to the political and ecclesiastical changes which it produced. We think it much more natural to understand the words as equivalent to—' I will make a great change, not only in the external, but in the spiritual state of the Church.' The *earth* was shaken; *i.e.*, the external form and state of the Church was completely altered. But that was not all: the heavens were shaken; a clearer and more extensive revelation of spiritual truth was made,—a more abundant and powerful dispensation of divine influence was given. The whole system of the Church was put into a new order. He who sits upon the throne saith, "Behold, I make all things new."

But the Apostle refers not only to the extent of the change, but also to its permanence, especially as that permanence, established as it is by change, involves in it the entire abrogation of the state of things whose place the new economy occupies. The ancient oracle not only indicates the extent, but the permanence of the change; "for," says the Apostle, "this word," or oracle, "*Yet once more*,"—the Apostle quoting only the first words, while he plainly refers to the whole passage, though his argument is more particularly grounded on the words, "*Yet once more*,"—" this word, *Yet once more*, signifieth the removing of those things that are shaken, as of things that are made, that those things which cannot be shaken may remain." The general idea is: The language intimates that this shaking of the heaven and earth of the Church is to be the last shaking; and, of course, that nothing in her constitution henceforward remains of a perishable kind—or that can be shaken; all is permanent and immovable. The order of things now introduced is not, like that which preceded it, to give way to another. The things which are shaken are removed. The things shaken are the earth and the heaven of the Church; that is, the external and the spiritual state of things: they are to be so shaken as to be removed; a complete change is to take place. The law was *added* to the promise as a temporary appendage, and did not abrogate it; but the Gospel takes the place of the law, and thus abolishes *it*. The law was but a change on *the earth* of the Church, and left *the heaven*, which was regulated by *the promise*, unshaken, unchanged; but the Gospel reaches both *the earth* and *the heaven* of the Church, and " old things pass away, and all things become new."

The clause, " as of things which are made," is considerably obscure. The " things that are shaken"—the state of the heaven and the earth of the Church under the former economy—" are removed, as things which are made." " Things that are made;" what is the meaning of this? Some have considered these words as equivalent to—' frail, perishing things,' as things of a corporeal and created kind generally are: ' The heavens and the earth of the Church under the old economy were like the material heaven and earth: they were to perish. But the new heavens and earth, which were to be the result of this ultimate shaking, were to endure for ever.' They consider the Apostle's idea as the same as that of the prophet, when he says, in reference to the very same event, " Lift up your eyes to the heavens, and look upon the earth beneath; for the heavens shall vanish away like smoke, and the earth shall wax old like a garment, and they that dwell therein shall die in like manner: but My salvation shall be for ever, and My righteousness shall not be abolished."[1] The only difficulty here is in getting these ideas out of the word *made*. Others, with much less probability, have explained the word as equivalent to—' destined, or doomed;' and others, as equivalent to—' fashioned so as to make a great show;' and others have, without any sufficient reasons, suspected a slight change in the text, and that the word originally written by the Apostle was one which signifies *labouring*,[2] like a ship tossed in the waves, ready to go to pieces; or to vary the figure, and use the words of the Apostle, " become old, and ready to vanish away." Admitting the first mode of interpretation, the words, " that those things which cannot be shaken may remain," are equivalent to—' so that those things which cannot be shaken may remain;' *i.e.*, the declaration in the passage, that the change referred to is to be the ultimate change in the state of the Church, is an intimation that the things which remain unchanged by it are to remain unchanged for ever.

I cannot help thinking that the words, " as of things which are made," are not to be viewed as a separate clause, but as most intimately connected with what follows. " Things which were made, in order that the things which cannot be shaken

---

[1] Isa. li. 6.   [2] πεπονημένων for πεποιημένων.

might remain," is the description of the heavens and earth of the Church under a former dispensation. They were made not to continue; they were made in reference to a system which was to continue; and when they had served their purpose, they passed away. Just as, in building a bridge across a wide ravine or mighty river, there is a cumbrous and unsightly mass of scaffolding and enginery erected, till the work is completed and the key-stone fixed; and then there is a shaking among the scaffolding, till it gives way, and is entirely removed. It seems a work of entire destruction; but it is but the removal of what was never anything better than necessary preparation—what, now that the end is gained, is unsightly encumbrance.[1] And now the work of art, which had been but obscurely seen when rising to perfection, bursts on the delighted eye, self-supported,—

"—— Like the cerulean arch we see,
Majestic in its own simplicity."

Everything in the new dispensation is solid. We have not the emblem of Divinity, but God Himself; not a typical expiation, but a real atonement; not bodily purifications, but spiritual holiness: all is spiritual, all is real, all is permanent. How happy is the individual who is interested in this new and better economy! The living during the period of this economy does not secure an interest in its blessings; the belonging to a visible society called a church does not secure an interest in its blessings. He who belongs to this new creation must himself become " a new creature;" he " must be born again;" he must be " transformed, by the renewing of his mind." Faith in the truth as it is in Jesus is the only way in which we can be introduced into this new and better world, and be made participants of its high and holy blessings. Just in the degree in which we understand and believe the truth do we become participants of these blessings. And now " may the God of our Lord Jesus Christ, the Father of glory, give unto you the spirit of wisdom and revelation in the knowledge of Him: the eyes of your understanding being enlightened; that ye may know what

---

[1] A similar meaning is brought out by connecting μείνῃ with τὰ σαλ., not with τὰ μὴ σαλ.; thus, " The removal of the things which were made, *that*—for the purpose that—they might wait for the things that cannot be shaken,—remain until these came, or were established, and no longer."— BAULDRY, quoted by Carpzov.

is the hope of His calling, and what the riches of the glory of His inheritance in the saints, and what is the exceeding greatness of His power to us-ward who believe, according to the working of His mighty power, which He wrought in Christ, when He raised Him from the dead, and set Him at His own right hand in the heavenly places, far above all principality, and power, and might, and dominion, and every name that is named, not only in this world, but also in that which is to come ; and hath put all things under His feet, and gave Him to be the head over all things to the Church, which is His body, the fulness of Him that filleth all in all."[1]

The concluding words of the chapter contain in them an account of the practical improvement which the Apostle wished the Hebrew Christians to make of the view he had given them of the glories of the Gospel economy. Vers. 28, 29. "Wherefore, we receiving a kingdom which cannot be moved, let us have grace, whereby we may serve God acceptably with reverence and godly fear: for our God is a consuming fire."

To "receive a kingdom," is to be invested with royalty—to be made a king; and to "receive a kingdom which cannot be moved," is permanently to be invested with royalty—to be made a king for ever. From the connective particle, *wherefore*, it is plain that to receive an immovable kingdom is but another mode of expressing what is meant by "coming to Mount Sion," etc. It is another figurative mode of expressing the privileges and honours which, under the new economy, men obtain by the faith of the truth as it is in Jesus.

It is a common thing in Scripture to represent the privileges and honours of Christians under the figure of a kingdom. The figure is, however, not always employed in the same way. Very frequently the whole of the new economy is represented as a kingdom : "the kingdom of God"—"the kingdom of heaven." Of this kingdom Messiah is the Prince, and true Christians are the subjects. When a man believes the Gospel, he enters into this kingdom, and becomes a partaker of its numerous and invaluable rights and privileges. At other times the blessings enjoyed by Christians are represented under the figure of a kingdom ; and in this case they are represented, not as subjects, but as kings—possessors of royalty. They are "a royal priest-

[1] Eph. i. 17-23.

hood;" they "reign in life by Christ Jesus;" they are "kings and priests." It is plainly in the last way that the figure is employed in the passage before us. "We," says the Apostle—that is, obviously, we Christians—"have received a kingdom"—have been invested with royalty—have been made kings.[1]

Royalty is the most exalted form of human life. The kingly state is the most dignified known on earth; and, however mistakenly, men have been accustomed to consider royal happiness as the consummation of mortal blessedness. When the Apostle says, then, "We have received a kingdom," he means, in plain words, we have obtained happiness and honour, of which the most dignified and happy state known among men affords but an imperfect representation. And who that knows the truth on this subject, and is capable of rightly appreciating the value of things, can hesitate as to the justness of the Apostle's representation? To enjoy the peculiar favour of, to be admitted to familiar intercourse with, the greatest and best of beings; to be associated with angels and "the spirits of just men made perfect;" to have the inheritance of the world; to be secured that everything in the universe is ours, so far as it is necessary to promote our true happiness; to be loved and esteemed by all the wise, and holy, and benignant beings in the universe,—surely this is real dignity, true happiness. This is royalty indeed; and " this honour"—this felicity—"have all the saints."

But they not only receive a kingdom, but "a kingdom which cannot be moved;" they not only are made kings, but "they shall reign for ever and ever." The privileges conferred on them are indefeasible privileges, they never can be taken from them. Jehovah said to Israel, when at Sinai He constituted them His people, "Ye shall be to Me a kingdom of priests;" but the kingdom bestowed on them was a kingdom which could be moved. It was shaken; it was removed. The royal, sacred dignities of Israel after the flesh are no more; they have passed away with the economy out of which they originated. But it is otherwise with the kingdom of which we Christians, by the belief of the truth, become possessors. The blessedness and the honour arising from the favour, the image, and the fellowship of Jehovah, are substantial and real. The vicissitudes of time cannot affect them; over them death can have no power; and

[1] Οὗτος γὰρ παραλαβὼν βασιλείαν, 2 Mac. x. 11.

eternity will but develop their excellence and demonstrate their indestructibility. Well then might the Apostle say, "We have received a kingdom which cannot be moved." We have been made kings unto God, and we shall reign for ever and ever. We have obtained, through the faith of the truth, privileges and honours of the very highest kind; and they are stable as the throne, endless as the years, of Him who has conferred them.

Privilege and duty are closely, are indissolubly connected. The more valuable the privilege, the stronger the obligation to gratitude and obedience to Him who has graciously conferred it. This is a principle which pervades the whole of the Apostle's writings; and we find him applying it here when he says, "Wherefore, we having received"—*i.e.*, since we have received—"a kingdom which cannot be moved, let us have grace, whereby we may serve God acceptably with reverence and godly fear: for our God is a consuming fire."

The exhortation, "let us have grace," has been variously interpreted. Grace, in the language of systematic theology, is divine influence; and it is common to understand the exhortation as if it were—'Let us seek divine help, which is necessary in order to our acceptably serving God, and which we shall obtain if we seek it.' This is good enough sense, but it is impossible to bring it out of the Apostle's words. It gives to the word *grace* a sense which it is very doubtful if it ever has in Scripture; and to the phrase, *have grace*, a meaning which it is certain it never has. *Grace* in Scripture signifies the free favour of God. That is its primary and proper signification; but it is often used to denote particular manifestations of the divine favour,—in other words, divine benefits. It has been supposed that here it refers—as in the passage, "We beseech you that ye receive not the grace of God in vain"—to that remarkable manifestation of the divine favour, that invaluable divine benefit, the revelation of mercy; and that the word *have* is here—as it is apparently in some passages of Scripture, 1 Tim. i. 19, iii. 9; Rev. vi. 9—equivalent to *hold;* and that the Apostle's exhortation is, 'Let us hold fast that divine favour, the revelation of mercy, by means of which we have obtained the kingdom which cannot be moved; let us continue stedfast in the faith, notwithstanding all the temptations to apostasy to which we are exposed, by which continued faith alone we can serve God acceptably.'

This also gives a good sense, but it is not the sense which the words naturally suggest.[1]

The phrase translated *have grace* is idiomatical (like the Latin *ago gratias*), and is used to signify, 'to be grateful, to express gratitude.' Of this use of the phrase we have a number of instances in the New Testament. Luke xvii. 9, "Doth he *thank*?"[2] literally, 'Does he have grace?' 1 Tim. i. 12, "I *thank*;"[3] literally, 'I have grace.' 2 Tim. i. 3, "I *thank*;" literally, 'I have grace.' This, I apprehend, furnishes us with the key to the expression. 'Let us be thankful; let the reception of blessings so invaluable excite a corresponding gratitude.' "Having received a kingdom which cannot be moved, let us be thankful."

Gratitude is, as it were, the soul and the sum of the Christian's duty. Where it is absent, no duty can be performed aright; where it is present in due energy, every duty will be performed aright. The duty which the Apostle enjoins on the Hebrew Christians he himself habitually performed. Who can read his Epistles without being struck with the deep, habitual gratitude which he discovers to Jesus Christ, and to God as the God and Father of Jesus Christ? "I thank God," exclaims he, "through Jesus Christ our Lord." "Thanks be to God, who giveth us the victory through our Lord Jesus Christ." "Thanks be to God for His unspeakable gift."[4] How frequently, how affectionately, does he urge this duty on Christians! "Give thanks always to God and the Father in the name of Jesus Christ."[5] "Give thanks to the Father, which hath made us meet to be partakers of the inheritance of the saints in light; who hath delivered us from the power of darkness, and hath translated us into the kingdom of His dear Son." The Apostle's exhortation, then, is, 'Let us be grateful to Him who has conferred on us blessings so rich and honours so high—who has given us a kingdom, a kingdom which cannot be moved.'

Let us be grateful, "that we may serve God acceptably." The words, "whereby we may serve God acceptably," are parenthetical, and contain the reason why we should cultivate gratitude to Him who has conferred on us such benefits. We ought to serve Him. Our service will be of no use if it is not accept-

---

[1] It would, I apprehend, require the article: τὴν χάριν, instead of χάριν.
[2] μὴ χάριν ἔχει;
[3] χάριν ἔχω.
[4] Rom. vii. 25; 1 Cor. xv. 57; 2 Cor. ix. 15.
[5] Eph. v. 20.

able; and it cannot be acceptable if it is not the result of gratitude, the expression of thankfulness. The word rendered "*serve*"[1] God, properly refers to religious worship. I do not think that it is here to be restricted to religious duties properly so called; but I apprehend it is used to express the idea, that every duty on the part of a Christian should have a religious character. Whatever he does should be in the name of the Lord Jesus, giving thanks to God the Father through Him. The presenting of himself a living sacrifice to God in all the duties of life, is "rational worship."[2] The Christian, though invested with royal dignity, must remember that there is a King of kings, and that his true honour, as well as duty, consists in serving Him. External acts of duty will serve no good purpose if they are not acceptable; *i.e.*, if they are not regarded with complacency by Him to whom they are performed. Now they will not be regarded with complacency by Him, unless they are the expression of gratitude. The only homage which is acceptable to Him is the homage of the heart—of the heart penetrated with gratitude for His "unspeakable gift," and of which the native language is, 'We love Him who hath so loved us.'

But while the Apostle calls on the Hebrew Christians to be thankful, seeing they have "received a kingdom which cannot be moved," he calls on them to be thankful "with reverence and godly fear." Their gratitude and its expressions were not to be of that light character which the reception of temporal and temporary blessings is calculated to excite, but of that grave, chastened, solemn, sublime character, which corresponds with the spiritual, heavenly, and eternal benefits that had been conferred on them. There is something awful in everything connected with God; and when Christians rejoice, they should "rejoice with trembling." When a Christian considers how the blessings which he enjoys were obtained, such a manifestation of the divine holiness and righteousness, as well as benignity, is brought before the mind, as, while it does not in the slightest degree impair his joy in the Lord and his confidence in His mercy, excites an overwhelming sense of His infinite majesty and purity, and induces him to say, "Who shall not fear Thee, and glorify Thy name? for Thou only art holy."

The ground of that holy fear, with which our grateful, joy-

[1] λατρεύωμεν. [2] λογικὴ λατρεία, Rom. xii. 1.

ful services to Him who has given us "a kingdom that cannot be moved" should be accompanied, is stated in the concluding verse of this chapter: "For our God is a consuming fire." Hence the necessity and propriety of "reverence and godly fear." The Apostle obviously refers to the words of Moses, Deut. iv. 24, where God is termed a *consuming fire*. The ideas intended to be conveyed seem to be absolute moral purity, connected with irresistible power. Our God is glorious in holiness, and inflexible in justice. He will "by no means clear the guilty," without complete satisfaction to the injured honours of law and government. He shows Himself "a consuming fire" in not sparing His Son when He took our place, but wounding and bruising Him even to the death, "the Just One in the room of the unjust;" and He shows Himself "a consuming fire" in punishing with peculiar severity those who neglect and despise the revelation of grace, reigning through righteousness unto eternal life. The God of the law and the God of the Gospel is the same God—unchanged, unchangeable. His mercy beams forth more gloriously in the Gospel than in the law, but His holiness is not obscured by the effulgence of His mercy. No, the displeasure of God against sin is more strongly marked in the sacrifice of His Son, than in all the hecatombs of victims which bled on the Jewish altars; and we may rest assured, that "if he who despised Moses' law died without mercy, he will be accounted worthy of much sorer punishment, who treads under foot the Son of God, treats as unclean the sanctifying blood of the covenant, and does despite to the Spirit of grace." The Gospel despiser, the impenitent apostate, will find that there is no wrath like the wrath of contemned, abused mercy, and that it is indeed "a fearful thing to fall into the hands of the living God." The belief of the infinitely energetic holiness of God, manifesting itself both in the sufferings of Christ and in the peculiarly sore punishment of the despiser and neglecter of the Gospel, is admirably fitted to produce that "reverence and godly fear," which is in perfect harmony with that grateful love which arises from the faith of the truth as it is in Jesus.

It is a just remark of a judicious expositor and divine, "God does not leave our compliance with the Gospel merely to the generosity and gratitude of the human heart; for, however noble these principles are, the hearts of believers themselves are not always under their vigorous influence. Indeed, the human heart is not so generous and grateful in this imperfect state as many imagine; and he must be a stranger to his own heart who does not feel this. We need to have our fears as well as our hopes stimulated, and the Gospel affords sufficient motives for both."[1] Let us then, in the careful study of the character of God, as manifested in the person, work, and doctrine of our Lord Jesus Christ, the great Revealer of Divinity, lay our minds and hearts open to all the motives, of whatever kind, which it suggests; and having obtained such high and holy privileges, and such "exceeding great and precious promises," let us "cleanse ourselves from all filthiness of the flesh and of the spirit, and perfect holiness in the fear of God."

§ 2. *Particular Exhortations.* Chap. xiii. 1–14.

This chapter may be considered as dividing itself into two parts,—the first being an exhortation to a variety of duties, the second being the conclusion of the Epistle. The duties enjoined are some of them *moral*, and others *religious*. The moral duties recommended are—the love of the brethren, and its appropriate manifestations in hospitality towards strangers and sympathy with sufferers; chastity; freedom from covetousness; contentment; a grateful recollection and pious improvement of the instructions and examples of their deceased pastors; and liberality and beneficence. The religious duties recommended are—fidelity to God; unshaken steadiness in the faith and profession of the Gospel, notwithstanding all the suffering and reproach to which it might subject them; thanksgiving; dutiful subjection to their pastors; and prayer for the Apostle and his brethren. The conclusion of the Epistle consists of three parts: a prayer to God; a request to his brethren; and a parting salutation and benediction. Let us examine these various parts as they lie in order.

The chapter begins with a recommendation of brotherly love. Ver. 1. "Let brotherly love continue."

The persons to whom this Epistle was addressed were at once *Jews* and *Christians;* and according as we view them in the one or other of these aspects, the phrases, "brotherly love,"

[1] M'Lean.

and the "continuance" of brotherly love, must be somewhat differently interpreted. The Jews had a peculiar regard to each other, as distinguished from the Gentile nations; and it was one of the charges which the unbelieving Jews brought against their Christian brethren, that they had become enemies to their nation. Now, the Apostle may be understood as saying, 'Give no occasion for this reproach. Show that in becoming Christians you have not ceased to be, in every good sense of the word, Jews—that the expansion of your philanthropy has not lessened the ardour of your patriotism. Let all the regard you ever had for your brethren, your kinsmen according to the flesh, continue; only let your mode of manifesting it correspond with the juster views which you have now obtained of their true interests.' Paul's "own brotherly love," in this sense, continued. What a striking expression of it have we in these words! Rom. ix. 1-5, x. 1.

But the persons whom he was addressing were not only *Jews*, but *Christians*; and as Christians they formed part of a spiritual brotherhood bound together by ties more intimate and sacred. They were all "the children of God by faith in Christ Jesus." They all stood in the relation of children to God; they had all been formed to the character of the children of God; and the faith of the truth, by which at once the relation was constituted and the character formed, naturally and necessarily led to mutual esteem and love. This is, we apprehend, the view the Apostle is here taking of the Christian Hebrews; and this peculiar affection with which genuine Christians regard each other, is that brotherly affection the continuance of which is the subject of the Apostle's exhortation. All true Christians are taught of God to love one another. "He who loves Him who begat, must also love those who are begotten of Him." He who does not love the children of God, is not himself a child of God.

The degree in which this love is felt depends on a great variety of circumstances. It obviously was felt in a very great degree in the earlier days of the primitive Hebrew Church: Acts ii. 44, 45, iv. 32, 34. To this the Apostle refers in chap. vi. 10, and x. 32, 33, 34: "Ye became companions of those who were made a gazingstock; and ye had compassion of me in my bonds." It is not unlikely that, owing to a variety of circumstances, the ardour of their first love had abated. "Iniquity," according to the Saviour's prophecy, "was abounding, and the love of many," both towards the Saviour and towards one another, "was waxing cold." The Apostle's exhortation is, "Let brotherly love continue." 'Persevere in that warm, disinterested affection towards each other as Christians, by which, after ye were illuminated, ye were so remarkably characterized.'

The instruction afforded by this exhortation is suited to Christians in all countries and in all ages. Love to the brotherhood is a duty wherever the brotherhood exists. From the impure state of Church communion, in consequence of which there are so many in external fellowship whom an enlightened Christian cannot regard as brethren in Christ, and from the division of the Christian Church into a variety of hostile factions, there are difficulties thrown in the way of the cultivation of this Christian virtue; but the obligation to cherish this disposition is in no degree diminished. Wherever you see the image of your Lord—wherever there is a consistent profession of the faith of Christ—there ought we to fix our Christian affections; and having fixed them, we are not easily to allow them either to abate or to be transferred. It is finely remarked by the illustrious divine to whom I have already more than once referred: "The love which is among His disciples is that whereon the Lord Christ hath laid the weight of the manifestation of His glory in the world. But there are only a few footsteps of it left in the visible Church, some marks that it hath been, and dwelt there of old. It is, as to its lustre and splendour, retired to heaven, abiding in its power and efficacious exercise only in some corners of the earth and secret retirements. Envy, wrath, selfishness, love of the world, with coldness in all the concerns of religion, have possessed the place of it. And in vain shall men wrangle and contend about their differences in opinions, faith, and worship, pretending to advance religion by an imposition of their persuasion on others: unless this holy love be again re-introduced among all those who profess the name of Christ, all the concerns of religion will more and more run to ruin. The very continuance of the Church depends secondarily on the continuance of this love. It depends primarily on faith in Christ, whereby we are built on the Rock and hold the Head. But it depends secondarily on this mutual love. Where this faith and love are not, there is no Church. Where they are, there is a Church materially, always capable of evangelical form and order."[1]

Having enjoined the continuance of brotherly love, the Apostle goes on to point out some of the ways in which the existence and continuance of this principle were to be manifested; and he particularly mentions the appropriate display of love to stranger brethren, and to suffering brethren. With regard to stranger brethren, he says, ver. 2, "Be not forgetful to entertain strangers: for thereby some have entertained angels unawares." With regard to suffering brethren, he says, ver. 3, "Remember them that are in bonds, as bound with them; and them which suffer adversity, as being yourselves also in the body." Let us attend to these commanded methods of displaying the love of the brotherhood in their order.

The duty enjoined in the 2d verse is repeatedly in the apostolical Epistles termed "hospitality," but is something considerably different from what is now ordinarily meant by that word. To be hospitable, in the common use of the term, is descriptive of the disposition and habit of liberally entertaining friends, relations, neighbours, or acquaintances. Where such entertainments proceed from genuine kindness, and are unstained by excess, where they do not occupy too much time, where they do not in their expense trench on the demands of justice and benevolence, they are at least innocent, and may serve a number of useful purposes. The Christian duty here enjoined is something totally different. It is the gratuitous and kind entertainment of Christian brethren who are "strangers." In the primitive age, Christians, in consequence of persecution, were often driven from their habitations and native countries, and Christian teachers travelled into strange lands to plant and water the churches. It was the duty of Christians to show the love of the brotherhood by receiving such persons into their houses, and supplying them with the necessaries and comforts of life. For his exemplary discharge of this duty, John pronounces an eulogium on "the well-beloved Gaius," 3 John 5-8. Besides, Christians travelling even on secular business were, in consequence of their Christianity, exposed to inconveniences among pagans of which we can form no very distinct concep-

[1] Dr Owen.

tion; and it was of much importance, both to their comfort and their improvement, that they should live with a Christian family. Accordingly, we find Phœbe, who seems to have gone from Corinth to Rome on business, commended to the kind attentions of the Roman Christians, that they should not only "receive her in the Lord as becometh saints," but that they should "assist her in whatsoever business she had need of them." The Apostle's injunction then is, 'Be ever ready, according to your ability, to receive into your houses, and entertain with kindness, such Christian strangers as, in the service of the Gospel, from the force of persecution, or in the ordinary course of business, stand in need of your hospitality.'

The motive which the Apostle employs to enforce this exhortation is drawn from the unlooked-for honour and advantage which in former times had arisen from the performance of a similar duty. "For thereby"—*i.e.*, by entertaining strangers— "some have entertained angels unawares." There is plainly here a reference to Abraham and Lot, who entertained angels hospitably in their houses, supposing that they were human strangers. It is quite possible that the same thing may have happened to other good men under the former dispensation. The force of the motive does not seem to lie in any probability that they might have the same honour, but in this general principle, that they might derive advantage from the exercise of hospitality greater than they anticipated; that they might have the honour and happiness of entertaining men distinguished for their Christian worth and excellence, and who, by the spiritual communications made by them, would far more than compensate for the external accommodations afforded them.

The circumstances of Christians are greatly changed in the course of ages, but the spirit of Christian duty remains unchanged. It is still the duty of Christians to open their houses as well as their hearts to their stranger brethren, especially to such as are occasional visitants on business connected with the kingdom of our Lord Jesus. I do not think it creditable to the state of Christian feeling among us, that ministers occasionally visiting our city on public business are in many cases under the necessity of seeking accommodation at their own cost, or at the expense of the public cause which they are promoting. I am persuaded wealthy Christians would find a rich reward in performing the duty of Christian hospitality. In entertaining such strangers, they would entertain occasionally men who have much of the spirit of angels. A more powerful recommendation of the duty than even that contained in the passage before us, is to be found in the words of our Lord at the great day, when He is to "come in His glory, and all the holy angels with Him." "Then will He say to those on His right hand, I was a stranger, and ye took Me in." And when they answer, "Lord, when saw we Thee a stranger and took Thee in?" He shall reply, "Inasmuch as ye did it to the least of these My brethren, ye did it to Me."

Another way in which the Christian Hebrews were to manifest their brotherly love, was by "remembering them who were in bonds, as bound with them; and them who suffer adversity, as being themselves in the body." "Those who were in bonds" are plainly the Christians who for their religion had been committed to prison. This was a very common occurrence in the primitive age. These were to be remembered by their brethren. They were to be often thought of with affection and interest; they were to be prayed for; they were to be visited; they were to be supplied with food and clothing and other comforts, and every lawful means employed to mitigate the rigour of their confinement and to obtain their liberty. Onesiphorus, whose conduct Paul mentions with so much gratitude, is an example of the mode of behaviour here recommended: "The Lord give mercy unto the house of Onesiphorus; for he oft refreshed me, and was not ashamed of my chain: but, when he was in Rome, he sought me out very diligently, and found me. The Lord grant unto him that he may find mercy of the Lord in that day: and in how many things he ministered unto me at Ephesus, thou knowest very well."[1]

They were to "remember those who were in bonds, as bound with them." The language is very emphatic. When Saul was persecuting the Church, Jesus called to him from heaven, "Saul, Saul, why persecutest thou *Me*?" and in answer to the question, "Who art Thou, Lord?" He replied, "I am Jesus whom thou persecutest." He considered Himself as bound and persecuted in those who were bound and persecuted in His cause. In like manner Christians are to sympathize with their

[1] 2 Tim. i. 16-18.

imprisoned brethren as if they themselves were in bonds. They are to make the same exertions for them that they would be disposed to make for themselves if they were in their circumstances.

But " bonds and imprisonment" are but one of the many evils to which Christians are exposed ; and therefore the Apostle adds, " Remember them who suffer adversity, as being yourselves in the body." To " suffer adversity," when by itself, may signify every species of affliction, whether personal or relative, mental or bodily—sickness, pain, loss of relatives or property. At the same time, I think it probable that the Apostle had a direct and principal reference to afflictions undergone in the cause of Christ. To be reproached, turned out of secular employment, spoiled of goods, banished, or in any other way to be exposed to suffering on account of the profession of the Gospel, —all this is included in suffering adversity.

Now, such Christians were to be remembered by their more prosperous brethren, " as being themselves in the body." These words admit of two modes of interpretation. It may mean that they ought to sympathize with, comfort, and assist them, as being themselves members of the same mystical body with them, according to the Apostle's statement ; "For as the body is one, and hath many members, and all the members of that one body, being many, are one body ; so also is Christ. For by one Spirit are we all baptized into one body, whether we be Jews or Gentiles, whether we be bond or free ; and have been all made to drink into one Spirit.—That there should be no schism in the body ; but that the members should have the same care one for another. And whether one member suffer, all the members suffer with it ; or one member be honoured, all the members rejoice with it. Now ye are the body of Christ, and members in particular."[1] Or it may mean—and, we rather think, does mean —' Pity them and help them ; for ye too are yet in the body—ye too are liable to the same afflictions under which they now labour. Their situation may soon be yours.' Christians in our country and age are not exposed in the same degree to affliction on account of their religion ; but there is still, and there ever will be, suffering on account of religion ; and wherever this is to be found in any form, or in any degree, it ought to draw out the

[1] 1 Cor. xii. 12, 13, 25-27. This is Calvin's exegesis.

tenderest sympathies of their fellow-Christians. How admirably fitted is Christianity to improve at once the character and the situation of mankind! It is plainly calculated to make mankind happier, in the most afflicted conceivable situation, than without it they could be in the most prosperous conceivable circumstances.

A family is the elementary form of human society, the germ of nations and churches; and the relation in which families originate is the foundation of all other human relations. The institution which forms that relation must of course be of peculiar importance. That institution is of direct divine appointment, and is nearly coeval with the existence of the human race. In its primitive and only legitimate form, it is the union of one man and one woman for life; and just in proportion as it has preserved this form, has it served its purpose, in distinguishing man from the brute creation, in excluding the disorders of licentiousness, and in cultivating the best affections of the heart. It has been well said, that whatever there is of virtue, honour, order, or comeliness among men—whatever is praiseworthy and useful in all societies, economical, ecclesiastical, or political—depends on this institution; and that by all to whom children are dear, relations useful, and inheritances valuable, marriage should be accounted honourable.

Marriage, as an institution, has in every age received the approving sanction of every enlightened philosopher and every wise legislator; and the opinion of those who would banish or degrade it, has always been considered by sober thinkers as a sentiment indicative of a dark mind and a depraved heart, and which, if brought into action, would be found equally hostile to the worth and to the happiness of mankind. The Holy Scriptures stamp this important institution with the broad seal of the divine approbation. They lead us back to its commencement in Paradise; they inform us that a divine benediction rests on it; they borrow from it an image to illustrate the tender and intimate relation between Christ and His people; they unfold its duties and enforce them by the most cogent motives; they class its prohibition with the " doctrine of devils;"[1] and in the passage before us they pronounce it " honourable in all."

Ver. 4. "Marriage is honourable in all, and the bed undefiled: but whoremongers and adulterers God will judge."

[1] Jay.

At the period this Epistle was written, and among those to whom it was addressed, there seem to have prevailed a variety of mistaken notions respecting marriage, and some subjects closely connected with it. In the corrupt age of the Jewish as of the Christian Church, a false notion of the superior sanctity of a state of celibacy seems to have been entertained; and the opinion, which was universal apparently among the Pagans, seems also to have been common among the Jews, that if the marriage vow was not violated—if the seventh commandment was not broken in the letter—no harm was done, no moral guilt was contracted. Whether we view these words before us as an assertion or a precept, they seem to be directed against these false and dangerous opinions.

If, with our translators, we consider them a statement, their meaning appears to be—'Marriage is a state which itself is honourable among all classes of men; and the bed undefiled is honourable,'—*i.e.*, there is nothing morally degrading, there is nothing polluted, as the Jewish Essenes alleged, in the marriage relation, if its duties be strictly observed; on the contrary, it is worthy of respect,—'among all classes of men; but the unbridled indulgence of that principle of our nature which makes marriage a wise and benevolent institution, and for the proper regulation of which marriage is intended, is in a very high degree displeasing to God, and will draw down tokens of His righteous displeasure.'

This is excellent sense, but still, I apprehend, it is not just the meaning of the Apostle. I apprehend the words are a precept, and not a statement.[1] They stand in the midst of a set of moral precepts, and the sentence is constructed on precisely the same principles as the next verse, which cannot otherwise be rendered than as an injunction. We have, we are afraid, in the manner in which the words are rendered, an instance of the undue influence of the wish to obtain an argument against an enemy's doctrine. That the passage, rendered as a statement, contains in it a stronger and more direct condemnation of the detestable doctrine of the Roman Catholic Church respecting the celibacy of the clergy, and the peculiar sanctity of a state of celibacy, than when translated as a precept, seems to have been the true reason why the first mode of rendering has been preferred by our

[1] The word to be supplied is not ἐστί, but ἔστω.

own and by many other of the Protestant translators. Considered as a precept, which for the reasons already assigned we are disposed to do, the words are, "Let marriage be honourable among all, and let the bed be undefiled; for[1] whoremongers and adulterers God will judge:" *i.e.*, 'Let marriage be accounted a sacred and venerable thing, both by those who have and by those who have not entered into it. Let the purity of the marriage bed be equally respected by the married and the unmarried; for impurity of every kind is hateful in the estimation of God; and all its perpetrators will assuredly be subjected to the righteous judgment, and will as assuredly meet with the unqualified condemnation, of God.'

These words are not less applicable to us than they were to those to whom they were originally addressed. From the peculiarities of modern society, especially in large cities, peculiar facilities are afforded both for the commission and the concealment of the sins against which this divine injunction is particularly directed; and it is to be feared that even among the professors of Christianity there are persons who avail themselves of these facilities. If there be any such who may read these pages, in the name of God I assure them that their sin will find them out; and that, however they may cloke these abominations from the eye of man, they must one day be made manifest before the judgment-seat of Christ, and have their final doom determined by that law that declares that "no whoremonger nor unclean person hath any inheritance in the kingdom of God or of Christ." "Let no man deceive you with vain words; for because of these things cometh the wrath of God upon the children of disobedience."

The next moral precept refers to the repressing of covetousness, and the cultivation of contentment. Vers. 5, 6. "Let your conversation be without covetousness; and be content with such things as ye have: for He hath said, I will never leave thee, nor forsake thee. So that we may boldly say, The Lord is my helper, and I will not fear what man shall do unto me."

"Conversation," in modern English, signifies colloquial discourse. When our translation of the Scriptures was made, it is obvious that its meaning was more extensive. It plainly

---

[1] The Vulgate translates δὲ *enim;* Griesbach and Lachmann read γὰρ instead of δέ.

then was equivalent to—' character and conduct.' "Let your conversation be such as becometh the Gospel of Christ," is plainly equivalent to—' Let your whole frame of sentiment, affections, and habits correspond to the revelation of mercy.' " Having your conversation honest among the Gentiles " is equivalent to—' Habitually conducting yourselves in such a manner as to impress even the unconverted heathen with sentiments of respect for you.' The word is plainly used in this extensive sense in the passage before us. " Let your conversation be without covetousness " is equivalent to—' Let your manners be without covetousness. Let not covetousness characterize your behaviour ;' in other words, ' Be not covetous.'

The word generally rendered *covetousness* in the New Testament[1] is a term expressive of an undue regard for anything present and sensible, seen and temporal. The word here rendered " covetousness"[2] is of a more limited signification ; it denotes one variety of the love of the world—the love of worldly wealth, the love of money. The injunction is, Be not inordinately fond of worldly possessions. This is an important Christian duty at all times ; but it was peculiarly called for from the Hebrew Christians at the time this Epistle was written. A man could not become a Christian without exposing his worldly property to great hazards, and in many instances to certain loss. Important worldly advantages were to be gained by concealing or renouncing Christianity. A man under the powerful influence of the love of money was in danger of employing means for obtaining it inconsistent with his duty as a Christian—was in danger of "making sacrifices of faith and a good conscience" to retain it ; and when deprived of it, was in danger of mourning its loss as if it were the loss of his happiness. The danger of this principle to a Christian is very graphically described by the Apostle, when he says, " They that will"—that are determined to—" be rich fall into temptation and a snare, and into many hurtful and foolish lusts, which drown men in destruction and perdition. For the love of money"—the same word as in the text—" is the root of all evil, which, while some have coveted after, they have erred from the faith, and have pierced themselves through with many sorrows." It is an evil against which Christians in every country and age ought carefully to

[1] πλεονεξία, ἐπιθυμία. [2] φιλαργυρία.

guard; and never perhaps was there a country and an age in which it was of more importance to guard against it than our own.

In opposition to this love of money, so dangerous, so ruinous to a Christian, the Apostle enjoins the cultivation of contentment. "Be content with such things as ye have,"—literally, 'Be content with present things.'[1] "Godliness with contentment is great gain. For we brought nothing into the world, and it is certain we can carry nothing out; and having food and raiment, let us be therewith content." We are to be satisfied with food and raiment; and if we are not, "our conversation" is not "without covetousness." But it may be said, 'There are different kinds and qualities of food and raiment. The rich man and Lazarus had equally food and raiment; but the one was clothed in purple and fine linen, and fared sumptuously every day; the other was covered with rags, and fed with the crumbs from the rich man's table. What is to be the standard of contentment as to food and raiment?' The Apostle furnishes us with it in the words before us: "Be content with present things." Indeed, if we do not make this the standard of contentment, we will never be content at all. The Apostle himself admirably exemplified the virtue which he here recommends. "Not that I speak in respect of want: for I have learned, in whatsoever state I am, therewith to be content. I know both how to be abased, and I know how to abound: everywhere, and in all things, I am instructed both to be full and to be hungry, both to abound and to suffer need."[2] This contentment is not at all inconsistent with a duly regulated desire to improve our circumstances, and the use of the lawful means fitted for obtaining this purpose. It does not consist in a slothful neglect of the business of life, or a real or pretended apathy to worldly interests. It is substantially a satisfaction with God as our portion, and with what He is pleased to appoint for us. It is opposed to covetousness, or the inordinate desire of wealth; and to unbelieving anxiety—dissatisfaction with what is present, distrust as to what is future.

Numerous powerful motives to the repressing of covetous-

---

[1] τὰ παρόντα. "Facultates quæ ad vitæ usum utut parvæ præsto sunt—natura paucis contenta."—CARPZ.

[2] Phil. iv. 11, 12.

ness and the cultivation of contentment might be brought forward, but the Apostle confines himself to one; but that one is a most cogent and persuasive one: "For HE hath said, I will never leave thee, nor forsake thee."[1] The passage quoted is a promise made to Joshua, on his being intrusted with the great work of bringing in God's chosen people into the inheritance of the Gentiles, Josh. i. 5. Similar promises are to be found in various parts of the Old Testament. These words have a direct reference to Joshua, but they lay a foundation for the faith of every saint. God stands in the same relation to all His people. The promise here quoted was really made to Joshua alone; but the Apostle argues on the obviously fair principle, that the unchangeable God will do like things in like cases. God promised to be constantly with Joshua amid all the difficulties and trials of his situation; and He will be with His people in every age, in all their difficulties and trials.

There is something peculiarly emphatic in the way in which he introduces the motive: "For HE hath said." It is somewhat similar to—"We know *Him* that has said," ch. x. 30. It is more emphatic than if it had been said—'God hath said.' HE has said; and His power is omnipotent, and His wisdom unsearchable, and His faithfulness inviolable. "*He* is not a man, that He should lie; neither the son of man, that He should repent: hath He said, and shall He not do it? or hath He spoken, and shall He not make it good?" And if HE be with us—if infinite power be our defence, and infinite wisdom our guide, and infinite love and excellence our portion—what need of covetousness, what ground of contentment! What would we have more than Divinity with us? What is all the wealth, and honour, and pleasure of the world, if He is not with us? If He leave us, what matters it what is left behind; and if He does not leave us, what matters who or what forsake us? Well may we without anxiety, and with sweet inward satisfaction, pass through floods and fires if He is with us. The one will not drown, the other will not consume us. "The floods will not overwhelm, the fires will not kindle on us." Yea, when we walk through the shadow of death, we need fear no evil; for still *He* is with us; His staff and His rod they will sustain us.

[1] This is perhaps the strongest negation in the Bible. There are five negative particles: οὐ μή—οὐδ' οὐ μή.

"So that WE may boldly say, The Lord is my helper, and I will not fear what man shall do to me." If HE has said, I will never leave, WE may well say, What shall MAN do. The quotation here is from Ps. cxviii. 6. The best commentary on these word is to be found in the 8th chapter of the Epistle to the Romans: "If God be for us, who can be against us? He that spared not His own Son, but delivered Him up for us all, how shall He not with Him also freely give us all things? Who shall lay any thing to the charge of God's elect? It is God that justifieth; who is he that condemneth? It is Christ that died, yea rather, that is risen again, who is even at the right hand of God, who also maketh intercession for us. Who shall separate us from the love of Christ? shall tribulation, or distress, or persecution, or famine, or nakedness, or peril, or sword? (as it is written, For Thy sake we are killed all the day long; we are accounted as sheep for the slaughter.) Nay, in all these things we are more than conquerors through Him that loved us. For I am persuaded, that neither death, nor life, nor angels, nor principalities, nor powers, nor things present, nor things to come, nor height, nor depth, nor any other creature, shall be able to separate us from the love of God, which is in Christ Jesus our Lord."[1] "If God be for us, who can be against us?" God is for us, for He has not spared His Son; and He will continue for ever to be for us, for nothing can separate us from His love. What abundant consolation, what strong support, have Christians amid the evils of life! and how shameful is it when they allow either the hope of worldly good things, or the fear of worldly evils, so to influence their minds as to induce them to act a part inconsistent with their obligations to Him who has said, "I will never leave thee, I will never forsake thee!" Surely we should be ready to say, We will never leave Him, we will never forsake *Him*. But we must look to *Him* to enable us to form and to keep this resolution; for it is only by His not forsaking *us* that we can be secured from not forsaking *Him*.

The great design of the Apostle in the Epistle to the Hebrews, as I have frequently had occasion to remark since I commenced its exposition, is to fortify those to whom it is addressed against the numerous and powerful temptations to apostasy to which they were exposed, and to induce them to

[1] Rom. viii. 31-39.

continue "stedfast and unmoveable" in the faith of the truth as it is in Jesus, in the profession of that faith, and in the performance of the duties which rise out of that faith and profession. This leading object is scarcely ever for a moment lost sight of by the inspired writer. Everything of the nature of statement, argument, or motive throughout the Epistle, will be found to bear more or less directly on this point; and almost everything of the nature of injunction or exhortation will be found to have for its object, either directly the persevering faith and profession and practice of Christianity, or something that is fitted instrumentally to promote, *to secure* this persevering faith and profession and practice.

Among the motives which the Apostle employs, those derived from example hold a conspicuous place. The whole of the 11th chapter consists of a most persuasive recommendation of persevering faith, from the achievements it had enabled holy men under a former dispensation to perform, the trials it had enabled them to sustain, and the attainments it had enabled them to realize. In the passage before us, he brings the motive derived from example to bear on the minds of his readers in another, and, if possible, a still more impressive form. He brings before their mind the faithfulness even unto the death of those venerable men who in former years had presided among them, and calls upon them to go and do likewise.

Ver. 7. "Remember them which have the rule over you, who have spoken unto you the word of God; whose faith follow, considering the end of their conversation." To a careful reader of this passage, it must be plain that it refers, not to the present, but to the former, not to the living, but to the dead rulers of the Hebrew Church. The "conversation" or life of the persons spoken of had come to an end, and they were thus the proper objects of remembrance. In this case it would have been better to have rendered the words translated "them who have the rule over you"—a phrase which describes living pastors—simply, "your rulers,"[1]—an expression which merely designates the office, without fixing anything as to whether they now filled it or had formerly filled it.

To understand the divine injunction contained in this verse, it will be proper that we consider, first, the description here

---

[1] τῶν ἡγουμένων ὑμῶν.

given us of the persons in reference to whom a variety of duties are enjoined on the Hebrew Christians; and then, that we attend to these various duties that are enjoined in reference to these persons.

The persons in reference to whom the Apostle speaks, are described as their rulers, and as having spoken to them the word of God. There can be no doubt that the persons referred to were the *pastors*, or elders, or bishops of the Hebrew Church. These pastors are represented as at once *rulers* and *teachers*. In every orderly society there must be rulers; and our Lord Jesus, who is not the author of confusion, but of peace, in all the churches of the saints, among the gifts which He has bestowed on these churches, has included "governments," or rulers. The pastors, or bishops, or elders of the primitive Church had no arbitrary power over their brethren. The command of our Lord to the primitive rulers of His Church was, "Be not ye called masters;" and His command equally to the pastors and to the flock was, "Call no man master on earth." "The princes of the Gentiles," said our *one* Master in heaven, "exercise dominion over them, and they that are great exercise authority upon them; but it shall not be so with you."[1] But though they had no arbitrary power, they yet bare rule. Chosen by their brethren, they presided in their assemblies; they declared the will and executed the laws of the supreme and sole King of the Church; they reproved, they rebuked, they exhorted with all authority. They enjoined the believers to "observe all things whatsoever Christ had commanded them;" they reproved them when they neglected or violated His laws; and when any individual was obstinate and impenitent in transgression, they excluded them from the communion of the faithful. In all this they exercised no legislative authority: they had no power to enjoin new laws, to institute new ordinances, to invent new terms of communion. Their authority was entirely subordinate to the authority of Christ. Yet, within the limits He prescribed to them, they were *rulers*; and it was the duty of the brethren, who had chosen these pastors to be over them in the Lord, to obey them, and submit themselves to them.

There never has been any change introduced by Him who alone has the power of alteration in such a case, into the con-

[1] Matt. xx. 25.

stitution of His Church; and it is of equal importance that the office-bearers in a church should not aspire to a higher degree of authority, and should not be content with a lower degree of authority, than that which their Master has assigned them; and that the members of a church should equally guard against basely submitting to a tyranny which Christ has never instituted, and lawlessly rebelling against a government which He has appointed.

These pastors are represented as not only rulers, but as teachers. They " spoke the word of God" to them. Indeed, it was in a great measure as teachers that they were rulers and guides. They ruled and guided their brethren by declaring to them the will of God, and bringing to bear on their consciences the numerous and powerful motives which urge them to yield obedience to it. It does not seem that, in the primitive age, rulers were uniformly teachers. The Apostle speaks of " the elders who rule well, especially those who labour in word and in doctrine;" which seems to indicate that there were elders who ruled, and who ruled well, who yet did not labour in word and in doctrine. And this is our scriptural authority for that class of church officers commonly, though absurdly, called '*lay elders.*' The terms, 'clergy' and 'laity,' are not scriptural terms, and the ideas they are intended to express are not scriptural ideas. If the term, 'clerical,' or 'clergy,' be equivalent to—'vested with ecclesiastical office'—elected and ordained to rule in Christ's Church (and this is the least objectionable sense which can be given to the term)—the elders who only rule are as really clerical as the elders who both rule and teach. The individuals referred to by the Apostle, however, were obviously among those who both ruled and laboured in word and doctrine.

The manner in which the Apostle describes this last and most important part of their duty deserves our attention. "*They spoke the word of God.*" They made plain to their brethren the meaning and evidence of the divinely inspired revelation of the will of God. It is very possible some of the persons referred to were inspired men; but the description is perfectly applicable to the duty of Christian teachers in all countries and ages, though uninspired. Their great business is just to "*speak the word of God.*" The more Christian teachers realize this description in their mode of teaching, the more good are they likely to do. We who are teachers are in danger of indulging too much in speculations of our own about the things which are the subjects of the word of God; and those who are hearers are in danger of being so pleased with the exercise which this species of teaching gives to the imaginative and reasoning powers, as to consider it as the best species of teaching. But, in truth, it is only in the degree in which we "speak the word of God"—in which we clearly exhibit its meaning and evidence, in which we bring man's mind into contact with God's mind—that we discharge our duty to our Master, or promote the real spiritual improvement of our hearers. To have made a single doctrinal statement of Scripture better understood and more firmly believed—to have made a man in his conscience feel more strongly the obligation of a single religious or moral duty—is in reality doing more solid good than sending away an audience delighted and astonished with the ingenuity of the preacher's speculations, the force of his reasoning, the splendour of his imagery, and the resistless force of his eloquence. To "speak the word of God" is the grand duty of the Christian teacher. Such are the persons in reference to whom the Apostle enjoins a variety of duties—the deceased pastors of the Hebrew Church, men who had ruled them and spoken the word of God to them.

The duties he enjoins in reference to them are the following: They were to "remember" them; they were to "follow their faith;" they were to "consider the end of their conversation."

The Christian Hebrews were to "remember" their pastors who had guided and taught them; *i.e.*, they were not to forget them, they were often to think of them, to recall to mind the wholesome instructions they had given them, and the holy example they had set before them. It is not one of the creditable points in the character of human nature that we are so apt to consign to oblivion those to whom we have been deeply indebted. This tendency operates in reference to deceased pastors as well as other benefactors. He who consults his own spiritual improvement will guard against it. We are so constituted that religious truth makes a deeper impression on us, and a holy example exercises a more powerful influence on us, when the one is stated and the other exhibited by an individual to whom we are closely connected, and whom we personally esteem and love; and if we do not give way to an ungrateful forgetfulness, the circumstance of that individual being no more on earth, instead of diminishing, will increase that impression and influence. In this way departed friends, and especially departed pastors, will promote the spiritual improvement of those with whom they were connected long after their death.

While the Apostle exhorts them generally to remember with affectionate gratitude their departed pastors, he particularly urges them to " follow their faith." It is not very easy to fix the precise import of these words. " Faith," as I have often had occasion to state, usually signifies one of two things: either that act or state of mind which we term believing, or that which is the object of the mind in that state or act, *i.e.*, the thing believed. It also sometimes signifies the virtue of fidelity, or faithfulness.

Understanding the word in the first sense, the meaning is, ' Your departed teachers were eminent believers. They were strong in faith, and thus gave glory to God. They remained unshaken in their belief of the doctrines of Christ, and did not yield to the impulses of the evil heart of unbelief. Follow them. Be ye also strong in faith. Let nothing shake your conviction, that in having received the Gospel, you have not followed a cunningly devised fable; but that it is a faithful saying, and worthy of all acceptation, the very truth most sure.'

Understanding the word in the second sense, the meaning is, ' There are many diverse and strange doctrines now taught you; beware of giving heed to them. Do not change your creed; hold by the belief of your deceased pastors; follow their faith. They were, many of them, inspired men, who spake to you as they were moved by the Holy Ghost. The doctrine they taught you was the true doctrine of Christ, and they gave you the fullest evidence of this. Do not be carried away by the pretences of these innovators. Recollect your original instructors; and hold fast the form of sound words which ye have learned of them, in faith and love which is in Christ Jesus.'

Understanding the word " faith" in the last sense, as equivalent to 'fidelity,' the meaning is, ' Your departed teachers continued stedfast in the faith, and profession, and practice of Christianity till the close of their life. They were faithful to their great Master—faithful even to death. Imitate their fidelity. Be followers of them, as they were of Christ.'

In whichever of these senses you understand the words, they convey an important and appropriate meaning. I confess that I find it difficult to determine which is the preferable mode of interpretation. I hesitate between the second and the third. When I consider the injunction as connected with that contained in the 9th verse, I am disposed to prefer the second : ' Hold fast the faith of your primitive and inspired instructors, now with God, and do not adopt the diverse and strange doctrines which are pressed upon you by new and self-appointed teachers.' When I look at it in its connection with the clause to which it is immediately attached—" considering the end of their conversation"—I am disposed to prefer the third : ' Reflecting on the manner in which they finished their course. Be imitators of their fidelity.'

The third duty which the Apostle enjoins on the Christian Hebrews in reference to their departed pastors, is the consideration of "the end of their conversation." " Conversation " here is just equivalent to—' manner of life :' their sentiments, affections, and habits as Christians. " The *end* of their conversation" is the result, the termination—or, to use rather a familiar, but still a very expressive word, the *upshot*, of their Christian course. These good men continued faithful to the death, and died in the faith of Christ, and the hope of eternal life in Him. Some of them, like Stephen and James the brother of John, suffered martyrdom, but they were " more than conquerors through Him that loved them." The dying scenes of such men were well fitted to confirm the faith of their surviving brethren. When the Christians returned from witnessing Stephen's martyrdom, must they not have said within themselves, ' Jesus Christ is well worth dying for !' and, instead of fearing, must they not rather have coveted a similar end to their conversation ? When ministers on their deathbed are enabled to exhibit an example of the power of the faith of the Gospel to sustain and console the mind, amid exanimating sickness and agonizing pain, and in the prospect of the awful solemnities of judgment, and the untried realities of an eternal and unchangeable state, it is very much fitted to operate as a motive on their people to imitate at once their faith and their fidelity.

I am rather disposed to think that the phrase, "end of their conversation," looks beyond death into the unseen world. The Apostle's exhortation seems to be, 'Consider not only how their course closed in this world, but consider in what it has terminated in a future world.' He seems to turn their mind to the same glorious scene which was presented to the mental view of John the divine. He as it were bids them contemplate their departed pastors "standing before the throne, and before the Lamb, clothed with white robes, and palms in their hands, and crying with a loud voice, Salvation to our God, that sitteth on the throne, and to the Lamb;" and says to them, 'These are those who had the rule over you, and who spoke to you the word of God. They have overcome by the blood of the Lamb, and by the word of their testimony; and they loved not their lives to the death. "They have come out of great tribulation, and have washed their robes and made them white in the blood of the Lamb. Therefore are they before the throne of God, and serve Him day and night in His temple. And He that sitteth on the throne shall dwell among them. They shall hunger no more, neither thirst any more; neither shall the sun light on them, nor any heat; for the Lamb, who is in the midst of the throne, shall feed them, and lead them to fountains of living water; and God shall wipe away all tears from their eyes." This is the end of their conversation. Faithful unto death, they have obtained a crown of life.' The consideration of the state of glory and blessedness into which their departed faithful pastors had entered, was certainly very well fitted to induce the Hebrew Christians to hold fast their faith, and to emulate their faithfulness.

To this exhortation to remember their departed pastors, and especially so to consider the termination of their Christian course as to imitate their faith and fidelity, the Apostle subjoins the emphatic words, "Jesus Christ the same yesterday, and to-day, and for ever." One is almost tempted to suspect that these words have fallen out of their proper place. They would come in well between the 5th and 6th verses. But this conjecture is unsupported by external evidence, and therefore cannot be entertained.

These words are obviously elliptical. The ellipsis may be supplied in two ways: Jesus Christ is the same yesterday, to-day, and for ever;' or, 'Let Jesus Christ be the same yesterday, to-day, and for ever.' Understanding the words as an assertion, the meaning is not, I apprehend, 'Jesus Christ is the unchangeable Jehovah,' though that is a truth, and an infinitely important one; but, 'Jesus Christ never changes;' *i.e.*, either, 'His mind, as that mind has been made known to you by your inspired teachers, who are now with Him, can never change, so that any new doctrine brought to you under His name must be false. Men's opinions are constantly changing, but Jesus Christ is "the same yesterday, to-day, and for ever," —His doctrines are invariable.' Or, 'He ever lives; and His affection and care of His people are unchanged and unchangeable. Your most valuable pastors must die, but He ever lives; and He ever lives to protect and bless those who put their confidence in Him.'

I am disposed to understand the words rather as an exhortation than as a statement. The same reasons which led me to consider the fourth verse as an exhortation, influence me in taking a similar view of the verse now before us. It stands in the midst of exhortations, a number of which are expressed in the same elliptical manner. 'Let Jesus Christ be the same yesterday, to-day, and for ever;' *i.e.*, let Him be the same to you. He is the same in Himself; His person is as certainly divine, His doctrine is as true, His promises are as trustworthy, His laws as wise and good, as ever they were. You have embraced Him as your Saviour, and your Teacher, and your Lord. Why should you abandon Him? He really is what your pastors, now with the Lord, represented Him to be, and what you, believing their representations, have acknowledged Him to be. By your steady adherence to Him in all His characters, make it plain that to you, in your estimation, He is "the same yesterday, to-day, and for ever."

The exhortation which follows naturally rises out of this. Ver. 9. "Be not carried about with divers and strange doctrines: for it is a good thing that the heart be established with grace; not with meats, which have not profited them that have been occupied therein."

"Divers doctrines" are doctrines different from the doctrines of pure Christianity; "strange doctrines" are doctrines foreign to, alien from, these doctrines. "To be carried about," or carried hither and thither, by these doctrines, is to have the mind brought into an unsettled state, which naturally produces a corresponding unsteadiness of conduct. The doctrines spoken of by the Apostle, as is plain from what follows, referred to the Jewish doctrines respecting clean or unclean meats, according as they were or were not to be offered on the altar; and probably he has in view the attempt, which was very early made, to connect Judaism with Christianity.

"For it is a good thing that the heart be established with grace; not with meats, which have not profited them that have been occupied therein." "To have the heart established," is a Jewish phrase, directly referring to the effect of food in producing refreshment, and used as equivalent to—'to obtain real satisfaction.' The Apostle's sentiment is this: '*Grace*'—*i.e.*, the free favour of God to sinners, as revealed in the Gospel—'is far more fitted to give solid, permanent satisfaction to the mind and heart, than a superstitious regard to distinction of meats.' The man who understands and believes the truth with regard to the grace of God bringing salvation, walks at liberty, keeping God's commandments, is taught to "deny ungodliness and worldly lusts, and to live soberly, righteously, and godly in this present world;" but the man who is fettered with notions that this species of food is lawful and that unlawful,—that the first may be safely eaten, but that the other must be avoided, under the penalty of incurring God's displeasure,—has his mind occupied with trifles, which lead away from the great fundamental duties of piety and virtue, and, having no solid ground of hope towards God, can have no settled or rational tranquillity of mind.

The Apostle adds, what indeed to us must be very obvious, that "they who have occupied themselves with these things had not been profited." Every deviation from the purity of primitive truth, and from the simplicity of primitive usage, must be hurtful to those who indulge in it. The advice contained in these words, though having a peculiar reference to the circumstances of the Hebrew Christians, is full of important instruction to us. For more than a hundred years the Church in this country has not been so much harassed as of late with "divers and strange doctrines."[1] Had the description been meant for

[1] This was originally written in 1830, when what were called the Row heresies were exciting very general attention.—ED.

those dogmas which have been, and are still, so sedulously inculcated, it could not have been more appropriate. The doctrines of the sinfulness of our Lord's human nature, of universal pardon, and of the identity of the faith of the Gospel with an assurance of personal salvation, are certainly " divers and strange doctrines ;" and the duty of Christians in general in reference to them, is very distinctly stated in the passage before us. They are not to be " carried about" by them ; they are not to be tossed to and fro with these words of doctrine. They will " not profit those who occupy themselves therewith."

It is a fact as honourable to Christianity as disgraceful to human nature, that the difficulty with which that religion has hitherto made its way in our world has been owing, not to its faults, but to its excellences ; and that those qualities which chiefly recommend it to the admiration of the higher and uncorrupted orders of intelligent beings, as " the manifold wisdom of God," are the very qualities which have excited the contempt and loathing, the neglect and opposition of mankind, and led the great majority of those in every age to whom its claims have been addressed, to consider it as absolute foolishness. Purity, simplicity, and spirituality are the leading features of Christianity ; and it is because it is pure, and simple, and spiritual that it is so much admired in heaven, and so much despised on earth— that holy angels " desire to look into" it, and that depraved men " make light of it."

The fondness of man for what is *material* in religion, and his disrelish of what is *spiritual*, is strikingly illustrated in the extreme difficulty which was experienced by the primitive teachers of Christianity in weaning the Jews, even such of them as by profession had embraced the Gospel, from their excessive attachment to a system which had so much in it to strike the senses as Judaism. The manner in which these inspired men laboured to attain this end, discovers " the wisdom from above" by which they were guided. They showed the Jews, whether converted or unconverted, that everything that was excellent under the former economy had a counterpart under the new order of things still more excellent ; that the spiritual reality was far better than the material shadow ; and that what was glorious had now no glory, " by reason of the glory that excelleth." They showed them, that if we Christians have no visible, material manifestation of the divine glory on earth, towards which we bodily draw near when we worship, we have the spiritual Divinity in heaven, to whom in spirit we approach, in exercises which employ our highest faculties, and interest our best affections; that, if we have no splendid temple like that of Jerusalem, within whose sacred precincts acceptable homage can be presented to Jehovah, we have access to the omnipresent God at all times, and in all circumstances; that, if we have no order of priests like that of Aaron to transact our business with God, we have, in the person of the incarnate Son of God, " a great High Priest," who has by the sacrifice of Himself expiated our sins, and who " ever lives to make intercession for us."

In the passage which comes now before us for explication, we find the Apostle applying this mode of reasoning to the subject of *sacred meats*, on which the Jews seem to have valued themselves. Of many of the offerings which were laid on the altar of Jehovah part only was consumed, and the rest reserved as food, either for the priests, or for the offerer and his guests. This food was considered as peculiarly sacred, and the eating of it viewed as an important religious privilege. In the verse which immediately precedes the passage for exposition, the Apostle, in reference to these sacred meats, had said in effect, ' The grace of God—the free favour of God to sinners, manifested in the Gospel—understood and believed, will do the heart more good than the use of any kind of food, however sacred.' And in the paragraph, on the illustration of which I am about to enter, he shows that Christians had a species of spiritual sacred food, far more holy than any which the Jewish people, or even the Aaronical priesthood, were permitted to taste.

Vers. 10-12. " We have an altar, whereof they have no right to eat which serve the tabernacle. For the bodies of those beasts, whose blood is brought into the sanctuary by the high priest for sin, are burnt without the camp. Wherefore Jesus also, that He might sanctify the people with His own blood, suffered without the gate." I shall endeavour first to explain the meaning of these words, and then illustrate the general sentiment which they express.

Before doing this, however, I shall quote Tholuck's beautiful sketch of the Apostle's train of thought:—" The asyndeton gives greater emphasis to the thought. The reference to what precedes is this: 'If ye would indeed hold by βρώματα, or meats, ye have surely far more excellent βρώματα, or meats, in Christianity than in Judaism.' The thought contained in the image that Christians have a higher altar, leads first of all to the idea, that Jesus, as the great sacrifice of atonement, is the true βρῶμα, or meat, of the faithful. The sacrifice of Christ naturally suggests the idea of His sufferings. Then comes the thought, we should be the companions of His sufferings, and even for His sake go out of the city, the emblem of this earthly existence, and endure a death like His, of pain and shame. And then comes the additional thought, that as Christ is the true sacrifice, all our sacrifices are of a figurative and spiritual kind,—no longer sin-offerings and expiatory sacrifices, but simply sacrifices of praise; and these are not to consist merely in words, but also in good works. Such is the brilliant chain of thought from ver. 10 to ver. 16."

It is quite plain that the language in the 10th verse is elliptical. Nor is it difficult to supply the ellipsis: "We"—*i.e.*, we Christians as opposed to Jews—" we have an altar, of which we have a right to eat, but of which they who serve the tabernacle have no right to eat." By "the altar" we are either to understand the sacrifice laid on the altar, or, what comes to the same thing, the phrase, "to eat of," or from, "the altar," is to be understood as meaning, to eat of the sacred food which had been offered on the altar. "Those who serve the tabernacle," or rather, 'those who minister in the tabernacle,' are, I apprehend, the Levitical priesthood. There were, as we have already remarked, certain sacrifices of which the offerer and his friends were allowed to eat a part; and of by far the greater number of sacrifices a considerable portion was assigned to the priests.[1] But there was a class of offerings of which the priest was not allowed to appropriate the smallest part to himself: the animal was considered as entirely devoted to God, and was wholly burnt with fire, either on the altar, or in a clean place without the camp, while Israel was in the wilderness, and without the city, after the erection of the temple at Jerusalem.[2]

Now it appears to me that the Apostle says, 'We Christians are allowed to feast—spiritually, of course—on a sacrifice belong-

---

[1] Lev. vi. 26; Num. xviii. 9, 10; Lev. vii. 34; Num. vi. 19; Lev. vii. 15, xix. 6.

[2] Lev. xvi. 14-16, 27; iv. 3-12.

ing to that class of which not only no ordinary Israelite, but no priest, was under the law allowed to taste.' The sacrifice referred to is plainly the sacrifice which our Lord, as our great High Priest, offered up once for all, even the sacrifice of Himself. Of the class of sacrifices to which the Apostle refers, and which was not a large class, the sacrifice for the sins of the people on the great day of atonement was the most remarkable; and I think there can be no doubt that this sacrifice was directly in his view when he made the statement which we are considering. That sacrifice was not to be used as food: the blood was to be brought into the holy place, which is here equivalent to the holy of holies; and after certain portions had been burnt on the altar, all the rest was to be taken without the camp, or without the city, and there burnt to ashes. Instead of being allowed to be eaten, it was considered as entirely a devoted thing; and he that touched it was not permitted to mingle with the congregation of Israel till he had submitted to certain lustratory rites. Now the sacrifice of our Lord Jesus belongs to this class. When He suffered, it was that by the shedding of His blood " He might sanctify the people;" *i.e.*, expiate the sins of the spiritual Israel of God, and fit them for acceptable spiritual intercourse with God. His sacrifice was a propitiatory sacrifice for the sins of all His people, answering to the sacrifice for the sins of all Israel on the great day of atonement. And that our Lord's sacrifice was of this character, was marked by His suffering death without the gates of Jerusalem, as the bodies of the victims offered for the sins of the Israelitish people were consumed without the camp, or without the city. Maimonides says, What originally was not lawful to be done in the camp, it was afterwards unlawful to do in the city.

The sacrifice of Christ plainly, then, belongs to that class of sacrifices of which not only the Israelites generally, but the priests, ay, even the high priest, were forbidden to participate. We Christians are permitted spiritually to feast on this sacrifice—to " eat the flesh and to drink the blood of the Son of man." We are allowed to feed on the sacrifice offered up for our sins, and not for our sins only, but for the sins of the whole people of God. And we thus have a far higher privilege in reference to sacred food, not merely than the Israelites, but even than the priests themselves enjoyed. Such seems to me the general meaning of the passage. The meaning of the Apostle does not seem to be, as some have supposed, 'We Christians have an altar'—meaning the Lord's table—' to which no Jew, continuing to practise the rites of Judaism, can be admitted;' nor, 'We have a sacrifice on which we spiritually feed, but of which no Jew, continuing to practise the rites of Judaism, can participate;' but, 'We Christians are allowed to feed on the propitiatory sacrifice for our own sins, the sins of the people of God, which even the priests under the Old Testament economy were not permitted to do.'

Thus it appears that these words contain a statement, and a proof of that statement. The statement is, 'We Christians, with regard to sacred food, have higher privileges, not only than the Jews, but even than the Jewish priests. We are allowed to feast on a sacrifice of the highest and holiest kind, which they were not.' The proof is, 'The highest and holiest kind of sacrifice was that which was offered on the great day of atonement for the sins of the people of God. Of that sacrifice even the priests were not permitted to eat. The blood was brought into the holy place, and what was not burnt on the altar was consumed without the camp, or without the city. The sacrifice of Jesus Christ was a sacrifice of this highest and holiest kind. It was a sacrifice for sin—it was a sacrifice for the sins of the whole spiritual people of God; and to mark it as the antitype of the sacrifice for sin on the great day of atonement, He suffered without the gates of Jerusalem. On this sacrifice we Christians are permitted to feed. We eat the flesh and we drink the blood of the Son of man, offered in sacrifice for our sins.' The conclusion is direct and inevitable : 'We Christians have higher privileges in reference to sacred food, not merely than the Jews, but than the Jewish priests. We have an altar of which they have no right to eat who serve the tabernacle.'

Having thus endeavoured to ascertain the meaning of the Apostle's words, let us proceed to illustrate the sentiment which they contain. Fully to perceive the meaning and design of this statement, thus most satisfactorily proved, it will be necessary to inquire into the nature and value of the privilege of the Jews and the Jewish priests in feeding on sacrifices; then to inquire into the nature and value of the privilege of Christians in feeding spiritually on the sacrifice of Christ; and then, by a comparison of these, to evince the superiority of the latter to the former.

With regard to the privilege of the Jews and the Jewish priests, it is quite plain, whatever superstitious notions might be entertained by them, that the flesh which had been offered in sacrifice was not better as food than any other flesh of the same quality, and that the mere eating it could be of no spiritual advantage to the individual; just as, whatever superstitious notions may be entertained respecting the bread and wine in the Lord's Supper, they have no qualities as bodily nourishment different from common bread and wine, and the mere eating the one and drinking the other can communicate no spiritual benefit. Sacrifice was emblematical, and feasting on sacrifice was emblematical also. Eating the flesh of the sacrifice was, I apprehend, emblematical of two things, or perhaps, to speak more accurately, of two aspects of the same thing. Eating of the sacrifice was a natural emblem of deriving from the sacrifice the advantages it was intended to secure—expiation of ceremonial guilt, removal of ceremonial pollution, and access to the external ordinances of the tabernacle and temple worship. As the altar is in Scripture represented as God's table—Mal. i. 7; Ps. l. 12, 13; Ezek. xxxix. 20, xli. 22—eating of the sacrifice is emblematical of being in a state of reconciliation with God: sitting at His table, and eating of the sacrifice which had been presented to Him, interested in the blessings promised, and secured from the evils threatened, in the Old Covenant. This, whatever extravagant notions the Jews might entertain on the subject, seems to have been the true nature and value of the privilege of feeding on sacrifices.

Now let us inquire into the nature and value of the privilege enjoyed by Christians. They "eat the flesh and drink the blood of the Son of man," who gave Himself a sacrifice and an offering in the room of His people. I need scarcely say the language is figurative; that eating and drinking are not to be understood literally, but spiritually. But what is meant by spiritually feeding on the sacrifice of Christ—spiritually eating His flesh and drinking His blood? It is, in plain words, our deriving from the sacrifice of Christ the blessings which it is intended and calculated to obtain. This we do by the belief of the truth respecting this sacrifice. Believing that truth, we have the forgiveness of our sins, the sanctification of our natures, and spiritual favourable intercourse with God as our reconciled Father. We have in Him the redemption that is through His blood, even the forgiveness of sins; we are washed and sanctified; we have access with boldness to the throne of grace. We have not merely the emblems of these in the Lord's Supper, but in the faith of the truth of the Gospel respecting the sacrifice of Christ we have these invaluable blessings themselves; and seated spiritually at the table of a reconciled Divinity, we feast along with Him. That which satisfied His justice, magnified His law, glorified all His perfections, and gave Him perfect satisfaction, is that which quiets our conscience, transforms our nature, rejoices our heart. We find enjoyment in that in which He finds enjoyment: "our fellowship is with the Father." We hear Him saying, as it were, in reference to the sacrifice of His Son, 'I am fully satisfied;' and our souls echo back, 'So are we.' He says, "This is My Son, in whom I am well pleased;" and we reply, 'This is our Saviour, and He is all our salvation and all our desire.'

It will not require many words to show the superiority, the infinite superiority, of the privilege of the Christian as to *sacred food*, above that of the Jewish people, and even of the Jewish priests. They had merely, in eating the sacrifices, the *emblem* of blessings; we, in spiritually feeding on the sacrifice of Christ, have the blessings themselves. They had but the emblems of expiation, and forgiveness, and purification, and fellowship with God; we have expiation, and forgiveness, and purification, and fellowship with God. But this is by no means all. The blessings of which, in eating the sacrifices, they enjoyed the emblems, were of a kind far inferior to the blessings of which we, in eating spiritually the sacrifice of Christ, actually participate. What is expiation and forgiveness of ceremonial guilt to the expiation and forgiveness of moral guilt? What is external purification to inward sanctification? What is external communion to spiritual fellowship? Nor is even this all. The circumstance that it was but a part of the sacrifice that was set before them that they were allowed to eat of, probably intimated —and the circumstance that there were certain sacrifices, and those of the most solemn and sacred nature, of which they were not permitted to participate at all, certainly intimated—

that complete atonement had not been made for them, and that God and the worshipper were not yet altogether at peace; whereas we, in the faith of the truth, are permitted to feast on the whole sacrifice of Jesus Christ. We not only eat His flesh, but we do what none of the priests durst do with regard to any of the sacrifices, we drink His blood. We enjoy the full measure of benefit which His sacrifice was designed to secure. We are allowed to feed freely on the highest and holiest of all sacrifices. Our reconciliation with God is complete, our fellowship with Him intimate and delightful.

The bearing of this statement on the Apostle's object is direct and obvious. It is a striking illustration of the general principle of the Epistle. 'In Christ you have all that you had under Moses, and much more. Let your unbelieving brethren boast of their privileges with regard to *sacred food*: you enjoy far higher privileges than they, or even than their venerated priests. Even *they* durst not eat of the sacrifice of atonement for all the people of Israel. But *you* are permitted daily, hourly, without ceasing, to feast on the sacrifice of the incarnate Son of God, who suffered, the Just One in the room of the unjust, who gave Himself an offering of a sweet smelling savour in the room of all the sanctified ones.'

From this statement the Apostle draws an important practical inference in the 13th verse. "Let us go forth therefore unto Him without the camp, bearing His reproach."[1]

The meaning and force of this exhortation are not difficult to perceive. If Jesus, the incarnate Son of God, in order to expiate our sins, submitted to become a sin-offering—voluntarily subjected Himself to so much suffering and shame, and if we, from our interest in this sacrifice, enjoy such invaluable privileges; let us cheerfully submit to whatever suffering and shame we may be exposed to in cleaving to Him and His cause. There He is, hanging on a cross as one accursed—cast out of the holy city as unworthy even to die within its walls. But who is this? "A man approved of God"—"the Holy One and the Just"—"the Brightness of the Father's glory"—"God mani-

---

[1] No Seceder should be ignorant that this was the text from which William Wilson of Perth, one of the illustrious four who were the fathers of the Scottish Secession, preached on the day that by civil authority he was prevented from officiating in the parish church.

fest in flesh;" and "He is wounded for our iniquities, and bruised for our transgressions, and the chastisement of our peace is on Him, and our healing is in His wounds." Shall we then seek to enjoy worldly honour and pleasure by remaining among His murderers? Shall we not leave the city, and take our place by the cross of our Saviour, and willingly bear whatever reproach and suffering may be cast on us for our attachment to Him? Is it not quite reasonable and right that we should even be willing to be crucified for Him who was crucified for us?

It is impossible to conceive the duty of the Christian Hebrews, readily to sacrifice worldly advantages, and submit cheerfully to suffering and reproach for the cause of Christ, more cogently recommended than in these words. And it does seem probable that the Apostle meant to suggest, by this way of stating the truth, that an entire separation from their unbelieving countrymen, and an entire abandonment of the overdated Mosaic institution, were called for on their part, in order to an unreserved devotement of themselves to Jesus Christ; and that this, whatever it might cost them, should be immediately made by them.[1] The Apostle adds, in the 14th verse, a powerful additional reason for their thus willingly submitting to such reproaches and sufferings as an honest attachment to Jesus Christ might bring upon them. Ver. 14. "For here have we no continuing city, but we seek one to come."

Some have supposed that the Apostle refers here to the approaching destruction of Jerusalem, and the final overthrow of the temple worship and the economy to which it belonged. We rather think his idea is, 'The sacrifices we may be called on to make, the sufferings we may be called on to endure, the reproaches which may be cast on us for our attachment to Christ, ought not to make any very deep impression on us. We are but pilgrims and strangers here; we have no fixed residence, no continuing city. This is not our home. But we have a home, at which in due time we shall arrive. To get safely

---

[1] Chrysostom is a good interpreter in many cases, but he does not sustain his character when from this passage he, in his 32d Hom. on this Epistle, teaches that Christians, after the example of Christ, should be buried *extra urbem*. It would have been well, however, if the practice, for which so whimsical a reason is assigned by the Byzantine bishop, had been universally followed.

there, is the great matter. This is what we are seeking; and if we succeed in this—of which, if we be real Christians, there is no doubt—that home will far more than make amends for all the toils and sufferings we have met with on our road to it. These reproaches and sufferings for Christ's sake will soon pass away; and in the heavenly Jerusalem above, from which we shall never be called on to go out, we shall meet with an abundant compensation for all the sufferings, the privations, and reproaches we may be called to sustain in the cause of our Lord while here below.'

While there is a peculiar propriety in these words, viewed as addressed to the Hebrew Christians, in their substance they are applicable to Christians in every country and in every age. All who by faith have feasted on the sacrifice of Christ, are bound by gratitude and duty cheerfully to submit to all the reproach and suffering which may be involved in an honest and open profession of attachment to Him, and dutiful observance of all His ordinances. It is their duty to renounce the world, and all that is in it, even their lawful enjoyments, when these come in competition with their adherence to Christ. They are not, as it has been very justly remarked, to steal out of the camp or city, but they are boldly to go forth, making a public profession of their dependence on Christ's atonement, and their subjection to His authority. And they are to do this under a deep conviction that all that is earthly is transitory, and that what is spiritual is alone permanent. All the worldly advantages which may be purchased by unfaithfulness to our Lord will soon be as if they had never been; nothing will remain but the shame and punishment. All the worldly disadvantages which may be incurred by faithfulness to our Lord will also soon be as if they had never been, and nothing will remain but "the recompense of reward," the "exceeding and eternal weight of glory." May we all who name the name of Christ be enabled to be "faithful to the death, that we may obtain the crown of life."

CONCLUSION.

PRIVILEGE and duty are very closely connected under the Christian economy. All the Christian's duties, when rightly understood, will be found to be privileges, and all his privileges will be found sources of obligation and motives to duty. We have, in the paragraph of which our subject of exposition forms a part, a very interesting view of the leading privileges and duties of Christians in their intimate mutual connection. The description is given in language borrowed from the Jewish economy. Christians, as they need a high priest, have such an high priest as they need in Jesus Christ, the incarnate Son of God. On that all-perfect sacrifice for sin which He has offered up in His own spotless obedience unto the death, they as a holy priesthood are allowed spiritually to feed; enjoying thus a higher privilege than belonged to the Jewish people, or even to the Jewish priesthood, under the former dispensation. They have no sacrifice of atonement to offer for themselves: that is not necessary; for "by His own sacrifice He has for ever perfected"—*i.e.*, completely expiated the sins of all—"them who are sanctified," of the whole body of the separated ones. They do not need to present a sacrifice of expiation: that has been done in their room. What remains for them is to feast on that sacrifice; or, in other words, to enjoy the glorious results of this all-perfect sacrifice, in reconciliation with God, peace of conscience, and the joyful hope of the glory of God.

But while they have no sacrifice of atonement to offer, they still, as a spiritual priesthood, are required to offer spiritual sacrifices to God; and the fact that the perfection of the Saviour's atoning sacrifice supersedes entirely the necessity of their attempting to do anything for the expiation of their own sins, is the most powerful of all motives to their diligent discharge of their duties as spiritual priests, in presenting themselves to God a "living sacrifice, holy and acceptable, which is their reasonable service."

What are some of those sacrifices which gratitude to Christ, for giving Himself for our sins a sacrifice and offering, should induce Christians to present, may be learned from the 15th and 16th verses. Vers. 15, 16. "By Him therefore let us offer the sacrifice of praise to God continually, that is, the fruit of our lips, giving thanks to His name. But," or *and*, "to do good and to communicate forget not: for with such sacrifices God is well pleased."

The Jews were required to offer not only sacrifices of expiation, but sacrifices of thanksgiving. "The thank-offering consisted in the presentation of an ox, sheep, or goat, which was brought by the offerer to the altar, and slain by him at the south side of it. The priest received the blood and sprinkled it round the altar. The fat was burnt on the altar. The breast and the shoulder—the former of which was to be heaved, and the latter waved by the offerer—belonged to the priest. The rest was applied to the purpose of a sacrificial feast for the offerer and his friends. These offerings were sometimes presented in token of gratitude for some particular blessing received from God, and sometimes as an expression of a habitual sentiment of thankfulness for God's continual kindness. The first of these kinds of thank-offerings was united with meat-offerings, consisting of unleavened cakes and a leavened loaf, which went to the priests."[1]

Under the Christian dispensation there were no such material thank-offerings, but there was something far better. We Christians are bound by obligations peculiarly strong and tender to present a thank-offering to God; but the thank-offering we are to present is not anything material: it is "the fruit of the lips, giving thanks to God's name." What we present is not the offspring of an animal; but, as the Prophet Hosea expresses it, "the calves of our lips;" not the fruit of the earth, but "the fruit of our lips." The words, "giving thanks to His name," are to be joined in construction with the word "lips:" 'our lips giving thanks to His name.' "The fruit of our lips giving thanks to God's name"—*i.e.*, giving thanks to God as revealed to us—is just a circumlocution for our grateful acknowledgments. "Let us offer the sacrifice of praise, the fruit of our lips giving thanks to His name," is just equivalent to—'Let us gratefully acknowledge the divine kindness.'

What is the particular divine benefit for which the Apostle here calls on Christians to give thanks, it is not difficult to perceive. It is indicated by the word *therefore*, which plainly looks back to the preceding statement. A sacrifice of expiation has been presented for us, in the offering of the body of Christ once for all. That sacrifice has been accepted of God; and this is intimated to us by our being permitted spiritually to feast on this sacrifice. "We have been redeemed to God by the blood of His Son;" "Christ has died for us, the Just One in the room of the

[1] *Winer's Bib. Dict.*, as quoted by Dr Pye Smith.

unjust," and "His blood cleanses us from all sin;" and "in Him we have redemption through His blood, the forgiveness of sin, according to the riches of divine grace." It is *therefore* that we ought to "offer the sacrifice of praise" to Him who appointed, to Him who accepted, the great atoning sacrifice—to Him who gave His Son for us—to Him who gives His Son to us.

This spiritual sacrifice of thanksgiving we are to present to God *continually*. The sacrifices under the law could only be presented at particular times, and in particular places; but our spiritual services may be presented at any time, in any place. And as they may, so they ought, to be presented continually. Not that we are to be uninterruptedly engaged in praise, but that we are frequently to be so employed; and that we are constantly to cherish a grateful sense of the divine kindness in the appointment and acceptance of the great sacrifice of atonement, and in permitting us habitually spiritually to feast on it, so as always to be ready to avail ourselves of every proper opportunity of expressing these sentiments in praise and thanksgiving.

This spiritual sacrifice of thanksgiving to God we are continually to present *by Christ Jesus*. By *Him*. All the sacrifices of the people of Israel under the law were offered by, through the medium of, the priests. All our religious services must be presented through the mediation of our Lord Jesus Christ—in a dependence on what He did on earth, and is doing in heaven. It is only when viewed in connection with His atonement and intercession that any of our religious services can be acceptable to God.

But praise is not the only species of thank-offering which Christians are required to present to God. "Thanksgiving is good," as Mr Henry quaintly but justly remarks, "but thanksliving is better." The Apostle accordingly adds, ver. 16, " To do good and to communicate forget not."

The connective particle rendered " but," is merely *connective*. It is equivalent to 'moreover.' I can scarcely doubt that the Apostle here refers to the custom of the Jews, who were accustomed to send portions of the sacrificial feast, on the eucharistic sacrifices, to the poor: Lev. vii. 14; Deut. xii. 12, xiv. 29, xvi. 11. It is the duty of Christians to express their gratitude to God for His goodness to them, through Christ Jesus, by doing good; *i.e.*, by performing acts of beneficence—in feeding the hungry, clothing the naked, relieving the distressed; and in this way communicating to their poor and afflicted brethren of the blessings Providence has conferred on them,—"doing good to all men, especially to those who are of the household of faith." While the terms are of that general kind as to express beneficence and the communication of benefits generally, it seems probable that the Apostle had a direct reference to doing good by communicating to others those blessings for which they were especially bound to give thanks. It is the duty of Christians to do good to their fellow-men by communicating to them, so far as this is competent to them, those heavenly and spiritual blessings for which they are bound continually to give thanks to God by Christ Jesus.

The motive by which the Apostle enforces the duty of offering these spiritual sacrifices of praise and beneficence, and the communication of benefits, is a very powerful one: "With these sacrifices God is well pleased." These were sacrifices with which God at all times was well pleased—better pleased than with external, positive religious duties. "I will have mercy," said He, "and not sacrifice." With regard to praise, we find the psalmist saying, "Whoso offereth praise glorifieth Me: and to him that ordereth his conversation aright will I show the salvation of God." "I will praise the name of God with a song, and will magnify Him with thanksgiving."[1] And with regard to well-doing and communicating we find the prophet saying, "Is it such a fast that I have chosen? a day for a man to afflict his soul? is it to bow down his head as a bulrush, and to spread sackcloth and ashes under him? wilt thou call this a fast, and an acceptable day to the Lord? Is not this the fast that I have chosen? to loose the bands of wickedness, to undo the heavy burdens, and to let the oppressed go free, and that ye break every yoke? Is it not to deal thy bread to the hungry, and that thou bring the poor that are cast out to thy house? when thou seest the naked, that thou cover him; and that thou hide not thyself from thine own flesh? Then shall thy light break forth as the morning, and thine health shall spring forth speedily; and thy righteousness shall go before thee: the glory of the Lord shall be thy rere-ward."[2] But it is probable that the

---

[1] Ps. l. 23, lxix. 30. [2] Isa. lviii. 5-8.

Apostle's design was to convey the idea, that these were now the only kind of thank-offerings which were acceptable to God. The ceremonial thank-offerings had ceased to be pleasing to Him; for the economy to which they belonged had come to an end. These spiritual eucharistic sacrifices are the only ones which, under the new and spiritual dispensation, are agreeable to Him.

When the Apostle says that praise, and kindness, and liberality, are sacrifices which are acceptable to God, I trust I need scarcely say he does not intend to represent them as available to remove the divine displeasure, or to propitiate the divine favour. They are not expiatory sacrifices at all. Expiatory virtue is to be found only in the great atoning sacrifice of our Lord. He merely means,—God approves of them; they are well pleasing to Him. This surely is a very strong incitement to offer such sacrifices, " an exceeding great reward" for offering them. Beyond this the highest aspirations of a Christian cannot go. It is all he can wish; it is above all that he can think. To have the approbation of good men is delightful; to have the approbation of our own conscience is more delightful still; but to have the approbation of God, this is surely the highest recompense a creature can reach. This approbation is very strongly expressed in the word of God already. "God is not unrighteous, to forget your work and labour of love which ye have showed toward His name, in that ye have ministered to the saints, and do minister." "My God shall supply all your need according to His riches in glory by Christ Jesus."[1] It will be still more illustriously displayed when the Son appears in the glory of the Father, and in the presence of an assembled universe proclaims to those who, as a token of gratitude to God for the blessings of the Christian salvation, have " done good and communicated :" " For I was an hungered, and ye gave Me meat: I was thirsty, and ye gave Me drink : I was a stranger, and ye took Me in : naked, and ye clothed Me : I was sick, and ye visited Me : I was in prison, and ye came unto Me. Then shall the righteous answer Him, saying, Lord, when saw we Thee an hungered, and fed Thee? or thirsty, and gave Thee drink? When saw we Thee a stranger, and took Thee in? or naked, and clothed Thee? Or when saw we Thee sick, or in prison, and came unto Thee? And the King shall answer and

---

[1] Phil. iv. 19.

say unto them, Verily I say unto you, Inasmuch as ye have done it unto one of the least of these My brethren, ye have done it unto Me."[1]

The next duty which the Apostle enjoins on the Hebrew Christians, is obedience to their spiritual rulers. He had formerly pointed out to them their duty in reference to their deceased pastors, ver. 7; now he points out their duty to their living pastors, and enforces its performance by very powerful motives. Ver. 17. " Obey them that have the rule over you, and submit yourselves : for they watch for your souls, as they that must give account; that they may do it with joy, and not with grief : for that is unprofitable for you."

I have already had an opportunity of explaining to you the nature and extent of Church rule.[2] The Hebrew Christians were to be obedient to their spiritual rulers. They were to consider the Christian ministry as an ordinance of Christ; and they were to yield obedience to those who filled it, in so far as they taught them the doctrines and commandments of Jesus Christ. They were not to obey them with a slavish, implicit respect to their authority, but they were to obey them from an enlightened regard to Christ's authority; and they were to submit themselves, not only in receiving with humility their instructions, but also their faithful reproofs and admonitions.

The motives to the conscientious performance of these duties are contained in the concluding part of the verse :—" They watch for your souls, as those who must give an account." Christian pastors, if they are at all what they ought to be, " watch for the souls" of those who have called them to take the oversight of them in the Lord. The spiritual improvement, the everlasting salvation of their people, is their great object: and to gain this great object, they *watch*. They know, that to gain it, constant attention is necessary ; and they endeavour to yield it. They occupy a place of trust : they have not only been called by their people, but they have been commissioned by their Lord. They have been entrusted with the care of a portion of that " Church which He purchased with His own blood ;" and they know that " they must give account." They must do so at the close of life, when the command comes forth, " Give an account of thy stewardship ; thou must be no longer

---

[1] Matt. xxv. 35–40.   [2] *Vide* pp. 234, 235.

steward;" and at the great day of judgment, when both ministers and people " must give an account to God." But this is not all: they must give account even here. Ministers ought to keep up a constant intercourse with their great Master. They ought to bear their people on their hearts before the Lord. If their work prospers,—if the souls of their people seem to prosper and be in health,—then they ought with joy and thankfulness to give an account of this to Him; and if, on the other hand, the souls of their people seem languid and diseased,—if ignorance and carelessness prevail,—if " questions gendering strife rather than godly edifying" occupy their attention,—if there " be among them roots of bitterness," or " enemies of the cross of Christ,"—then too ought the Christian minister to pour out his sorrows before the Lord, giving his account " with grief." It is to this giving account that, I apprehend, the Apostle refers in the passage before us.

The consideration of these facts should induce the Christian people to " obey" their pastor, and " submit themselves." He may urge on you unpalatable truth—he may utter sharp reproofs; but recollect he has no choice; remember he is " a man under authority." Put the question, Has he said anything that Christ has not said? If he has, disregard him; if he has not, blame him not,—he has but discharged his duty to his Master and to you; and recollect, you cannot in this case disregard the servant without doing dishonour to the Master. If he had been appointed to amuse you, to " speak smooth things" to you, you might reasonably find fault with him for his uncompromising statements and his keen rebukes. But he " watches for your souls." Your spiritual improvement, your everlasting salvation, is his object; and therefore he must not, to spare your feelings, endanger your souls. It were cruel kindness in the physician, to save a little present pain, to allow a fatal disease to fix its roots in the constitution, which must by and by produce far more suffering than what is now avoided, and not only suffering, but death.

The last clause of the verse is connected with the first clause: " Obey them that have the rule over you, and submit yourselves, that when they give in their account, they may give it in with joy, and not with grief; for that is unprofitable to you." If a minister is but *faithful*, so far as he himself is concerned, he may, he must, give in his account with joy. Whether the Gospel, as administered by him, be " the savour of life unto life" or " of death unto death," if he is but faithful, he will be " a sweet savour of Christ unto God," in them that perish as well as in them that believe; his unsuccessful as well as his successful labours will meet the approbation of the great Master, and obtain an abundant " recompense of reward." But so far as his people are concerned, the account given in by him will be joyful or sorrowful just in proportion to his success; and for him to give in a joyful account, is profitable for them; for him to give in a sorrowful account, is unprofitable. It affords the purest satisfaction to a Christian minister to find that his labours among his people are " not in vain in the Lord;" that the thoughtless are becoming serious; that those alarmed about their spiritual interests are seeking and finding rest in the faith of the truth, and the well-grounded hope of eternal life; and that those who have believed through grace are growing up in all things to Him who is the Head, becoming more intelligent and active, more harmless and useful, more weaned from earth, more fit for heaven. Every Christian minister, if he deserve the name at all, can in some measure say, with the Apostle John, " I have no greater joy than to hear that my children walk in truth;"[1] or with the Apostle Paul, " For what is our hope, or joy, or crown of rejoicing? are not even ye in the presence of our Lord Jesus Christ at His coming? For ye are our glory and joy."[2] In these circumstances he gives his account to his Master with joy, and thus is profitable to his people. His holy joy enables him to prosecute with growing alacrity the duties of his office; and the great Head of the Church, by a still further communication of divine influence, shows His satisfaction with His obedient children. On the other hand, if the members of a Christian church do not obey their pastor in the Lord and submit themselves, and if their souls obviously are not prospering under his ministry, it must be with a sad heart that he gives in his account to his Lord.

It is very strikingly said by Dr Owen, With what sighing, and groaning, and mourning, the accounts of faithful ministers to Christ are often accompanied, He alone knows, and the last day will manifest. For the accounts of ministers to be given

[1] 3 John 4.   [2] 1 Thess. ii. 19, 20.

in in this way, is not profitable for their people.[1] The heart of the minister is discouraged; the great Master is displeased; the tokens of His favour are withdrawn; spiritual barrenness prevails; and the clouds seem, as it were, commanded to rain no rain on the unfruitful vineyard.

The Apostle now solicits from the Hebrew Christians an interest in their prayers, ver. 18. "Pray for us." The Apostle was fully persuaded of two things: that all the blessings he stood in need of could be obtained from God, from God alone; and that prayer was the appointed means of obtaining these blessings. Hence we find him very frequently requesting the prayers of the churches: 2 Cor. i. 11; Eph. vi. 19; Col. iv. 3; 2 Thess. iii. 1. By soliciting the prayers of the Hebrew Christians, he also intimates the high opinion he entertained of them as righteous men, whose prayers would "avail much." He adds, "For we trust that we have a good conscience, willing in all things to live honestly."

There never was a man more exposed to obloquy than the Apostle Paul; and it seems likely that unfavourable reports had been circulated among the Hebrew Christians respecting him. It is in reference to these that he says, "We trust we have a good conscience, in all things willing to live honestly." 'Though my name may be cast out as evil, and I may suffer as if I were an evil-doer, yet I am conscious of my own integrity and faithfulness in the ministry committed to me. I am desirous of conducting myself *honourably* in all circumstances. I do not walk in craftiness, nor do I handle the word of God deceitfully; but my rejoicing is this, the testimony of my conscience, that in simplicity and godly sincerity, not with fleshly wisdom, but by the grace of God, I have had my conversation in the world.'[2]

---

[1] ἀλυσιτελές, one of the ἅπαξ λεγόμενα, so far as regards the New Testament. By a common figure, it is used to mean more than it expresses. It is = 'hurtful.' We have a curious illustration of the meaning of the word in the address which the comic poet, in Athenæus l. iv., puts in the mouth of a drunkard, to an abstinent philosopher or water-drinker,—a teetotaller of those days:—

'Ἀλυσιτελὴς εἶ τῇ πόλει, πίνων ὕδωρ,
Τὸν γὰρ γεωργὸν καὶ τὸν ἔμπορον κακοῖς·
Ἐγὼ δὲ τὰς προσόδους μεθύων καλὰς ποιῶ.

[2] This passage is quoted with great effect by Richard Alleine in his valedictory discourse to his people, on leaving them in consequence of the Act of Conformity, 1662.

He presses his request on them from a reference to his present circumstances. The Apostle had been among the Christian Hebrews formerly; he wished to be restored to them. He considers their prayers as means well fitted for gaining his desire, knowing that, in the government of His Church, Jesus Christ has a great regard to the prayers of His people. Whether the Apostle obtained his wish or not, we do not know, nor is it at all material. Whatever appears to us duty in any particular case, we may, we ought to desire and to pray for, though the event we wish for may never take place. The secret purposes of God are not the rule of our prayers. If Apostles needed the prayers of the churches, how much more ordinary ministers! " Brethren, pray for us."

One of the best methods of enforcing our recommendations of duties to others, is to exemplify them ourselves. This is the plan which the Apostle adopted in reference to the duty of mutual intercession. He had just been requesting an interest in the prayers of the Hebrew Christians, and he immediately shows them that they had an interest in his. He had just been bidding them pray for him, and he straightway commences praying for them. He had just said, " Brethren, pray for us," and he now says, vers. 20, 21, " Now the God of peace, that brought again from the dead our Lord Jesus, that great Shepherd of the sheep, through the blood of the everlasting covenant, make you perfect in every good work to do His will, working in you that which is well-pleasing in His sight, through Jesus Christ; to whom be glory for ever and ever. Amen."

This sublime and comprehensive prayer—which, properly speaking, forms the appropriate conclusion of the Epistle, for what follows is plainly a kind of postscript—deserves, and will reward, our most considerate attention. Our attention must be directed in succession—(1) to the descriptive appellation under which the Apostle addresses the object of prayer—"The God of peace, who brought again from the dead our Lord Jesus, that great Shepherd of the sheep, by the blood of the everlasting covenant;" (2) to the prayer itself—that God, as the God of peace, would " make them perfect in every good work to do His will, working in them that which was well-pleasing in His sight, by Jesus Christ;" and (3) the doxology or ascription of praise with which the prayer closes—" To Him be glory for ever and ever. Amen."

Let us then, first, consider the import of the descriptive appellation under which the Apostle addresses the great object of prayer. Before we enter on an inquiry into the meaning of this appellation, it will be proper to endeavour to settle a question respecting the construction of this clause of the verse, the determination of which materially affects the sense. The words, " through the blood of the everlasting covenant," may either be connected with the phrase, " brought again from the dead," or with the dignified title given to Jesus Christ, " the great Shepherd of the sheep ;"—they may either be viewed as descriptive of the manner in which His resurrection was accomplished, or of the manner in which He became " the great Shepherd of the sheep." A good sense may be brought out of the words according to either of these two modes of connecting them. The usage of the original language admits of either. Looking merely at the Greek words, I should be disposed to say the latter method of connecting them is the more natural of the two, and that the Apostle's idea is, that Christ became the great Shepherd of the sheep by means of His voluntary oblation of Himself; *i.e.*, obtained for Himself that supreme authority over the Church which is implied in His being " the great Shepherd of the sheep." Yet when I consider that—though it is most true that Christ purchased the Church with His own blood, and was exalted on account of His expiatory sufferings as " Head over all things to His Church"—" in the days of His flesh" He takes to Himself the appellation, " the good Shepherd," and that it was as " the good Shepherd," in the discharge of the duties rising out of this character, that He " laid down His life for the sheep," it appears to me more probable that the first method of connecting the words is that which gives us the Apostle's idea: that His resurrection from the dead was " through the blood of the everlasting covenant." What is the meaning of that assertion, will appear, we trust, by and by.

Having settled this question of construction, let us proceed to the exposition of the descriptive appellation here given to the object of prayer. In order distinctly to bring out the thoughts involved in such a complicated form of expression as that now before us, it is often found advisable to reverse, or at any rate

considerably to change, the order in which they stand. The
following are the thoughts in what I apprehend is their natural
order—the order in which they presented themselves to the
Apostle's mind:—Jesus Christ our Lord is the great Shepherd
of the sheep. As the great Shepherd of the sheep He submitted to death. As the great Shepherd of the sheep He has
been brought again from the dead by God. When God brought
Him again from the dead, He did so through the blood of the
everlasting covenant. In bringing Jesus our Lord from the
dead by the blood of the everlasting covenant, God acted as the
God of peace; and it is to God, as having manifested Himself
to be the God of peace by bringing our Lord Jesus from the
dead through the blood of the everlasting covenant, that the
Apostle addresses his prayers in behalf of the Hebrew Christians. Let us shortly illustrate these most important truths.

(1.) Jesus our Lord is "the great Shepherd of the sheep."
What class of persons is described under the figurative denomination, "the sheep?" What is to be understood by Jesus
our Lord being their Shepherd? and what by His being the
great Shepherd? To the first of these questions a most satisfactory answer will be found in the words of our Lord in the
tenth chapter of the Gospel by John. The description extends from the 11th verse down to the 30th. The sum of His
statement is, that the sheep are those whom the Father has
given Him, both Jews and Gentiles, for whom He laid down
His life, who hear His voice and follow Him, to whom He gives
eternal life, and who "will never perish, because none can pluck
them out of His, and out of His Father's hand." They are
plainly that innumerable multitude out of every kindred, and
people, and tongue, and nation, which He redeems to God by
His blood,—the same class of persons who in the preceding
part of the Epistle are represented as "the heirs of salvation;"
"the many children to be brought to glory" through "the
captain of their salvation being made perfect through suffering;" the "holy brethren" of the Messiah; the "partakers of
the heavenly calling;" those that through believing do enter into
the promised rest; "partakers of Christ;" "the heirs of the
promise;" "they that are called;" "they that come to God by
Christ;" "the sanctified" ones by the offering of Christ's body
once for all; those who have "received the kingdom that can-

not be moved." "The sheep" is just another name for genuine Christians, viewed as separated from the rest of the world, and placed under the peculiar care of Christ as their Shepherd.

This naturally leads us to inquire what is meant by His being termed the Shepherd of the sheep. Many very learned interpreters have considered that the figurative expression "shepherd" is intended chiefly, if not solely, to convey the idea of *teacher, instructor.* I apprehend, however, that this is a mistake, and that this idea, if included, is but a subordinate one; that the word "shepherd," when used figuratively, both in the Old and New Testament, denotes one who presides over a collection of people, who governs, guides, and protects them—a leader, a guard, a defender, a chief, a king. David's being raised to the supreme government of the Israelitish people is represented as his being made their shepherd: Ps. lxxviii. 70-72. In the First Epistle of Peter, chap. ii. 25, *shepherd,* and *bishop,* or overseer, are used as equivalent expressions. The idea intended to be conveyed is obviously this: He is placed over them for the purpose of doing everything that is necessary for promoting their happiness. It is just a figurative expression equivalent in meaning to the literal expression "Saviour."

But our Lord is not only termed "the Shepherd," but "that great Shepherd of the sheep." He may receive this appellation to distinguish Him from all others who are called shepherds, as He is termed "the King of kings, and the Lord of lords;" or to mark Him as the superior of all those who in His Church receive the name of shepherds or pastors—in which case the phrase is equivalent to that used by Peter—the chief Shepherd; or to mark His transcendent personal dignity, as in the use of the same epithet in the expression, "A great High Priest, Jesus the Son of God." I have sometimes thought that, both in this expression, and in our Lord's own expression, "the good," or that good "Shepherd," there is an allusion to the numerous predictions of the Messiah under the character of a Shepherd in the Old Testament prophecies. The following are specimens of the predictions I refer to: "O Zion, that bringest good tidings, get thee up into the high mountain; O Jerusalem, that bringest good tidings, lift up thy voice with strength: lift it up, be not afraid; say unto the cities of Judah, Behold your God! Behold, the Lord God will come with strong hand, and His arm shall rule for Him: behold, His reward is with Him, and His work before Him. He shall feed His flock like a shepherd; He shall gather the lambs with His arm, and carry them in His bosom, and shall gently lead those that are with young." "And I will set up one Shepherd over them, and He shall feed them, even My servant David; He shall feed them, and He shall be their Shepherd. And I the Lord will be their God, and My servant David a prince among them: I the Lord have spoken it."[1] The full import of the expression seems to be—'Jesus our Lord, the Divine Saviour of the spiritual people of God, promised to the fathers.'

(2.) This "great Shepherd of the sheep" submitted to death. This is not indeed stated in so many words, but it is obviously implied, both in the phrase, "brought again from the dead," and in that of "the blood of the everlasting covenant." He submitted to death; and He submitted to death as a victim. His blood was the blood of a victim, or expiatory sacrifice, shed to ratify a covenant of peace. "The good Shepherd gave His life for the sheep." "All we like sheep had gone astray; we had turned every one to his own way; and the Lord laid on Him the iniquity of all. Exaction was made, and He became answerable. And He was wounded for our transgressions, He was bruised for our iniquities: and the chastisement of our peace was upon Him; and by His stripes we are healed. He gave His soul a sacrifice for sin." But as "the great Shepherd" laid down His life in order to save His sheep, in obedience to the will of His Father, so He laid it down "that He might take it again." It was not possible that *He* should continue bound with the fetters of death.

(3.) God "brought Him again from the dead." These words represent the resurrection of our Lord as an act of divine power. No power inferior to divine could have accomplished it. The question of the Apostle to king Agrippa, "Why should it be thought a thing incredible that God should raise the dead?" implies that it might well be accounted an incredible thing that any one else should. The resurrection of Jesus Christ is sometimes spoken of as His own work. "Destroy this temple," He says, "and in three days I will raise it up again. This He said of the temple of His body." And, "As the Father raiseth up the

---

[1] Isa. xl. 9–11; Ezek. xxxiv. 23, 24.

dead, and quickeneth them, even so the Son quickeneth whom He will." This will not, however, in any degree appear to be inconsistent with the declaration in the passage before us, by any one who understands the principles of the economy of redemption. The Father in that economy is the representative of divinity—the sustainer of its majesty, the vindicator of its rights. The Son acts in a subordinate character. Whatever He says, He says in the name of the Father; whatever He does, He does by the power of the Father. "The Father who dwelleth in Me, He doth the works." When He was raised from the dead, He was raised by the power of the Father; *i.e.*, by the power of God. But the words before us do not so much represent the resurrection as an act of mere power, as an act of rectoral justice.

(4.) God brought "the great Shepherd of the sheep"—who had given His life for the sheep—"from the dead, by the blood of the everlasting covenant." The covenant here referred to is obviously that divine constitution or arrangement by which spiritual and eternal blessings are secured for the guilty and depraved children of men, through the mediation of the incarnate Son of God. This covenant is termed "the everlasting covenant" to distinguish it from other covenants or arrangements made by God, and especially from that covenant or arrangement which was made with the Israelites at Sinai, and which, as it referred directly to temporal blessings, was intended only for temporary duration. This new covenant is never to give place to any other.

"The blood" of this covenant is the blood by the shedding of which this covenant was ratified. When illustrating the ninth chapter of the Epistle, I had occasion at considerable length to show you that it is the doctrine of the Apostle, that in all covenants or arrangements made by God for conferring blessings on sinful men, there has always been an assertion of His rights as the just and holy Moral Governor of the world; and that the form this assertion of His rights has uniformly taken, has been that of the death of a propitiatory victim; and that the dignity of the victim necessarily bore a proportion to the value of the benefits secured by the covenant. The blood of animal propitiatory victims confirmed the first covenant. The blood of the incarnate Only-begotten of God confirmed the new and better covenant; *i.e.*, the obedience to the death of the incarnate Son of God as the substitute of sinners, makes it consistent with, illustrative of, the divine holiness, and justice, and faithfulness, as well as goodness, to bestow pardon on the guilty, and salvation on the lost children of men, believing in Jesus.

The resurrection of our Lord is represented as the result of this shedding of His blood, by which the everlasting covenant was confirmed. He was "brought again from the dead by the blood of the everlasting covenant." His obedience to the death was the procuring cause of His own resurrection, as well as of the salvation of His people, which is the result of that resurrection. The Father loved the Son, had complacency in Him, because, in compliance with His will, He laid down His life for the sheep; and this was the manner in which He manifested His complacency. Because He humbled Himself, therefore He highly exalted Him.

(5.) In bringing our Lord Jesus from the dead, God acted in the character of "the God of peace." This is an appellation of the Divinity peculiar to the Apostle Paul, and frequently occurring in his writings: Rom. xv. 33, xvi. 20; 1 Cor. xiv. 33; 2 Thess. iii. 16. The word "peace" is often used as equivalent to 'prosperity,' happiness in general; and "the God of peace" may be considered as equivalent to—'the God who is the author of happiness.' The proper signification of the word, however, is 'reconciliation;' and I think there can be but very little doubt that it has its proper primary signification here. "The God of peace," or reconciliation, is the pacified, the reconciled Divinity. It is just equivalent to the more fully expressed character of God—"God in Christ, reconciling the world to Himself, not imputing to men their trespasses; seeing He has made Him to be sin for us, who knew no sin, that we might be made the righteousness of God in Him." God was displeased with man on account of sin; *i.e.*, in plain words, not merely was man's sin the object of His moral disapprobation, but, in the ordinary course of things, man's final happiness was inconsistent with the honour of His character as the righteous Governor of the world, and (what is but another way of expressing the same truth) with the principles of His moral administration, and the happiness of His intelligent subjects generally. This incompatibility could be removed only by some display of the divine displeasure against sin, and of the righteousness and reasonableness of the law man had violated, fully equivalent to that which would have been given by the condemning sanction of the law being allowed to take its course in reference to the offenders. This has been given in the substituted obedience and sufferings of the incarnate Son. These have "magnified the law, and made it honourable." God is now "just, and the justifier of the ungodly" —"the just God and the Saviour." "His righteousness is declared through His Son being set forth a propitiation in His blood." And the first display, and the satisfactory proof, that God is now "the God of peace," is His raising His Son, our Surety, from the dead, and giving Him "all power in heaven and earth," "that He may give eternal life to as many as the Father has given Him."

It is finely said by Dr Owen: "The well-spring of the whole dispensation of grace lies in the bringing again our Lord Jesus Christ from the dead, through the blood of the everlasting covenant. Had not the will of God been fully executed, atonement made for sin, the Church sanctified, the law accomplished, and the threatenings satisfied, Christ could not have been brought from the dead. The death of Christ, if He had not risen, could not have completed our redemption; we should have been yet in our sins. For evidence would have been given that atonement was not made. The bare resurrection of Christ, or the bringing Him from the dead, would not have saved us; for so any other man may be raised by the power of God. But the bringing of Christ again from the dead by the blood of the everlasting covenant, is that which gives assurance of the complete redemption and salvation of the Church."

Now, it is to God as having manifested Himself to be "the God of peace"—the pacified Divinity—by "bringing again from the dead our Lord Jesus," when, as "the great Shepherd," He had given His life for the sheep, that the Apostle addresses his prayers in behalf of the Hebrew Christians. Indeed, this is the only character in which the Divinity can be rationally addressed by sinful men, or in behalf of sinful men. Without a reference to that atonement which was completed in the death of the Son of God, and the completeness of which is demonstrated by His resurrection, no spiritual and saving blessing can be reasonably expected by sinners from Him who is "glorious in holiness," and "can by no means clear the guilty." But from the pacified Divinity every heavenly and spiritual blessing may be expected; and, contemplating God in this character, we may go near Him, even to His seat, asking blessings both for ourselves and others—"drawing near with boldness to the throne of grace," in the faith of Him "who was given for our offences, and raised again for our justification," "that we may obtain mercy, and find grace to help in the time of need." Such is the appellation under which the Apostle addresses his intercessions for the Hebrew Christians to the object of prayer—the pacified Divinity, manifesting His reconciled character in the resurrection of Jesus, "the great Shepherd," on the ground of His having fully satisfied the demands of His law and justice, in giving His life for the sheep, in giving Himself a sacrifice and an offering that He might bring them to God.

We proceed now to inquire into the import of the prayer which the Apostle here presents. He prays that "the God of peace" would make the Hebrew Christians "perfect in every good work to do His will, working in you that which is well-pleasing in His sight."

The prayer consists of two parts; the one referring to the end, and the other to the means of gaining that end. The Apostle prays that the Christian Hebrews might be "made perfect in every good work to do His will;" and He prays that, in order to do this, He would "work in them that which is well-pleasing in His sight, through Jesus Christ."

The first petition is, that God would "make them perfect in every good work to do His will." These English words do not convey any very clear and distinct signification. The word translated "make perfect," properly signifies 'to set to rights what is out of order,' thus preparing it for its proper use. Its meaning will be best illustrated by referring to some of the passages where it occurs. Rom. ix. 22, the "vessels of wrath" are represented as "*fitted*"—the same word as that used here—"for destruction." "The worlds" are said to have been "*framed*" —*i.e.*, 'arranged, put in order from the chaotic state,' and thus fitted for their several purposes—"by the word of God:" Heb. xi. 3. "A body" is said to be "prepared" for our Lord: Heb. x. 5. And it is said, Eph. iv. 13, that Christ "gave some teachers, for the perfecting of the saints, for the work of the ministry"—*i.e.*, to fit or prepare holy men for the work of the ministry,—"that the body of Christ—*i.e.*, the Church—"may be edified." We apprehend the word has the same meaning here as in the passages to which I have just referred. The Apostle prays that "the God of peace" would fit or prepare the Hebrew Christians "to do His will in every good work." We are all by nature utterly unfit to obey the divine will; we do not know it, we do not love it. God alone can render us fit for doing His will; and this is true, not only with regard to unregenerate, but with regard to regenerate men. "Without Him we can do nothing." "Our sufficiency is of God."

The Apostle's prayer is a very extensive one. He wishes not only that they might be prepared to do the will of God, but to do the whole will of God—"to do His will in every good work;" *i.e.*, in the performance of every duty, moral and religious. The will of God is our sanctification—our sanctification wholly, in the whole man—"soul, body, and spirit;" and it is the Apostle's prayer that the Hebrew Christians might be enabled by God to be perfect and entire, wanting nothing.

The second petition refers to the means by which this end is to be gained. The Hebrew Christians are to be prepared for doing the will of God "in every good work," by God's "working in them that which is well-pleasing in His sight, by Jesus Christ."[1] In order to external good works, there must be internal good principles. In order to conformity to the law of God in the life, there must be conformity to the will of God in the heart. That in us which is "well-pleasing in God's sight," is just a mode of thinking and of feeling which is conformable to His will. The way in which God does this, is not by miraculously implanting such a mode of thinking and feeling within us. That God could do this, if it so pleased Him, we have no reason to doubt; but He acts according to the laws of our intelligent and moral nature. In His word He has given us a plain, well-accredited revelation of His *mind*. By the influence of His Spirit, which our depravity renders absolutely necessary, He leads us to understand and believe this revelation. The revealed mind of God, understood and believed by us, becomes our mind; and our mind being brought into accordance with God's mind, our will, according to the constitution of our

[1] εὐάρεστον ἐνώπιον αὐτοῦ = טוֹב לְפָנָיו.

nature, is brought into accordance with God's will. It is thus that God, by His word and Spirit, "works in us that which is well-pleasing in His sight."

It is plain from these remarks, that God's working in us does not make us passive. It is plain that, in order to our having in us "that which is well-pleasing in His sight," we must carefully study the Scriptures, and accompany our study of the Scriptures with earnest prayer to God for that divine influence without which they cannot be understood and believed. While we use the means—and we act like madmen if we do not use the means—and look for the end, we are never to forget that His *working in us* is necessary to enable us "both to will and to do;" and when the use of the means is effectual, we are to ascribe to Him all the glory, saying, 'It was not I, but the grace of God that is in me. It is not so much I that live as Christ that lives in me.'

The expression, "by Jesus Christ," admits of a twofold connection, and, of course, of a twofold explication. It may either be connected with the phrase, "that which is well-pleasing in His sight," or with the phrase, "working in us." In the first case the meaning is, that whatever good is wrought in the mind of man is acceptable to God, through Jesus Christ. We owe to Him, not only the pardon of our sins and the sanctification of our nature, but we owe also the acceptance of our imperfectly sanctified hearts and lives to His mediation. In the second case the meaning is, that, while the Holy Spirit is the direct agent, all God's sanctifying operations on the mind of man, are carried on with a reference to the mediation of our Lord Jesus Christ. There is no communication of divine influence from "the God of peace," but in and by Jesus Christ, and by virtue of His mediation.

The third thing in the Apostle's prayer which requires consideration is, the doxology or ascription of praise with which it closes : " To whom be glory for ever and ever." It is impossible, from the construction, to determine with absolute certainty whether this ascription of praise refer to "the God of peace" or to Jesus Christ. We know that both are worthy of eternal honour and praise, and that both shall receive them. We find that glory is ascribed to each separately, and to both together, in other passages of Scripture. To the Father separately : Phil.

iv. 20, "Now unto God and our Father be glory for ever and ever. Amen." To the Son separately: Rev. i. 5, 6, "Unto Him that loved us, and washed us from our sins in His own blood, and hath made us kings and priests unto God and His Father; to Him be glory and dominion for ever and ever. Amen." To both together: Rev. v. 13, "And every creature which is in heaven, and on the earth, and under the earth, and such as are in the sea, and all that are in them, heard I saying, Blessing, and honour, and glory, and power, be unto Him that sitteth upon the throne, and unto the Lamb, for ever and ever." It appears to me, however, that though Christ be the nearest relative, yet, as "the God of peace" is the person addressed and principally spoken of in the prayer, the ascription of praise is to be considered as addressed to Him. "The God of peace" well deserves to be praised and glorified for ever, for all He has done for, and for all He has done in, His redeemed people. The "bringing again from the dead our Lord Jesus, that great Shepherd of the sheep," and His "preparing His people in every good work to do His will," by "working in them that which is well-pleasing in His sight," are themes worthy of the songs of eternity. In these dispensations He displays a power and a wisdom, a holiness and a grace, which richly deserve everlasting praise. And as they deserve it, so they shall receive it. The Apostle's pious wish, in which every Christian will cordially acquiesce, will be fully realized. A song ever new shall be unceasingly raised by the nations of the saved to "the God of peace," who reconciled them to Himself by the blood of His Son, and declared the reconciliation by His glorious resurrection; and who, by the instrumentality of His word and the power of His Spirit, "prepared them for doing His will in every good work, by working in them that which is well-pleasing in His sight." "Amen," adds the Apostle. So it ought to be, so let it be, so shall it be. "And let all the people say, *Amen, and Amen.*"

This is, properly speaking, the conclusion of the Epistle; and a more appropriate one could not have been conceived. What follows in the four following verses is of the nature of a postscript. This is a usual practice with the Apostle. Similar postscripts are attached to the Epistles to the Romans and Philippians, and to both the Epistles to Timothy.

The 22d verse contains an affectionate request that they would take kindly what on his part was meant kindly. "I beseech you, brethren, suffer the word of exhortation; for I have written a letter to you in few words." The Hebrew Christians were, like all other Christians, Paul's spiritual brethren; but I think it very likely he here referred to the natural relation in which they stood to him as Hebrews. It was as Hebrews—as persons possessed with Jewish prejudices—that they especially needed, and were in danger of not " suffering, the word of exhortation." It is equivalent to—'Remember, I am your brother, and both feel the affection, and am warranted to use the freedom, of a brother.'

"The word of exhortation" is just equivalent to—'this hortatory discourse.' Some have supposed that the Apostle refers only to those parts of the Epistle that consist of direct exhortation, such as the beginning of the 2d chapter, the 6th, the latter part of the 10th, the 12th, and the 13th chapters. We rather apprehend that he means 'this hortatory discourse' as a general description of the whole Epistle. And a juster one could not be conceived; for what is the Epistle, from beginning to end, but a most impressive and well-supported exhortation to persevere in the faith and profession of the Gospel, notwithstanding all the temptations to abandon them to which they were exposed?

To "suffer," or bear, this hortatory discourse, is a phrase which obviously implies, that in it there were many things opposed to their prejudices, and which, therefore, they might be dissatisfied and displeased with. I do not know that the meaning of the exhortation can be better given than in the words of Dr Owen : " Let no prejudices, no inveterate opinions, no apprehension of severity in its admonitions and threatenings, provoke you against it, render you impatient under it, and so cause you to lose the benefit of it. Christians should beware of turning away from statements and exhortations merely because they are not very agreeable to them. That may be the very reason why they are peculiarly required by them."

The reason of this injunction is given in the close of the verse: "For I have written a letter to you in few words."[1] It may appear strange that the Apostle uses such language with regard to this Epistle, as it is the largest of his Epistles, with the

---

[1] διὰ βραχέων (ῥημάτων); *i.e.*, δι' ὀλίγων,—1 Pet. v. 12.

exception of that written to the Romans, and as he seems to have considered his Epistle to the Galatians a long one: " Ye see how long a letter I have written to you with mine own hand." The remark in the Epistle to the Galatians refers either to the size and form of the Greek characters, which the Apostle does not seem to have been accustomed to write, or to the letter being long for an autograph, he being in the habit of employing an amanuensis. Length and shortness are comparative terms. A very short letter on an unimportant subject may be too long, and a very long letter on an important subject may be too short. The Apostle's meaning is, 'I have written to you concisely.' And who that has read the Epistle is not convinced of this?[1] I have delivered nearly one hundred lectures of an hour's length on this Epistle; and yet I am persuaded I have but very imperfectly brought out those "treasures of wisdom and knowledge" which are contained in these brief terms.

The force of the conciseness of the Apostle's style, as a reason why his brethren should "bear the word of exhortation," is not difficult to perceive. It is equivalent to—'If there be anything apparently harsh and unpalatable in the exhortation, impute it to the circumstance that I have had so much to communicate within a moderate compass, that there was no room to smooth down all asperities.'

The 23d verse gives some interesting information respecting a distinguished Christian evangelist, and the Apostle's intention of speedily visiting the Hebrew Christians: "Know ye that our brother Timothy is set at liberty; with whom, if he come shortly, I will see you." Timothy, of whose history we have a number of notices in the Acts of the Apostles, seems to have accompanied the Apostle in very many of his journeyings, and to have served with him as a son with a father in the work of the Gospel. Having been with him in Judea, his worth and excellences were well known to the churches there. He does not seem to have gone to Rome with the Apostle, but he probably followed him there; and it would appear from this passage that he had been cast into prison as an associate of Paul, or for preaching the Gospel himself. From this imprisonment he had

---

[1] "It is reasonable to suppose that the writer means to say that he had written briefly, considering the importance and difficulty of the subjects of which he had treated. And who will deny this?"—STUART.

been delivered; and it seems to have been his intention to avail himself of his deliverance to visit the brethren in Judea. The Apostle intimates his intention to accompany Timothy in this journey, if he should undertake it soon; at the same time, hinting that, if Timothy could not come speedily, it was doubtful whether his work would permit him to do so or not. We do not know whether these expectations were ever fulfilled.

The words in the 24th verse seem plainly addressed to those individuals to whom the letter was sent, and by whom it was to be communicated to the Church. He charges them to "salute" —*i.e.*, to express his kind and respectful affection, first to the office-bearers, and then to the members of the churches of Judea. The members are called *saints—separated ones*, set apart by God for Himself—separated from "the world lying under the wicked one"—devoted to the love, and fear, and service of God and His Son. Such are the only proper members of the visible Church; such are the only true members of the Church invisible. "They of Italy salute you;"[1] that is, 'The Christians in Italy send you the assurance of their cordial regard.' How does Christianity melt down prejudices! Romans and Jews, Italians and Hebrews, were accustomed to regard each other with contempt and hatred. But in Christ Jesus there is neither Roman nor Jew, neither Italian nor Hebrew: all are one. Christians of different countries should take all proper opportunities of testifying their mutual regard to each other. It is calculated to strengthen and console, and to knit them closer and closer in love. Proper expressions of love increase love on both sides.

The Epistle is concluded with the usual sign in the Apostle's Epistles, written probably by his own hand. "Grace be with you all. Amen." "Grace" here is the grace of God—the divine sovereign kindness. What a comprehensive, kind wish is this: 'May you be the objects of the continued love of the greatest, the wisest, and the best Being in the universe; and

---

[1] Οἱ ἀπὸ τῆς 'Ιταλίας may signify, 'those who have come from Italy'— those Italians who have been obliged to leave their country and come to some other country. In this way some interpreters render it, especially those who deny the Pauline origin of the Epistle. It may signify Italians generally, including Romans; but supposing the Epistle to have been written from Rome, it probably signifies the Christians from other parts of Italy, at the time residing in Rome. Tholuck's note deserves to be read.

may He constantly bestow on you proofs of His peculiar love and care!' "His favour is life, His loving-kindness is better than life." Nothing better, for time or for eternity, can be desired for ourselves or for others than the grace of God. Infinite power to guard, infinite wisdom to guide, infinite excellence and love to excite and gratify all the affections of the heart for ever and ever.

And now I close these illustrations of the Epistle to the Hebrews. Happier hours than those which I have spent in composing these expository discourses, I can scarcely expect to spend on this side the grave. I trust the study of the Epistle has not been without some improvement, as well as much enjoyment, to myself. I shall rejoice if at last it shall be found that others also have been made better and happier by it. All is now over with the author and his readers, as to his illustrating the Epistle, and their listening to these illustrations; but there remains the improvement to be made, and the account to be given in. God requireth the things which are past, and so should we. Let me request those who have accompanied me thus far, seriously to review the whole Epistle, and ask themselves, Do we understand it better, and do we feel more strongly the sanctifying and consoling influence of the doctrines which it unfolds? Can we say with greater conviction of the truth than formerly, We need a High Priest—we have a High Priest—we are well pleased with our High Priest; we have acknowledged Jesus as our High Priest; we will hold fast our acknowledgment; He died for us—we will live for Him; and if He calls us, we will die for Him; we will trace His steps on the earth, we will wait His coming in the clouds? If this be the case even in one individual, I shall not have laboured in vain: if it has been the case with a number of individuals, I shall have received a full reward.

Πρὸς Ἑβραίους ἐγράφη ἀπὸ τῆς Ἰταλίας διὰ Τιμοθέου.

The 23d verse of the 13th chapter sufficiently proves that this hypograph is not genuine. Like many of the other hypographs of the Apostolical Epistles, it is the mere conjecture of an ignorant and inconsiderate transcriber. "These inscriptions are," as Hallett well says, "not of the least authority. It is a pity they should be printed in the Bible." In some MSS., after ἐγράφη, Ἑβραιστὶ is added. Instead of ἀπὸ τῆς Ἰταλίας, one codex has ἀπὸ Ῥώμης, and another, ἀπ' Ἀθηνῶν.

DISCOURSES

ON SELECT PORTIONS OF THE

EPISTLE TO THE HEBREWS.

DISCOURSES

ON

SELECT PORTIONS OF THE EPISTLE.

DISCOURSE I.

THE CHRISTIAN'S PRIVILEGE AND DUTY.

HEB. IV. 14–16.—" Seeing then that we have a great High Priest, that is passed into the heavens, Jesus the Son of God, let us hold fast our profession. For we have not an High Priest which cannot be touched with the feeling of our infirmities; but was in all points tempted like as we are, yet without sin. Let us therefore come boldly unto the throne of grace, that we may obtain mercy, and find grace to help in time of need."

THERE is an intimate connection between truth and holiness, doctrine and precept, faith and practice, the illumination of the mind and the transformation of the heart and life. The principle now announced is deeply founded in the constitution of human nature; and it is one of the many corroborative evidences of the divine origin of the Scriptural revelation, that it uniformly recognises this principle. Its statements of truth always look forward to practical results, and its injunctions to duty look back to announced principles. *This* is *true;* therefore *that* is *right*. This is *right*, because that is *true*.

We have an exemplification of this in the passage of Scripture which forms the subject of discourse. It consists of a *statement* and an *exhortation;* the statement originating the exhortation, the exhortation based on the statement. The statement is fourfold:—We Christians have a High Priest. Jesus Christ is our High Priest. He is a great High Priest, being the Son of God, and having passed into the heavens. He is a compassionate High Priest; He is "not a High Priest who cannot be touched with the feeling of our infirmities; but was in all points tempted like as we are, yet without sin." The exhortation is twofold:—"Let us hold fast our profession;" and, "Let us come boldly to the throne of grace, that we may obtain mercy, and find grace to help in time of need." The duties enjoined in the exhortation are inferences from the doctrines contained in the statement. The doctrines contained in the statement are motives to the duties enjoined in the exhortation. The Christian's *privilege*, the Christian's *duty*, and the influence which the one ought to have on the other, are all here strikingly placed before us.

The statement runs thus: "We have a great High Priest, that is passed into the heavens, Jesus the Son of God. We have not a high priest who cannot be touched with the feeling of our infirmities; but was in all points tempted like as we are, yet without sin." This complex statement naturally resolves itself into these four simple ones: We Christians have a High Priest; Jesus Christ is our High Priest; He is a great High Priest; He is a compassionate High Priest. Let us attend to these in their order.

I. In the first place, then, the text teaches us that "we Christians have a *High Priest*." Had man continued innocent, and therefore safe and happy, there would have been no high priest, for man would have had no need of one; and had his fall been irremediable—had it been impossible to avert the dangers, to escape the miseries, in which he was involved—there would equally have been no high priest, for there would have been no use for one. "The angels who kept their first estate" have no high priest; and neither have they who, having sinned, are "reserved under everlasting chains to the judgment of the great day."

The high-priesthood is an institution rising out of the peculiar circumstances of our race, as lost, but not hopelessly lost. "A high priest is a person taken from among men, ordained for men in things pertaining to God, that he may offer both gifts and sacrifices to God."

While man was innocent, he needed no one to come between him and God and transact his business with *Him*, with whom principally every intelligent accountable being has to do. God was pleased with His innocent child, and delighted to do him good: and man, full of veneration, and love, and confidence, found his happiness in such fellowship with God as was competent to his nature.

But the introduction of sin produced a sad revolution. God became displeased with man, and man alienated from God. All direct favourable communication was at end, and must have been at an end for ever, if some means were not employed at once to make the restoration of man to the enjoyment of the favour and fellowship of God consistent with the perfections of the divine character, and the principles of the divine government, and to effect such a change in man's dispositions as would fit him for acceptable intercourse with God.

To make atonement for sin, so that it might be pardoned, and so to purify men as that they should be capable of yielding acceptable obedience to God, and of finding supreme ultimate happiness in God—this was the great design of the institution of a high priest.

The priesthood under the patriarchal and Mosaic economies could not effect these purposes; but it was at once a striking representation of what was necessary to effect them, and a gracious intimation that, in the fulness of the times, they should be effected. So far as the heathen priesthood was not a corrupted resemblance of the patriarchal or Mosaic institution, it was the expression of the natural feelings of fallen man, conscious of guilt, and afraid of punishment.

The High Priest man needs, we Christians have. We know that an atonement of infinite value has been offered and accepted, and that an influence has been secured, fitting men for that renewed favourable intercourse with God, a way for which has been opened through the merits of the great sacrifice of expiation.

A high priest is the first necessity in a religion for fallen man. Clear statements of truth and duty, with corresponding evidence and motive, are good, necessary things; but what can they do where there is no atoning sacrifice, no sanctifying influence? Teachers, lawgivers, are very valuable; but they cannot make up for the want of a high priest.

Under the Christian dispensation, all the external appearances of a priestly institution are wanting. No material temple, in the proper sense of the word—no altar—no human priest—no animal sacrifices—no lustratory rites. Yet *we* have a High Priest; and it is just because we have Him that we have none of these. The unbelieving Jews would be very apt to say to their Christian compatriots, Your new religion is deficient in the very first requisite of a religion for fallen men. You have no high priest. How are your sins to be pardoned? you have none to make expiation for you. How are your pollutions to be cleansed? you have none to sprinkle you that you may be clean. How are your wants to be supplied? you have none to make intercession for you.

The answer to the cavil is contained in the words of our text, "We have a High Priest." The high priest among the Jews was the principal religious minister of that economy, the inferior priests being merely his deputies, executing such parts of his office as he could not personally overtake. The import of the institution was, as I have already remarked, that God was offended with man, and would not have direct favourable intercourse with him; that He was disposed to be reconciled to him; and that the medium through which He was disposed to confer saving blessings on him, was that of vicarious sacrifice and intercession. When, then, the Apostle says, "We have a High Priest," he means, We have one who has offered up an availing expiatory sacrifice in our room; who has done what renders it consistent with, and illustrative of, the divine character to pardon and save us; and one, too, who makes intercession for us—continually interposes in our behalf with God, so as to secure for us everything that is necessary to final and complete salvation. Such is the import of the statement, "We have a High Priest."

II. I remark, in the second place, that *Jesus Christ* is our High Priest.

None could be our high priest unless divinely commissioned to be so. None can be our high priest who has not executed, and is not executing, the functions peculiar to that office. In Jesus Christ—in Him alone—are to be found those necessary and indubitable evidences of being our High Priest.

"No man taketh this honour of high-priesthood to himself, but he that is called of God, as was Aaron." So also Christ glorified not Himself to be made a high priest; but His Father God thus glorified Him. He who said to Him in a divine oracle, "Thou art My Son, this day have I begotten Thee," said also in another divine oracle, "Thou art a Priest for ever, after the order of Melchisedec." He came not of Himself— His Father sent Him; and He came to give His life a ransom for many—to give His flesh for the life of the world. I have power, says He, to lay down My life for the sheep. I have power to take it up again. "This commandment have I received of My Father."

And as Jesus Christ was commissioned to be our High Priest, so He performs for us the functions of high-priesthood. He is "the Mediator, the one Mediator between God and man." He has offered for us an atoning sacrifice of infinite value. He did not, indeed, offer animal sacrifices in that temple which "served as an example and shadow of the heavenly things;" but He did offer a sacrifice, of which all the sacrifices offered in that temple were figures. Being a High Priest, He was ordained to offer gifts and sacrifices. It was of necessity, therefore, that He should have somewhat to offer. The Eternal Son, our appointed High Priest, though the Inheritor of all things, the Proprietor of the Universe, had in that character nothing that He could offer as a sacrifice. The suitable, the only available, victim must be obtained by His becoming incarnate. "A body was prepared Him;" and in that body, once for all, He offered Himself for us, a sacrifice and an offering of a sweet-smelling savour. He laid Himself as the Lamb of God, bearing, and bearing away, the sin of the world, on the altar of divine justice. His perfect conformity in disposition to the divine law, his spotless obedience to all its commands, and His cheerful submission to its penal sanction in the room of men—this was the sacrifice by which the requisitions of justice and the purpose of mercy were harmonized. We are "sanctified by the offering of the body of Jesus Christ once for all." "The blood of Jesus Christ, God's Son, cleanseth us from all sin."

And on the ground of this all-perfect atonement, having obtained eternal redemption for us, He has entered into the true holy place, the heaven of heavens. There He ever liveth, making intercession for us, so as to be able to save to the uttermost all coming to God by Him. By the blood of His atoning sacrifice sprinkled on the conscience—that is, by the effect of the truth respecting this atoning sacrifice, understood and believed, under the influence of the Holy Spirit, whom God has shed forth on us abundantly through Jesus Christ our Saviour—we are at once disposed and qualified for habitual holy intercourse with God, in Christ reconciling the world to Himself, and are enabled to present ourselves to Him as living sacrifices—sacrifices of eucharist, not of atonement—holy, acceptable, which is rational worship. Thus is Jesus Christ our High Priest—our only High Priest.

None can, without imminent hazard, intrude on His functions. They are strictly appropriated to Himself. Whosoever attempts to take His place, or to substitute any other in His room, will not only lose the advantage of His priesthood, but incur guilt peculiarly deep, and expose himself to punishment peculiarly dreadful.

III. I proceed to remark, in the third place, that the text teaches us that Christ Jesus is a *great High Priest*. "We have a great High Priest, that is passed into the heavens, Jesus the Son of God." Our High Priest is a great High Priest. He is so both comparatively and absolutely—great in contrast to the Gentile high priests, who were impostors; great in comparison with the Jewish high priests, who were but shadows. He was the reality as a High Priest: *a* real High Priest in opposition to pretended high priests; *the* real High Priest in contrast with figurative high priests. And He was a *great* reality. In the nature and measure of qualification for the office which He possessed and displayed, in the manner in which He discharged the functions of that office, and in the nature, variety, and value of the results of His discharge of these functions, there is a manifestation of an intellectual and moral grandeur such as the universe never before witnessed—a display of infinite knowledge, and wisdom, and righteousness, and kindness.

The greatness of our High Priest is a boundless theme. The studies of eternity will not exhaust it. Here it is brought before our minds in two aspects, similar to those in which His greatness, viewed alongside of that of the angels, is exhibited in the previous context of this Epistle, when it is said that He has been made as much higher than the angels, as He has obtained by inheritance a more excellent name than they. In essential and in official greatness He is infinitely exalted above all other high priests. His essential greatness is marked by the expression, the Son of God; His official greatness, He is passed into the heavens. Let us look a little at these two aspects of our High Priest's greatness.

First, our High Priest is a great High Priest; for He is *the Son* of God. This is an appellation which is peculiar to Him. It is not applied, it cannot be applied, to any other being in the universe. Holy angels and sanctified men—to mark their origin as intelligent holy beings, their likeness to God, their being the objects of His complacential regard, and His being the object of their supreme veneration, love, and confidence—are termed sons of God; but Jesus only receives the name of *the* Son. He is "the only-begotten Son"—"God's own Son"—"the Son of Himself." To none but Him did God ever say, "Thou art My Son, this day I have begotten Thee." This name indicates identity of nature, and, of course, equality of perfection.

The proper Deity of Him who is our High Priest is one of the foundation principles of our most holy faith. The names most descriptive of divine excellence are given Him—God, the Lord, Jehovah. The attributes most strictly peculiar to Deity are ascribed to Him—Eternity, Immutability, Omniscience, Omnipresence, Omnipotence. Works competent only to Deity are represented as performed by Him—He is the Creator, Upholder, Ruler, Judge of the world; and He is the object of worship on earth and in heaven.

We need go no further than the first chapter of this Epistle to learn how infinitely great is our High Priest as the Son of God. He who has purged our sins,—made the worlds, is the Inheritor of all things, is the brightness of the Father's glory, the express image of His person, upholds all things by the word of His power, has obtained by inheritance a more excellent name than the angels, even that of the only-begotten Son, while their highest name is, created spirits, spiritual creatures. He in the beginning laid the foundations of the earth, and the heavens are the works of His hand. They shall perish, but He remaineth; they all shall wax old as doth a garment, and as a vesture will *He* fold them up, and *they* shall be changed: but He is the same, and His years shall not fail.

Such is the essential greatness of Him who is our High

Priest. And this essential greatness must stamp an inconceivable grandeur on all that He is and does in His official character. What limits can be set to the value of the sacrifice, to the importance of its results, and to the dignity of Him who presents the sacrifice, and works out its results—

> " When *God* Himself comes down to be
> The Offering and the Priest!"

But, secondly, our High Priest is a great High Priest; for " He has passed into the heavens," or rather, He has passed through the heavens. The fact stated here, and, still more, that which is necessarily implied in the fact, are striking proofs of the greatness of the High Priest of our profession.

The fact proves His greatness. The fact referred to is His ascension through these heavens into the heaven of heavens. It is thus described in the Gospel history : Forty days after His passion, having given His disciples " many infallible proofs" that He was risen from the dead, and having "through the Holy Ghost given commandment to them," and spoken to them "the things pertaining to the kingdom of God," " He led them out as far as Bethany, and lifted up His hands and blessed them ; and it came to pass, while He blessed them, He was parted from them." " He was taken up, and a cloud received Him out of their sight. And, while they looked stedfastly toward heaven as He went up, behold, two men stood by them in white apparel ; which also said, Ye men of Galilee, why stand ye here gazing up into heaven ? this same Jesus, which is taken from you into heaven, shall so come in like manner as ye have seen Him go into heaven." Thus was Jesus our High Priest "taken up into heaven, and sat on the right hand of God ;" " angels, and authorities, and powers being made subject to Him."

The mere fact is a proof of transcendent greatness ; but we do not see half the evidence which it affords of the greatness of Jesus as our High Priest, if we do not attend to the import of the fact, as that is distinctly unfolded to us in Scripture. The vail which divided the holy place from the holy of holies was an emblem of the visible heavens—the vail between the earth which is the outer, and heaven which is the inner, temple of Jehovah. Through the vail the Jewish high priests passed once a year, on the great day of atonement, after having offered up expiatory sacrifice for the people, to present before the Lord the evidence that atonement was made according to the due order, and to receive tokens that Jehovah was reconciled to His offending people. Our Lord's going up through these visible heavens into the heaven of heavens, was a function of His high-priesthood; and places in a striking point of view His greatness as a High Priest, whether you consider what led to *it*, or what it led *to*.

What led to it? His incarnation, obedience, suffering, and death. The Son of God, taking to Himself a holy human nature, full of the Holy Ghost, qualified Himself for His priestly functions. In His obedience, sufferings, and death, we have the great expiatory sacrifice which He came to offer up—that which was to make the salvation of man consistent with, and illustrative of, the perfections of the divine character and the principles of the divine government, and lay a foundation for that change of character in men which would fit them for holy happiness in the service and enjoyment of God. In the resurrection from the dead and the ascension to heaven, we have the most satisfactory evidence that this sacrifice has served its purpose—that the supreme Judge is satisfied—that the sacrifice, as it was a sacrifice of infinite worth, and in every point offered up in entire agreement with divine appointment, is indeed a sacrifice of a sweet-smelling savour to God. The High Priest of our profession, raised from the dust of death to never-ending life, is raised from earth to heaven; and as a token at once that what has been done by Him is acceptable, and that it never can require to be repeated, He is set down for ever on the right hand of the Majesty on high. Is He not a great High Priest, who has done what numberless priests, divinely appointed, had by numberless sacrifices, during a long course of ages, been attempting in vain? This proclaims: He has finished transgression; He has made an end of sin; He has brought in everlasting righteousness; His blood cleanses from all sin. He has, by His one offering, perfected for ever all them who are sanctified. He is set forth a propitiation in His blood. God is just, and the justifier of the ungodly believing in Jesus. God is in Christ reconciling the world to Himself, not imputing to them their trespasses; seeing He hath made Him who knew no sin to be sin for us, that we might be made the righteousness of God in Him. Who shall lay anything to the charge of God's elect? It is Christ that died, yea, rather, that is risen again, who is even at the right hand of God.

If the consideration of what led to our High Priest passing through those heavens places in a strong light His greatness as a High Priest, the consideration of what this passing through the heavens led to, gives additional evidence of the same truth. It led to His receiving from His Father power over all flesh,—all power in heaven and in earth. Jehovah said to Him, Sit on My right hand, till I make Thine enemies Thy footstool. The Lord sware, and He will not repent, Thou art a Priest for ever, after the order of Melchisedec. There, then, sits our High Priest, a Priest on His throne—the regal and sacerdotal dignities gloriously harmonized in Him—a covenant of peace between them both—having the government of the universe committed to Him, external event and inward influence being equally under His control, coming and going at His bidding. He is able to save to the uttermost all coming to God by Him. Nothing without them, nothing within them, can withstand His saving omnipotence. Having made His soul an offering for sin, He sees His seed, He prolongs His days, and the pleasure of the Lord prospers in His hand. He sees of the travail of His soul, and is satisfied. The righteous Servant of Jehovah, the great High Priest, justifies many through the knowledge of Himself, having borne their iniquities. All this is the result of His successful discharge of the functions of high-priesthood. It is all because He poured out His soul unto death, and was numbered among the transgressors, and bare the sins of many. Such is the result of Jesus our High Priest passing into the heavens; and is He not then a great High Priest, every way qualified for the work of a high priest—to bring men to God, to His favour, image, fellowship, and enjoyment?

IV. I proceed to the illustration of the fourth statement. 'Jesus Christ, our High Priest, is a compassionate High Priest.' In Christ Jesus, our great High Priest, who has passed into the heavens, " we have not a High Priest who cannot be touched with the feeling of our infirmities; but we have a High Priest who was in all points tempted like as we are, yet without sin," and who therefore can be touched with the feeling of our infirmities. After explaining these words, I will shortly illustrate the sentiment they convey, and then proceed to the illustration of the exhortations founded on the statements.

"Our infirmities," is a term expressive generally of our weaknesses and afflictions. The Apostle explains his declaration, "I will glory in my infirmities,"—I take pleasure in infirmities,—*i.e.*, " in reproaches, in necessities, in persecutions, in distresses."

To have a fellow-feeling with, or to sympathize in our infirmities, is to compassionate us while suffering under these weaknesses and afflictions,—so to compassionate us, as he only can who has himself sustained similar weaknesses and afflictions. Sympathy is a law of our nature: when we see our fellow-creatures in distress, we are affected with a feeling similar to theirs. The foundation of this feeling lies in the possession of a common nature; and its proximate cause seems to be the excitement of those feelings which we have experienced, or know that we should experience, placed in similar circumstances with the sufferer. A benevolent being, incapable of suffering, may, must pity sufferers, but cannot, in the strict sense of the word, sympathize with them.

Our High Priest can sympathize with us; for He is a man— a suffering man. He is not a holy angel, who has never experienced weakness or pain. He is not merely a Divine Being, who is, because merely divine, essentially impassible. While He is the Word who is God, He is " the Word made flesh;" while " God's own Son," He is " the man Christ Jesus." " Forasmuch as the children were partakers of flesh and blood, He also Himself likewise took part of the same." And He not only, in consequence of His incarnation, became capable of suffering —suffering as men suffer; but He has actually suffered—suffered as men suffer. " We have not a High Priest who cannot be touched with the feeling of our infirmities; but," on the contrary, we have a High Priest who " was in all points tempted like as we are," and therefore *can* be touched with the feeling of our infirmities.

Our High Priest " was tempted;" that is, He was tried. The strength and steadiness of His loyal regard to the divine honour, as connected with the execution of the great work committed to Him, were subjected to numerous, varied, severe, searching tests. He experienced in an unparalleled degree "the ills that flesh is heir to;" and they were all to Him, as they are to us, trials; so that He could sympathize with us in them both as sufferings and as trials. He knows from experience what bodily uneasiness, fatigue, pain, agony are; and knows, too, all that man can suffer from grief, sorrow, shame, fear, disappointment, and regret.

He was tempted " in all things"—in every point. He was exposed to trials suited to all the various principles of human nature; so that, wherever the test of affliction was applicable, it was applied. With the single exception of the misery necessarily connected with remorse and depraved feeling, there is no kind of suffering of which He was not participant.

He was thus tried " like unto us." The precise force of this expression, which, literally rendered, is, " according to likeness," is not very easily determined. It may signify, what our translators obviously understood by it, ' In every way in which we are tried He has been tried;' or it may signify, He was tried in all things in a conformity to the likeness of His nature and circumstances to ours. That conformity was extensive, but it was not complete. He was made in the *likeness* of sinful flesh—He was made flesh; but He was not made sinful flesh. He was tried in all things, so far as His conformity to us admitted. To all trials, except those which are inseparably connected with present guilt and depravity, He was exposed. The general meaning is plain—' being assimilated to us in all manner of trials.'

The qualifying words, " yet without sin," may be variously understood. They may either indicate that His trials did not *originate*, as all ours do, in our personal sin; or that they did not *lead* to sin in Him, as they always, in some degree or other, do in us. Both are truths. We are sufferers, because we are personally sinners. He, though the greatest of sufferers, was completely free from personal fault and depravity. He suffered for sins, but not for His own sins. " Messiah was cut off, but not for Himself." He was " holy, harmless, undefiled, separate from sinners." If He had had sins of His own to expiate, He never could have expiated ours. As our trials originate in our sins, so none of them are undergone by us without discovering that we are morally imperfect—that we are depraved beings. There is always something wanting—something wrong. Our trials, even when they are ultimately salutary and sanctifying, bring out our deficiencies and faults. It was otherwise with our High Priest. He could say to Him who tried Him, the Holy, Holy, Holy One, the Searcher of the hearts, the Trier of the reins, what the holiest mere man never durst say,—" Thou hast proved My heart; Thou hast visited Me in the night; Thou hast tried Me, and shalt find nothing in Me." When the tempter comes to us, he finds something of his own in us on which to practise; and his temptations, in consequence of being imperfectly resisted, even when not entirely complied with, seldom leave us without our contracting additional guilt,—a strong reason why we should avoid unnecessary trials, and earnestly present the petition, Lord, lead us not into temptation.

There is something peculiar in the language of the Apostle in describing the compassion, the sympathy of the Saviour, in the passage before us. He is " not a High Priest who cannot be touched with the feeling of our infirmities." We should have expected him to say, We have a High Priest who can be touched, or who is touched, with the feeling of our infirmities. There must be a reason for his adopting so strange a circumlocution; and I do not think we have far to seek for it. In the preceding verse he had represented our Lord as a *great* High Priest—both essentially and officially great—the Son of God; and as having " passed through these heavens" into the heaven of heavens. The thought would naturally occur: Such a High Priest cannot be touched with the feeling of our infirmities. He is too high above us to enter into our perplexities, and fears, and sorrows. No, says the Apostle; this High Priest, notwithstanding all His essential and official grandeur, is not incapable of sympathizing with you, for in His assumed nature on earth He was in all things tempted like as ye are; and though unlike you in this, that before trial, under trial, after trial, He was without sin, this no more than His essential and mediatorial greatness interferes with His capacity of thoroughly sympathizing with you under all your infirmities.

His sympathy is not impaired by His divine perfection, nor by His glorified state. His divinity, which did not hinder Him, when on the earth, from suffering, cannot, now that He is in heaven, interfere with the capacity and exercise of the sympathy growing out of these sufferings. His exaltation to the right hand of God has not made Him less a man than He was on the earth. The same human heart beats in the bosom of Him who reigns in heaven, as in Him who on earth shed tears at Lazarus' grave, and as He drew near to Jerusalem. "His compassion is the same essentially as it ever was. A change has taken place in its degree and mode of exercise. Everything that was painful in it, as felt by Him in the days of His flesh, is now removed. He no longer groans and weeps; but He retains a lively recollection of all He suffered on earth, and of the manner in which He was affected by it, which, acting on the essential principles of His humanity, prompts Him to exert His boundless mercy and power in supporting, and relieving, and comforting His afflicted people."[1]

Nor does our Lord's entire freedom from sin make Him " a High Priest who cannot be touched with the infirmities" of His people. It is finely remarked by the writer quoted above, that " the consciousness of their own moral infirmity, or liability to sin, was fitted to make the priests under the law, and should make the ministers of the Gospel still, tender in their dealings with fellow-sinners, ' considering themselves, lest they also be tempted.' Yet sin dwelling in any man is itself an evil; and in proportion as it prevails, instead of helping, hurts the exercise of compassion, as well as of every other good disposition, rendering him less qualified for discharging his duties to others. From this sinful infirmity our Lord was perfectly free; yet being made sensible of its power over us, by His having felt all the natural infirmities which in us are connected with sin, and by which we are often drawn into its commission, He is perfectly qualified for sympathizing, not indeed with the sin, but with the weakness which gives occasion to, and, in our case, yields to the temptation." " As a person who successfully resists the violence which may be used to draw him from the king's highway, knows the strength of the assailant better than one who yields, with little or no resistance, so Christ knows the force of temptation, which He uniformly resisted, better than we who but too easily comply with it."

From these illustrations of the words in which the Apostle asserts the sympathy of the Redeemer, it appears that his sentiment may be thus expressed: 'The divine nature, the media-

[1] M'Crie.

torial glory, and the absolute sinlessness of Jesus Christ, while they fit Him to perform for us the great functions of effectual atonement and intercession, in no degree prevent His tender sympathy with His people—His being to them "a merciful and faithful High Priest in things pertaining to God;" for "in the days of His flesh" "He suffered, being tempted, so that He is able to succour them who are tempted." "He was in all things tempted like as we are," so that He is not—as might be supposed, from thinking merely of His absolute sinlessness and His divine and mediatorial glories—a High Priest who cannot be touched with the feeling of our infirmities; but even more than the Jewish priests, who were compassed with moral infirmities, as well as those for whose benefit they performed the priestly functions, He can have compassion on the ignorant, and them that are out of the way.' It is plain that, while this is the direct force of the statement, it seems intended also to suggest the idea, that our High Priest is not only not a High Priest who cannot be touched with the feeling of our infirmities—who *can* be touched, but also that He *is* touched, that He *cannot but be* touched, with them.

How full of comfort to the people of Christ—"compassed about as they are with infirmity," liable to suffering in such a variety of forms—is this consideration that they are sure of their Saviour's sympathy in them all! Are they in languor, debility, pain, agony? He who sat by the well of Sychar, weary and way-worn—He who felt the pain of the scourge, and the deeper agony of the cross—comprehends all they feel, pities them, and can and will give them the necessary support. Are they poor, and do they find it difficult to meet the demands made on them? He who had not where to lay His head, and, when the tax-gatherers came to Him, had nothing to meet their demands —He sympathizes with their honest anxiety, and, though He may not send the needed supply in a fish's mouth, can and will give the needed relief. Are they mourning the death of valued relatives and friends? He who wept at the grave of Lazarus— He who had pity on the bereaved widow of Nain—feels for them, and will comfort them. Are they pained by the unkind conduct of living friends? He whose relations did not believe in Him, whom one disciple betrayed and another denied, and whose best friends deserted Him in the hour of trial,—He has a fellow-feeling with this affliction, and will prove Himself "a friend that sticketh closer than a brother." Are they persecuted and reproached for righteousness' sake? He who for the sake of His Father's honour and their salvation bore reproach, and was persecuted even unto death, cannot but take a deep interest in those who suffer in the same cause; and they cannot take a more ready way to prevent their being "weary and faint in their minds," than "considering Him who endured such contradiction of sinners against Himself," and realizing His promised presence, sympathy, and relief. Are they suffering from the temptations of the wicked one? He who experienced the hour and power of darkness "will not suffer them to be tempted above what they are able to bear"—He will pray for them, that their faith fail not.

"He knows what sore temptations are,
For He has felt the same."

Are they weighed down with a sense of guilt, oppressed with a feeling of the loathsomeness of sin? Though He never knew remorse—for He always, in thought and feeling, language and action, was entirely conformed to the will of God; though He never knew what it is to say, "Wretched man that I am, who will deliver me from this body of death?"—for sin never dwelt in Him, never found entrance into Him;—yet none know as He knows the demerit and the hatefulness of sin; and none can understand as He does how a sense of these pains weigh down the heart; and none but He, in His atoning blood sprinkled on the conscience, and by His purifying Spirit shed forth abundantly on the heart, can give the needed relief. Are they deprived of divine consolations, and going mourning as those without the sun? He who agonized in Gethsemane—He who on the cross uttered the bitter cry, "My God, My God, why hast Thou forsaken Me?"—He can understand, what their friends can only very imperfectly do in many cases,—He can understand their sorrows, and, touched with compassion, will give seasonable comfort and deliverance. Are they, through fear of death, subject to bondage? He whose human sensibilities would have led Him to say, "Father, save Me from this hour," can pity and remove these distressful feelings. Finally, are they in the article of death? There no mortal friend can help, no mortal friend can fully sympathize with them. He, the First and Last and Living

THE CHRISTIAN'S PRIVILEGE AND DUTY. 295

One, became dead—died that, among other and higher ends, this might be gained, that He should be able to sympathize with His people when dying. He knows the great secret of what it is to die; and His compassionate heart moves His powerful arm to give His dying people all the needed help in that peculiarly trying hour. When heart and flesh faint and fail, when no man hath power over the spirit to retain the spirit; but when, naked and alone, so far as earthly friends are concerned, it must wend its mysterious course to Him who gave it,—even then, moved by sympathy, He is with them, and they find they are not alone— the Saviour is with them.

Surely, then, the Christian, amid all his trials, may, ought to make this his song in the house of his pilgrimage:—

> "Where high the heavenly temple stands,
> The house of God not made with hands,
> A great High Priest our nature wears,
> The guardian of mankind appears.
>
> "Though now ascended up on high,
> He bends on earth a brother's eye;
> Partaker of the human name,
> He knows the frailty of our frame.
>
> "Our fellow-sufferer yet retains
> A fellow-feeling of our pains;
> And still remembers in the skies
> His tears, His agonies, and cries.
>
> "In every pang that rends the heart,
> The Man of Sorrows had a part;
> He sympathizes with our grief,
> And to the sufferer sends relief."

Now for the application of these glorious truths:

> "When gathering clouds around I view,
> And days are dark, and friends are few,
> On Him I lean, who not in vain
> Experienced every human pain.
> He sees my wants, allays my fears,
> And counts and treasures up my tears;
>
> "If aught should tempt my soul to stray,
> From heavenly wisdom's narrow way,—
> To flee the good I would pursue,
> Or do the ill I would not do,—
> He, who has felt temptation's power,
> Will guard me in that dangerous hour.

"If wounded love my bosom swell,
  Deceived by those I priz'd too well,
  He shall His pitying aid bestow,
  Who felt on earth severer woe;—
  At once betray'd, denied, and fled
  By those who shared His daily bread.

"When vexing thoughts within me rise,
  And sore dismay'd my spirit dies,—
  Then He, who once vouchsafed to bear
  The burden of our guilt and care,
  Shall sweetly soothe, shall gently dry,
  The throbbing heart, the streaming eye.

"When mourning o'er some stone I bend,
  Which covers all that was a friend,
  And from his hand, his voice, his smile,
  Divides me for a little while,—
  My Saviour marks the tears I shed,
  For 'Jesus wept' o'er Laz'rus dead.

"And when I shall have safely passed
  Through every conflict but the last,
  Th' unchanging Friend will watch beside
  My dying bed, for He has died;
  Then point to realms of cloudless day,
  And wipe the latest tear away."

So much for the illustration of the Apostle's fourth statement, that in Jesus Christ we have a compassionate High Priest.

Having thus considered the Apostle's fourfold statement, let us now turn our attention to the double exhortation he grounds on it. "Let us hold fast our profession;" and, "let us come boldly to the throne of grace, that we may obtain mercy, and find grace to help in time of need."

I. The first exhortation the Apostle gives is, "Let us hold fast our profession." "Our profession" is a phrase equivalent to—'our acknowledgment.' "The High Priest of our profession" is 'the High Priest whom we have acknowledged;' and the profession or acknowledgment here referred to, is our profession or acknowledgment with regard to *Him*. Now, what is our profession with regard to Him? It is just that contained in the Apostle's statement: 'We *have* a High Priest, as we as sinners deeply need one; Jesus Christ is our High Priest; He is a great High Priest—essentially great, officially great; and He is a compassionate High Priest.' This is what we profess to believe.

Now, to "hold fast" this profession includes two things: the holding fast, the continuing stedfast in, the *faith* of what we profess; and the holding fast, or persevering in *professing* this faith—publicly acknowledging it as our faith.

Christians should continue in *the faith* of what they have acknowledged respecting Christ Jesus. They should hold fast their acknowledgment. It must not be let go. It must not be lost sight of. We must habitually keep it before our minds, and keep it before our minds as the truth—the truth which we have acknowledged. The great reason why we should do so is, that it *is* the truth most sure. What we profess about our High Priest is the testimony of God, who cannot lie. When we received it, we "set to our seal that God is true." We cannot let it go without calling Him a liar. While this is the primary reason for holding fast the truth we have professed in reference to our High Priest, another very powerful reason is, that it is only in holding fast this truth that we can enjoy the advantages connected with Jesus being our High Priest. All the saving results of His high-priesthood come to us through the belief of the truth. Pardon, justification, free access to God, sanctification, support under trials, consolation amid afflictions, all come to us through faith, and are enjoyed by us as believers, and according to our faith. Hence the great weight which the inspired writers place on faith—true faith, persevering faith.

But to hold fast our profession refers not merely to the holding fast the *truth* professed, but to the holding fast the *profession* of that truth. Some might be disposed to say, It is quite right we should hold fast the truth, but may we not "hold it to ourselves before God," and shield ourselves from the evils to which we are sure to expose ourselves by an open profession of it? No, says the Apostle; we have professed this truth; we have openly avowed that this is our profession; and we must persevere in this open avowal. Faith in the heart is the first thing; confession with the mouth, the second. Both are required to make a consistent Christian. The profession referred to includes in it not only the acknowledgment made by connecting ourselves with the Christian community, and observing the ordinances of Christ, but also the giving expression to our inward convictions on every proper occasion to our fellow-men, and the exhibiting, in the entire conformity of our temper and behaviour to the law of our Lord, that our profession is an honest one. We must not be "ashamed of the testimony of our Lord Jesus," which we have made our profession.

A regard to Him, a regard to ourselves, a regard to our fellow-men, all require this at our hand. Is our High Priest not worthy to be acknowledged? Have we any cause to be ashamed of Him? Has He not required us to acknowledge Him in terms as explicit as He has required us to believe in Him? Is not confession with the mouth to salvation conjoined with faith of the heart to right conversion? And is not our interest deeply involved in this matter? Has He not told us what will be the result of our not being ashamed of Him, and of our being ashamed of Him, in that day when He appears in the glory of His Father, in His own glory, and in the glory of the holy angels? It is the honest, open, consistent professor of the truth as it is in Jesus that has the promise of the crown of righteousness at last, and who only, in the very nature of the case, can have the joys and consolations which even here are bestowed on those who hold fast what they have received. And, still further, this holding fast the profession of our faith is the way of our doing good to our fellow-men;—to our fellow-Christians, by strengthening and comforting them; to our unbelieving fellow-men, by holding forth to them the word of truth, by the knowledge and faith of which alone they can be saved.

We have but to look into the Apostle's statements to find abundant reason why we should comply with his exhortation. If it be indeed so, that we have a High Priest—that Jesus Christ is our High Priest, and is such a High Priest as becomes us, as we absolutely need, as completely suits our circumstances as guilty, depraved, weak, helpless creatures—a High Priest so great, a High Priest so compassionate,—surely, having acknowledged Him as such on abundant evidence, we should hold fast the truth acknowledged, and hold fast, too, the acknowledgment of the truth. Where can we find a substitute for Him? Who can be compared to Him? Where shall we find expiation, forgiveness, acceptance, sanctification, comfort, eternal life, but in Him? What is there that we want, that is not to be found in

Him? And can the universe of being do for us what He has done, what He is doing, for us? What blood but the blood of our High Priest's sacrifice can cleanse us from all, from any sin? And who but HE, who ever lives to make intercession for us, can be able to save us—as we need to be saved—to the uttermost, and for ever? Does He not deserve to be clung to by persevering faith? Does He not deserve to be honoured in persevering public acknowledgment?

II. The Apostle's second exhortation is, "Let us come boldly to the throne of grace, that we may obtain mercy, and find grace to help in the time of need." The language and the imagery, here, exactly correspond to the view the Apostle has been giving us of Jesus Christ as the High Priest of our profession. They are borrowed from the most sacred and recondite portion of the Old Testament worship. In the expression, "the throne of grace," there is without doubt an allusion to the mercy-seat in the holy of holies, over which the Shechinah, or cloud of glory —the emblem of the divine presence—occasionally, if not constantly, hovered, and which therefore might with propriety be represented as the throne of Jehovah, who dwelt between the cherubim.

The question of greatest importance here is, What is that which, under the new economy, answers to the mercy-seat under the old dispensation, which was a figure of good things to come? What is that throne of grace to which the Hebrew Christians are exhorted to come boldly? Some consider the mercy-seat as emblematical of our Lord Jesus Christ, grounding their opinion chiefly on what the Apostle says, Rom. iii. 25: "Whom"—that is, Jesus Christ—"He hath set forth to be a propitiation;" or, as they would render it, 'propitiatory or mercy-seat.' There is no doubt that it is the same word which is rightly rendered 'mercy-seat' in the 5th verse of the 10th chapter of this Epistle; but in the passage in the Romans there can be little doubt that the word refers to a propitiatory victim or sacrifice, and not to the sacred gold-covered chest, on which the blood of the sacrifice of atonement for the congregation was sprinkled; and it obviously better suits the whole connected system of emblems, to consider the whole of the mystic furniture of the holy of holies—the Shechinah hovering over the ark of the covenant containing the law, sprinkled with atoning blood—as a figurative representation of the Divine Being, the Righteous Governor, propitiated by sacrifice.

It is common in our own language, as well as in that in which this Epistle was originally written, to speak of a monarch under the name of things which are characteristic of his royal dignity. We speak of the prerogatives of the crown, and of addressing the throne, when we mean the distinguished individual who wears the crown and sits on the throne. In like manner, the throne of grace is a figurative expression for God, as seated on a throne of grace, dispensing pardon and all saving blessings to sinners—the God of Peace, the pacified Divinity, who was angry, but whose anger is turned away; God in Christ reconciling the world to Himself, not imputing to men their trespasses, seeing He has made Him who knew no sin to be sin for us, that we might be made the righteousness of God in Him; for, as the Apostle expresses it in his Epistle to the Ephesians, chap. iii. 12, it is "in," or by, "Christ Jesus that we have boldness and access—that is, to God—in the faith of Him."

To this propitiated Divinity the inspired writer exhorts the believing Hebrews to "come"—to draw near. It is plain that this expression is figurative, denoting mental, not local movement. To draw near to the propitiated Divinity, as seated on His throne of grace, is, in the firm faith of the truth respecting His reconciled character, and in the exercise of those affections which the belief of this truth naturally excites, to render Him religious homage—to present the desires of our heart before Him.

When Christians thus worship the reconciled Divinity, they are to do it "boldly;" that is, not with the trembling apprehension with which the Israelites approached, not *to*, but towards the mercy-seat, who, when their high priest, having offered a sacrifice of atonement for their souls, had entered in their name within the vail, to present and sprinkle the blood of the sacrifice there, were ignorant what might be the event—whether the sacrifice would be accepted or rejected,—but with a holy reverential confidence, arising from the assurance that our High Priest, having completed His one infinitely valuable and availing sacrifice on the earth, has passed through these heavens into the heaven of heavens, with the blood which cleanseth from all sin, and, ever living there to make intercession for us, is able to save us to the uttermost, coming to God by Him. Boldness is not here opposed to reverence, but to slavish apprehension and appalling terror, which estrange men from God.

The object of our coming thus boldly, like cherished children, to Jehovah propitiated in Christ, is, "that we may obtain mercy, and find grace to help in time of need." The words mercy and grace seem nearly synonymous; and so do the two phrases, to "obtain mercy," and to "find grace." Both of the words are primarily expressive of the principle of benignity in the divine mind: the first, in its exercise to us as miserable; the second, in its exercise to us as undeserving. But here, as in many other places, they, by a common figure of speech, are used to denote the manifestations of this principle. To obtain mercy, to find grace, is to receive manifestations of God's mercy to us as miserable, and of His grace towards us as undeserving—to receive proofs that God is our loving Father, our eternal Friend, who for His own sake, for His name's sake, for His Son's sake, will supply all our need. And those proofs are afforded by Him in answer to our believing prayers, in his conferring upon us such assistance as is needful for us in the time of trial, to enable us to hold fast our profession. The words literally are, "that we may obtain mercy, and find grace for seasonable help." The direct reference here is not, as ordinarily supposed, to pardon of sin—though we are to be ever coming to the throne of grace for that blessing, of which we are ever in need —but to those kind assistances of the good Spirit which are requisite amid the trials of life, to enable us to hold fast our profession.

This exhortation is plainly based on the statements which precede it. We were at variance with God. As the righteous Judge, He had condemned us. But a High Priest, a great High Priest, the Son of God, has interposed in our behalf. He has given Himself a sacrifice for us; and as a token that that sacrifice has been accepted, He has passed through these heavens into the heaven of heavens, and is there a Priest on His throne. This High Priest is as gracious as He is great; and notwithstanding His divine and mediatorial glories, notwithstanding our sinfulness and His sinlessness, He is, both physically and morally, capable of such sympathy with us in all our infirmities, as to secure that His unbounded powers of supplying our need shall be put forth at the right time, for the supply of all our wants, in the best and kindest way. The way into the holiest is made manifest; and why should not the believer by faith enter in and approach the throne of mercy? Why should he hesitate? Why should he fear? Having *such* a High Priest—having acknowledged Him as our High Priest —should we not hold fast our profession? And that we may hold fast our profession, should we not be constantly, in the exercise of faith in the truth, going to our Father and God, that we may obtain from Him, for the sake of our great High Priest, everything that is necessary to secure our holding fast our profession?

DISCOURSE II.

CHRIST, THE AUTHOR OF ETERNAL SALVATION, MADE PERFECT
BY SUFFERING IN THE DAYS OF HIS FLESH.

Heb. v. 7–9. "Who in the days of His flesh, when He had offered up prayers and supplications, with strong crying and tears, unto Him that was able to save Him from death, and was heard in that He feared: though He were a Son, yet learned He obedience by the things which He suffered; and being made perfect, He became the Author of eternal salvation unto all them that obey Him."

In reading, we must have often found that nothing is of greater importance towards the right understanding of an author's particular statements, illustrations, and arguments, than a distinct apprehension of his general object. Without this, the most accurate statements may seem incorrect, the most apposite illustrations irrelevant, and the most cogent arguments inconclusive. For example, there is no understanding the meaning of the passage which I have read as my text, unless we perceive the design the Apostle had in writing it. Happily, it is not difficult to discern that design; and in apprehending it, we may find the key which unlocks the precious treasures which this somewhat difficult passage contains.

Those words form part of the Apostle's demonstration of the superiority of the priesthood of our Lord Jesus Christ to that of Aaron and his sons. He introduces the subject by asserting the fact, that in Christ Jesus we Christians have a High Priest; a great High Priest—essentially great, for He is the Son of God; officially great, for He has passed through these heavens into the true holy place, the heaven of heavens; and a compassionate High Priest—one who can be, who is, who cannot but be, touched with the feeling of our infirmities—having been tempted like unto us in all things, yet without sin. Having asserted this fact, he has proceeded to produce the evidence that Jesus Christ is a High Priest—such a High Priest. As a necessary preliminary, he has given a concise but comprehensive description of what a high priest is: 'A man divinely selected and ordained to manage the religious concerns of his fellow-men, by offering in their stead, and for their benefit, gifts and sacrifices for sin;' and on the basis of this description, he proceeds to prove that Jesus Christ is a Priest, having been divinely selected and ordained to the priesthood, and having successfully performed its functions. The substance of his first argument is this: He did not take this honour to Himself, He was called of God as was Aaron; He did not glorify Himself in making Himself a High Priest, but *He* who in one ancient oracle had said to Him, "Thou art My Son, this day I have begotten Thee," had said to Him in another ancient oracle, "Thou art a Priest for ever, after the order of Melchisedec."

The three verses now before us form the second branch of the evidence of the reality of our Lord's priesthood. As He has been divinely appointed to the office, so He has successfully performed its functions. At first view the words may not seem very distinctly, if at all, to convey this idea. But if we will but examine them with sufficient care, it will become clear that this is their meaning.

These three verses form one long and complicated sentence. To the right interpretation of such a sentence, the first step is its right construction. A distinct apprehension of what is the main body of the sentence, and what are the members attached to it,—or, to vary the figure, what is the trunk, and what are the branches which grow out of it,—often goes far to make a sentence perspicuous which at first view appears obscure or even unintelligible. The leading idea becomes distinctly marked, and the subsidiary ones are seen in their relation to their principal.

The body of this sentence—expressing the great leading idea, that Jesus Christ has successfully performed the functions of the high-priesthood to which He has been divinely appointed—is to be found in these words, "He learned obedience by the things which He suffered, and is become the Author of eternal salvation to all who obey Him." He has done what He, as a High Priest, was appointed to do; He has obtained what, as a High Priest, He was appointed to obtain. The other clauses are, all of them, expressive of subsidiary ideas, defining and qualifying the primary ones. The body of the sentence divides itself into two parts: "He, as a High Priest, learned obedience by the things which He suffered;" and, "He, as a High Priest, is become the Author of eternal salvation to all who obey Him." The three clauses, "In the days of His flesh;" "when He had offered, or, having offered, up prayers and supplications, with strong crying and tears, and was heard in that He feared;" and, "though He were a Son," qualify the first statement, " He learned obedience by the things which He suffered :" the first of them defining the term of His priestly obedience ; the second being illustrative of the nature and extent of those sufferings by which Christ, as a High Priest, learned obedience; and the third intimating that the dignity of His nature did not prevent in any degree the learning of all the obedience and the enduring of all the suffering which were required of Him as a High Priest. The clause, " being made perfect," qualifies the second part of the sentence, connecting it with the first, and showing how His "learning as a High Priest obedience by the things which He suffered"—which is just the same thing with His being, as "the Captain of salvation, made perfect through suffering" —led to His being the Author of eternal salvation to all who obey Him—the same thing with "bringing the many sons to glory."

If we have at all succeeded in resolving this considerably complicated sentence, it expresses this great thought : 'Jesus Christ has successfully performed for us the functions of a High Priest.' And it offers two very important and appropriate topics for our consideration. First, what He *did* as our High Priest ; and secondly, what He has *obtained* as a High Priest by doing this—His discharge, and His successful discharge, of the priestly functions. As to the first—He learned obedience by the things which He suffered ; He did this "in the days of His flesh." While doing so, He offered up prayers and supplications, with strong crying and tears, to Him who was able to save Him from death, and was heard in that He feared; and He *thus* learned obedience though He was a Son. As to the second, He was made perfect as a High Priest by thus learning obedience; and having been thus made perfect, He is become "the Author of eternal salvation to all who obey

Him." Such is the outline I will attempt to fill up in the remaining part of this discourse.

Let us first, then, consider the account contained in the text of what our Lord *did* as our High Priest: He "learned obedience by the things which He suffered." (1.) "He suffered;" and (2.) "He learned obedience by the things which He suffered."

First, "He suffered." And what were the things He suffered? We may rather ask, What were the things He did not suffer? What suffering, of which an innocent, holy man is capable, did the Saviour not endure? He was "the man who saw affliction by the rod of God's wrath"—"a man of sorrows, and acquainted with griefs." To borrow the words of an old divine: "If hunger and thirst, if revilings and contempt, if sorrows and agonies, if stripes and buffetings, if condemnation and crucifixion, be suffering, Jesus suffered. If the infirmities of our nature, if the weight of our sins, if the malice of man, if the machinations of Satan, if the hand of God could make him suffer, our Saviour suffered."

These sufferings He was subjected to as our High Priest. He stood in our place. He was appointed to offer sacrifice for our sins. He suffered, "the Just One in the room of the unjust." Being without sin, He was not personally liable to suffering at all. But "the Lord laid on Him the iniquity of us all." "Exaction was made" of the desert of our sins; "and He answered" to the exaction. "He bare our sins." "He was wounded for our transgressions; He was bruised for our iniquities; the chastisement of our peace was upon Him." These are the things which He suffered,—the multiplied, severe, varied, penal, vicarious sufferings which He endured.

Now, secondly, by these sufferings, it is said by the Apostle, our High Priest learned obedience. "He learned obedience by the things which He suffered." The meaning of these words is, I apprehend,—' In these sufferings He became practically acquainted with the full amount of that obedience which the divine law exacted from Him, as our divinely appointed high-priest,'—submission to these sufferings forming the great act of atoning sacrifice, to perform which was His primary duty as our High Priest.

The words have often, usually indeed, been otherwise interpreted; but this seems the only interpretation which equally suits the facts of the case, and the purpose for which the Apostle introduces the statement in the passage before us. It is readily admitted, that when it is said of a person, ' He learned obedience by the things which he suffered,' the thought naturally suggested by the words is that of a person, originally indisposed to obey, disciplined into obedience by a course of suffering rising out of his disobedience. But the language is, in this meaning, utterly inapplicable to the High Priest of our profession. He never disobeyed; there never was in His mind or heart the slightest bias towards disobedience, in the form of nascent error, or rising irregular desire. He never was in the way of disobedience, to be driven out of it by being made to feel that the way of transgressors is hard. It was as natural to Him to obey as it was to breathe.

Not more satisfactory is the mode of interpretation which makes " learned obedience by the things which He suffered" equivalent to—learned by sufferings how hard and difficult a thing obedience is, how painful it is to be entirely subject to the will of another. For it is our depravity, in the form of pride and desire of independence, which makes obedience a painful thing to us. These principles did not exist in His mind. What in itself was disagreeable, became to Him desirable, just because God had enjoined or appointed it. This sweetened to Him the bitterest cup; this lightened to Him the heaviest load. So far from obedience being to Him a difficult thing, as obedience, " it was His meat to do the will of His Father, and to finish His work." " To do Thy will I take delight," says He; " Thy law is within My heart;"—though He knew that that will was " the offering of His body once for all,"—that law, " that He should redeem men from the curse, by becoming a curse in their room." When the intensity of His sufferings suggested the question, " Shall I say, Father, save Me from this hour?" the reply was, " For this cause came I to this hour. Father, glorify Thy name."

To learn obedience, is to become practically acquainted with obedience,—to know what it is,—to experience the length and breadth of that obedience which He, as the Saviour of men, was required to yield in order to their redemption. When it is said of our Lord, that " He knew no sin," the meaning is not, that He did not know what is sin, or what sin is in its nature and desert. In both these senses, none ever knew sin as He did. But the meaning is, He was experimentally unacquainted with sin; He was an entire stranger to depraved principle and to guilty conduct. So, when it is said, He learned obedience, the meaning is not, that He did not before fully understand what was required of Him as our High Priest in order to the gaining of the great object of His appointment—the expiation of our sins; but, that it was by the means of the sufferings laid on Him in that character that He obtained an experimental knowledge of the obedience which was requisite for this purpose. He could *thus* learn this obedience in no other way. The commandment which our High Priest received from Him who appointed Him, was that He should lay down His life for the sheep; and He learned what obedience to that commandment was in the only way in which it could be learned, by His becoming obedient to death, even to the death of the cross. The Jewish high priest could become practically acquainted with the duties of his office only by performing them; and so it was with the great High Priest of our profession. The law of the Levitical high priest was, that he should offer gifts and sacrifices for the sins of Israel; and he learned obedience in performing these functions. The law of our High Priest was, that He should offer Himself for us a sacrifice and an offering in our room; and it was not till that sacrifice was completed that He experimentally knew the full extent of the obedience required of Him.

The language seems to intimate two things: the docile spirit in which He thus gradually acquired an experimental acquaintance with obedience; and the absolute completeness of this experimental knowledge. He was a learner, seeking to know all. "The Lord opened His ear, and He was not rebellious; neither turned He away back." He was always ready, to use a familiar phrase, for the next lesson. "He gave His back to the smiters, and His cheeks to them who plucked off the hair: He hid not His face from shame and spitting." And He persevered in learning till there was no more to learn. Who of the sons of men knows experimentally the full extent of the precept of the divine law? Who knows the power of God's anger, as the penalty of that law? are questions which can be answered in the affirmative only of our High Priest. He knew the breadth of the divine law by perfectly obeying it. He knew the power of the displeasure of God against sin by enduring it. He knew what was necessary to finish transgression, make an end of sin, make reconciliation for iniquity. He continued learning obedience, so long as obedience was required, till, knowing in Himself that the things concerning Him had come to an end, He said, It is finished. The work was done; obedience had been completely learned. He had experienced the full demands of the divine law on Him, the High Priest and Surety of men, and fully met them all. The law was satisfied, atonement was made. He has no more to suffer—no more to learn. He was obedient unto death, the death of the cross.

This, then, is the grand statement in the first division of the text. The reality of our Lord's high-priesthood is proved not only by His divine appointment to that office, recorded in an ancient divine oracle, but by His actually performing its functions—becoming personally acquainted, by His sufferings, with every part of the obedience required of Him as our High Priest. This general statement is attended by three subsidiary clauses.

1. It was in *the days of His flesh* that He learned obedience by the things He suffered.

2. While learning obedience by the things He suffered, *He offered up prayers and supplications, with strong crying and tears, and was heard in that He feared.*

3. He thus learned obedience, *though He was a Son.*

Let us attend to these in their order.

1. It was in the days of His flesh that He thus suffered, and thus learned obedience by His sufferings. The word "flesh," and the phrase "flesh and blood," are often expressive just of human nature. "All flesh" is "all men;" "no flesh," no man. The Word was made flesh, means, The divine person called the Word became man. "Inasmuch as the children were partakers of flesh and blood"—*i.e.*, of human nature—"He also likewise took part of the same." The expressions are, however, sometimes used to signify human nature, with the superadded idea of that frailty and liability to death that belongs to it in its fallen state, when "*made* lower than the angels;" as, "He remembered that they were flesh," poor, weak, dying creatures—"a wind that passeth away and returns not again." "Flesh and blood"—*i.e.*, human nature

in its present frail, mortal state—"cannot inherit the kingdom of God, neither doth corruption inherit incorruption." In the former sense, the "days of our Lord's flesh" commenced with His incarnation, and will continue for ever; in the latter sense, they commenced at His incarnation, and terminated at His resurrection or ascension. There can be no doubt that it is in the latter sense that they are here to be understood. The days of our Lord's flesh are plainly contrasted with His present condition, as having been "made perfect, and the Author of eternal salvation to all who obey Him." During the whole of His humbled state, from Bethlehem to Calvary, from His cradle to His grave, "He learned obedience by the things which He suffered." He was always suffering—always learning obedience by His suffering. The whole of His humbled life was that one great continuous act of obedience to the will of God of the Second Adam, which is opposed by the Apostle to the one act of disobedience of the first Adam, that "brought death into the world, and all our woe." This is the great act of expiation, by which the sin of the world was taken away.

2. While, "in the days of His flesh," our High Priest learned obedience by that which He suffered, "He offered up prayers and supplications, with strong crying and tears, to Him who was able to save Him from death, and was heard in that He feared." From the manner in which the words are rendered in our version, it is natural to conclude that our Lord's learning obedience was something posterior to His offering up prayers and supplications, and being heard: 'When He had offered up—when He had been heard—He learned obedience.' This does not, however, appear to be the Apostle's meaning. He seems to intimate to us what was the fact, that the learning of obedience and the offering up of prayers were contemporaneous.

The word rendered "prayers," properly signifies, requests for support under, or deliverance from, evil already experienced; as, "Father, let this cup pass from Me." The word rendered "supplications," means prayers against evil viewed as impending; as, "Lead me not into temptation." These prayers of our Lord were offered up "with strong crying and tears;" they were expressive of keen sensibility and intense desire—they were urgent, importunate prayers.

These prayers, the utterance of His inmost soul and heart,

were presented to " Him who was able to save Him from death." They were addressed to God His Father, under the character of Him who was able—*i.e.*, who had at once a boundless capacity and disposition—to save Him from death, and who He knew would assuredly save Him from death. It is worthy of notice that our Lord's express words in one of these prayers are, " Abba, Father, all things are possible with Thee. Take away this cup from Me."

To "save from death" does not here seem to mean, to deliver from the necessity of dying. Death—death under the curse—was the ultimate term of that obedience which Jesus as our High Priest was learning by suffering. It was necessary to the gaining of the great object for which He had become a High Priest, it was necessary to the completion of the sacrifice of atonement He was appointed to offer, that He should be obedient to death—to the death of the cross. Any suffering, any obedience, short of this, would not have gained the end. No doubt, abstractly speaking, God, who is omnipotent, could have prevented His incarnate Son from dying; but He could not do so in consistency with the economy of human salvation. To save or deliver from death means, here, to deliver from the power of death,—after that power has been exerted, to deliver from the state of the dead. God manifested Himself as Him who is able to save from death, when, as the God of peace—the reconciled Divinity, whose law had been magnified, whose justice had been satisfied, in the obedience completed on the cross—" He brought again from the dead our Lord Jesus, that great Shepherd of the sheep, by the blood of the everlasting covenant."

It has been common to consider the Apostle, in these words, as referring entirely to the "prayers and supplications" offered up by our Lord in the immediate prospect, and in the midst, of His last sufferings. I do not see any satisfactory reason for such a restriction. "The days of His flesh" include more than the hours of agony in Gethsemane, or of torture on the cross: they include the entire period of His humbled life. As the pressure of human guilt habitually weighed down His spirits, so His love to, confidence in, His Father habitually led Him to pour out His heart into His bosom; so that He was at once a man of sorrows and a man of prayer. We read in one instance, that, after He had dismissed the multitude and His disciples, He retired, not to repose, but to devotion: "He went up into a mountain apart to pray." On another occasion we read, that "in the morning, rising up a great while before day, He went out and departed into a solitary place, and there prayed." On a third occasion, we find Him going out "into a mountain to pray, and continuing all night in prayer to God." And we are told that, after the observance of His last Passover, He went, as He was wont, to the Mount of Olives; and we know He then went there to offer up prayers and supplications, "with groans, and blood, and tears." According to the ancient oracle, "He cried in the day-time; and in the night season there was no silence for Him."

But although I see no reason for supposing that there is an exclusive reference here to what took place in the immediate prospect of His death, yet, at the same time, as His prayers then are more circumstantially recorded than those on any other occasion, as a specimen of His devotional exercises, they are strikingly illustrative of the declaration in the text, and in all probability were directly in the Apostle's view when He made it. "Now is My soul troubled, and what shall I say? Father, save Me from this hour? But for this cause came I unto this hour. Father, glorify Thy name." "Then cometh Jesus with them to a place called Gethsemane; and when He was at the place, He saith to His disciples, Sit ye here, while I go and pray yonder. And He took with Him Peter and the two sons of Zebedee, James and John, and began to be sorrowful, sore amazed, and very heavy. Then said He to them, My soul is exceeding sorrowful, even unto death. Tarry ye here and watch with Me. And He went forward a little, withdrawing from them about a stone's cast, kneeled down, and fell on His face on the ground, and prayed that, if it were possible, the hour might pass from Him. And He said, Abba, Father, all things are possible to Thee. O My Father, if it be possible, take away this cup, and let it pass from Me: nevertheless not what I will, but what Thou wilt. And He cometh to the disciples, and findeth them sleeping, and saith unto Peter, Simon, sleepest *thou?* couldest *thou* not watch one hour? Watch ye and pray, lest ye enter into temptation. The spirit truly is willing, but the flesh is weak. And again He went away the second time, and prayed and spake the same words, saying, O My Father, if this cup may not pass away from Me except I drink it, Thy will be done. And when He returned, He found them asleep again; for their eyes were heavy, neither wist they what to answer Him. And He left them and went away again, and prayed the third time, saying the same words: Father, if Thou be willing, remove this cup from Me: nevertheless not My will, but Thine be done. And there appeared an angel unto Him from heaven, strengthening Him. And being in an agony, He prayed more earnestly, and His sweat was, as it were, great drops of blood falling down to the ground." "About the ninth hour Jesus cried with a loud voice, saying, Eloi! Eloi! lama sabachthani? that is to say, being interpreted, My God! My God! why hast Thou forsaken Me?" Such were the prayers and supplications which our High Priest, when learning obedience by the things which He suffered, offered up in the days of His flesh, with strong crying and tears, to Him who was able to save Him from death.

Nor did He offer up those prayers in vain. "He was heard in that He feared." He was "heard"—all His supplications were ultimately answered. The sum of all He asked, was support under them while they continued, and deliverance from them when they had served their purpose. And both were granted. Even the prayer, "Let this cup pass from Me," which many interpreters, considering as referring to death, have represented as arising unheeded and unheard, received a gracious and speedy answer. "This cup" seems to refer to that intense mental agony which He at that moment experienced, and which threatened, if prolonged, to dissolve the connection between soul and body. That cup passed from Him, inasmuch as an angel was sent to comfort Him, and He regained composure to act with propriety before His judges, and to suffer with unshrinking firmness what He had yet to endure before He reached the appointed hour of dissolution. The whole history of our Lord's humbled life may be summed up in the words of the Psalmist: "This poor man cried, and the Lord heard him, and saved him out of all his troubles." His prayers for support under and deliverance from particular evils were heard, even in the days of His flesh; and all His prayers were fully answered when God brought Him from the dust of death, and crowned Him with glory and honour. Then "the Man of Sorrows," who had said, "O My God, I cry in the day-time, but Thou hearest not; and in the night season, and am not silent,"—exclaimed, "Thou hast heard Me: I will declare Thy name unto My brethren; in the midst of the congregation will I praise Thee. Ye that fear the Lord, praise Him; all ye the seed of Jacob, glorify Him; and fear Him, all ye the seed of Israel. For He hath not despised nor abhorred the affliction of the afflicted; neither hath He hid His face from Him; but, when He cried unto Him, He heard."

"He was heard in that He feared." This last clause, "in that He feared," has occasioned much trouble to expositors. Some have rendered it—'He was heard on account of His pious reverence for God;' as if in meaning it was equivalent to the oracle in Ps. xlv. 7: "Thou lovest righteousness, and hatest iniquity: *therefore* God, Thy God, hath anointed Thee with the oil of gladness above Thy fellows." There is no doubt that the words thus rendered convey a truth, and an important one; but I do not think that either the original words or the coherence of the thoughts will warrant us to consider it as the truth taught here. Others consider the expression, heard, as equivalent to—deliver, as in Job xxxv. 12: They cry, but none giveth answer, or heareth; *i.e.*, delivers. Ps. xxii. 21: Thou hast heard Me; *i.e.*, Thou hast delivered Me. Ps. cxviii. 5: The Lord answered, heard Me—*i.e.*, delivered Me—in a large place. In this case the clause would run: He was delivered from that which He feared—from His fear—from all those evils which, according to the constitution of His human nature, could not but be the object of aversion and fear; *i.e.*, from all suffering in every form, and in every degree. A third class, with our translators, consider the words as meaning, "was heard in reference to that which He feared"—had His prayers, for alleviation of, support under, and deliverance from, the evils to which He was exposed, completely answered.

It may be asked, What was the Apostle's object in connecting this statement with his leading assertion—that, by His sufferings, Christ, as our High Priest, became experimentally acquainted with the obedience He owed as the divinely appointed High Priest, or, in other words, fully performed all the functions of that office? Now, I think he had a threefold object: first, to mark the peculiar character of His obedience as pious obedience ; secondly, to indicate the severity of His sufferings, and the intensity of His desire that His work should be completed in the most perfect way ; and thirdly, to intimate that the sufferings were over, and the obedience perfected. The obedience was prayerful obedience. He set the Lord always before Him. "Lo, I come to do Thy will." When our High Priest, the God-man, obeyed, He did what God required—in the way God required it—depending on the promised divine assistance, and seeking it in the appointed way of prayer and supplication ; thus setting us an example, that we should follow His steps. The severity of the sufferings, and the intensity of His desire to have His work of obedience completed in the most perfect form, are also indicated in this subsidiary clause. No ordinary suffering could have produced in Him strong crying and tears. The work of our High Priest was no easy work. If the question be asked, Whence? The answer is: The expiation of our sin required a whole burnt-offering. The prayers and supplications were expressive of intense desire, as well as of severe suffering. They embody the same sentiment as the emphatic words : I have a baptism to be baptized with ; and how am I straitened till it be accomplished ! With desire have I desired to eat this Passover before I suffer. The clause referred to also intimates that the sufferings are over—the obedience is completed. He has been heard—He has nothing now which can be an object of fear. He has obtained His heart's desire, and the request of His lips has not been withholden from Him. It is finished. The will of God is fully done : no need for additional obedience or suffering ; suggesting the idea which, in the next clause, is expressed : He is made perfect. The days of His flesh are over. Frailty and mortality are left in the grave ; the body of His humiliation is superseded by the body of His glory.

There is still a third clause dependent on the Apostle's general statement—He learned obedience by the things which He suffered—which requires consideration ; and that is, " though He were a Son." " Though He were a Son, yet learned He obedience by the things which He suffered." These words look back to the declaration in the 14th verse of the preceding chapter : " We have a great High Priest, Jesus the Son of God." Son of God, as applied to Jesus Christ, intimates that He was a person of the same nature with His Father, intimately related to Him, dearly beloved by Him. Now, though this was the truth with regard to Him, yet, notwithstanding, by severe suffering, He became experimentally acquainted with the full amount of obedience He owed as the divinely appointed High Priest. The mention of our Lord's dignity is fitted to suggest the thought of the infinite efficacy of His priestly functions; but the direct purpose of the Apostle seems to have been to indicate that the divinity of His nature, and His infinite dearness to His divine Father, did not interfere with His fully meeting and discharging the obligations to do and suffer, which rose out of His being divinely appointed our High Priest. As they did not lead to sparing Him from suffering, they did not lead to sparing Him in suffering. "Though in the form of God," He "emptied Himself"—"took on Himself the form of a servant, humbled Himself, and became obedient to death, to the death of the cross." Though "the brightness of the Father's glory, and the express image of His person," He yet "purged our sins by Himself."

I may be permitted to remark in passing, that this is one of the many passages which prove that Son of God and Messiah, though appellations of the same person, are not convertible terms; and that the first of these expressions is often, indeed usually, the expression of an essential personal relation, not of an ordained official relation. Suppose that Son of God, here, were just equivalent to Messiah, or divinely appointed Saviour, and there is no point in the Apostle's remark. In that case we would have expected him to say, Because He was a Son, He learned obedience by the things which He suffered; not, Although He were a Son, yet learned He obedience by the things which He suffered. But considering Son of God as an appellation descriptive of identity of nature and equality of perfection with His divine Father, there is inexpressible energy in the remark: Though He was the fellow of Jehovah, He yet learned obedience by the things which He suffered. He did all and suffered all that was necessary to the full accomplishment of His duties as our divinely appointed High Priest, in offering gifts and sacrifices for sin.

Thus have we considered the account contained in the text of what our Lord *did* as our divinely appointed High Priest. During His humbled state, He became experimentally acquainted, by the severe sufferings which He endured, with the obedience required by His office, in offering sacrifice for sin; and, while acquiring this painful but necessary experimental knowledge, the severity of His sufferings, the intensity of His desire to accomplish His work, and the holiness of His character, were manifested in His habitual, earnest supplications—all which supplications were, as a token of His Father's approbation, heard and answered. The reality of His priesthood is thus proved by the discharge of its duties. It is further proved by the *successful* discharge of His duties. The second statement in the text refers to this. It informs us of what He has *obtained* by thus learning obedience by the things which He suffered:—" Being made perfect, He is become the Author of eternal salvation to all who obey Him." A few illustrative remarks on this part of the subject will form the conclusion of the discourse.

Allow us, in the meanwhile, to call on you to yield your minds to the impressions which the truths we have been considering are calculated to make on the heart; wondering at the condescension and kindness of the Son of God, our Divine Redeemer, in voluntarily becoming our High Priest, and cheerfully submitting to such degradation and suffering in order to the full discharge of the functions and attainment of the object of this office; penetrated with a deep sense of the malignity of sin, the expiation of which required such labours and sufferings on the part of one so great and excellent; rejoicing in the abundant evidence we have, that the Saviour's work has completely served the purpose for which it was intended—in the answer He has received to all the prayers and supplications offered up by Him during its performance; determined, by the promised help of His good Spirit, in our immeasurably inferior sphere, " to learn obedience by the things we suffer;" and in the midst of our labours and sufferings in the days of our flesh, seeking support and deliverance, in prayers and supplications, from Him who has saved Him from death, who is able to save us through Him from death—who has heard and answered all His prayers, and who for His sake will hear and answer ours, offered up in His name—delivering us, as He has delivered Him, from evil felt or feared, in every form, and for ever and ever.

Let me now turn your attention for a little to what your Lord, as your High Priest, has thus obtained both for Himself and you. "He has been made perfect," and has "become the Author of eternal salvation to all who obey Him."

"He has been made perfect:" this is what He has obtained for Himself. The perfection here spoken of, as well as in the parallel passage—" It became Him, for whom are all things, and by whom are all things, to make the Captain of our salvation perfect through sufferings "—does not refer to moral excellence, but to official qualification. In the first sense, the Captain of our salvation, the High Priest of our profession, was ever perfect—holy, harmless, undefiled, separate from sinners—without sin—knowing no sin—without imperfection or fault; He needed not to be perfected. In the second, from the very nature of the case, He did require to be perfected. There was merit, rising out of voluntary obedience to the precept, and submission to the penalty, of a law which man had broken, but to which the great High Priest was not naturally subject, necessary as the means of expiation, the ground of forgiveness; there was *authority*, to be bestowed as the reward of this merit, to warrant Him to bestow the blessings of salvation on mankind, who deserved nothing but punishment; and there was *sympathy*—the capacity of entering fully into the sufferings of those whom He was appointed to save. All these were necessary to His being an accomplished High Priest, a perfect Saviour. None of these belonged to the Son of God as a divine person; all of them had to be acquired by the God-man. He had thus to be made perfect. And it was by the obedience which He learned by the things that He suffered that He obtained these accomplishments—that He acquired this perfection. His obedience to the death is the price of our souls. He took on him our demerit, and suffered its legal effects; and He obtained for Himself such a fulness of merit, so magnified the law and made it honourable, that it became a righteous thing in God to treat as innocent—as righteous—the greatest sinner united to Him; so that God is just, and the justifier of him that believeth in Jesus. His obedience to the death in our room, as it obtained *merit* on the ground of which sinners might be pardoned, obtained for Him that power and authority in His official character which are necessary to this merit becoming availing to the salvation of men. It was because He finished the work given Him to do, that the Father gave Him all power in heaven and earth, that He might give eternal life to all whom He had given Him—exalted Him a Prince and Saviour, to give repentance and remission of sin. And, still further, it was by this obedience, which He learned by what He suffered, that our High Priest, the incarnate Son of God, became capable, both physically and morally—obtained both the capacity and disposition—to sympathize with those whom He was appointed to save in all their anxieties, fears, afflictions, and sorrows. It was necessary that He should be made like unto His brethren, that He might be a merciful and faithful High Priest. Had He not Himself suffered, being tempted, He could not, in the same way and degree, have been able to succour them who are tempted. But having been in all points tempted like as we are, yet without sin, He is not a High Priest who cannot be touched with the feeling of our infirmities. No; He is a High Priest who can be touched, who cannot but be touched, with the feeling of our infirmities. Thus did our High Priest, by the obedience which He learned by the things which He suffered, become an all-accomplished High Priest. He obtains all the merit, all the authority, all the sympathy, necessary to the gaining, in the most perfect manner, to the fullest extent, of the great ends for which He assumed the priestly office.

And being thus "made perfect, He is the Author of eternal salvation to all who obey Him." This is what He has obtained for you. Salvation is deliverance from sin and all its effects, including restoration to the divine favour, image, fellowship, and enjoyment—perfect, holy happiness.

The epithet *eternal* is emphatic. The Jewish high priest, when he had performed his functions in behalf of his countrymen in the due order—when, accomplished for his work, with his hands filled with the blood of the completed sacrifice and the sacred incense, he entered into the holy place made with hands—obtained for them a salvation, a deliverance from certain evils to which they were exposed, according to the principles of the peculiar economy under which they were placed. But that deliverance, as it was inferior in nature to that which our High Priest has accomplished, so it was temporary in its duration. The Jewish atonements could not remove moral guilt, and therefore could not secure permanent salvation. But Jesus Christ has secured a complete and never-ending deliverance from evil, in all its forms, and in all its degrees. The gift of God is eternal life, through Jesus Christ our Lord.

Of this eternal salvation our perfected High Priest is the Author. To be the Author of salvation, is, in the fullest sense of the word, to be the Saviour. He is the procurer and the bestower of salvation. It is He who, by His obedience unto death, has done all and suffered all that was necessary to make the salvation of men consistent with, and illustrative of, the perfections of the divine character, and the principles of the divine government; and it is He, too, who—in the dispensation of the Holy Spirit, and in the administration of the government of the world, obtained as the reward of this obedience—actually saves His people from guilt, depravity, and misery; actually makes them really holy and happy here, and will certainly make them perfectly holy and happy hereafter.

Our all-accomplished High Priest is thus "the Author of eternal salvation to all who obey Him." Obedience necessarily presupposes a revelation of the will of the person to be obeyed. I cannot obey Christ if I do not know the will of Christ. It not merely presupposes a revelation of the will of Christ, but a belief of that revelation. Without faith there cannot, in the nature of things, be anything that deserves the name of obedience. And where the revelation of the mind and will of Christ is really understood and believed, obedience to that will, according to the measure of faith, is the natural and uniform consequence. He then obeys Christ who, crediting God's testimony concerning Him, submits to be saved by Him in the way of His appointment, and, trusting to Him as the only Author of eternal salvation, acknowledges Him as his Lord and Master, who has bought him with His blood, and subdued him by His Spirit—pays a conscientious regard to His will, so far as he knows it, and seeks to walk in all His commandments and ordinances blameless.

To all persons of this description, and to persons of this description alone, will Jesus Christ ultimately prove the Author of eternal salvation. All, whether Jew or Gentile, however great their previous guilt and depravity, who thus obey Him, will be assuredly saved by Him. But there is, there can be no salvation through Christ to any man living and dying in impenitence, unbelief, and disobedience.

Those persons miserably misunderstand and abuse this passage, who consider it as forbidding the greatest sinner, believing the truth as it is in Jesus, to hope, and immediately to hope, for eternal salvation through Christ, and as making our sincere, but imperfect obedience to the will of Christ, in any degree the ground of our expectation of eternal life through Him. It merely characterizes the persons who are saved by Christ Jesus, and teaches that it is only in obeying Him, in believing the truth about Him, and in living under the influence of this faith, that we can enjoy that eternal salvation which He died to procure, and is exalted to bestow.

Such are the glorious results of our Lord, as our High Priest, learning obedience by the things which He suffered; and so direct and abundant is the evidence that we Christians are not destitute of a High Priest, but have in Christ Jesus, the Son of God, one who, taken from among men, has offered an all-efficacious sacrifice for sins, the blood of which, sprinkled on the conscience, cleanses from all sin, and the merit of which has opened up for Him the way into the holiest of all, where at the right hand of God, with all power in heaven and earth, He is able to save to the uttermost all coming to God through Him.

These views of the character and work of our great High Priest have not served their designed and appropriate purpose, if they do not send us away with hearts full of admiration, and love, and joy, and hope,—with entire confidence in the perfection of His sacrifice, the prevalence of His intercession, the power of His Spirit, the freeness and the fulness of His salvation,—with stronger yet humbler resolutions than ever, that, constantly looking to Him as the Author of our salvation, we shall, taught by His grace, "deny ungodliness and worldly lusts, and live soberly, and righteously, and godly; while we look for that blessed hope, the glorious appearing of the great God, our Saviour Jesus Christ, who gave Himself for us, that He might redeem us from all iniquity, and purify us to Himself, a peculiar people, zealous of good works." That they may do so, may the Father Himself, who loves us, shed forth on us abundantly the good Spirit, through Christ Jesus the Saviour. And to the Father, Son, and Holy Ghost, the one Jehovah and our God, be glory for ever and ever. Amen.

DISCOURSE III.

CHRIST'S CHARACTER AND MINISTRY AS A HIGH PRIEST.

HEB. IX. 11, 12.—"But Christ being come an High Priest of good things to come, by a greater and more perfect tabernacle, not made with hands, that is to say, not of this building; neither by the blood of goats and calves, but by His own blood, He entered in once into the holy place, having obtained eternal redemption for us."

THESE words naturally call our attention to two important topics. First, the official character with which our Lord is invested. He is come a High Priest of good things to come. And secondly, the ministry which He performs in that character. He obtains eternal redemption for His people; and having obtained eternal redemption for His people, He enters into the holy place; He enters in there through a greater and more perfect tabernacle; He enters in there, not by the blood of goats and of calves, but by His own blood; and He has thus entered in there once for all. This is the outline which I will endeavour to fill up in the sequel of the discourse.

I. Let us then, first, turn our attention for a little to the official character which our Lord is here represented as sustaining. "Christ being come a High Priest of good things to come." Our Saviour is spoken of by the Apostle, in this Epistle, under a great variety of appellations. Sometimes He is termed *Jesus*, sometimes *Christ*, sometimes *Jesus Christ*, sometimes *the Son*, sometimes *the Son of God*. These appellations are all of them significant. Each of them is descriptive of some aspect of the many-sided character and work of our Lord; and they are by no means used indiscriminately by the inspired writer. The attentive, well-informed reader will find little difficulty, in most cases, in discovering the reason why, in a particular place, one of these appellations is employed in preference to all the others. It is easy to do so in the case before us. *Christ*—or the Messiah, the Anointed One—describes our Lord as the great, divinely *appointed, qualified,* and *accredited* Saviour, promised to the fathers as a High Priest after the order of Melchisedec; and the sum of the declaration in the text is, The 'Messiah, in the person of Jesus, having come in the character in which He was promised, has done all that it was predicted He should do.'

The character in which our Lord came, according to the promises which went before concerning Him, was that of " the High Priest of good things to come." " Good things to come," here, is a description of that economy, dispensation, or order of things, under which Jesus Christ is the High Priest, viewed in contrast with the Mosaic law—the Jewish economy, under which Aaron and his sons were high priests. This economy receives the name of *things to come,* to mark its enduring nature, as— what is and is to come—in contrast with the Jewish economy, which had been, but was passed away; and *good* things to come, to characterize it as a salutary system,—an order of things, the great design of the establishment of which is the securing for, and communicating to men good things—blessings of the highest order, which well deserve the name of good things—better things than any preceding divine dispensation made provision for. The idea does not seem to be, as some interpreters suppose, that the best blessings of the economy under which Christ is the High Priest are future blessings, not to be enjoyed on earth, but laid up in heaven—not things of time, but things of eternity. This is no doubt an important and delightful truth; but here the Apostle seems to have in view the distinction which prevailed among the Jews as to the times before the Messiah, and the times under the Messiah. They spoke of the Messiah as " the Comer,"—He that should come; and of the state under Him as " the world to come." " Things to come," as opposed to things that are or have been, thus came naturally to be employed as a description of the state of things under the Messiah; and as the object of His mission was exclusively and in the highest degree salutary, this state of things was termed not only " things to come," but " good things to come." The Messiah was not to be *a* High Priest of the old covenant; He was to be *the* High Priest of the new covenant, which was to be an everlasting covenant, and transcendently good—the better covenant, established on better promises, or in reference to better promised blessings.

Of this covenant our Lord Jesus is *the* High Priest. He, He alone, is under this economy " ordained for men in things pertaining to God, that He may offer both gifts and sacrifices for sin." His sacrifice of Himself is the only sacrifice of expiation under this economy; and it is on the ground of this sacrifice, and through means of His intercession founded on this sacrifice, that all the transcendently good things, the heavenly and spiritual blessings of this economy, are conferred on men. The appellation, " the High Priest of good things to come," is, as to meaning, quite equivalent to that appellation repeatedly given to our Lord in other parts of this Epistle,—" the Mediator of the new covenant," " the Mediator of the better covenant."

II. Having thus endeavoured, with as much clearness and brevity as I could, to explain the import of the terms in which our Lord's official character is described in the text, I proceed to consider what I mean to make the chief subject of discourse—the account which the text gives of the ministry which in this official character our Lord has accomplished. That account is contained in these words :—Christ, as the High Priest of good things to come—the divinely appointed and divinely qualified manager of the religious interests of man under the new and better economy—ordained for men in things pertaining to God, " having obtained eternal redemption for us, has entered *by*, or rather *through*, a greater and more perfect tabernacle, that is not of this building, *by*—that is, by means of—not the blood of calves or of goats, but His own blood." His ministry as a High Priest is thus represented as consisting of two great parts, the one rising out of the other. First, the obtaining eternal redemption for His people, by the sacrifice of Himself; and secondly, the entering into the holy of holies, to present the blood of that sacrifice before the mercy-seat. Let us shortly attend to these two great acts of our Lord's sacerdotal ministry.

The first great act of our Lord's ministry as the High Priest of good things to come, is *the obtaining eternal redemption for His people*. Men, in consequence of sin, in consequence of being guilty and depraved, are exposed to the judicial displeasure and the moral disapprobation of God; and if this guilt is not expiated, if the removal of this depravity is not secured, this judicial displeasure, this moral disapprobation, must continue, as long as God and man continue to exist, that is, for ever; and must manifest themselves in a way fitted to display to other intelligent beings the holiness and justice of God, and the intrinsic malignity of human transgression. What man needs, is redemption, deliverance,—eternal redemption, everlasting deliverance. Now, what man needs, Jesus Christ as our High Priest has obtained. The high priests under the law obtained, by the offering of certain appointed expiatory sacrifices on the great day of atonement, redemption or deliverance for the Jewish people; but it was only a temporary redemption—from external evils. It was deliverance from the evils to which their transgression of the law of Moses had exposed them,—the being shut out, cut off, from the congregation of the Lord,—exclusion from taking part in the worship of the temple, and other evils connected with this. And it was but a temporary deliverance from these evils: new transgression incurred new guilt, and required new expiation. "The sacrifices which they offered year by year continually, did not make the comers thereunto perfect: for then would they not have ceased to be offered?" "In these sacrifices there was a remembrance again made of sin every year."

"The High Priest of good things to come," by the offering of Himself, according to the will of God, as a sacrifice in the room of His people, obtained for them redemption, or deliverance; but it was redemption not only from a certain class of external evils, it was redemption from all evils,—from evil physical and moral, in every form and every degree, and redemption from all these—for ever. The *expiation* made by the Jewish high priest was shadowy and imperfect,—that made by the High Priest of good things, real and complete.

In plain words, the incarnate Son of God has, by yielding a perfect obedience to the law of God, which man had violated, and by a satisfactory endurance of the evils in which God's displeasure against sin is expressed,—this obedience and endurance being the voluntary fulfilment of a special divine appointment for man's salvation, and invested with infinite merit from the *divine* nature of Him who obeyed and suffered,—made the deliverance of mankind from guilt, and from all the consequences of guilt throughout eternity, compatible with all the glories of the divine character, and all the interests of the divine government, and has absolutely secured such a deliverance for all whom God from the beginning had chosen to salvation, through sanctification of the Spirit and the belief of the truth. He took away sin by the sacrifice of Himself. He finished transgression, He made an end of sin, He brought in an everlasting righteousness. His blood cleanseth from all sin. In Him we have redemption, eternal redemption, through His blood, the forgiveness of sins. The effect of the act of sacrifice in the case of the Jewish high priests, and of the High Priest of good things to come, respectively, is very strikingly represented in the words which follow the text :—" The blood of bulls and goats, and the ashes of an heifer sprinkling the unclean, sanctified to the purifying of the flesh ;" and thus obtained a temporary redemption from external evils. "The blood of Christ, who through the eternal Spirit offered Himself without spot, purges the conscience from dead works, and qualifies and disposes to the service of the living God ;" and thus obtains eternal redemption from all evils. So much for the illustration of the first great act of our Lord's sacerdotal ministry as the High Priest of good things to come,—the obtaining of eternal redemption for His people by His infinitely meritorious vicarious sacrifice.

The second great act of our Lord's ministry as the High Priest of good things to come, is *His entering into the holy place.* When the Jewish high priest, on the great day of atonement, had finished the first part of his ministry, in obtaining redemption for the people from ceremonial guilt, by the expiation of their sins by the appointed vicarious sacrifice, he went through the outer sanctuary into the holy of holies, with the blood of atonement to present before Jehovah, the covenanted God of Israel, dwelling between the cherubim—sitting as it were on the blood-sprinkled mercy-seat as a throne of grace,—evidence that atonement had been made according to the due order; and to make intercession, if not verbally, emblematically by the offering of incense, that as the reconciled Divinity He would pardon and bless His people. The whole of what he did in the holy place, as well as the act of going into it, is pointed out by the phrase, " entering into the holy place." In like manner, Christ, as the High Priest of good things to come, the substance of these shadows, when He had finished on the cross that great work of expiation, which embraces all He did and all He suffered from the manger to the sepulchre, entered into the true holy place, of which the inner sanctuary in the tabernacle and temple was the figure, to present there, as it were, in the immediate presence of God, the Judge of all, the evidence of the completeness of the atonement which He had made, and to follow it up by a never-ceasing interposition in behalf of His people, founded on his all-perfect, infinitely meritorious atoning sacrifice. All this is included in *His* entering into the holy place.

By the holy place, into which Christ as the High Priest of good things to come has entered, we are to understand the heaven of heavens,—the place where the Divinity most remarkably manifests His excellences and communicates His blessings to the unfallen and restored portions of His intelligent offspring, the elect angels and the redeemed from among men. "Christ," says the Apostle at the 24th verse, "is not entered into the holy places made with hands, which are the figures of the true; but into heaven itself, now to appear in the presence of God for us." When our Lord entered into heaven, he entered in His public character—as an accomplished High Priest—with His hands full of atoning blood, and incense of a sweet-smelling savour to God, having been made perfect through suffering.

His very entrance there was a proof of the perfection of His sacrifice. And additional proof of this delightful truth is to be found in the place which He occupies there, and the manner in which He is employed there. When He entered there, it was not to stand there for a short period ministering before the throne of God, and then to come forth, that He might again resume the work of expiation by sacrifice; it was to sit down for ever on the throne of God, on the right hand of His Father. It was to reign along with God; for the Lord said to our Lord, Sit on My right hand, till I make Thine enemies Thy footstool. And He must reign there till even the last of His enemies be destroyed. Power over all flesh, ay, all power in heaven and in earth, has been given Him; and all this power He employs in completing the salvation of those whom He has redeemed from their sins by His own blood, in conferring the eternal redemption which He obtained by His sacrifice. The following is the prophetic testimony respecting the exalted and beatific state of Messiah, the Priest upon His throne, when He had entered into the holy place: "The King joys in the strength of Jehovah: in His salvation how greatly does He rejoice! He has given Him His heart's desire, and has not withholden from Him the request of His lips. He has prevented Him with the blessings of goodness: He has set a crown of pure gold on His head. He asked life" for Himself and His redeemed ones, the covenanted recompense of His atoning death, "and He gave it Him, even length of days for ever and ever. His glory *is* great in Jehovah's salvation: honour and majesty has He laid upon Him. He has made Him most blessed for ever: He has made Him exceeding glad with His countenance."

And this is the apostolic testimony: Christ having become dead in the flesh, " the just in the room of the unjust, has been quickened in the Spirit, and is gone into heaven; and is at the right hand of God, angels, and authorities, and powers being subject to Him: able to save to the uttermost all coming to God by Him, for ever; seeing He ever liveth to make intercession for them." In the intercession which, as " the High Priest of good things to come," He makes in the true holy place, there is nothing humiliating. His intercession, and His mediatorial power and dominion, are but two phases of the same glorious object. The great primary truth contained in both these representations of our Lord's present state is, 'that it is in consequence of *His* expressed will that every exertion of divine power, directly or indirectly connected with the salvation of men, whether in the production of external event or the putting forth of inward influence, is made.'

Into this glorious state and place, " Christ, the High Priest of good things to come," is said by the Apostle to have " *entered by a greater and more perfect tabernacle*, that is not of this building." What is the meaning of this? By this tabernacle some pious and judicious interpreters have understood our Lord's human nature, in which as in a tabernacle He dwelt among us, and in which He performed His sacrificial functions as a High Priest; and they have explained the phrase, *entered by this tabernacle*, as if it were equivalent to—entered in through means of, in consequence of, services performed in this tabernacle. No doubt this is truth; but we much doubt if it is the truth here stated. That the entrance was the result of sacrifice offered, is stated in the second clause: " not by the blood of calves or goats, but by His own blood." The allusion does not here seem to be to the priest entering into the holiest of all in consequence of what he did in the holy place—for the sacrifice was offered, not there, but on the altar of burnt-offering, before the first tabernacle; but to his passing through the holy place—the holy place being the only way to the holiest—bearing the atoning blood into the holy of holies. Nowhere in this Epistle is the human nature of Christ represented as emblematized by the outer tabernacle, though in one place it has been supposed, I think erroneously, to be emblematized by the *vail* which divided the holy place from the holiest of all. The meaning of the inspired writer may, I apprehend, be thus correctly represented:—Our Lord offered *His* sacrifice on the earth, as the Jewish high priests did theirs before the tabernacle; and having offered His sacrifice on the earth, He passed through the visible heavens into the heaven of heavens, as they passed through the holy place into the holiest of all, the emblem of heaven. He entered into the holy place through the visible heavens, which are represented in the Old Testament Scriptures as the tabernacle of Jehovah, His antechamber, as earth is His outer court,—an ante-chamber replete with manifestations of beauty and grandeur, suitable to the entrance into the presence-chamber of the great King, the Lord of hosts—a tabernacle certainly incomparably greater, more magnificent, and more perfect, more highly finished than the Mosaic tabernacle, with all its curious embroidery and costly ornaments—a tabernacle formed immediately by the hand of God, "who in the beginning stretched out the heavens alone—stretched them out as a curtain, and spread them out as a tent to dwell in."

This tabernacle through which our Lord passed is said to be "not of this building," or of this creation or establishment. The words are plainly intended to complete the implied antithesis between the High Priest of good things to come and the Jewish high priests. They offered animal sacrifices; He offered Himself. They obtained temporal, temporary redemption; He obtained spiritual, eternal redemption. They entered into the holy of holies made with hands, on earth; He entered into the celestial sanctuary created by God, in heaven. They entered into that material, earthly holy place, through a tabernacle, suited to it, framed in the same way, forming a part of the same constitution or building; He entered into the heaven of heavens, which Jehovah had formed for His own dwelling-place—the adytum of His temple—through the visible heavens, which He too had formed as a glorious vestibule to the presence-chamber of His majesty.

The following is the inspired history of the glorious event to which the Apostle refers :—Having " showed Himself alive after His passion by many infallible proofs, He," on a day never to be forgotten on earth or in heaven, " led forth His disciples as far as to Bethany, and He lifted up His hands and blessed them : and it came to pass, as He blessed them, He was parted from them—He was taken up; a cloud received Him out of their sight—and carried Him up into heaven. And while they looked stedfastly up towards heaven, as He went up, behold, two men stood by them in white apparel, which also said, Ye men of Galilee, why stand ye gazing up to heaven ? This same Jesus that is taken up to heaven shall so come in like manner as ye have seen Him go into heaven."

What took place when, far beyond the sight of mortal eye and hearing of mortal ear, He entered into the holy place in the temple above, the sacred history does not tell us. But the Spirit of prophecy, which is the witness of Jesus, does. " God—*God with us*—is gone up with a shout, the Lord with the sound of a trumpet." " The chariots of God are twenty thousand, thousands of angels. The Lord is among them, as in Sinai, in the holy place." " The Son of man came to the Ancient of days, and they brought Him near before Him; and there was given Him dominion, and glory, and a kingdom, that all people, nations, and languages should serve Him : His dominion is an everlasting dominion, and His kingdom that which shall not be destroyed." " The Lord said to my Lord, Sit on My right hand, till I have made Thine enemies Thy footstool. The Lord hath sworn, and will not repent, Thou art a Priest for ever after the order of Melchizedek." We cannot doubt that the whole of the attendant cherubim in the heavenly holy of holies, if not awed into reverent silence, poured forth their choicest melodies when the perfected High Priest of good things to come sat down on the burning throne, sprinkled with His own blood, on the right hand of Him who lives and reigns for ever and ever. " Worthy is the Lamb that was slain to receive power, and riches, and wisdom, and strength, and honour, and glory, and blessing.

Blessing, and honour, and glory, and power, be to Him that sitteth on the throne, and to the Lamb, for ever and ever." Indeed, the oracles in the 7th chapter of Daniel and in the 5th of Revelation seem to refer to the same event—that described in the text as the entering in of the High Priest of good things to come into the true holy place.

It is still further stated in this account of the ministry of the High Priest of good things to come, that He entered into the holy place by blood—"not by the blood of calves or of goats, but by His own blood." The reference does not appear to be to the Jewish priest entering with blood, to be sprinkled with his finger upon and before the mercy-seat seven times on the great day of atonement, but to that of which this was the appointed sign and evidence. The reference is to the fact, that the Jewish high priest entered in consequence of the shedding of the blood of the bullock and the goat, as sin-offerings for himself and the congregation. Without this bloodshedding, there was no entrance into the holy of holies. It was on the ground of the expiation thus made that there was warrantable safe entrance there. In like manner, it was on the ground of the all-perfect expiation made by the blood of the sacrifice of the High Priest of good things to come, which sacrifice was Himself, that He has entered into heaven, sat down on the right hand of God, and, ever living to make intercession, is able to save to the uttermost all coming to God by Him. He ever lives, because He once died, the just in the room of the unjust. He lives and reigns in the power of God, because He died in weakness, the victim for the sins of men. Because He humbled Himself, and became obedient to death, the death of the cross, God has highly exalted Him. His being a Priest on His throne is the result of His being a Priest on the cross.

The only other circumstance mentioned in the text respecting the ministry of our Lord as "the High Priest of good things to come," is, that He entered into the holy place *once*,—*i.e.*, once for all. The Jewish high priests had to enter often—once every year. A new year accumulated much new guilt; this guilt required a new sacrifice, and a new entrance into the holy place. But by the sacrifice of Himself, a sacrifice of infinite worth, the High Priest of good things to come has obtained eternal redemption for us; and the expiation being complete—having by one offering perfected for ever all them that are sanctified—the entrance into the holiest of all is *final*, once and for ever. The Jewish high priest could not abide in the holy place: he had work to do which could not be performed there. He must return to the altar to offer sacrifice for unatoned-for transgressions. But our High Priest comes no more out to perform the ministry of atonement. That is over, completely over. He has finished transgression, made an end of sin, taken away sin by the offering of Himself. Jehovah has heard His vows, and "He abides before God for ever." He will indeed once more come forth. Behold, He cometh with clouds, and every eye shall see Him. When He came the first time, it was with a sin-offering—with a human nature so constituted as to be a fit sacrifice for the sins of men; but when He comes the second time, it will be without a sin-offering: not without a human nature; for He who entered is to come forth, and that was the God-man Christ Jesus. But the human nature He brings with Him, as it is not fitted, so it is not intended, to be a sacrifice for sin. He comes to confer, in all its glorious completeness, the eternal redemption which He obtained by His sacrifice. "For Christ is not entered into the holy places made with hands, which are the figures of the true; but into heaven itself, there to appear in the presence of God for us: nor yet that He should offer Himself often, as the Jewish high priests entered into the holy place every year with the blood of others; but now once in the end of the world hath He appeared, to put away sin, and sin-offering, by the sacrifice of Himself. And as it is appointed unto men once to die, but after this the judgment; so Christ was once offered to bear the sins of many: and unto them that look for Him will He come the second time, without sin, unto salvation." There is a striking analogy between the *death* of men and the *sacrifice* of Christ, which was consummated in His death. They are both events which, by the constitution of God, *can* take place but *once*. And this is not the only analogy. Death is not the end of man: the *sacrifice* is not the close of our Lord's saving work. *Men* must come back again to this world; but it is not again to *die*—they die no more; it is to be judged. The High Priest of good things to come also comes back again: He comes forth from the holy place into which He has entered. But it is not again to offer sacrifice: there is, for there needs not be, any more sacrifice for sin. He comes forth to judge the world, and to complete the salvation of those whose sins He expiated in His death, and who, having believed in Him, are looking for Him. May we, my brethren, all be among that happy company who, when He cometh, cometh to judge the world, will welcome Him with holy exultation, saying, This is our Lord; we have waited for Him: He has come, and He will save us;—who, when at the sound of the archangel's voice, and at the sign of the Son of man, the kindreds of the earth are wailing because of Him, shall, unmoved amid the solemnities of a dissolving world, have all feelings lost in delight in the thought that He comes to take all His redeemed ones, soul and body, a glorious assembly, without spot or wrinkle, or any such thing, into the many mansions in the heaven of heavens which He entered in to prepare for them. May our ears be opened to the voice which is ever coming forth from the holy of holies, within the vail, from above the skies—"Lo, I come;" and let the response of our heart be, "Amen. Even so come; come quickly, Lord Jesus."

Thus have I shortly illustrated the view which the text gives us of the official character of our Lord as the High Priest of good things to come, and His ministry in this official character. And "of the things which have been spoken, this is the sum:"—Under the new and better economy, Jesus Christ is the one Mediator between God and man, who opens up, and keeps open, favourable intercourse between them; and in this character He has, by an all-perfect, infinitely meritorious sacrifice, obtained eternal redemption for His people; and, on the ground of this sacrifice, He has, as an all-accomplished High Priest, passed through these heavens into the heaven of heavens, where, "for ever blessing and for ever blessed," on the right hand of the Father, He reigns Head over all things to His body, the Church, communicating to them the eternal redemption He has obtained for them.

What gratitude, then, my brethren, is due by us to the High Priest of good things to come, for what He has done, is doing, will do for us as *our* High Priest! How confidently may we rely on His infinitely meritorious sacrifice, His all-prevalent intercession! How should we rejoice in Him, as rich in mercy, mighty to save; and how gladly should we embrace every opportunity offered of expressing these sentiments in a believing, affectionate observance of His ordinances, in which He puts us in mind of what He did for us in order to obtain eternal redemption for us, and in which He bids us look for Him from heaven to complete the communication to us of that eternal salvation, the obtaining of which for us was completed on the cross! Jesus the Saviour, who will deliver us from the wrath that is to come; Jesus, the Saviour, who will bestow on us "the salvation that is in Him, with eternal glory!" O let us make melody to Him in our hearts; and let *this*, as it has been the theme of our discourse, be the subject of our song.

"The true Messiah now appears,
　　The types are all withdrawn;
　So fly the shadows and the stars
　　Before the rising dawn.

"No smoking sweets, no bleeding lambs,
　　Nor kid nor bullock slain;
　Incense and spice of costly names
　　Would all be burnt in vain.

"Aaron must lay his robes away,
　　His mitre and his vest,
　When God Himself comes down to be
　　The Offering and the Priest.

"He took our mortal flesh to show
　　The wonders of His love;
　For us He paid his life below,
　　And reigns for us above."

"Not all the blood of beasts,
　　On Jewish altars slain,
　Could give the guilty conscience peace,
　　Or wash away the stain.

"But Christ, the Lamb of God,
　　Takes all our sins away—
　A sacrifice of richer blood
　　And nobler name than they.

> "Believing, we rejoice
> To see the curse remove;
> We bless the Lamb with cheerful voice,
> And sing His bleeding love."

Worthy is the Lamb that was slain. To Him that loved us, and washed us from our sins in His own blood, and made us kings and priests to God, even His Father, be glory and dominion. Hallelujah.

DISCOURSE IV.

THE SACRIFICE OF CHRIST SUPERIOR IN EFFICACY TO THE LEGAL SACRIFICES.

HEB. IX. 13, 14.—" For if the blood of bulls and of goats, and the ashes of an heifer sprinkling the unclean, sanctifieth to the purifying of the flesh; how much more shall the blood of Christ, who through the eternal Spirit offered Himself without spot to God, purge your conscience from dead works, to serve the living God?"

JESUS CHRIST, the High Priest of our profession, has received from God a more excellent ministry than that conferred on Aaron and his sons. This proposition is laid down by the Apostle in the 6th verse of the preceding chapter; and the illustration of it occupies him down to the conclusion of the doctrinal part of the Epistle, at the 18th verse of the next chapter. The particular point which the Apostle states and establishes in our text, is the superior *kind* of efficacy which belongs to the expiatory sacrifice offered up by Jesus Christ, as the High Priest of our profession, when compared with that which belonged to the expiatory sacrifices presented by the Aaronical priesthood. It was intended to gain—it was fitted to gain—it has actually gained—a much, an infinitely higher, object than *they* gained, or indeed were intended or fitted to gain.

This most important proposition, lying at the foundation of all our hopes for eternity, is in the text clearly stated, and satisfactorily proved. The *statement* is in these words: "The blood of bulls and of goats, and the ashes of an heifer sprinkling the unclean, sanctified to the purifying of the flesh. The blood of Christ purges the conscience from dead works, to serve the living God." The *argument* is thus expressed:—"*If* the blood of bulls and of goats, and the ashes of an heifer, sanctifieth to the purifying of the flesh; *how much more* shall the blood of Christ, who *through the eternal Spirit* offered *Himself*, purge the conscience from dead works, to serve the living God?" To point out the meaning of the statement, and the force of the argument, are the two objects which I mean to prosecute in the remaining part of the discourse.

I. Let us then attend, in the first place, *to the Apostle's statement;* and first, to his statement as to *the efficacy of the Levitical sacrifices.* " The blood of bulls and goats, and the ashes of an heifer sprinkling the unclean, sanctified to the purifying of the flesh." " The blood of bulls and of goats," here plainly refers to the blood of animals offered as sacrifices for sin, according to the law of Moses.[1] The phrase, " the ashes of an heifer," refers to a remarkable usage, of which we have a minute account in the 19th chapter of the book of Numbers, vers. 2–9. There it is commanded that a red heifer, or young cow, without blemish, on which no yoke had come, should be taken without the camp and slain in the presence of the priest, who was to sprinkle of the blood seven times before the tabernacle of the Lord; that the carcase should then be burned entire; that into the midst of the fire should be cast by the priest cedar wood, hyssop, and scarlet wool; that the ashes which remained should be preserved; and that, on a person having contracted ceremonial defilement, from contact or contiguity to a dead body, a portion of these ashes, mixed in running water, should with a bunch of hyssop be sprinkled on him by a person free from ceremonial defilement. The sprinkling of the blood of these sacrifices, or of this mixture of the ashes of the heifer and running water, was the appointed means of interesting the defiled individual in the expiatory and cleansing virtue of the death of the victims; and when the sacrifice had been offered, and the lustral water prepared according to the due order, this sprinkling availed to the removal of the ceremonial defilement—unfitting for fellowship with Jehovah and His people in the services of the sanctuary—which had been contracted, freed from the punishment which had been incurred, and restored to the privileges which had been forfeited. It " sanctified to the purifying of the flesh." It " sanctified :" it set apart the individual from the great body of the *common*, or *profane*—those who were unfit for the divine service, who were by statute debarred from taking part in it,—and anew consecrated him as a servant of Jehovah; it removed that which had excluded him from the

[1] Lev. xvi. 14, 15; i. 2–5, 10, 11.

congregation of the Lord; it made him, in a ceremonial sense, "holy to the Lord."

"It thus sanctified *to the purifying of the flesh.*" "The purifying of the flesh" does not mean the cleansing of the body; for sprinkling with blood, or with a mixture of ashes and water, was fitted to soil rather than to purify. It marks the kind of sanctification or purifying. It was of the flesh, as contrasted with the spirit—of an external, not an internal kind—of a ceremonial, not of a moral kind. The purifying of the *flesh* is contrasted with the purifying of the *conscience*—the inner man—the seat and subject of moral guilt and pollution, and of the corresponding forgiveness, justification, and sanctification. The sprinkling of the blood, and of the mixture of ashes and water, was the vehicle and the token of that forgiveness of ceremonial guilt and removal of ceremonial pollution, which the expiatory sacrifices procured—of the offering of which, this blood and mixture were, as it were, the evidence; so that the person thus sprinkled was, as to his relation to Jehovah, and his right and fitness for engaging in His service, in the same state in which he was before the guilt and defilement had been contracted, and thus placed on a level with his fellow-worshippers.

The sacrifices of the Mosaic institution are often spoken of by divines as if they had been utterly, and in every sense, inefficacious. This is, however, by no means an accurate representation. It is utterly irreconcilable with the statement in the text, which at once declares the efficacy of these sacrifices, and, in explaining the nature of that efficacy, defines its limits. If they had not had efficacy, complete efficacy, for their own purpose, they would have been quite unfit to serve the end for which we know they were intended—to foreshadow the all-efficacious sacrifice of the great Redeemer of mankind. They had no efficacy, indeed, for removing moral guilt and spiritual defilement. "It was not possible that the blood of bulls and goats," shed in sacrifice, "should take away sin;" and therefore it was not possible that that blood, when sprinkled on the body, could sanctify to the purifying of the conscience. It could not expiate moral guilt, so as to lay a foundation for forgiveness, and sanctification, and final salvation to him who had contracted that guilt. The sanctifying efficacy of a sacrifice must be appropriate and proportioned to its expiatory power; and both must correspond with the nature of the sacrifice, and the purpose it was appointed to serve.

These sacrifices, then, were efficacious, completely efficacious, for their own appointed purpose. This is very distinctly stated in the law of Moses, Lev. vi. 1, 7 : " If a soul sin, and commit a trespass against the Lord, he shall bring his trespass-offering unto the Lord, a ram without blemish out of the fold, to the priest, and the priest shall make an atonement for him before the Lord ; and it shall be forgiven him for anything of all that he hath done in transgressing therein." And it is stated of the person defiled by the dead, that " if the water of separation has not been sprinkled on him, he defileth the sanctuary of the Lord," if he approach it ; but if he be sprinkled with it according to the due order, " he is clean."

It is of importance to remark here, that though these rites were efficacious only to the purifying of the flesh, to the removal of ceremonial guilt and defilement, they were the figure of that which is efficacious to the removal of moral guilt and defilement. They were " shadows." In these rites were embodied these principles: that God is displeased at sin ; that the violation of His law forfeits the high privilege of favourable intercourse with Him, and unfits for its enjoyment; that God is not inexorable ; that though He is disposed to restore sinning man to His favour and fellowship, this must be in the way of showing His displeasure at sin, and of their being qualified for the enjoyment of His blessings—it must be by the removing, the taking away, of the guilt and the defilement. And how this is to be done, was dimly shadowed forth by vicarious suffering, and by that vicarious suffering being made to bear on the conscience of the sinner. In the degree in which this reference was apprehended by the Jewish worshipper (and what that degree was, we have but imperfect means of determining—it was likely very different in different individuals, even among the truly pious of the Jews— but in that degree), these rites were the means of a higher kind of purification. The Gospel in a figure, like the Gospel in plain words—in the promises and predictions—wherever it was understood and believed, produced its appropriate effects on the believing mind and heart; but in this case it was not the efficacy of the Jewish sacrifices, but the efficacy of the Great Sacrifice prefigured by them, which produced the effect. The sins that were forgiven under the old covenant, were forgiven with a reference to the propitiation which was completed on the cross, and is set forth in the Gospel; and all purification of the conscience under that economy proceeded from the same source. It is this purification the Psalmist prays for, under figures borrowed from the Levitical economy: " Purge me with hyssop, and I shall be clean; wash me, and I shall be whiter than the snow."

For the illustration of the Apostle's statement as to the efficacy of the Jewish sacrificial rites, it is only necessary further to remark, that this was an efficacy confined to the Jewish people, and the proselytes joined to them. It would have been a profanation of the sacrificial blood and the water of separation, to have sprinkled them on one of the uncircumcision. The Gentiles could have neither part nor lot in this matter. They had no portion, nor right, in these rites of expiation and lustration.

Of what the Apostle states on this point, this then is the sum: The sacrifices for sin under the law, when duly offered by the priests and applied to the worshippers, were effectual in expiating ceremonial guilt, and removing ceremonial defilement from the ancient people of God.

Let us now, secondly, consider his statement with regard to *the efficacy of the sacrifice of Christ*, offered by Himself, and applied to all who believe. " The blood of Christ purges your conscience from dead works, to serve the living God." The blood of Christ is the blood which He shed, when by His death on the cross He finished the great sacrifice which He came to offer for the sins of mankind. This blood is in the text represented as " sprinkled" on the conscience. The conscience is the soul, the spiritual part of our nature, the inner man. It is obvious, then, that the language must be figurative. The soul can neither be sprinkled with blood nor washed with water. It is not, however, difficult to perceive at once the meaning and the fitness of the metaphorical representation. It was by sprinkling the blood of the animal sacrifices under the law on the individual for whom they were offered, that that individual became personally possessed of the advantage to obtain which they were offered,—that is, deliverance from the ceremonial guilt and defilement which prevented him from drawing near to God in the temple along with His people. Now the question is, What is it under the new covenant which answers to this? How is a man interested in the expiatory, justifying, sanctifying efficacy of the sacrifice which Christ Jesus finished on the cross by pouring out His blood, His life, His soul unto death? An answer to that question will explain what the sprinkling of the blood of Christ on the conscience, so as to cleanse it from dead works, is. The priest who offered the sacrifice, sprinkled the blood on those for whom it was offered; and it is the work of the great High Priest of our profession to sprinkle His own blood on the conscience. Let us translate these figures into literal language. By the effectual operation of the Holy Spirit, Christ leads the individual so to apprehend the meaning and evidence of the truth respecting His sacrifice, exhibited in the Gospel revelation, as that, according to the arrangements of the new covenant, he becomes personally interested in the blessings obtained by that sacrifice. The expiatory, justifying, sanctifying influences of the atonement are thus shed abroad in the heart by the Holy Ghost given us; the man is pardoned, and accepted, and sanctified; the conscience is thus " purged from dead works."

The phrase, " dead works," is a singular one, and has been variously explained. It plainly denotes that from which the blood of Christ, when sprinkled upon the conscience, purifies. In other words, it refers to that spiritual pollution which makes man the object of the divine rectoral displeasure and moral disapprobation, which prevents favourable intercourse with God, making man both unworthy of it and unfit for it—that state of guilt and depravity in which all men are by nature; and it is likely that *that* is here described by the somewhat strange phrase, " dead works," with a reference to that defilement by contact with dead bodies, from which sprinkling with the water of separation was intended to cleanse, spoken of in the preceding verse. " Dead works" are " defiling works," having, in common with dead bodies, this quality, that they produce defilement.

The word " works " is not to be restricted to external acts, but includes all the activities of the thinking, feeling, acting being—the workings of the mind and heart as well as of the hands.

By these sinful works man is *defiled;* and that defilement is removed by the sprinkling of the blood of Christ. He who, under divine influence sent forth by the Saviour, believes the truth respecting His sacrifice, is purified from the defilement of *guilt*, which sin's dead works produce. He that believeth is not condemned; he is justified. He cannot be condemned, for he is united to Him who was delivered for his offences, and raised again for his justification. The blood of Jesus Christ, God's Son, cleanseth him from all sin. And he is also delivered from the defilement of *depravity*, which sin's dead works at once indicate and increase: his heart is purified by faith. The belief of the truth respecting the sacrifice of Christ destroys his natural alienation and enmity, and leads him to love God, and to delight in His fellowship and service. It becomes a fitting thing in God to admit him to favourable intercourse, and he is qualified for this high and holy privilege.

The conscience being thus purified from dead works through the sprinkling of the blood of Christ's sacrifice, the man formerly shut out from, as unworthy of, unfit for, favourable intercourse with God, in consequence of the pollution rising from his dead works, "now serves the living God." The proper meaning of the word "serve" here is, religious ministration—worship. The Israelite who violated Moses' law, and incurred ceremonial guilt and pollution, shut himself out of the enjoyment of his highest privilege—that which, indeed, may be considered as including them all—access to Jehovah as his covenant God. The sacrifices of the law, when duly attended to, restored him to this privilege. He went up to the temple and mingled with the congregation of the Lord. Men, by the pollution connected with dead works, are shut out from the favour and fellowship of God—*i.e.*, from true holiness and true happiness. The sacrifice of Christ, applied to the conscience by the truth in reference to it being understood and believed, brings men to *God*—opens their way into the favourable presence of the Divine Being, as God in Christ reconciling the world to Himself, not imputing their trespasses to them; seeing He hath made Him who knew no sin to be sin for them, that they might be made the righteousness of God in Him. They are made priests to God, and are enabled, influenced by the mercies of God manifested in the sacrifice of Christ, to go boldly to the throne of grace, and to present themselves living sacrifices to Him, the living God, holy and acceptable, which is rational worship, or service. They who are thus interested in the effects of the great sacrifice, are even here "a people near to Him." They dwell in His house; they serve Him without fear, in righteousness and holiness; they offer to Him continually the sacrifices of praise; and the ultimate result of the great sacrifice, the blood shed and sprinkled, will be their being taken, like their great High Priest, body and spirit, fully sanctified, without spot or wrinkle or any such thing, into the immediate presence of their God and Father, where they shall no more go out, but serve Him day and night in His temple, for ever and ever, the living worshippers of the living God. Such, then, is the Apostle's statement respecting the efficacy of the sacrifice of Christ when applied to the conscience.

It only remains, on this part of the subject, to remark, that the efficacy of the Saviour's sacrifice is not, like that of the Levitical sacrifices, confined to the Jewish people. He gave Himself a ransom for all; He is the propitiation for the sins of the whole world. It was predicted, not only that He should bear the sins of many, but that He should "sprinkle many nations." The guiltiest and the most depraved of our race are not excluded from the benefits of the blood of this sacrifice, shed and sprinkled. "The blood of Jesus Christ cleanseth from all sin." However defiled the previous state of the inner man, the sprinkling of this blood purges from dead works, and converts the dead worker into a living minister of a living God—the holy, happy participant of the mind, and will, and enjoyments of the holy, holy, holy, ever blessed God. It must, however, never be forgotten, that though the value of the shed blood is in itself infinite, it is only in the event of its being sprinkled on the conscience that it is efficacious in reference to individuals. It is by the blood of sprinkling—the sprinkled blood—by it alone, that there is sanctification.

II. Having explained the Apostle's *statement* as to the superior efficacy that belongs to the sacrifice of Christ, in comparison with the sacrifices of the old economy, let us now proceed to illustrate *the force of his argument in support of this statement.* "*If* the blood of bulls and of goats, and the ashes of an heifer sprinkling the unclean, sanctifieth to the purifying of the flesh, *how much more shall the blood of Christ, who through the eternal Spirit offered Himself without spot to God, purge your con-*

science from dead works, to serve the living God?" The argument is twofold. If the legal sacrifices had efficacy to cleanse from ceremonial guilt and defilement, the sacrifice of Christ has efficacy to cleanse from moral guilt, spiritual defilement; and if the legal sacrifice had efficacy for its appointed subordinate purpose, the sacrifice of Christ must much more have efficacy for its appointed far higher purpose. Let us endeavour to place in a clear light the force of these two arguments.

The first of these arguments rests on this fact, that the sacrifice of Christ possesses all that gave the legal sacrifices their efficacy. If the question be put, What was it that gave the legal sacrifices their efficacy? the answer plainly is, Their divine appointment. In themselves, they could have no efficacy. They were instituted by God to serve a particular purpose, and they served it just because they were so instituted. Now, it is not more certain that these sacrifices were divinely appointed for *their* purpose, than that the sacrifice of Christ was divinely appointed to serve *its* purpose. "God gave His Son to be the Saviour of the world;" He "laid on Him the iniquities of us all;" He has "set Him forth a propitiation in His blood;" He came, sent by His Father, to "take away sin by the sacrifice of Himself;" and "God made Him, who knew no sin, to be sin in our room, that we might be made the righteousness of God in Him." He who said to Him, "Thou art My son, this day I have begotten Thee," said also to Him, "Thou art a Priest for ever, after the order of Melchisedec." The legal sacrifices were efficacious for their purposes, for they were divinely appointed; and for the same reason, the sacrifice of Christ is efficacious for its purposes.

The second argument will require a somewhat more extended illustration. Its substance is, "If the legal sacrifices served their purpose, much more must the sacrifice of Christ serve its purpose." This argument rests on facts which the Apostle brings forward. Not only is the element which gave efficacy to the legal sacrifices for their purposes present in the sacrifice of Christ, but there are other and most potent elements, fitted to secure for it the far higher efficacy which was necessary to its answering its far higher purposes. The legal sacrifices owed all their efficacy to their divine appointment. The sacrifice of Christ could not have been efficacious, it could not have existed, without divine appointment; but it was in its own nature fitted to be efficacious, and it is to this fact that we are to trace its divine appointment. The legal sacrifices cleansed because of their appointment. The appointment of our Lord's sacrifice took place because it was fitted and adequate for cleansing. (1.) The blood of His sacrifice was "the blood of Christ;" (2.) The sacrifice He offered was the sacrifice of "Himself;" (3.) That sacrifice was offered "without spot;" and, what most of all goes to prove its efficacy, (4.) That sacrifice was offered "through the eternal Spirit." Let us look a little at these statements, and we will see that they fully bear out the Apostle's argument, that the sacrifice of Christ must be held much more to have efficacy to serve its purpose than the legal sacrifices to serve theirs.

The blood of His sacrifice is "the blood of Christ." And who is *Christ?* The Messiah, the Anointed One. And what does that mean? Nothing less than the divinely qualified, appointed, sent, accredited Saviour. His blood must surely be precious blood. His blood—His sacrifice—must be fitted to be effectual for any purpose, however great, that sacrificial blood can answer. What, in comparison of this, is the blood of the cattle on a thousand hills? What, in comparison of this, the sacrifice of the whole race of man? It is likely that the Apostle meant here, a contrast not only between the Levitical sacrifices and our Lord's sacrifice, but between the Levitical high priest and our Lord Himself. They, the priests of a nation; He, the Anointed One—the Priest of mankind—" the Christ," according to the Samaritan creed, "the Saviour of the world."

Then, the sacrifice offered by our High Priest was the sacrifice of "Himself." There is much more in that expression than is ordinarily apprehended. What our Lord offered was nothing extrinsic; it was Himself, His whole self. The sacrifice offered by our Lord was *all* He was—all that He had done; that entire, most willing subjection both to the precept and to the sanction of the law—holy, just, and good, and exceeding broad—which man had violated; a subjection reaching from the moment of His incarnation to the moment of His death—so continuous and perfect as to be represented by the Apostle as *one* act of obedience, corresponding with the one act of him who was His figure, by which death and all our woe came into the world:

it was this which He, as the appointed, qualified High Priest, presented to God as that which was fitted to be a declaration of His righteousness in the salvation of man—that which should take away sin, in procuring the expiation of sin, the forgiveness of sin, the absolute destruction of sin. Who that knows *what* that sacrifice was, and *who* it was that offered it, can doubt that it must have been efficacious for its purposes; and that, when offered to God, it must have been a sacrifice of a sweet smelling savour in His estimation,—a magnifying of the law, and a making of it honourable, so as that " grace might reign through righteousness unto eternal life ?"

Still further, when He who is the Christ, by the shedding of His blood, offered Himself an offering to God, the offering was *a spotless* offering. This is, indeed, implied in the sacrifice being the sacrifice of Himself. But it is separately mentioned, from its essential importance. The absolute sinlessness, the absolute perfection of our Lord, is an essential element of the efficacy of His sacrifice. Had Jesus been a sinner in any degree—had His flesh been sinful flesh—had His humanity been, strictly speaking, fallen humanity, He would not have been " Christ, the Holy One of God;" He would have been utterly disqualified for achieving the great work of our salvation. He would have needed for Himself that blessing He came to confer upon others. The Levitical law made men priests having moral infirmity, who had to offer sacrifice for their own sins as well as for the sins of the people; but our High Priest is such an one as became us, " holy, harmless, separate from sinners." He needed not to offer sacrifice for His own sins, for He had no sin. He was thus fitted to serve the purpose for which He was manifested—to take away sin; for in Him was no sin. As a High priest, He was perfect; as a victim, spotless. The blood by which we are redeemed is the blood of Christ, as of a lamb without spot and blemish. We have thus, in the sacrifice of Christ, a perfect oblation, offered up in a perfect manner by a perfect High Priest. How much more, then, must it be efficacious?

But the primary element of efficacy in the sacrifice of Christ, for the purposes it was meant to serve, remains to be stated. This sacrifice of Himself which Christ offered to God without spot, was offered " through the eternal Spirit." There is some difficulty of fixing the reference of the appellation, "the eternal Spirit," and the meaning of the phrase, " through the eternal Spirit." Some consider the appellation as referring to the Holy Spirit, the third Person of the Holy Trinity, and view the expression as equivalent to—Christ, in whom the Holy Spirit dwelt, offered Himself; or, under the influence of the Holy Spirit, He offered Himself; or, according to the declarations of the Holy Spirit in the Old Testament Scriptures, He so offered Himself, as Paul says, He died for us, according to the Scriptures. Each of these interpretations brings out a meaning true in itself, and not alien from the argument of the Apostle. But I am disposed to go along with those interpreters who consider " the Eternal Spirit" as descriptive of our Lord's divine nature,—" the spirit of holiness," according to which He is the Son of God, while " according to the flesh" He is the Son of David,—" that Spirit" in which He was justified when He was manifested in flesh,—that eternal life which was with the Father, the eternal Word in which was life. The words are strictly applicable to the divine nature, as existing in the Person of the incarnate Son; and it would have been strange if the Apostle, in indicating how the blood of Christ's sacrifice was much more efficacious than that of the legal sacrifices, had omitted that which was necessary to its efficacy, and which more than all other things put together demonstrates that efficacy— His true divinity. When it is said that our High Priest offered Himself " through the eternal Spirit," we apprehend the thought meant to be conveyed is, that the efficacy of that sacrifice was closely connected with, indeed primarily produced by, " that union with the eternal Spirit of Godhead" which formed the most extraordinary feature in His person. Had not Christ been a *divine* person—a person not naturally subject to the law man had violated—meritorious obedience and satisfaction would have been in the nature of things impossible, no creature being capable of doing more than his duty in obeying or submitting to the divine will. When he has done all those things which are commanded him, he must still say, I am an unprofitable servant; I have done that which was my duty to do. It is otherwise with Him who is the Word made flesh—God manifest in flesh. " The assumption of human nature by the eternal Spirit, in the person of the Word, or Son, was the act of an infinite mind, looking to all the results of that assumption. The union, once formed, was constant and invariable; so that all that He did, in and for the execution of His mediatorial office and work, were impressed with the essential dignity and moral value of His divine perfection."[1] This, then, requires us to attribute to our Lord's sacrifice a value properly infinite. He is worthy, with all the worthiness of the Godhead.

It is deserving of notice, how closely connected in the inspired declarations are the divinity of our Lord and the efficacy of His atonement. "Look to Me and be saved," says the Messiah by the prophet, "for I am God." "Surely in *Jehovah*," says the Church, "I have righteousness"—justification. "In HIM," says the Apostle, "we have redemption through His blood, the forgiveness of sins; in *Him*, who is the image of the invisible God, the first-begotten of every creature, the Prince of the whole creation, by whom, for whom all things were created, who is before all things, and by whom all things subsist." "The Son of God, the appointed heir of all things, by whom also He made the worlds—the brightness of His glory, the express image of His person—*by Himself*, i.e., by the sacrifice of Himself—being what He was—what He only was—purged our sins." When we think what "purging the conscience from dead works" is, and what is requisite to its accomplishment, we see that the labours and sufferings of men and angels combined could not effect it; but what can the labours and sufferings of Him who is an incarnation of God not effect? "Is anything too hard for the Lord?" We thus see, that beside the element of divine appointment—which equally belongs to the sacrifices under the law and to our Lord's sacrifice, and warrants the conclusion, that they both must be efficacious for the purposes they are respectively meant to serve—there are in our Lord's sacrifice elements peculiar to itself,—in the nature of the sacrifice—" Himself," in the manner in which it was offered— " without spot," in the official character—" Christ," and in the personal dignity—divinity—" the eternal Spirit," of Him that offered it,—elements which warrant the conclusion, that if the legal sacrifices were efficacious for their purpose, *much more* must His sacrifice be effectual for *its* purpose.

There is yet one other remark necessary to complete our view of the Apostle's argument. From His sacrifice possessing

[1] Pye Smith.

these qualities, it follows that it has the quality of intrinsic suitableness. It is quite adequate to the purpose—the " purging the conscience from dead works ;" *i.e.*, as we have seen, expiation, justification, sanctification. There is a more glorious display given of the holiness and justice of God, of the excellence of the law, and of the demerit of the transgression of it, and at the same time of the love and mercy of God, than there would have been in the everlasting destruction of a sinning world, or in the everlasting happiness either of an unsinning world, or of a sinning world pardoned by mere amnesty, without satisfaction. And this glorious display, when made the subject of a revelation—if understood and believed, under that divine influence for the communication of which it makes provision—delivers from the power of sin, and at once disposes and qualifies men for that favourable intercourse with God in which consist their holiness and happiness, and which it is now consistent with, illustrative of, His righteousness, as well as His grace, to vouchsafe to them. It would take a volume to exhibit fully the truth packed up in these two sentences. I repeat them, that you may employ your thoughts in comprehending and unfolding them. " For if the blood of bulls and of goats, and the ashes of an heifer sprinkling the unclean, sanctifieth to the purifying of the flesh ; how much more shall the blood of Christ, who through the eternal Spirit offered Himself without spot to God, purge your conscience from dead works, to serve the living God ?"

I have thus illustrated the Apostle's statement and argument. —His twofold statement : The blood of bulls and goats, and the ashes of an heifer sprinkling the unclean, sanctifies to the purifying of the flesh. The blood of Christ purges the conscience from dead works to serve the living God. His argument, which is twofold also :—If the blood of bulls and goats sanctifies to the purifying of the flesh, the blood of Christ must purge the conscience from dead works. If the blood of bulls and goats does the one, the blood of Christ will *much more* do the other. The two contrasted sacrifices have equally the element of divine appointment ; therefore, if the one is efficacious, so must the other. But the second has additional elements, in the nature of the sacrifice, in the manner in which it was offered, in the official character and essential dignity of Him who offered it, and in the intrinsic suitableness to serve its purposes, resulting from these elements; therefore it may much more be held to be efficacious for its specific purposes. Most appropriately does the Apostle express the last conclusion interrogatively,—How much more? This is a question which neither man nor angel will be able to answer to all eternity.

And now for the all-important question, Has this efficacy of the Saviour's sacrifice, so clear a point of Christian doctrine, become a matter of personal experience with us? Have we had *our* conscience purged from dead works, so as to become the holy, happy worshippers of the living God?

If we have not, how miserable is our condition! Our hearts and conscience are defiled; we *are* guilty and depraved; there is no other sacrifice for sin—no other means of sanctification. Unforgiven, unsanctified, unworthy of, unfit for God's fellowship and worship, what is, what can be before us, continuing in this condition, but banishment from Him, condemnation, ever-growing guilt, depravity, and misery in the lake of fire, prepared for the devil and his angels?

But why should we continue strangers to the efficacy of this sacrifice? The value of the sacrifice is absolutely infinite: no sin it cannot expiate, no pollution it cannot cleanse. The blood, through which alone there can be expiation and sanctification, is still being sprinkled; and its power is put forth on all who believe. If you are strangers to its efficacy, it is just because you do not believe the truth respecting it. And why do you not believe the truth respecting it? Is it because it is so abstruse that you cannot understand it,—so self-contradictory, or ill supported, that you cannot believe it? No, no. It is because, however you might like expiation and forgiveness, you have no heart for the purified conscience and the spiritual service of the living God; and rather than submit to be thus made holy and happy, you will run the hazard, nay, incur the certainty, of being miserable for ever,—trampling under foot the Son of God,—treating the blood of the covenant, through which alone there can be sanctification—the purifying of the conscience—as a common thing, and doing despite to the Spirit of grace. Can madness go beyond this? Yet this is the madness which is in the heart of men while they live; and afterwards they go to the dead.

DISCOURSE V.

CHRIST THE MEDIATOR OF THE NEW COVENANT.

Heb. ix. 15.—"And for this cause He is the Mediator of the new testament, that by means of death, for the redemption of the transgressions that were under the first testament, they which are called might receive the promise of eternal inheritance."

The Bible is a book very imperfectly understood by the great body of those who profess to receive it as a divine revelation. In many cases, this is very easy to be accounted for. Multitudes who profess to receive the Bible as a divine revelation, seldom or never read it; and it would be a strange thing, indeed, if a book could be understood without being read. Multitudes more read the Bible more or less regularly and frequently; but they read it with such an almost entire absence of everything like intellectual effort, that understanding it is quite out of the question. Indeed, understanding it is not the object they have in view. Where there is any design—where it is not the mere result of early education and confirmed habit, it is not to find out the meaning of the Bible: it is to be able to quiet an ill-informed, but still not entirely benumbed conscience, by telling it, I have not only said my prayers, but read my chapter.

But there are instances in which it is not so easy to account for the fact of the Bible being but very imperfectly understood. There are persons who read the Bible with an honest, ay, with an anxious, desire to understand it, who are painfully conscious, that while there is in it much that is plain to them, there is not a little also that is obscure; that there are many passages to which they can attach only very indistinct and unsatisfactory ideas, and not a few to which they can attach no idea at all. In many cases, they cannot see what it is that the inspired writer is illustrating or proving; or they cannot see the appositeness of his illustrations, or the conclusiveness of his arguments. It is not my purpose just now to make a full enumeration of the causes why such persons so imperfectly understand the Holy Scriptures. These causes are of very various kinds in different individuals, and even in the same individual. But I have no hesitation in saying, that the imperfection of the translations, through the medium of which the great body of Scripture readers must derive their acquaintance with the inspired writers, is one of these causes. All translations of the Scriptures are the work of uninspired men, and therefore they are necessarily imperfect. This is true of all versions from the inspired originals, and of our own very excellent translation among the rest. There are some worthy men who are exceedingly indisposed that such a statement as I have just made should even go forth among Christians at large, lest it should shake their confidence in the infallibility of the Holy Scripture as the rule of faith and duty. But surely he must be very ignorant who needs to be told, that translations are the work of uninspired men, and therefore must bear the traces of the imperfections of their authors; and if any man among us is so deplorably ignorant as not to know this, it is surely desirable that without loss of time he should be better informed. And I cannot satisfy myself that a Christian teacher acts an honest part, who, though he is persuaded the translation he, in common with his audience, is using, does not in a particular place accurately express the mind of the inspiring Spirit, yet conceals this from them, and leaves them uninformed, or misinformed, about the mind or will of God in that particular passage, for the purpose of preserving unbroken their undue veneration for the work of great and good, learned and pious, but still fallible men. He acts a part worse than foolish who finds fault with our translation merely for the sake of finding fault, and thus figuring, in the estimation of the thoughtless and superficial, as an acute or learned man, or who indeed suggests changes that are not absolutely required to bring out clearly and fully the meaning of the inspired writer; but, on the other hand, he surely does not deserve the praise of wisdom, who, from reverence for man, or fear of possible bad consequences, does neither more nor less than " shun to declare the whole counsel of God." Here, I believe, as in every other similar case, the safest as well as the most dutiful course, is to tell the truth—all the truth—nothing but the truth. Indeed, every Christian minister, when expounding Scripture, should speak as warily and as explicitly as if he were on oath. An intelligent hearer, if he find his minister always treating the English version of the Scriptures as if it were immaculately correct, must arrive at one of three conclusions: that his teacher is very imperfectly acquainted with the original Scriptures; or that he does not use the knowledge of this kind he may possess as an instrument of interpretation; or that, for some reason, he is afraid to tell what he knows respecting the occasional mistranslations, which are universally admitted to exist, in that, as in all other versions of the sacred writings. While, on the other hand, when by a well-informed teacher the whole truth is unostentatiously told, an enlightened impression of the general accuracy and excellence of our translation is deeply lodged in the mind, when it is seen how comparatively few are the passages in which one who has devoted himself, as every minister should, to the study of the original text, and who is obviously fettered by no superstitious veneration for the translators, and no fear of the bad consequences of telling all the truth, if it be but the truth, finds it necessary to represent it as exhibiting an imperfect or mistaken representation of the divine original.

The paragraph of which the text is the commencement, must undoubtedly be numbered among those which mistranslation has rendered obscure, and indeed unintelligible. I say it considerately, that no mere English reader can make a consistent, satisfactory sense out of the paragraph, beginning at the 15th verse of this chapter and ending with the 23d. What meaning can he attach to the phrase, " mediator of a testament," or last will? In a testament, we have a testator, and legatees, and executors; but a mediator of a *testament* is as incongruous an expression as the testator of a league or bargain. It is difficult, not to say impossible, to see how the new covenant, whether in its formation—the purpose of mercy, or in its execution—the plan of salvation, can be represented as a testament or latter will. The only point of resemblance is, that death in it, as in the case of a testament, was necessary to the enjoyment of its blessings; though, even in this case, this leading idea is not accurately expressed, the death of a testator not being the procuring cause of the blessings to the legatees, as the death of Christ is to those who enjoy the blessings of the new covenant, but merely a conditional occasion of the obtaining the legacies. Besides, if the new covenant were figuratively represented as a testament, the testator would not be Jesus Christ, but God the Father; for it is God who blesses us with all heavenly and spiritual blessings in Christ Jesus, and He never dies. And even supposing that Jesus Christ was considered as the testator, it is plain that His resurrection destroys the congruity of the figure. It is, if possible, still more difficult to attach any consistent idea to the term "testament," as descriptive of the "first covenant," or the order of things established at Sinai. Who was the testator here, and how was the testament confirmed by death? It was a law imperatively enjoined: and what is the meaning of transgressions under the first *will*, which the maker of the second will dies to redeem? Besides, it is impossible to make out the force of the Apostle's reasoning, on the supposition that the word rendered testament means a latter will. He is obviously accounting for the death of Christ, dignified and exalted as He was, by showing that it was absolutely necessary to the gaining of the great object for which He was constituted the High Priest and Mediator of the new covenant. Now, it requires but little perspicacity to see that there is absolutely no force in such an argument as the following:—' The new covenant may be considered as a testament, inasmuch as its blessings cannot be enjoyed without the death of Christ, who in that case is viewed as testator. Now a testament, in order to be valid, requires that the testator should be dead; *therefore* it was necessary that Christ should die.' That is the argument as it stands in our English translation,—an argument which, taking for granted what it professes to prove, proves nothing. Setting his inspiration out of the question altogether, the author of the Epistle to the Hebrews was obviously a person of too clear a mind to argue in this way. Now, all this perplexity, in which an intelligent English reader of this paragraph, determined, if possible, to understand it, must feel himself involved,—and the more intelligent and inquisitive he is, he will be but the more perplexed,—arises out of a mistranslation of a very few words, in which our excellent translators have paid less regard than they ordinarily do to the original, and more than enough to the old Latin translation, which the Church of Rome holds as authentic. It is right that all readers of the Bible should know that the word translated "testament" in this paragraph, is the same word that in the preceding and in the following context is rendered "covenant;" and not only there, but wherever it occurs in our New Testament, with the exception of Matt. xxvi. 28, Mark xiv. 24, Luke xxii. 20, 1 Cor. xi. 25, 2 Cor. iii. 6, 14, Heb. vii. 22, Rev. xi. 19, in every one of which it ought to have been rendered covenant. The substitution of the word covenant—understanding by that, arrangement, economy, order of things—in the room of the word testament, with a few slight changes which necessarily rise out of that substitution, gives perfect distinctness of meaning and conclusiveness of argument to a passage obviously of high significance and importance, which, as it stands in our version, appears to me altogether inexplicable.

Let us now proceed to a somewhat minuter inspection of the various parts of the text; but before doing so, it will be requisite to say a word or two as to the design of the paragraph of which the text forms a part, and the manner in which it is introduced.

The Apostle is proving that Jesus Christ, as our High Priest, has received a more excellent ministry than Aaron or any of his sons. He has briefly described in succession their ministry and His. He has, in the words immediately preceding, shown that His ministry excels theirs in the *kind* of efficacy that belongs to it: theirs was efficacious to remove ceremonial guilt and defilement, and to fit for ceremonial worship; His was efficacious to remove moral guilt and pollution, and to fit for spiritual worship. And in the paragraph, from the 24th to the 28th verse, he shows that His ministry had a corresponding superiority to theirs, in the completeness and permanence of its efficacy; theirs requiring to be indefinitely repeated, His being performed once for all. The paragraph to which our text belongs, comes in between these two proofs of the superiority of our Lord's ministry. It is a kind of digression, but a digression closely connected with, naturally rising out of, the argument. It is intended to meet the Jewish prejudice, which may be expressed in the question—a prejudice having a deep root in human nature—But why did this great High Priest die? And the substance of the answer is just this:—Death, and the death of a person so illustrious, was, in the nature of things, absolutely necessary to the gaining of the great ends of that new and better covenant, of which Jesus Christ, as our High Priest, is Mediator.

I intend to confine myself to the illustration of the 15th verse, which resolves itself into the following propositions:— Jesus Christ is the Mediator of the new covenant. The great design of the new covenant was, that they who are called may obtain the promise of everlasting inheritance. In order to this, there must be a redemption of the transgressions which were under the first covenant. To the redemption of them, death, and death of adequate value, is necessary. Such a death is the death of Jesus Christ. And for this cause, for all these things taken together, Jesus Christ is "the Mediator of the new covenant." What a rich field of spiritual pasture opens before us here!

I. The first proposition in the text is,—Jesus Christ is the Mediator of the new covenant. The word covenant, in our language, means a league, or a bargain. The words in the original Scriptures rendered by that word are of more comprehensive meaning. They signify a disposition, arrangement, settled order of things. A league is a covenant, and so is a bargain; and they are so, because they are arrangements. But so also is a law, or a promise, or a testament, or, indeed, any regularly fixed disposition of things. The arrangement that there is not to be another general deluge, and that the seasons are to follow each other in regular order, is called God's covenant with the earth. God's promise to Abraham and his seed is called a covenant. The institution of circumcision is called a covenant. The law at Sinai is called a covenant. The Messiah, as God's ordinance, appointed means for saving men, is termed "a covenant to the people." We are accustomed from our infancy to hear of two covenants,—the covenant of works and the covenant of grace. The first of these is the arrangement under which mankind were placed immediately after the creation, and by the violation of which we all became guilty. I am not sure that this arrangement is ever termed a covenant in the Scriptures, though quite certain that it might have been so. The second of these covenants is the arrangement by which God, in the exercise of His sovereign mercy, saves lost man, through the mediation of His Son. In the New Testament we read also of two covenants. The first of these is the old covenant,—the arrangement made known in the law of Moses, according to which the people of Israel became in a peculiar sense the people of God, and had secured to them a variety of privileges. The second, or new covenant, nearly, if not entirely, coincides with the second in the former division—is the arrangement, fully revealed in the writings of the New Testament, by which an innumerable multitude from among mankind, of all nations, in all ages, become God's people in a peculiar and much higher sense, and have secured for them much more exceeding great and precious blessings. The Aaronical priesthood was the mediator of the first covenant. Of the second covenant Jesus Christ, the High Priest of our profession, is the Mediator. He comes between us and God. He brings us into a state of reconciliation; He keeps us in a state of reconciliation. It is through what He has done, and is doing, that all the blessings of the new covenant come to those who are interested in it. That is what is meant by His being the Mediator of the covenant. We come to God through Him, and God comes to us through Him. But what are the blessings which this new covenant is intended to secure for those interested in it? The text informs us; and this is the *second* point to which we must attend.

II. The great object of the new covenant is, "that they who are called might receive the promise of eternal inheritance." They who are called, or "the called ones," is a descriptive appellation of the true spiritual people of God, borrowed, like so many other of their descriptive appellations, from a denomination bestowed on the Israelites, the external people of God. The appellation originates in the call of Abraham out of the idolatry of Ur of the Chaldees, and of his posterity out of the bondage of Egypt. "I called Abraham alone. Israel is My son, My first-born; I called him out of Egypt." Abraham and his posterity were supernaturally *called* by God to the enjoyment of peculiar privileges in the land of Canaan; and hence we find the Israelites termed by Isaiah, Jehovah's called ones. The leading idea is, invited and led by God into the enjoyment of certain privileges. In the New Testament this appellation is transferred to the spiritual people of God, the spiritual descendants of Abraham, whether they be his natural descendants or not. They are often termed the called of God the Father, called in Christ Jesus, called to be saints, called unto the kingdom and glory of God. These are those whom the Apostle represents as saved and called with a holy calling,—men who, under the influence of the Holy Spirit, are made to listen to, understand, believe, and obey the call of God in the word of the truth of the Gospel,—to whom the word comes, not in word only, but in power; with the Holy Ghost, and with much assurance. These called ones are the same as the chosen ones, predestinated in love before the foundation of the world; for it is whom He did predestinate that He calls. Their calling is not according to their works, but according to His own purpose and grace, given us in Christ Jesus before the world began. To these, the spiritual Israel, pertains the new covenant, as the old did to Israel after the flesh; and the great design of the covenant with regard to them is, " that they may receive the promise of eternal inheritance,"—literally, of *the* eternal inheritance. We will mistake the meaning of these words if we consider them as signifying, that they might have the everlasting inheritance promised to them—that they might obtain a promise of at some time receiving it. That is secured in the covenant; but there is much more than that secured. The intelligent reader of the New Testament must notice the word " promise" often means ' the thing promised,' just as " faith" often means ' the thing believed,' and " hope," the thing expected. To " inherit the promises," is to enjoy the blessings promised. The patriarchs " died, not having received the promises,"—not having obtained in this world the promised blessings. " The promise of the Spirit," in Gal. iii. 14, as well as " the Spirit of promise," Eph. i. 13, means the promised Spirit; and in like manner, " the promise of the eternal inheritance" is equivalent to ' the promised eternal inheritance.' Under the old covenant there was a promised inheritance, the inheritance of Canaan, to be enjoyed by the called Israelites in peace, under the peculiar blessing of Jehovah. A promise was given them of entering into this rest of God; and the various arrangements of the covenant were intended to fit them for that inheritance, to secure their entrance on it, and their continued enjoyment of it. It was only through the covenant that these ends were to be gained. Now to *us*, under the new covenant, as well as to those under the old, are good news proclaimed. An inheritance—a better inheritance than Canaan—a spiritual, a heavenly, an everlasting inheritance—holy happiness, in being acknowledged by and knowing God, being loved by God and loving God, being like God, thinking along with Him, choosing along with Him, enjoying along with Him,—this is the inheritance incorruptible, undefiled, and that fadeth not away, laid up for us in heaven. This inheritance, this everlasting inheritance, is promised to all the called ones. For thus runs the covenant of promise,—" God so loved the world, that He gave His only-begotten Son, that whosoever believeth in Him should not perish, but have everlasting life." " He that believeth on the name of the Son of God hath everlasting life." Now, as the arrangements of the old covenant were intended to secure for the Israelites their promised inheritance, so the arrangements of the new covenant are intended to secure for " the called ones" their inheritance. The question naturally arises, And what was necessary for this purpose? Many things were necessary, all of which were secured by the covenant; but the Apostle fixes our attention specially on one thing absolutely necessary, and which, if secured, would secure everything else. This he does in the third proposition, to the consideration of which we now proceed.

III. In order to the called receiving the everlasting inheritance, " there must be a redemption of the transgressions which were under the first covenant." The transgressions which were under the first covenant, is not an expression equivalent to that in Rom. iii. 25, " sins that are past, through the forbearance of God;" that means, ' sins that had been pardoned, though not expiated,' from a regard to the fore-appointed propitiation which is set forth in the Gospel. Nor does it appear to be synonymous with sins that were committed under the old covenant. Looking at the expression in connection with what is said in the preceding context, vers. 11-14, and in the succeeding context, ver. 23, it seems impossible to doubt that the words mean, those transgressions of the divine law which remained transgressions, and therefore unforgiven, because unexpiated, under the old covenant,—for the expiation of which, in other words, the old covenant made no provision. It made provision for making atonement for ceremonial guilt, for removing ceremonial pollution, and thus for obtaining and enjoying the earthly inheritance. But the deeper transgressions remained; they still were. The transgressions which draw down on man the judicial displeasure and the moral disapprobation of God, and thus stood in the way of God's bestowing and man's enjoying the spiritual eternal inheritance of perfect holy happiness, in the favour, image, and fellowship of God,—these must be removed, or the promised eternal inheritance can never be received by the called ones. God can by no means clear the guilty. It was not possible that the blood of bulls and of goats could take away sin. The old covenant can open the way to the unclean Israelite unto the temple—it can, by its rites properly observed, secure to him the possession of Canaan; but it cannot save *man*, whether Jew or Gentile, from *hell*—it cannot carry them to heaven. This species of transgressions, the most serious of all, which *were*, notwithstanding all the expiation and ablutions of the law,—these must be dealt with, or not one of the called can receive the promised eternal inheritance. There must be a redemption of them. The phrase is peculiar; but, viewed in its connection, it can scarcely be called obscure. A ransom, a redemption-price, must be paid, in order to these transgressions being forgiven,—without the forgiveness of which, the everlasting inheritance is unattainable by any of the called ones. Expiation must be made. Something must be done to make God's conferring the inheritance on the called ones, who had been guilty of these transgressions, consistent with the perfection of His character, the honour of His law, the declarations of His word, the stability of His government. And what was this something, which all created intelligence would have sought for ever to discover in vain? The Apostle tells us in the fourth proposition.

IV. *Death*—an adequate death—must take place. It is "by means of death, for the redemption of the transgressions which were under the first covenant, that the called ones can obtain the promised everlasting inheritance." Nothing but *death* could serve the purpose. Death is the penalty of the law. Death is the wages of sin. Without the shedding of blood there is no remission. There must be a manifestation, an adequate manifestation, of the displeasure of God against the sin and the sinner, to make pardon honourable to God, or safe to the subjects of His moral government. No such thing as mere amnesty exists in God's government. There must be something besides repentance and reformation—something in order to true repentance and reformation. There must be blood. The blood of bulls and goats will not serve the purpose. That, vicariously shed, may serve as a protest against God's overlooking ceremonial guilt, and giving external benefits to those who deserve them not; but it cannot expiate moral guilt—it never can afford a fit reason why a just God should forgive a guilty, condemned malefactor. The death of all men can effect nothing in the way of expiation. It does not exhaust the curse; it lays no foundation for pardon. The death of the whole angelic host incarnate could not serve the purpose. They had neither the disposition nor the right to devote themselves victims for men. This sacrifice would have been deficient in both the constituent elements of an effectual sacrifice—divine appointment, and intrinsic infinite value. A death was necessary which would fully answer all the requisitions of the divine character and government. The death of one who had a right to lay down His life for such a purpose—for it was His own independent property,—and whose one life was in value incalculably superior to that of all the lives He by His death rescued from destruction;—such a death was the death of Jesus Christ. And His death is the only such death to be in the wide extent of God's universe, from eternity to eternity.

V. The fifth and concluding proposition comes out, then, with resistless power. "*For this cause* He is the Mediator of the new covenant." He is *Christ*, the divinely appointed, the divinely qualified Redeemer. He has paid the ransom for the transgressions which remained unexpiated under the first covenant. He has died for us in our room—died for our sins, on account of them—died, the just for the unjust. He has offered Himself unspotted, an all-perfect sacrifice—materially, formally perfect. He has done so through the eternal Spirit, His divine nature, which imparts an infinite value to His sacrifice. And the blood of that sacrifice can do what the blood of no other sacrifice ever could do: it can not only sanctify to the purifying of the flesh, it can cleanse from all sin—it can purge the conscience from dead works, to serve the living God. It can not only exhibit, but exhaust, the penal sanction of the divine law, and harmonize in the divine character and administration the apparently incompatible glories of perfect righteousness and infinite grace, the just God and the Saviour. And thus the death of the incarnate Only-begotten of God, which appears at first sight so unaccountable as to make us doubt the reality, the possibility of the whole economy, of which it is the chief constituent element, is seen to be indeed the unsearchable wisdom of God, though the wisdom of God in a mystery. It is *this*—which to the Jew is a stumblingblock, and to the Greek foolishness—which qualifies Him for being, what no other being in the universe is qualified for being, the successful Mediator of the new covenant. It is thus that He, crucified in weakness, is the power of God to salvation. It is thus that He secures for all the called ones the ineffable blessing of the promised everlasting inheritance, an inheritance which otherwise could never have been possessed by any of the fallen race of Adam. The meaning of our text, we trust, now stands out clear before you. "Because the blood of Christ, who through the eternal Spirit offered Himself without spot to God, purges the conscience from dead works, to serve the living God," while the blood of bulls and of goats, and the ashes of an heifer sprinkling the unclean, could do no more than sanctify to the purifying of the flesh,—for this cause He is the Mediator of the new covenant, that by means of death, "for the redemption of the transgressions which were under the first covenant, they which are called might receive the promise of everlasting inheritance."

If these things are so, is it not meet that this death should be held in everlasting, most grateful remembrance by those who, but for that covenant which it ratified, must have suffered for ever the fearful consequences of that forfeiture of the everlasting inheritance which their transgressions had incurred— transgressions which nothing could expiate but the blood of the everlasting covenant? The voice first uttered in the upper chamber in Jerusalem now comes forth from the most excellent glory: "This cup is the new covenant in My blood, shed for remission of sins unto many. Drink ye all of it." Over, then, the instituted memorial emblems of the ratification of the covenant by the death of Christ, who is the Mediator, both as the High Priest and as the atoning sacrifice, let us, when observing the holy ordinance of the supper, devote ourselves entirely to Him who devoted Himself entirely for us, and cherish an undoubting confidence that the confirmed covenant shall be followed out to all its blissful intended results; and that, as we have the promise and pledge, we shall in due time obtain the full possession, of the everlasting inheritance, blessing God that He has shown us, manifested to us, this His holy everlasting covenant, ordered in all things and sure. O that all of us, in the full assurance of faith, may be enabled, like David, to employ these as our last words, "This is all my salvation, and all my desire!"

> " 'Tis mine, the covenant of His grace,
>   And every promise mine,—
> All sprung from everlasting love,
>   And sealed by blood divine.
>
> " On my unworthy, favour'd head,
>   Its blessings all unite—
> Blessings more numerous than the stars,
>   More lasting, and more bright.
>
> " That cov'nant the last accents claim
>   Of this poor faltering tongue,
> And *that* shall the first notes employ
>   Of my celestial song."

With these views before you, Christian brethren, suffer, in conclusion, the word of exhortation; and this chiefly in the language of the Lord Himself, and His Apostles.

"Let your light so shine before men, that they may see your good works, and glorify your Father that is in heaven. Be the children of your Father in heaven, who maketh His sun to rise on the evil and on the good, and sendeth rain on the just and on the unjust. Lay not up treasures on earth, where moth and rust doth corrupt, and where thieves break through and steal; but lay up for yourselves treasures in heaven, where moth and rust doth not corrupt, and where thieves do not break through and steal: for where your treasure is, there will your heart be also. Let your eye be single, that the whole body may be full of light. Seek first the kingdom of God, and His righteousness, and all things shall be added to you. Whatsoever ye would that men should do to you, do ye even so to them; for this is the law and the prophets. Ask, and ye shall receive; seek, and ye shall find; knock, and it shall be opened to you. For every one that asketh receiveth, and he that seeketh findeth, and to him that knocketh it shall be opened. Pray, and do not faint. Fear not them who, after they have killed the body, have no more that they can do; but fear Him who, after He has killed the body, can cast both soul and body into hell-fire. Fear Him. Believe in God; believe in Me. Let not your heart be troubled, neither be afraid. Abide in Me, and I in you. Continue in My love. Ye are My friends, if ye do whatsoever I command you. Love one another. Love one another *as* I have loved you. Watch and pray, that ye enter not into temptation. Reckon yourselves to be dead indeed unto sin, but alive unto God. Let not sin reign in your mortal body, that ye should obey it in the lusts thereof. Neither yield ye your members as instruments of unrighteousness unto sin; but yield yourselves to God, as those that are alive from the dead, and your members as instruments of righteousness unto God. Present your bodies a living sacrifice, holy, acceptable to God, which is rational worship. Be not conformed to this world, but be transformed by the renewing of your mind, that you may prove what is that good and acceptable and perfect will of God. Know that your body is the temple of the Holy Ghost, which is in you, which ye have of God; and that ye are not your own, for ye are bought with a price: therefore glorify God in your bodies and in your spirits, which are God's. Whether ye eat or drink, or whatever ye do, do all to the glory of God. Covet earnestly the best gifts. Follow after charity. Let all things be done in charity. See that ye receive not the grace of God in vain. Come out from the world, and be separate. Touch not the unclean thing. Love not the world, nor the things that are in the world. Cleanse yourselves from all filthiness of the flesh and spirit, and perfect holiness in the fear of God. Stand fast in the liberty wherewith Christ hath made you free, and be not entangled with any yoke of bondage. Live in the spirit. Walk in the spirit. Be not deceived. Do not deceive yourselves. Be not weary in well-doing. Do good to all as you have opportunity, especially to the household of faith. Put off the old man; put on the new man. Be followers of God, as dear children; and walk in love, as Christ also hath loved you. Have no fellowship with the unfruitful works of darkness. Give thanks always for all things to God and the Father, in the name of our Lord Jesus Christ. Pray always, with all prayer and supplication for all saints. Let the mind be in you which was in Christ Jesus. Look not every man on his own things only, but every man also on the things of others. Let your moderation be known to all men, and be anxious about nothing. Seek the things that are above. Set your affections on *them*, and not on the things on the earth. Let the word of Christ dwell in you richly. Walk in wisdom to them who are without. Whatsoever ye do in word or in deed, do all in the name of the Lord Jesus, giving thanks to God and the Father by Him. Let the rich in this world not be highminded, nor trust in uncertain riches, but in the living God, who giveth us richly all things to enjoy. Let them do good; be rich in good works, ready to distribute, willing to communicate; laying up in store for themselves a good deposit against the time to come, that ye may lay hold on eternal life. Let the poor see that they be rich in faith, and heirs of the kingdom. Let husbands love their wives, as Christ loves the Church. Let wives be subject to their husbands, as the Church is to Christ. Let parents bring up their children in the nurture and admonition of the Lord. Let children be obedient to their parents in the Lord. Let masters give to their servants the things that are just and equal; and let servants obey not with eye-service, as men-pleasers, but with singleness of heart, as serving God. Let every soul be subject to the higher powers. Let the elders feed the flock of Christ; let them watch for souls as they who must give account; and let the brethren submit themselves to their self-chosen elders, and esteem them very highly in love, for their work's sake." These are some of the commandments of our Lord Jesus, and of His holy Apostles. Lay them up in your hearts, practise them in your lives; and remember that "this is love, that we walk after His commandments," and in keeping these commandments there is great reward. Look to yourselves, then, brethren, that we lose not the things which we have wrought, but that you and we may both receive a full reward. Finally, brethren, whatsoever things are true, whatsoever things are honest, whatsoever things are just, whatsoever things are pure, whatsoever things are lovely, whatsoever things are of good report, if there be any virtue and any praise, think on these things. Now may the God of all grace, who hath called you unto His eternal glory by Christ Jesus, make you perfect, stablish, strengthen, settle you. And unto Him who is able to keep you from falling, and to present you faultless before the presence of His glory with exceeding joy, to the only wise God our Saviour, be glory and majesty, dominion and power, both now and ever. Amen.

DISCOURSE VI.

ENTRANCE INTO THE HOLIEST BY THE BLOOD OF CHRIST.

Heb. x. 19-22.—"Having therefore, brethren, boldness to enter into the holiest by the blood of Jesus, by a new and living way, which He hath consecrated for us through the vail, that is to say, His flesh; and having an High Priest over the house of God; let us draw near with a true heart, in full assurance of faith, having our hearts sprinkled from an evil conscience, and our bodies washed with pure water."

The text resolves itself into two parts,—a statement of facts or principles, which are taken for granted, as already fully proved; and an exhortation to duty, grounded on the admission of these facts or principles. The statement is in these words:—" We have boldness to enter into the holiest by the blood of Jesus, by a new and living way, which He hath consecrated for us through the vail, that is to say, His flesh; and we have a great High Priest over the house of God." The exhortation is in these words:—" Let us draw near with a true heart, in full assurance of faith, having our hearts sprinkled from an evil conscience." To the illustration of this statement and of this injunction, in their order, I mean to devote the following discourse.

I. We begin with the statement of the principles taken for granted. These are two—the first of them more largely and particularly stated, the second more generally and briefly. The first principle which the Apostle takes for granted as sufficiently proved, as stated in our version, is, that "we have boldness to enter into the holiest by the blood of Jesus, by a new and living way, which He hath consecrated for us through the vail, that is to say, His flesh." What is this principle? What do these words mean? for they certainly are not self-obvious.

It is not often that we have reason to complain of our excellent translation of the Holy Scriptures, that it is not sufficiently literal. It is, indeed, in consequence of its extreme literalness, sometimes obscure, if not unintelligible. But in the passage before us, there is ground for such a charge. The words, literally rendered, are: " Having therefore," or 'thus,' " brethren, boldness, or confidence, in reference to the entrance into the holiest, by the blood of Jesus," or 'the entrance of Jesus by blood into the holiest,' " which"—*i.e.*, which entrance, or by which entrance—" He has consecrated for us a new and living way, through the vail, that is to say, of His flesh." The declaration, even thus rendered, is somewhat obscure, and, as a very acute and learned interpreter has remarked, " few seem to understand it."[1]

The first question to be resolved here is, What and where is that " entrance into the holiest," of which the Apostle here speaks? It has been common to consider the entrance into the holiest, here, as the entrance of believers; and that entrance has been explained of the thoughts and affections of Christians being fixed on, and their devotions directed to, the reconciled Divinity (of whom the glory hovering over the mercy-seat, sprinkled with blood, in the holy of holies, in the Jewish sanctuary, was an emblem) by which they, as it were, approach God, come to Him, even to His place, enter His peculiar dwelling-place,—in plain words, have all the intercourse with God which is compatible with a state in which the capacities and activities of the mind are limited by its union to a material body. But to this mode of interpretation there are strong objections; for throughout the whole of this Epistle, " the holy of holies" is the emblem of heaven; and to enter into the holy of holies, is, in other words, to go to heaven. Besides, it is plain that the Apostle is not here stating something new; he is referring to something which he had already illustrated. Now, what the Apostle has been illustrating, is neither that Christians have a present spiritual access to God, as a reconciled God, who is in heaven, nor that they shall have a future real bodily entrance into heaven; but that Christ, as our High Priest, has really and bodily entered into heaven, the true holy place, the antitype of the holy of holies in the tabernacle and temple. I cannot doubt, then, that the entrance here spoken of is this entrance of our Lord, by His own blood, on the ground of the accepted sacrifice which He finished in shedding His blood on the cross,—

[1] Valcknäer.

the entrance which took place in consequence of His ascension from Mount Olivet.

Thus has one main point been ascertained—' the entrance here spoken of is the entrance of our Lord into heaven;' but a few remarks on the construction of the passage, which is considerably involved, will be necessary, to open the way satisfactorily to a distinct apprehension of its meaning. These remarks I shall endeavour to make as brief and as plain as possible.

The words, " by a new and living way, which He has consecrated for us," are, literally, " by which entrance He has consecrated for us a new and living way," and are, I apprehend, parenthetical.

The phrase, " through the vail," if I mistake not, is immediately connected with the entrance of Jesus into the holiest of all by blood. It is a further description of this entrance. The entrance of Jesus by blood, through the vail, into the holy place, is just that described in chap. ix. 11, 12: " Christ being come a High Priest of good things to come, by a greater and more perfect tabernacle, not made with hands, that is, not of this building; neither by the blood of goats and calves, but by His own blood, entered in once into the holy place, having obtained eternal redemption for us."

The concluding explicatory phrase, " that is, His flesh," has commonly been supposed to refer to the expression which immediately precedes it—" the vail," and has been considered as teaching that our Lord's body, which He Himself compares to the temple, was the antitype of the vail which in the tabernacle and temple divided " the holy of holies" from the holy place, the second sanctuary from the first, and that the rending of that vail was symbolical of His death. However plausible this interpretation may be on a cursory survey, on a closer inspection, it will be found liable to great, and, as I conceive, insurmountable objections. Throughout the Epistle, as the holy of holies is the emblem of the heaven of heavens, the place of God's glory, so the holy place, the tabernacle and its vails, seem plainly to be the emblem of the visible heavens, by passing through which our High Priest entered into the heaven of heavens. Besides, though the rending of the vail, taken by itself, and in its consequences, as laying open the holy of holies, may not unfitly represent the death of Christ, by which the true way into the holiest of all was made manifest, yet the figure would not hold in the point here referred to. The high priest left the vail behind him, when through its opening he passed into the holy of holies; whereas Christ carried the human nature which suffered death, by its component parts being rudely torn asunder, with Him into heaven, and is there in the midst of the throne, " a Lamb as it had been slain."

On these grounds, I am disposed to consider these explanatory words, " that is, of His flesh," as referring not to our Lord's human nature, but to the entrance of that human nature into the holiest, the word entrance being understood here as repeated from the beginning of the sentence; just as in the parallel passage which I have quoted, " a greater and more perfect tabernacle, that is, not" the tabernacle " of this building." The passage, without the parenthesis, would read, " Having then, brethren, boldness, or confidence, respecting the entrance of Jesus by His own blood into the holiest of all, through the vail, that is, the entrance of His flesh." 'Being assured that Jesus Christ has, in His human nature, in consequence of His sacrifice, entered through the visible heavens into the heaven of heavens.' The parenthesis is, " which" entrance, or by which entrance, " He has consecrated for us a new and living way."

Having thus endeavoured to ascertain the true construction of this somewhat involved, and therefore obscure sentence, let us shortly illustrate the glorious truths which it unfolds. Jesus Christ, our great High Priest, has entered into the holiest. He has done so by His own blood; He has done so through the vail; He has done so bodily; and He has thus consecrated for us a new and living way into the holiest. In noticing these, we will perceive that these are just the great truths which the Apostle had been establishing, and were the heads of his discourse in the preceding section.

1. Jesus Christ is "entered" into heaven. He is no more on earth, dead or living. He has, as Mark says, been " received up into heaven, and set on the right hand of God." " He was carried up into heaven," says Luke. " This same Jesus," said the angels to the Apostles, "is taken up from you into heaven." " God," says Paul, " hath set Him at His own right hand in the heavenly places." " He is," says Peter, " gone into heaven,

and is on the right hand of God." This is what the Apostle has repeatedly stated in the previous context. Ch. i. 3, " He has sat down on the right hand of the Majesty on high." Ch. iv. 14, " Our great High Priest, Jesus the Son of God, has passed into the heavens." Ch. viii. 1, " We have an High Priest who is set on the right hand of the throne of the Majesty in the heavens." Ch. ix. 12, 24, " Christ has entered into the holy place"—" not into the holy places made with hands, which are the figures of the true, but into heaven itself."

2. Jesus Christ has entered into heaven " by His own blood." He has entered as a High Priest, not without blood— not with the blood of animal sacrifices, but by the blood of His own sacrifice. He could not have entered in this character, but on the ground of expiatory sacrifice offered and accepted. It was " because He humbled Himself, and became obedient to death, the death of the cross," that " God so highly exalted Him." His entrance into heaven was the fruit of His dying on earth. This, too, is stated in the previous illustrations. Ch. i. 3, " Having purged our sins by Himself, He sat down on the right hand of the Majesty on high." Ch. ii. 9, " For the suffering of death, He was crowned with glory and honour." Ch. ii. 10, " As the Captain of our salvation, He was made perfect through suffering." Ch. v. 9, " By learning obedience through the things which He suffered, He has become the Author of eternal salvation to all who obey Him." Ch. ix. 12, " He is entered in, not by the blood of goats and calves, but by His own blood." Ch. x. 12, " After He had offered one sacrifice for sin, He for ever sat down on the right hand of God."

3. Jesus Christ has by His own blood entered into heaven, "through the vail;" that is, as I have attempted to show, through those visible heavens which, like the vail in the temple, conceal the glories of the true holy of holies, and must, in our conception, be passed through in order to entering it. On that memorable day on which our Lord led out His chosen Apostles as far as to Bethany, and lifted up His hands and blessed them, "while He blessed them, He was parted from them, and carried up into heaven,"—" He was taken up, and a cloud received Him out of their sight." To this also the Apostle refers in the preceding context. Ch. iv. 14, which *may*, probably *should* be, rendered: " Our great High Priest, Jesus Christ the Son of God, has

passed through the heavens." Ch. ix. 12, " He is entered into the holy place by"—through—" a greater and more perfect tabernacle, not the tabernacle of this building,"—even that expanse which He has set as a " tabernacle for the sun."

4. Jesus Christ has entered *bodily* into heaven. The entrance is the entrance of " His flesh." " Flesh and blood," in their present state, " cannot inherit the kingdom of God." But the human nature of our Lord, though gloriously transformed, substantially went up into heaven. His entrance was not a metaphorical one; it was a real one. His entrance into heaven was as really a bodily entrance as that of the Jewish high priest into the holy of holies, which was its emblem. The same God-man Jesus, who died on the cross, ascended up through these heavens into the heaven of heavens, and there, as the representative of His people, He appears in human nature in the immediate presence of God. Thus Stephen, being full of the Holy Ghost, looked up stedfastly to heaven, and saw the glory of God, and Jesus standing on the right hand of God, and he said, " Behold, I see the heavens opened, and the Son of man standing on the right hand of God." Acts vii. 55, 56.

5. The only other truth contained in the words before us, is that expressed in the parenthetical clause, that Jesus Christ " has consecrated this entrance of His a new and living way to us into the holiest;" or, " by this entrance has consecrated for us a new, a living way into the holiest." To " consecrate" signifies to set apart, to open up, to sanction,—to make at once possible, lawful, and safe. Originally, there was a way for innocent, holy man into the holiest of all—the way of perfect personal obedience. Sin shut up that way. For man the sinner there is no entrance into the holiest. " There shall in no wise enter into *it* anything that defileth." But a way has been re-opened; and it has been re-opened in the entrance of Jesus by blood through the vail into the holy place, the entrance " of His flesh ;"—that is, in plain words, in consequence of this entrance of our Lord, provision is made that all who believe in Him—forgiven, justified, and sanctified through His atonement and Spirit, and raised and transformed by His mighty power, whereby He is able to subdue all things to Himself—shall, like Him, in their complete nature, body and soul, pass through these visible heavens into the heaven of heavens, enter into, and permanently dwell in,

the immediate presence of God. His entrance secures theirs. It was " as the Forerunner that He for them entered into that within the vail." "I go," said He, just as He was about to enter, "I go to My Father's house to prepare a place for you. And if I go, I will come again, and take you to Myself; that where I am, there ye may be also." "I am the way. No man cometh to the Father but by Me." The merit which opened the way to Him, and the power with which that merit has been rewarded, will open the way for them. Their spirits made perfect, in bodies changed like unto His glorious body, they shall, like Him, be caught up in the clouds, and go into heaven.

This way of entering heaven, for men, is "a new and living way." It is new—altogether different from the old original way of perfect personal obedience as the condition of eternal life, now inaccessible by man; it was not made manifest under the former covenant, but is a way belonging to the new covenant, where all is new—newly opened up, newly proclaimed. And it is living, life-giving. Any attempt to enter by the old way ends in the second death. This, this alone, is the way of life.

Perhaps there may be an allusion to its contrast with the entrance of the high priest into the holiest in the temple. He entered alone; and his entrance was not sanctioned as a pattern to others. He who should have attempted to follow him would have met death, not life. This, then, is the first great fact or principle which the Apostle states as a matter of undoubted certainty: We have confidence that Jesus has with His own blood, on the ground of the sacrifice of Himself, in His human nature passed through these visible heavens into the heaven of heavens, and has thus secured that, in due time, all His people shall do so likewise.

The second principle which the Apostle represents as the object of confident belief, will not require such extended illustration. It is, that "we have"—plainly in Him who has entered—"a great High Priest over the house of God." The figurative expression, "the house of God," does not seem here, as in chap. iii. of this Epistle, to represent 'the family of God,' but 'the temple of God.' An overseer belongs to a family; a high priest to a temple. For a high priest to be "over the temple of God," is rightfully to do, prescribe, and administer all that is necessary and fit in reference to the religious relations and interests of those for whom he acts. In Christ Jesus, gone into heaven, we have one who has offered an all-prevalent atoning sacrifice, and who, on the ground of that atoning sacrifice, is doing all for and in those for whom He ministers, which is necessary to bring them into the most intimate and permanent fellowship with God in the heavenly temple. This, indeed, is the sum of the things that have been spoken in the whole of the preceding discussions, from the close of the 4th chapter: "We have in Jesus Christ, the Son of God, a great High Priest," taken from among men, one ordained for men in things pertaining to God, to offer both gifts and sacrifices for sins; who has, by the one offering of Himself through the eternal Spirit, expiated their guilt, and, on the ground of the acceptance of that sacrifice, "is set on the right hand of the throne of the Majesty in the heavens, a minister of the sanctuary and of the true tabernacle, which the Lord pitched, not man;" "able also to save to the uttermost all that come to God by Him, seeing He ever liveth to make intercession for them."

II. Having thus cursorily illustrated the Apostle's *statement*, let us now consider the exhortation he founds on it. "Having confidence that Jesus has entered with His own blood through these visible heavens into the heaven of heavens, entered in His flesh, and that in Him we have a great High Priest over the house of God, let us draw near with a true heart, in full assurance of faith, having our hearts sprinkled from an evil conscience." Here there should be a point. What follows is connected with a second exhortation, contained in the 23d verse, based on its own proper foundation, which I do not intend at present to illustrate; thus: "And having our bodies washed with pure water,"—having in baptism made a solemn profession of our faith,—"let us hold fast that profession of faith without wavering." This, then, is the exhortation to which for a little our attention is to be turned: "Let us draw near with a true heart, in full assurance of faith, having our hearts sprinkled from an evil conscience."

Here three things call for our consideration: The duty recommended—"to draw near;" the manner in which it should be performed—"with a true heart, in full assurance of faith;" and the means by which we are to be enabled *thus* to perform it—"having our heart sprinkled from an evil conscience."

"To draw near" is an elliptical expression, but it is easy to supply the ellipsis—"to draw near to God." The reference seems to be to the Levitical service. When the high priest entered into the holy of holies, the congregation of Israel stood praying without in the court of the temple, not drawing near, and waiting for the return of their representative, who was never to lead them into the holy of holies. But Christians, having confidence that their High Priest has entered into the true holiest of all, and that He has thus made preparation for their entrance in due time there also, need not stand at a distance from the Divinity fully reconciled—God in Christ reconciling the world to Himself,—but may and ought to "draw nigh," waiting for the coming forth of the High Priest, which is to be the prelude of their being taken up,—looking for the blessed hope, the glorious appearance of Him who is the great God and our Saviour,—looking for His coming, not with a sin-offering, but for the complete salvation of those who are waiting for Him. The phrase is figurative. It does not express a movement of the body, but a state or exercise of the mind and heart. It is often explained as equivalent to worship; but it is an expression of wider extent of meaning. Man's natural state as a fallen being is a state of alienation from, non-intercourse with, dislike of, opposition to God. Men do not like to retain God in their knowledge. They think of Him as little as possible; they are afraid of Him; they have no complacency in worshipping and serving Him. To draw near to God is the reverse of all this. It is, in the knowledge and belief of the truth regarding Him, to make Him the chief subject of our thoughts, the supreme object of our affections; to cling to Him in love and confidence, habitually to realize His presence, and to seek happiness in conformity to and fellowship with Him; to have the mind and the heart always going forth towards Him, always drawing nearer and nearer to Him. Christians, on hearing the trumpet of the Gospel, are not, like the Israelites at Sinai, to "remove and stand afar off," but they are to "come near, even to His seat." This is to be their habitual temper, but specially exercised in the offices of religion, secret, private, and public.

The manner in which this duty of drawing near is to be performed is thus described: "With a true heart," and "in the full assurance of faith."

The first of these expressions is nearly equivalent to our Lord's description of acceptable worship—"in spirit and in truth:"—with the heart, the *inner* man, in opposition to formality; with the heart influenced by truth, really influenced by truth, in opposition to hypocrisy: not a bodily, but a mental approach; not a figurative, but a real approach: with the understanding enlightened with the truth, and the affections filled with the objects that truth reveals: not under the influence of the evil heart of unbelief, which leads away from the living God, but under the influence of the good and honest heart, made so by the Spirit through the truth, which unites man's mind and heart to the mind and will of God, and gives fellowship with Him, in knowledge, and holiness, and true felicity.

The second expression descriptive of the manner in which Christians are to draw near to God, is, "in the full assurance of faith." The phrase, "full assurance of faith," is just equivalent to 'the fullest, most assured belief.' The question naturally occurs, The full, assured belief of what? Not of our own individual salvation, though that assurance naturally rises out of this, but of the great truths respecting Jesus Christ as our great High Priest, especially of those stated in the immediate context:—that He has, on the ground of His perfect and accepted sacrifice, passed through these heavens into the heaven of heavens, there to appear in the presence of God for us; and that He has entered as the Forerunner,—having secured that in due time all His people shall, like Him, pass through these heavens into the heaven of heavens. It is the faith of the truth respecting the reality and the efficacy of the sacrifice of our Lord, and the hope that springs out of that faith, that emboldens us to draw near to Him, from whose presence, but for this faith and hope, had we just views of His holiness, justice, and power, we would seek for concealment under falling rocks and overturned mountains. It is well remarked by Dr Owen, that "'the full assurance of faith' here does not respect the assurance that any may have of their own salvation, nor any degree of such assurance; it is only the full satisfaction of our soul and conscience of the reality and efficacy of Christ's priesthood to give us acceptance with God, in opposition to all other ways and means thereof, that is intended."

It now only remains that we attend to the means by which Christians are to be enabled to comply with the Apostle's exhortation, to "draw near with a true heart, and in the full assurance of faith." "Having our hearts sprinkled from an evil conscience."

There is no drawing near to God with a heart defiled by an evil conscience. There is no obtaining deliverance from this defilement but by the sprinkling of blood on the conscience— "precious blood, the blood of Christ, as of a lamb without spot and blemish."

An evil conscience is a mind and heart burdened and polluted by unpardoned guilt. A man who has offended God, who knows that He has offended Him, and who has no solid ground of hope of forgiveness, is naturally alienated from God, indisposed to think of Him, altogether unfit for enlightened affectionate intercourse with Him. A stranger to confidence and love, he is full of jealousy, fear, and dislike. He must get rid of the evil conscience in order to his coming to God.

The removal of this obstruction in the way of drawing near to God, is described by the Apostle as the having "the heart sprinkled from an evil conscience." The evil conscience must be removed; and this is to be done "by the sprinkling of the heart" with the blood of atonement. There is here, as throughout the whole section, a reference to the Levitical order of worship. The Israelite could not be fitted for drawing near to God, through the sacrifice offered for him, unless he was sprinkled with its blood. Now, what in the spiritual economy answers to the sprinkling of blood under the external economy, which was its shadow and type? Plainly, that which gives the individual a personal interest in the expiatory and justifying efficacy of the great atonement, by which alienated man is enabled to draw near to God in spiritual service. Now, what is this, but the faith of the truth respecting salvation through Christ, produced in the soul by the effectual operation of the Spirit of Christ? When men believe this truth, God is seen in His true character —infinitely excellent, amiable, and kind; the enmity of the heart is slain, the jealousies of guilt are destroyed, and, instead of the constant attempt to exclude God from the mind and affections, with the heart they desire Him, with their spirit within them they seek Him early. The desire of their heart is to *Him*, and towards the remembrance of His name. They draw near to God, and find it good to draw near to Him; and the habitual language of their heart is, 'Whom have I in heaven but Thee? and there is none upon the earth whom I desire beside Thee.' It is just in the degree in which, through the faith of the truth, we realize the expiatory and forgiving, the soul-transforming and heart-satisfying influences of the atonement of Christ, that we can with a true heart draw near to God, and walk with Him in humility and love, " serving Him without fear, in righteousness and holiness, all the days of our life;" looking for the blessed hope, the glorious appearing of our Lord Jesus Christ, who has entered through these heavens into the heaven of heavens, and will be retained by them till the times of the restitution of all things; but who, according to His promise, will then return to earth, to gather together into one all His chosen people, and conduct them, soul and body, by the new and living way, which as the Forerunner He has opened up and consecrated, into the temple of God in heaven, where, before the eternal throne—near, very near, Him who sits on it—they shall serve Him day and night, uninterruptedly, eternally. And good reason have *we* thus to draw nigh. Our Saviour is in heaven; He has made all preparation for taking us there; He has promised to do so:—I go to prepare a place for you; and if I go, I will come again, and take you to Myself, that where I am, ye may be also. And He is faithful that has promised. All men have not faith—are not trustworthy; but the Lord is faithful. Though He is a man, He is not such a man that He can lie; though the Son of man, He is not such a son of man that He can repent. If it had not been so, He would not have told us so. So much for the illustration of the statement and exhortation of which our text consists.

It now only remains that, as the practical improvement of the discourse, we to-day endeavour to comply with the Apostle's exhortation, "Let us draw near." The command is not to us, as to Moses at Horeb, "Draw not nigh hither;" or to the Israelites at Sinai, "Go not up to the mount, touch not the border of it;" "break not through unto the Lord to gaze." No; it is, "Draw near. Come boldly." "We are not come unto the mount that might be touched, and that burned with fire, and unto blackness, and darkness, and tempest, and the sound of a trumpet, and the voice of words, which they that heard entreated that the word should not be spoken to them any more; but we are come to Mount Zion, and unto the city of the living God, the heavenly Jerusalem; and to an innumerable company of angels, the general assembly and the church of the first-born, whose names are written in heaven; and to God the Judge of all; and to the spirits of just men made perfect; and to Jesus, the Mediator of the new covenant; and to the blood of sprinkling, which speaketh better things than that of Abel." Seek, then, my brethren, that through the faith of the truth your hearts may be anew sprinkled from an evil conscience, your conscience purged from dead works, that you may be enabled to serve the living God, not in the oldness of the letter, but in newness of spirit—acceptably, with reverence and godly fear; but yet with holy boldness, free from the fear that has torment, in the full, assured belief of a completed and accepted atonement; in the firm though humble expectation of the salvation that is in Christ with eternal glory; in the *faith* that your Lord is bodily in heaven and spiritually here; and in the hope of seeing Him spiritually here, and in due time of seeing Him face to face, very near Him, and find it good for you to be thus near HIM. Thus will ye go not only to the altar of God, but to *God* Himself, your supreme portion, your chief joy. Thus shall you know that "truly your fellowship is with the Father, and with His Son Jesus Christ.

DISCOURSE VII.

THE JOINT PERFECTION OF OLD AND NEW TESTAMENT SAINTS IN HEAVEN.[1]

Heb. xi. 39, 40.—"And these all, having obtained a good report through faith, received not the promise: God having provided some better thing for us, that they without us should not be made perfect."

The remark of the Apostle Peter, that " in the Epistles of his beloved brother Paul there are some things hard to be understood," will be readily acquiesced in by all who have made these Epistles the subject of careful study ; and to none of these inspired letters does the remark apply with greater force, than to the Epistle to the Hebrews, to which he seems, indeed, to have had a direct reference in making the observation. What is hard to be understood, is, however, by no means equivalent to what is impossible to be understood. Of this I trust that we have had satisfactory proof, in some of the illustrations of select passages from this Epistle, which at intervals I have laid before you ; and that we have found, too, that when the Apostle's meaning is somewhat difficult to be apprehended, its importance, when discovered, far more than compensates for all the pains bestowed on the investigation. Another of these somewhat difficult passages comes now before us for consideration. May God open our understandings, that we may understand this portion of the Scriptures. May He open our hearts to receive the love of the truth which it contains, that it may thus contribute to our salvation.

The remarkable words before us are the conclusion of the Apostle's historical illustrations of the importance of faith, as that which can enable a man to do what otherwise he could not

[1] This was the last Action Sermon prepared by the lamented Author. On finishing it, he expressed his persuasion that his work was about done.

have done, suffer what otherwise he could not have suffered, obtain what otherwise he could not have obtained. They consist of two parts:—First, " And all these, having obtained a good report through faith, received not the promise." Second, " God having provided some better thing for them, that they without us might not be made perfect."

I. The words, " all these," have by some interpreters been considered as referring only to the whole of those who, in the immediate context, are represented as having suffered under the influence of faith, in contrast with those who, in the words preceding these, are represented as having *acted* under its influence. The latter, according to the Apostle, ver. 33, " by faith obtained promises;" the former, though they have " obtained a good report through faith, received not the promise." While Gideon, and Barak, and Jephthah, and Samson, and David, and Samuel, by their heroic deeds, performed under the influence of faith, " obtained promises," *i.e.*, obtained possession of the blessings promised to them, those who, when exposed to the fury of the Syro-Macedonian king, through faith endured tortures of the most exquisite kind, vers. 35-38, obtained indeed a good report, but died without obtaining any such blessings: " *they* received not the promise." On carefully looking at the passage, however, it is scarcely possible, I think, to doubt that the contrast is not between two different classes of the ancient worthies—between the *working* believers and the *suffering* believers, but between believers under the ancient economies—the patriarchal and Mosaic—the elders who received a good report, mentioned at the 2d verse of the chapter—and believers under the new economy—the Christian ; and that what he says is this, ' All these persons (to whose history the Apostle, in the preceding chapter, refers as an illustration of the power of faith,—all those whose names are so honourably recorded in the book of God, on account of their faith, or its results), " all these received *not* the promise." ' We should have expected just the reverse of this declaration—' All these *did* receive the promise ;' but the Apostle's assertion is, ' All these did *not* receive the promise.' What can this mean ?

The words, " did not receive the promise," taken by themselves, may signify, ' had not the promise made to them,' or, ' had not the promise fulfilled to them.' There are interpreters who adopt each of these views. Those interpreters who take the first view of the words, explain them thus:—' Those ancient believers had a number of promises made to them, " exceeding great and precious promises;" but there was one promise, which by way of eminence may be called *the* promise—the promise of " the resurrection," and " eternal life" in heaven,—that promise was not given to *them*. *They* obtained it not; we *have*. " Life and immortality are brought to light by the Gospel." This better thing is provided for *us*.'

This explication is, however, by no means satisfactory; for it is evident, from the statements made in the preceding part of this chapter, vers. 11, 13–16, as well as from our Lord's argument from the declaration made to Moses at the bush, in the desert, that the promise, " I am the Lord thy God,"—which all these worthies received in the sense of its being made to them,—included the promise of resurrection and immortal happiness, Luke xx. 37, 38; and it is clear also, that it was understood by them to include this promise. This promise, no doubt, is more fully unfolded to us than to them; it is expressed in much plainer terms in the New Testament than in the Old; but the promise of eternal life, though forming no part of the Mosaic law, was yet given to the people of God, both to those who lived before the giving of that institute, and to those who lived under it.

The expression here, " received the promise," must then be understood, not of the having the promise *made*, but of having it *fulfilled* to them; just as " to inherit the promises," Heb. vi. 12, means, to inherit the promised blessings. But still the question remains, What is that promised blessing, which none of the Old Testament worthies, though renowned for their faith, did receive? The great blessing promised to the ancient Church, both before the law and under the law, was salvation, in all the extent of meaning that belongs to that most comprehensive word, through the Messiah. It was promised to them that " the seed of the woman should bruise the head of the serpent; that in Abraham's seed all the families of the earth should be blessed; that to them a Child should be born, a Son given, whose name should be Wonderful, Counsellor, the Mighty God, the Everlasting Father, the Prince of Peace; and that Israel should be saved in the Lord with an everlasting salvation."

Now this blessing, which is indeed a congeries of blessings, these ancient believers did not receive during their mortal life. They died before the Messiah became incarnate, and suffered, and died, and rose again; and consequently they could not enjoy the blessings which originate in the fuller and clearer revelation of the truth respecting the salvation of the Messiah, and in that correspondingly enlarged communication of divine influence, which were the natural consequence of that great event. They saw the promised blessings afar off, and were persuaded of them, and embraced them, and lived under their influence; but they "received" them not (ver. 13). On their death, indeed, they entered on a state free from sin, and suffering, and fear; but still they "received not the promise." They were "saved," but "in hope." They waited in paradise—some of them thousands of years—expecting the manifestation of the mystery of mercy; but till that took place they could not have the full knowledge or enjoyment of the promised blessing. We have no reason to think that the departed spirits of good men, who died before the coming of Christ, knew more of the plan of salvation than the angels did, who had to learn from the divine dispensations to the Church that manifold wisdom of God: Eph. iii. 10. On the Word being made flesh, on His finishing the work on the earth which the Father had given Him to do, and on His taking possession of His mediatorial throne, great accessions were made both to the knowledge and blessedness of these happy spirits. But even yet "they have not" fully "received the promise." The promise of a glorious resurrection, and an immortal, celestial life in their entire natures, remains yet unperformed. It is not to them a matter of enjoyment, but of expectation. They are, in reference to these, but "saved in hope." Their flesh rests in hope, in the silence and quiet of the grave; and their spirits, looking forward to the glorious consummation, breathe out the longing desire, "How long, O Lord! how long!" Thus did all the ancient worthies, though celebrated for their faith, *not* receive the promised blessing.

It would have been, as I have already observed, more in accordance with our anticipations, had the Apostle said, 'All these, having obtained a good report through faith, did receive the promise.' After all the difficulties and trials, labours and suffering, to which they were exposed, they at last obtained, in the fulfilment of promises made to them, a rich recompense for them all. And this might have been justly enough said; for all true believers under the former economy did, immediately on death, obtain blessings which had been promised them, and which far more than compensated for all their toils and sorrows. And further, such a statement would have well comported with the Apostle's object, which was to support and animate the Hebrew Christians amid their trials. But the statement contained in the text, as we have seen, is equally true, that these excellent men, notwithstanding their faith, were not immediately, were not soon, put in possession of the great blessing; and it was at least equally fitted to prevent the Christian Hebrews from becoming faint in their minds because not fully invested immediately with the blessings of the Christian salvation, and to induce them to persevere in doing and suffering the will of God, though the promised blessing seemed long in being conferred on them. What a delight to sit down with Abraham, and Isaac, and Jacob, and Isaiah, and Paul, and all the prophets, in the kingdom of God! What a comfort to think, when parted by more than sea and land from a dear Christian friend, we are not parted for ever: we will meet again—meet again to be made perfect, to be made perfect together—perfected together with brethren—glorified together with our Lord!

Some have supposed that the intended practical application of the Apostle's remark may be thus brought out: 'These ancient believers persevered in their attachment to Jehovah and His cause in life and in death, though the great object of their faith and hope was not bestowed on them. How much stronger the obligation, how much greater the encouragement, to persevere in the case of the Hebrew Christians, and of all Christians in all ages, who *have* received the promise, to whom the promised Deliverer has come! How comparatively easy to continue to believe in a well-established, past fact, in comparison with continuing to believe in a future event, in itself very improbable, and for which there was no ground of expectation but the divine promise! How much more, then, are your circumstances calculated to facilitate perseverance than theirs!' There is undoubted force in this reasoning, but we do not think that it is the argument suggested by the Apostle's train of thought. It is obvious that he represents the enjoyment of the promised blessing as future—not yet realized even in the case of the Christian Hebrews. "*Ye* have need of patience," says he, chap. x. 36, "that *after ye have done the will of God*, ye may obtain the promise." It is as if he had said in the words before us, 'Let not the fact, that the great object of your expectation is yet future—something which you do not yet enjoy—something that you are never to enjoy in the present state—something that will not be realized till the mystery of God is finished, at the consummation of all things,—let not this prevent you from persevering. All those elders who, by living and dying in faith, obtained a good report—so noble a memorial, and are now entered, though but entered, on the possession of the promised inheritance,—all these, during their whole mortal life, many of them for ages after their death, did not obtain what is by way of eminence called "the promise." Nay, none of them even yet are in *full* possession of it. You have no cause to complain that you are to be here, or saved in hope, not in fruition—that you are to live in faith, die in faith—believing, not seeing or possessing.'

That this is the practical bearing of the words, will, I trust, become more apparent as we proceed to the illustration of the second part of our text, contained in the 40th verse, which is certainly one of the most difficult in the whole Epistle. "God having provided some better thing for us, that they without us should not be made perfect."

II. There can be no doubt that the pronoun "*us*," here, refers to Christians—to those who live under the new economy. For them "God has provided some better thing." The question naturally occurs, Better than what? And the answer ordinarily returned is, 'Better than anything which the saints under the former economies received.' They received many good things, of which you have a catalogue in the beginning of the third and ninth chapters of the Epistle to the Romans; but they received not *the* promise, *i.e.*, the promised blessing, by way of eminence. We have received it. The Messiah is come, and we are blessed with heavenly and spiritual blessings in Him. "Blessed," says our Lord, "are the eyes which see the things ye see: for verily I say unto you, That many prophets and righteous men have desired to see the things which ye see, and have not seen them; and to hear the things which ye hear, and have not heard them!" "The mystery which was kept secret from former ages and generations has been unveiled." The great propitiation has been offered to God, and "set forth" to men. The way into the holiest of all has been made manifest. The influence of the Holy Spirit has been more copiously shed forth, and more efficaciously exerted. Life and immortality have been placed in a clear, full light by the Gospel. A rational, spiritual, easy system of worship, has taken the place of the carnal, complicated, and burdensome ordinances of the law. The Church has passed from a state of minority, subjected to tutors and governors, a state of pupilage, into a state of mature sonship.

Now all this is truth, important truth, delightful truth, influential truth; but still I cannot but doubt if it be the truth here stated. The promise here spoken of does not seem to be the promise of the Messiah—the promise that the Messiah should come; still less the promise of those blessings of His reign which are to be enjoyed in this world; but "the promise of eternal inheritance,"—a promise, the full accomplishment of which the saints under the new economy do not obtain in the present state, any more than their elder brethren under the former economies —a promise, the full accomplishment of which they are not to obtain till after they have done the will of God, as the Apostle states, chap. x. 36. These better things, which God has provided for us, or foreseen concerning us, are to be enjoyed, not here below, but when we and our elder brethren are made perfect together above. It is this being "made perfect" that is the sum of the better things.

The answer, then, which we feel constrained to give to the question, What is the reference of the word "better" in the clause before us?—with what are the things provided by God for His New Testament people, and not for them only, but all His people equally, compared?—is this: The comparison is not between what the saints under the old economy enjoyed, and those which saints under the new economy enjoy on earth; but between what the saints under the new economy enjoy on earth, and what they are ultimately to enjoy in heaven. He marks, not what is the difference between the two classes of believers; he refers to something in which they do not differ, but agree. God has provided for *us* something better than anything we can attain to in the present state, just as He prepared for them something better than anything they could attain to in the present state. The ultimate object of their faith and hope lay beyond death and the grave, and so does ours. The good things provided for us by God are thus described by the inspired writers: "We know that when the earthly house of our tabernacle is dissolved, we have a building of God, a house not made with hands, eternal in the heavens. When we are absent from the body, we shall be present with the Lord. We know that them who sleep in Jesus, God will bring with Him. When He who is our life shall appear, shall be manifested, we also shall appear, shall be manifested, with Him in glory. When He shall appear, we shall be like Him, seeing Him as He is. Seeing His face in righteousness, we shall be satisfied with His likeness. We look for the Saviour from heaven, the Lord Jesus Christ, who shall change these vile bodies, and fashion them like unto His own glorious body. For this mortal shall put on immortality, and this corruptible shall put on incorruption; and then shall be brought to pass that which is written, Death is swallowed up in victory. And so shall we be for ever with the Lord. We shall dwell for ever in the presence of God and the Lamb. We shall serve them day and night in the celestial temple; and we shall go no more out for ever." These are the things which God hath provided for us; and surely *these* are infinitely *better* than anything, however good, we can attain to here below.

But it may be said, These things are not provided exclusively for us Christians; they are laid up for all that love God, who ever lived, whether under the patriarchal, the Mosaic, or the Christian dispensation. We very readily admit this, but do not think that there is anything in the Apostle's words to lead us to conclude that the good, the better things he is speaking of, are the exclusive possession of Christians. For, indeed, if his words are carefully weighed, it will appear, as I have already hinted, that he is pointing out, not a *contrast*, but a resemblance, in the circumstances of Old Testament and New Testament believers. Old Testament believers did not obtain the promise in the present state, and neither do New Testament believers; for God has provided for them better things, in the better world, than any bestowed on them in this world. We, as well as our elder brethren, must live believing, and die believing; we must die in faith, as well as live by faith.

It now only remains that we turn our attention to the concluding clause of the sentence, "That they without us should not be made perfect." Some interpreters connect these words with the first clause, considering the second as a parenthesis; thus: "All these, having obtained a good report by faith, received not the promise, that they might not without us be perfected." We consider them as equally connected with both clauses. Their meaning may, I apprehend, be brought out more distinctly by a very slight change, which the original warrants, if it do not require. "These all, having obtained a good report through faith, received not the promise: God having provided some better thing for us, that they not without us"—*i.e.*, that both they and we —"might be made perfect;"—made perfect simultaneously, not one after another, no one preventing or getting before the other (1 Thess. iv.), at once. God has so arranged matters that the complete accomplishment of the promise, both to the Old Testament and to the New Testament believers, shall take place together—at the same time. They shall be made perfect, but not without us. We and they shall obtain perfection together. The Old Testament saints died without receiving the promised blessing; yet their faith was by no means of no avail. In due season they shall be perfected—the promise, in its full extent, will be performed to them. And as God has provided for us, too, better things than any that are enjoyed by us here below, when *they* are perfected, *we* shall be perfected along with them. "To be made perfect," is the same thing as to receive the promise—for the promise is a promise of perfect, holy happiness,— or to obtain the better things that God hath provided for us; for this is better, far better, than anything enjoyed here below.

> " 'Tis heaven below to taste His love,
> To know His power and grace;
> But what is this to heaven above,
> Where I shall see His face?"

This exactly corresponds with the representations in other parts of Scripture. The whole, whether they lived under the old or new dispensation, of the saved are together, either through a resurrection, or a miraculous, instantaneous change, to obtain the perfected glorified body, and are together to be put in possession of the salvation that is in Christ Jesus, with eternal glory. There is to be a gathering together of all the saved at the coming of our Lord Jesus Christ: they shall be presented, not one by one, but a glorious church, not having spot or wrinkle, or any such thing. As one assembly they shall be invited to enter into the kingdom prepared for them from the foundation of the world; and, caught up to meet the Lord in the air, they shall be conducted to those many mansions, in the house of His Father and their Father, in which righteousness dwells, and into which imperfection in no form can find entrance for ever.

And is not this being made perfect—is not this some better thing than anything enjoyed here below? Here we know but in part—we see through a glass darkly; but when that which is perfect is come, that which is in part shall be done away. Then we shall see face to face; then shall we know even as we are known. How many heavenly and spiritual benefits are bestowed on the people of God—many exceeding great and precious promises fulfilled to them! They are made truly holy, truly happy; but till the resurrection of the dead they will not attain that perfect conformity to God and His Son in which perfect holiness and happiness consists. Then they shall be like their God and Saviour. They shall enter into the Saviour's joy, and be holy as God is holy, perfect as He is perfect—the objects of His entire moral approbation, His unmixed complacency. O how great is the goodness which He has laid up for them that fear Him! Eye has not seen it, ear has not heard it, heart has not conceived it.

What a glorious anticipation for every believer individually! And how is its delight increased by the consideration, that all are together to receive the promise, all together to be made perfect!—an innumerable multitude, out of every age and country, tongue and nation, made perfect at once!

This places in a peculiarly glorious light the power and grace of the Saviour—of Him who is the Author of all our blessings, good, better, best. Had all the dead saints at the resurrection of Christ—a goodly company, but still comparatively a little flock—been set free from the bonds of death, received in full the promise of eternal life; and had, since that time, every saint been freed from the necessity of dying, and been quietly clothed upon instead of being unclothed; the scene would have been incomparably less striking than that which will be exhibited on the last eventful day of the world's history, when the merit and the power of the Redeemer will bring the whole human race out of their graves and before His tribunal, and enable Him to confer on all of them an endless existence—on His own redeemed ones an endless existence of perfect holy happiness. What a day of triumph to the Redeemer as well as the redeemed! How glorious will the King of Israel be that day, at the head of His reanimated legions, all of them now more than conquerors, through Him that loved them! With what a benignant eye will the good Shepherd contemplate His sheep, now no more a divided and little flock, but a multitude no man can number, yet of that number not one lost! Oh, in that gathering together at His coming, how glorious will He be in His saints; how will He be admired by the angelic millions, *in* them that believe, who through faith have now obtained the promise!

Such views were surely well fitted to encourage the Christian Hebrews to persevere in believing and professing the truth, amid all the difficulties and trials they might be exposed to—to live by faith, to die in faith. Valuable as are the blessings they enjoy here, better things, absolute perfection is awaiting them at the coming of the Lord. This is promised, and He is faithful that hath promised. The blessed hope, the glorious appearance of our Lord, with which the receiving of the promise is connected, is absolutely certain. For yet a little while—as He reckons time with whom one day is as a thousand years, and a thousand years as one day—and He that shall come will come, and will not tarry. Living by faith, dying in faith, is the only way of realizing this better thing, this absolute perfection. They who draw back, draw back to perdition. It is they only who persevere in believing that attain to the salvation of the soul. That is, in every sense of the word, the end of our faith.

Such is the interpretation of this passage, somewhat hard to be understood, which appears to me the most probable. It is an interpretation that gives cohesion to every part of the Apostle's statement. The meaning brought out is in accordance with the doctrine of Scripture generally, and bears directly on the object which the Apostle has in view—the impressing on the minds of the Hebrews the pre-eminent importance of persevering faith. At the same time, it is but right to state that it is not the ordinary mode of interpretation, and it may be well to state in a few words the manner in which the passage is generally understood: "The ancient worthies persevered in their faith, although the Messiah was known to them only by promise. We are under greater obligations than they to persevere; for God has fulfilled His promise respecting the Messiah, and thus placed us in circumstances in which continued faith should be found a comparatively easy thing, and in which apostasy must incur guilt peculiarly deep, and expose to punishment peculiarly severe. So much is our condition superior to theirs, that we may say that their happiness is completed in the benefits bestowed on us." This is, no doubt, good sense and sound reasoning, but I cannot bring it out of the Apostle's words.

The practical use to be made of the important truth, that the great object of our hope, as well as of that of the ancient believers, is yet *future*, is abundantly obvious. It is to guard us against the undue influence of the present world, and to bring us under the power of the world that is to come; to make us look, not at the things that are seen and temporal, but at the things that are unseen and eternal; to walk by faith, and not by sight. Since our life is hid with Christ in God, and since we are not to appear in glory till we appear with Him, surely we should willingly be in the world even as He was in the world; surely we should set our affections on the things which are above, and not on the things that are on the earth; surely we should seek the things that are above, where He sits at God's right hand. We should mortify our members which are on the earth. We should crucify the flesh, with its affections and lusts. We should have our conversation in heaven, whence we are looking for the Saviour, our Lord Jesus Christ, who will change these vile bodies, and fashion them like unto His glorious body, according to the working whereby He is able even to subdue all things unto Himself. Surely we should be habitually looking for, longing for, the coming of our Lord Jesus, which has for its object the complete salvation of His people. We should gird up the loins of our mind, be sober, and hope to the end, for the grace that is to be brought to us at the revelation of Jesus Christ; and, taught by His grace, which brings salvation to all, of which we have heard in the word of the truth of the Gospel, which word we have received, not as the word of man, but, as it is in truth, the word of the living God, we should "deny ungodliness and worldly lusts, and live soberly, righteously, and godly in this world, looking for that blessed hope, the glorious appearance of our Lord Jesus Christ, who gave Himself for us that He might redeem us from all iniquity, and purify us unto Himself, a peculiar people, zealous of good works." Thus may we, my brethren, be enabled to improve it; thus may we, by a constant continuance in well-doing, seek for and obtain glory, honour, and immortality. May we all of us, habitually looking for the mercy of our Lord Jesus unto eternal life, find mercy of the Lord in that day; and, along with the venerable assembly of the patriarchs, the goodly fellowship of the prophets, the glorious company of the apostles, the noble army of the martyrs, the holy Church of God in all countries and ages, receive the promise—obtain the better thing provided for us—be made perfect in knowledge, holiness, and happiness; in one word, receive the complete salvation of the body and the soul, the "salvation that is in Christ Jesus, with eternal glory."

DISCOURSE VIII.

THE CHRISTIAN ALTAR.

Heb. xiii. 10.—" We have an altar, whereof they have no right to eat which serve the tabernacle."

It is a fact as honourable to Christianity, as disgraceful to human nature, that the difficulty with which that religion has hitherto made its way in our world, has been owing, not to faults, but excellences in it; and that those qualities which chiefly recommend it to the higher and uncorrupted orders of intelligent beings, are the very qualities which have excited the contempt and loathing, the neglect and opposition, of mankind, and led the great majority of those, in every age, to whom its claims have been addressed, to consider it as absolute foolishness. Purity, simplicity, and spirituality are the leading features of Christianity; and it is just because it is pure, simple, and spiritual that it is so much admired in heaven and despised on earth, that holy angels " desire to look into it," and that depraved men " make light of it."

The fondness of man for what is material in religion, and his dislike of what is spiritual, is strikingly illustrated in the extreme difficulty which was experienced by the primitive teachers of Christianity in weaning the Jews—even such of them as had in profession embraced the Gospel—from their excessive attachment to an order of things which had so much in it to strike the senses as Judaism. The manner in which these inspired men seek to attain this end, discovers " the wisdom from above" by which they were guided. They showed the Jew, whether converted or unconverted, that everything that was excellent in the economy which was vanishing away had its counterpart in the order of things which was in the process of introduction in something still more excellent; that the spiritual reality was far better than the material shadow; and that that which was glorious had no glory by reason of the glory that excelleth. They showed them, that if Christians have no visible, material representation of the divine glory on earth, towards which they draw near in bodily worship, they have the spiritual Divinity in heaven, to whom in spirit they approach, in exercises which employ their highest faculties, and interest their best affections; that if they had no splendid temple like that of Jerusalem, within whose sacred precincts, at appointed seasons, acceptable worship can be presented to Jehovah, they have access to the omnipresent God at all times, in all circumstances; that if they have no order of priests, like that of Aaron, to transact for them their business with God, they have, in the person of the incarnate Son of God, a great High Priest, who has by the sacrifice of Himself expiated all their sins, and, ever living to make intercession for them, is able to save them to the uttermost, coming to God through Him.

In the passage that lies before us now for explication, we find the Apostle applying this principle to the subject of sacred meats, on which the Jews seem to have valued themselves. Of many of the offerings which were laid on the altar of Jehovah, part only was consumed by fire, the rest being reserved for food, either for the priests, or for the offerer and his friends. This food was accounted peculiarly sacred, and the eating of it viewed as an important religious privilege. In the verse which immediately precedes our text, the Apostle had said in effect, in reference to these meats,—The grace of God—His free favour to sinners manifested in the Gospel—if understood and believed, will do the heart more good than the use of any kind of food, however sacred. And in the words we mean to fix your attention on, he goes on to say, that Christians had a species of spiritual sacred food far more holy than any which the Israelitish people, or even the Aaronical priesthood, were permitted to taste. "We have an altar, of which they have no right to eat who serve the tabernacle."

The train of thought in the paragraph these words introduce is natural and beautiful. It is as if the Apostle had said, ' If ye will hold to *meats*, know that as Christians you have a holier food than you, or even your priests, ever had as Jews. You have the flesh of Him who gave Himself as a sacrifice for you to feed on—that is meat indeed; His blood—that is drink indeed. The thought of His sufferings for them naturally introduces that of the fitness of their readily submitting to suffering for Him, under the beautiful image of going without the camp to Him, where He was crucified, bearing His reproach. And then comes the concluding thought, that as Christ is the true sacrifice, all our sacrifices are of a figurative and spiritual kind,—no longer sin-offerings and expiatory sacrifices, but simply offerings of thanksgiving, sacrifices of praise—praise to be expressed in the life as well as in the lips.

The language of the text is elliptical. Something must be supplied to make out the sense. But there is no difficulty in filling up the ellipsis. "We"—*i.e.*, we Christians, in opposition to "ye Jews"—"have an altar of which we have a right to eat, but of which they who serve, who minister, in the tabernacle—the Mosaic sanctuary, the temple—the Jewish worshippers, and even the Levitical priests—have no right to eat." By "the altar," we are either to understand sacrifices laid on the altar, or, what comes to the same thing, to "eat of," or from, "the altar," is to be understood as equivalent to—'to eat of sacred food which had been laid on the altar.' "Those who serve the tabernacle," or rather, "they who minister in the tabernacle," are, I apprehend, the Levitical priesthood.

There were, as I have already had occasion to observe, certain sacrifices of which the offerer and his friends were allowed to make a feast; and of by far the greater number of sacrifices a considerable portion was assigned as the food of the priests. You may consult Lev. vi. 26, vii. 15, 34, xix. 6; Num. vi. 19, xviii. 9, 10. But there was a class of offerings of which neither the offerer nor the priest was allowed to appropriate even the smallest part. The victim was considered as entirely devoted to God, and was wholly burnt with fire, either on the altar, or in a clean place without the camp while Israel was in the wilderness, and without the city after the erection of the temple in Jerusalem. For information respecting this class of sacrifices, you may consult Lev. iv. 3–12, xiv. 16, 27. Now it appears to me that the Apostle refers to this peculiarly sacred species of offering, of which even the priests were not allowed to participate as food; and that his assertion is, We Christians, as to sacred food, have higher privileges than the Jews—higher than even their priests. We are permitted to feast—spiritually, of course—on that sacrifice of which that class of sacrifices, of which not only no ordinary Israelite, but no priest, not even the high priest, was allowed to taste, was a typical representation.

The sacrifice referred to as being the food of Christians, is, without doubt, the sacrifice which our great High Priest, Jesus the Son of God, offered up once for all—the sacrifice of Himself. Of the class of Jewish sacrifices to which the Apostle alludes, which was not a large one, the sacrifice for the sins of the people offered up on the great day of atonement was the most remarkable; and it is probable that this sacrifice was in the view of his mind when he made the declaration we are now considering. No part of that sacrifice was to be used as food either by the people or the priests. The blood was to be brought into the holy place, that is, the holy of holies; and, after certain portions of the carcase had been burnt on the altar, all the remainder was to be taken without the camp, or beyond the walls of the city, and there consumed to ashes. Instead of any part of it being allowed to be eaten, it was considered as entirely a devoted thing; and he that even touched it was not permitted to mingle with the congregation of Israel till he had submitted to certain instituted lustratory rites. Now the sacrifice of our Lord was emblematized by this peculiarly sacred kind of offering. When He suffered, it was that He might, by the shedding and sprinkling of His own blood, sanctify the people, *i.e.*, expiate the sins of all the Israel of God, and fit them for acceptable intercourse with their covenant God. To mark the correspondence more closely, He suffered death beyond the gates of Jerusalem, as the bodies of the victims offered for the sins of Israel on the great day of atonement were consumed without the camp or the city. And this sacrifice, of the emblems of which no Israelite, no Israelitish priest, was permitted to taste, is the great staple article of spiritual food to Christians, who are all a holy priesthood, as well as a peculiar people. He "gave His flesh for the life of the world"—He shed His blood "for remission of sins to many;" and they who believe in Him are permitted to eat this flesh, which is meat indeed; to drink of this blood, which is drink indeed. It is their privilege to be allowed habitually to feast on the sacrifice which has been an effectual propitiation for their sins, and for the sins of the whole Israel of God.

The sentiment of the Apostle is not—We are allowed to eat the Lord's Supper, which no Jew, nor Jewish priest, continuing such, can have a right to do. It refers not to the Lord's Supper, but to that of which the Lord's Supper is an emblematical expression. Nor is it merely—We have a sacrifice, on which we spiritually feed, of which no Jew, no Jewish priest, continuing to be so, can participate. But, we are allowed—really, though spiritually—to feast on the propitiatory sacrifice for our own sins, and for the sins of all the people of God, which, even emblematically, the Jewish people and priests were not permitted to do.

It thus appears that these words contain a statement, and a proof of that statement. The statement is—We Christians have higher privileges with regard to sacred food than the Jewish people, or even the Jewish priesthood, possessed. We are permitted to feast on a sacrifice of the highest and holiest kind, which they were not. The proof is—The highest and holiest kind of sacrifice was that offered on the great day of atonement for the expiation of the sins of the whole congregation of Israel. Of that sacrifice even the priests were not permitted to eat. The sacrifice of Jesus Christ was a sacrifice of this highest and holiest kind. It was the sacrifice, of which all the sacrifices offered on the recurring great days of atonement, for ages, were but the shadow. On this sacrifice Christians are permitted freely to feed. They eat the flesh and drink the blood of the Son of God, offered as a sacrifice for the sins of men—for their own sins. The conclusion is direct and inevitable. The Christians have higher privileges with respect to sacred food, not merely than the Jewish people, but than the Jewish priests.

"We have an altar, of which they have no right to eat who serve the tabernacle." Fully to bring out the meaning and force of this statement, so satisfactorily proved, it will be necessary to inquire into the nature and value of the privilege possessed by the Israelitish people and priesthood in feeding on sacrifices; and then inquire into the nature and value of the privilege of Christians in feeding spiritually on the sacrifice of Christ; and then, by a comparison of these, to evince the superiority of the latter to the former.

I. With regard to the privilege of the Jewish people and priesthood in eating of the sacrifices, it is manifest that, whatever superstitious notions might be cherished by them, the flesh which had been offered in sacrifice was not better, as food, than other meat of the same quality, and that the mere eating of it could be of no spiritual advantage to the individual; just as, whatever superstitious notions may be entertained by professed Christians respecting the emblematical elements in the Lord's Supper—bread and wine—they have no qualities, as bodily nourishment, different from other bread and wine; and the mere eating the one and drinking the other can communicate no spiritual benefit. Sacrifice was emblematical; and feasting on sacrifice was emblematical also. Eating the flesh which had been offered in sacrifice seems to have been emblematical of two things, or, to speak perhaps more accurately, of two aspects of the same thing. Eating the flesh of the sacrifice was emblematical—plainly fitted to be emblematical—of deriving from the sacrifice the advantage it was calculated and intended to secure; namely, expiation of ceremonial guilt, removal of ceremonial pollution, and access, along with the people of God, to the external ordinances of the tabernacle or temple worship. Moreover, as the altar is in Scripture represented as God's table, and sacrifices as placed on that table,—for example, Mal. i. 7; Ps. l. 12, 13; Ezek. xxxix. 20, xli. 22,—eating of the sacrifice, implying sitting at table with God, is a natural emblem of a state of reconciliation and fellowship with Jehovah, in a state which gives an interest in the blessings promised, and security from the evils threatened, in the old covenant. This, whatever extravagant notions the Jews might have formed on the subject, seems to be the true nature and value of the privilege which they enjoyed, of feeding on sacrifices.

II. Let us now inquire into the nature and value of the corresponding blessing enjoyed by Christians. That privilege may be thus described: "They eat the flesh and drink the blood of the Son of man, who was also the Son of God, who gave Himself for them a sacrifice and an offering, that He might bring them to God." I need not say that these words are highly figurative. Eating and drinking the flesh and blood of Christ, are to be understood in a spiritual, not in a literal sense. The doctrines of transubstantiation and consubstantiation are insults to reason, and caricatures of Christianity. To eat the flesh and drink the blood of the Son of man, is to derive, by an appropriate exercise of mind—*believing*,—from the sacrifice of Christ, the advantages which it was intended and fitted to secure. As it is by eating and drinking that we derive nourishment from food, so it is by believing that we partake of the benefits obtained by the sacrifice of Christ. In the faith of that truth, we enjoy the forgiveness of sin, the acceptance of our persons and works, the spiritual transformation of our nature and character, and favourable intercourse with God as our reconciled Father. We have in Him redemption through His blood, even the forgiveness of sin. We are justified through the redemption that is in Christ Jesus. We are washed, justified, sanctified, in the name of the Lord Jesus. We have access with boldness, on the ground of His sacrifice, to the throne of grace, and are blessed with all heavenly and spiritual blessings in Him.

In the Lord's Supper we have an emblematical representation of all this. But we have not only the emblems,—we have, if we believe, the blessings emblematized. In the faith of the truth respecting the sacrifice of Christ, and the great end which that sacrifice was intended to serve, and has actually served, and been proved to have served by His resurrection, we personally enjoy all these invaluable blessings. In spirit sitting in the heavenly places, at the table of the reconciled Divinity, we, as it were, feast along with Him. That which satisfies His justice, magnifies His law, glorifies all His perfections, and gives Him perfect satisfaction—even the obedience to death of His incarnate Son—the sacrifice, without spot and blameless, which He offered up for the sins of men,—that quiets our conscience, transforms our nature, rejoices our heart. We find our enjoyment in that in which God finds His enjoyment. "Our fellowship is with the Father." Brought near to Him, we hear Him saying, in reference to the completed sacrifice of His Son, I am fully satisfied; and our souls re-echo the solemn declaration, So are we. And while He says, This is My Son, in whom I am well pleased, we say, This is our Saviour: He is all our salvation, all our desire. This spiritual feeding on the sacrifice of Christ, so as personally to realize the benefits that sacrifice was intended to procure,—this is the blessing enjoyed by Christians which corresponds to the privilege enjoyed by the Israelitish priests and people, in feasting on meats which had been offered in sacrifice, on the altar of Jehovah, in the tabernacle or temple.

III. It will not require many words to show the superiority—the infinite superiority—of the privilege of Christian believers, as to sacred food, above that of the Jewish people, or even priests. In eating of the sacrifices offered under the law, they had merely the emblems of blessings: we, in spiritually feeding on Christ's sacrifice, have the blessings themselves. They had but the emblems of expiation, and forgiveness, and purification, and fellowship with God: we have expiation, and forgiveness, and purification, and fellowship with God.

But this is by no means all. The blessings, the emblems of which, in eating of the sacrifices, the Jewish priests and people possessed, were of a far inferior kind to those of the substance, of which we Christians, in our spiritual banquet, participate. What a disproportion in value between the shadow and the substance—between expiation and forgiveness of ceremonial transgression, and expiation and forgiveness of moral guilt—between external purification and inward sanctification—between external communion and spiritual fellowship!

Nor is even this all. The circumstance, that it was but a part of any sacrifice that the Israelitish people and priests were allowed to eat, probably intimated—what the circumstance, that there were certain sacrifices, and those of the most sacred and solemn nature, of which they were not permitted even to taste, was undoubtedly meant to teach—that the expiations under the law, and the forgiveness founded on these expiations, were incomplete. The law made nothing perfect. They were allowed, as it were, crumbs from Jehovah's table, to show that He pitied them, and was kindly disposed to them; but they were not admitted to feast, along with Jehovah, on the great sacrifice of atonement. Christians, in the faith of the truth, are admitted into the presence of a reconciled God, and there have set before them the whole sacrifice which has taken away the sins of men. We eat the flesh of that sacrifice; we drink its blood. We enjoy the full measure of benefit which the sacrifice was intended to secure. Our reconciliation with God is complete—our fellowship with Him intimate and delightful.

There is yet another circumstance which must be adverted to, to show the superiority of the privilege of Christians to that of Jews as to sacred food. It was only at intervals—comparatively rare intervals on the part of the body of the people—that the Israelites enjoyed the privilege, such as it was, of eating meat which had been placed on the altar of God; whereas living by faith on the flesh and blood of the Son of God is the expression of the habitual experience of genuine Christians. This is their daily food. Their spiritual health and strength depend on their habitual use of it. On a communion Sabbath, there is, in eating the Lord's Supper, but an emblematical representation of what every Christian is habitually doing every day of his life,—exercising faith in Christ Jesus, delivered for his offences, and thus deriving from Him all things that pertain to life and godliness—all that is necessary to sustain and cherish spiritual life, and activity, and enjoyment. As there is a spiritual Sabbath to the believer every day, so there is a spiritual communion-table ever ready spread, at which, at all times, in all circumstances, he can eat the true bread of life, and drink of the wine of the kingdom.

The bearing of the statement, the meaning and evidence of which I have thus shortly attempted to lay before you, on the great design of the Apostle in the whole of this remarkable treatise, is direct and obvious. That design was to show the Hebrews that in Christ Jesus they had all that they had had under Moses, and much more. 'Let your unbelieving brethren boast themselves of their privileges with regard to "sacred food:" you enjoy far higher privileges than they, or even their venerated priesthood. Even *they* durst not taste of the sacrifice of atonement offered for the congregation of Israel; but you are permitted daily, hourly, without ceasing, at all times, in all circumstances, to feast on the sacrifice of the incarnate Son of God—the great victim for the sins of men, who suffered, the just in the room of the unjust, who gave Himself a sacrifice of a sweet-smelling savour for all the sanctified ones. Truly, "ye are complete in Him."'

The practical use which the Apostle would have the Hebrew Christians to make of the truth contained in the text, is indicated in the words that immediately follow. "Let us go forth therefore unto Him without the camp, bearing His reproach." The inference may seem inconsequent to a careless reader; but the connection is quite natural, and the conclusion is fairly drawn. This food of the soul, of which the Apostle was speaking, was the flesh of the Son of man who had come down from heaven, given in sacrifice for the life of the world. Jesus Christ, the great atoning sacrifice for men, to verify the type in reference to the remnant of the sacrifice of atonement for the people being burnt without the camp, was crucified beyond the walls of what was once the holy city—died for us in circumstances of deep degradation and bitter agony. He calls His people to the fellowship of His suffering. He requires of every disciple to deny himself, and take up the cross and follow Him; to hold himself ready for whatever sacrifice his allegiance to his Lord may require. This is to "go forth to Him without the camp." To come out from among the world lying under the wicked one, doomed to destruction, and be separate, and to cast in his lot with the Crucified One on earth and in heaven, for time and eternity, holding fast the faithful sayings: "If we be dead with Him, we shall also live with Him; if we suffer, we shall also reign with Him; if we deny Him, He will also deny us." And surely it is most meet that we should devote ourselves entirely to Him, who devoted Himself entirely for us; that we should at all hazards, by an honest profession and corresponding conduct, confess Him, who made a good confession before Pontius Pilate, and who has promised, if we confess Him before men, to confess us before His Father and the holy angels.

While there is a peculiar propriety and beauty in these words as addressed to the Hebrew Christians, in their substance they are thus applicable to Christians in every country and age. Christian faith and duty are unchanged, unchangeable. All who by faith have feasted on the great atoning sacrifice, are bound by duty and gratitude to submit cheerfully to all the reproach and suffering that may be involved in an open profession of attachment to Him, at once the Priest and the victim, and a regular observance of all His ordinances. It is their duty to renounce the world as a portion, and all that is in it. Even their lawful enjoyments are not to be clung to, when these come in competition with their adherence to Christ. We are not, as has been justly remarked, *to steal out* of the camp or city, but we are boldly *to go forth*. We are distinctly, in word and in deed, to say, We are not of the world, as He was not of the world. It was the *world* that murdered our Lord; and the world has not changed its character. Shall we not leave *them* and go to Him, though on His cross? There He is, cast out of the holy city, as unworthy even to die within its walls! But who is this hanging on the tree of shame and agony? A man approved of God—the Holy One and the Just. And He is wounded for our transgressions, He is bruised for our iniquities. He is undergoing the chastisement of our peace. He has borne our sins, our liabilities, in His body to that tree; and He will leave them there, no more to burden either Him or us. Shall we then seek to secure and enjoy the wealth, and honours, and pleasures of the world, by remaining among His murderers? Shall we not leave the city, and take our place by the Saviour's cross? Would it be anything unreasonable that, in support of His cause, we should be required to be crucified for Him who was crucified for us? Our hearts are not in the right place if we are not prepared for this, should this be required of us.

The period for exertion and suffering in His cause will soon be over. Here we have no continuing city; this is not our home. But we have a home. He has prepared for us a city—a stable residence, where we shall dwell for ever with Him. Let us be habitually seeking that city to come. It has foundations, and its builder and maker is God. Strengthened by the spiritual provision of which we have been discoursing, let us prosecute our pilgrimage, leaving every day the world, the city of destruction, more and more behind us, and drawing nearer and nearer that city of the living God of which we have become denizens—the citizens of no mean city, the freedom of which has been obtained for us at great price, not of corruptible things, as silver and gold, but of blood—the blood of a sacrifice —the sacrifice of the Son of God. And while moving onward and upward, let us through Him, our great High Priest, who offered for us Himself as the great, the only efficacious, atoning sacrifice, offer the sacrifice of praise to God continually, the fruit of our lips, giving thanks to His name; and in the ordinary duties of life, as well as in the solemn ordinances of religion, let us present our bodies a living sacrifice, holy and acceptable to God. This is reasonable service. This is rational worship.

DISCOURSE IX.

THE GREAT SHEPHERD OF THE SHEEP.

Heb. xiii. 20, 21.—"Now the God of peace, that brought again from the dead our Lord Jesus, that great Shepherd of the sheep, through the blood of the everlasting covenant, make you perfect in every good work to do His will, working in you that which is well-pleasing in His sight, through Jesus Christ; to whom be glory for ever and ever. Amen."

It has often been remarked, that one of the best methods that a teacher of morals can adopt for securing the desired practical effect of his instructions on the conduct of others, is to exemplify them in his own. Recommendations, however urgent, are not likely to be complied with, or indeed attended to, which are habitually disregarded by him who gives them. On the other hand, exemplified precept is calculated to serve the double purpose of direction and of motive. We find the Apostle adopting this plan, with reference to the duty of mutual intercession, in the passage which now lies before us for illustration. He had just been requesting an interest in the prayers of the Hebrew Christians: "Brethren, pray for us;" and he immediately proceeds to show that they had an interest in his. He asks them to do nothing for *him*, but what he himself does for *them*. He requests *from* them only what he was ready to give *to* them. It is as if he had said, 'Brethren, pray for me: I pray for you.' And what is his prayer? It is a brief, but a most comprehensive one. "Now the God of peace, who brought again from the dead our Lord Jesus, that great Shepherd of the sheep, by the blood of the everlasting covenant, make you perfect in every good work to do His will, working in you that which is well-pleasing in His sight, through Jesus Christ; to whom be glory for ever and ever. Amen."

This sublime prayer, which is to form the subject of our

discourse, well deserves, and will richly reward, our most considerate attention. It is full of instruction—full of consolation. "A glorious prayer it is," says Dr Owen, "enclosing the whole mystery of divine grace in its original, and in the way of its communication by Jesus Christ." It divides itself into three parts, to which, in succession, your attention shall be directed: The ADDRESS; the PETITION; the DOXOLOGY. The prayer is addressed to God, the only proper object of prayer, as " the God of peace, who brought again from the dead our Lord Jesus, that great Shepherd of the sheep, through the blood of the everlasting covenant." The petition presented to this God of peace is, that He would make the Hebrew Christians "perfect in every good work to do His will, working in them that which was well-pleasing in His sight, through Christ Jesus." And the doxology is contained in these words: " To whom be glory for ever and ever. Amen."

I. Let us then, in the first place, consider the address of the prayer, or, in other words, inquire into the import of the appellation here given to the great object of prayer,—" The God of peace, who brought again from the dead our Lord Jesus, that great Shepherd of the sheep, through the blood of the everlasting covenant."

Before, however, we enter on this inquiry, it will be proper that we endeavour to settle a question respecting the proper construction of the clause, " through the blood of the everlasting covenant," the determination of which materially affects the meaning of the passage. These words may be connected with the clause, " brought again from the dead," or with the dignified title here given to our Lord—" the great Shepherd of the sheep;" or finally, with the prayer that God would make the Hebrew Christians " perfect in every good work to do His will." A good sense may be brought out of the words according to any of these modes of connecting them. In the first case, they teach us that it was in consequence of, in reward of, our Lord Jesus shedding His blood, as the sacrifice by which the everlasting covenant was confirmed, that God raised Him from the dead. In the second case, they teach us that our Lord became the great Shepherd of the sheep by the shedding of this blood of the everlasting covenant. And in the third case, they teach us that the perfecting men in every good work to do

God's will,—*i.e.*, all divine influence and operation necessary to the sanctification of men,—are the result of the shedding of this blood. These are three important truths, all of them clearly revealed in other portions of the New Testament revelation. Looking merely at the words of the original, I would be disposed to say that the last mode of interpretation is the least probable, if not altogether inadmissible; and that, of the two others, the second seems at first sight the more natural mode of connecting the clause, bringing out this idea, that Christ became the great Shepherd of the sheep by the blood of the everlasting covenant; that is, in plain words, that He obtained for Himself that peculiar property in, and supreme authority over, the Church of redeemed men, which is indicated by the appellation—"the great Shepherd of the sheep." Yet when I consider, that though it is most true that Christ purchased the Church with His own blood, and was exalted in consequence of His expiatory sufferings as Head over all things to His body, which is the Church, "the fulness of Him who filleth all in all," He yet in the days of His flesh takes to Himself the appellation of the Good Shepherd, and that it was *as* the Good Shepherd—in the discharge of the duties rising out of this character—that He laid down His life for the sheep, it appears to me more probable that it is the first method of connecting the clause which brings out the Apostle's true meaning; and that he intends to represent our Lord's resurrection from the dead as having been effected by the God of peace through the blood of the everlasting covenant. What is the precise import, will, we trust, become apparent in the course of our illustrations.

Having thus endeavoured to settle the question of construction, let us now proceed to the exposition of the appellation here given to the object of prayer. In order to bring out distinctly the different thoughts in their natural connection, contained in such a complicated form of expression as that now before us, it is often found advisable to reverse, or at any rate considerably to alter, the order in which they stand. The following are the thoughts involved in these words, in what appears to be their natural order:—Jesus Christ our Lord is the great Shepherd of the sheep. As the great Shepherd of the sheep, He submitted to death. As the great Shepherd of the sheep, He has been brought from the dead by God. When

God brought Jesus Christ, as the great Shepherd of the sheep, from the dead, He did so through the blood of the everlasting covenant. In bringing Jesus Christ our Lord, as the great Shepherd of the sheep, from the dead through the blood of the everlasting covenant, God acted as the God of peace. And finally, it is to God, as having manifested Himself to be the God of peace by bringing again from the dead our Lord Jesus Christ, as the great Shepherd of the sheep, by the blood of the everlasting covenant, that the Apostle addresses his prayers in behalf of the Hebrew Christians. These are the truths involved in this appellation, and this seems to be their natural order. Let us endeavour shortly to illustrate them. They embody in them much that is most important and peculiar in the wondrous economy of human redemption.

I remark, then, in the first place, these words intimate that our Lord Jesus is the great Shepherd of the sheep. Here three questions meet us. Who are the sheep—what class of persons is described under this figurative denomination? what is to be understood by our Lord Jesus being their Shepherd? and what is to be understood by His being their great Shepherd?

To the first of these questions—Who are the sheep?—a most satisfactory answer may be found in the words of our Lord, in the tenth chapter of the Gospel by John, from the 11th to the 30th verses, which you will do well to read carefully in your retirement. The sum of our Lord's statement is, that the sheep are those whom the Father hath given Him, both Jews and Gentiles,—for whom He laid down His life,—who hear His voice, and follow Him,—to whom He gives eternal life, and who shall never perish, for none can pluck them out of His or His Father's hand. They are plainly that innumerable multitude, out of every kindred, and people, and tongue, and nation, whom He redeems to God by His blood,—the same class of persons who, in the previous part of this Epistle, are represented as the heirs of salvation,—the many children to be brought to glory by the Captain of their salvation being made perfect through suffering,—the holy brethren of the Messiah, to be presented by Him to His Father and their Father,—the partakers of the heavenly calling,—they that, through believing, do enter into the promised rest of God,—partakers of Christ,—the heirs of the promise,—they that are called,—they that come to God by Christ,—the sanctified ones, by the offering of the body of Christ once for all,—those who have received a kingdom that cannot be moved. The sheep is just another name for genuine Christians—Christians not in profession, but in reality possessing the peculiar privileges and distinguished by the peculiar character of Christians,—viewed as separated from the great body of mankind, and placed under the peculiar care of Christ, as their Shepherd.

We are now naturally led to inquire, What is meant by His being represented as the Shepherd of this flock? Many learned interpreters have considered the figurative expression, Shepherd, as intended chiefly, if not solely, to convey the idea of teacher, or instructor. This is, however, a mistake. If this idea be intended, as I do not doubt it is, it is a subordinate one. The word Shepherd, when used figuratively, either in the Old Testament or in the New, denotes one who *presides* over a collection of people,—who governs, guides, and protects them,—a leader, a guardian, a defender, a chief, a king. David's being raised to the supreme government of the Israelitish people is represented as his being made their shepherd. " He chose David also, His servant, and took him from the sheepfolds: from following the ewes great with young, He brought him to feed Jacob His people, and Israel His inheritance. So he fed them according to the integrity of his heart, and guided them by the skilfulness of his hands." In the First Epistle of Peter, ch. ii. 25, shepherd and bishop, *i.e.*, overseer, are used as synonymous expressions of our Lord,—" the Shepherd and Bishop of our souls." The thought intended to be conveyed is this: He is placed over them for the purpose of doing everything that is necessary to obtain and secure their happiness. It is just a figurative expression, intended to express some of the inexhaustible meaning that is contained in the literal expression, *Saviour*.

But our Lord is not only termed the Shepherd, but " that great Shepherd of the sheep." We come now to inquire, What is the meaning of that appellation? Our Lord may receive this title to distinguish Him from all others who receive it, just as He is termed the King of kings and the Lord of lords; or to mark Him as the official superior of all those who, in His Church, receive the name of shepherd or pastor,—in which case the appellation is equivalent to that used by Peter in the 5th chapter of his First Epistle—the Chief Shepherd; or the epithet, great, is used to mark His transcendent personal dignity, as when it is said, We have a *great* High Priest, Jesus the Son of God. I am strongly impressed with the conviction, that, both in the expression before us, and in our Lord's own declaration, I am the— or that—good Shepherd, there is a reference to those Old Testament predictions in which the Messiah is promised under the character of a Shepherd, a good Shepherd, a great Shepherd. The following are specimens of the predictions I refer to: " O Thou that bringest good tidings to Zion, get Thee up into the high mountain: O Thou that bringest good tidings to Jerusalem, lift up Thy voice with strength; lift it up, be not afraid: say unto the cities of Judah, Behold your God! Behold, the Lord God will come with strong hand, and His arm shall rule for Him; behold, His reward is with Him, and His work before Him. He shall feed His flock like a shepherd: He shall gather the lambs in His arms, and carry them in His bosom, and gently lead the ewes with the young. Thus saith the Lord God, I will take the children of Israel from among the heathen. I will make them one nation, and one king shall be king to them all. David My servant shall be king over them, and they all shall have one Shepherd." The full import, then, of the appellation, " Our Lord Jesus, that great Shepherd of the sheep," is, Jesus our Lord is the divine Saviour of the spiritual people of God, promised to the fathers.

I remark in the second place: The words before us intimate that our Lord Jesus, that great Shepherd of the sheep, submitted to death. This is not indeed stated in so many words, but it is plainly implied, both in the phrase, " He brought Him again from the dead," and in that other, " through the blood of the everlasting covenant." He submitted to death, and He submitted to death as a victim. His blood was the blood of an expiatory sacrifice—blood shed to ratify a covenant of peace or reconciliation. The good Shepherd had power to lay down His life, and He actually did lay it down for the sheep. All we, like sheep, had gone astray; we had turned every one to his own way; and the Lord laid on Him the iniquities of us all. Exaction was made, and He became answerable; and He was wounded for our transgressions, and bruised for our iniquities; and the chastisement of our peace was on Him, and by His stripes we are healed. He died, the just in the room of the unjust. He poured out His soul unto death, in making Himself a sacrifice for sin. But, as the good, great Shepherd laid down His life in the room of His sheep in order to save them, in obedience to the will of His Father, so He laid it down that He might take it again. It was not possible that He should continue bound by the fetters of death.

This leads me to remark, in the third place, that the words before us intimate that God brought this great Shepherd of the sheep, when He had died, again from the dead. These words represent our Lord's resurrection as the work of divine power. No power inferior to Omnipotence could have accomplished it. The question of the Apostle to king Agrippa, "Why should it be thought an incredible thing that God should raise the dead?" seems plainly to imply, that it might well be accounted an incredible thing that any one else should. The resurrection of our Lord is sometimes spoken of as His own work. Destroy this temple, said He to the Jews, speaking of the temple of His body, and in three days I will raise it up again. As the Father raiseth up the dead and quickeneth them, even so the Son quickeneth whom He will. I have power to lay down My life, and I have power to take it again. Such declarations will not, however, appear to be in any degree inconsistent with the statement made in the passage before us, to any one who understands the fundamental principles of the great divine economy of human redemption. In that economy the Father is the representative of divinity, the sustainer of its majesty, the vindicator of its rights. The Son acts in a subordinate character. Whatever He says, He says in the name of the Father; whatever He does, He does by the power of the Father. The Father who dwelleth in Him, He doeth the works. When He was raised from the dead, He was raised by the power of the Father, that is, by the power of God.

But the words before us do not bring the resurrection of our Lord before our minds so much as an exertion of divine power as the administration of divine righteousness. The resurrection of our Lord is the great manifestation of the entire satisfaction of Jehovah, as the supreme Governor, with the death to which He had submitted as the victim of human guilt. For

I proceed to remark, in the fourth place, that these words intimate, that when God brought again from the dead our Lord Jesus as the great Shepherd of the sheep, who had laid down His life for the sheep, it was "through the blood of the everlasting covenant."

The covenant here referred to, is undoubtedly that divine constitution or arrangement by which spiritual and eternal blessings are secured for the guilty and depraved children of men through the obedience unto death of the incarnate Son of God. Of this constitution or covenant we have a clear, though brief account, in the close of the 53d chapter of the prophecies of Isaiah. "When He shall have made His soul an offering for sin, He shall see His seed, He shall prolong His days, and the pleasure of the Lord shall prosper in His hand. He shall see of the travail of His soul, and shall be satisfied: by His knowledge shall My righteous Servant justify many; for He shall bear their iniquities. Therefore will I divide Him a portion with the great, and He shall divide the spoil with the strong; because He hath poured out His soul unto death: and He was numbered with the transgressors; and He bare the sin of many, and made intercession for the transgressors."

This covenant is called the everlasting covenant, to distinguish it from the other covenants or arrangements made by God, and especially from that covenant or arrangement made with the Israelites at Mount Sinai, and which, as it directly referred to temporal blessings, was intended only for temporary duration. This new covenant is never to give place to any other. It is an everlasting covenant, securing eternal blessings. The blood of this covenant, is the blood of the sacrifice by which this covenant was ratified. In the 9th chapter of this Epistle the Apostle shows, that in all covenants or arrangements made by God for conferring blessings on fallen man, there has always been an assertion of His rights as the just and holy moral Governor of the world, and that the form this assertion has uniformly taken, has been that of the death of a propitiatory victim, and that the dignity of the victim necessarily bare a proportion to the value of the benefits secured by the covenant. The blood of animal propitiatory victims confirmed the first covenant. The blood of the incarnate Only-begotten of God confirmed the second—the new and better covenant. That is—

The obedience to death of the incarnate Son of God, as the substitute of sinners, makes it consistent with, aye, illustrative of, the divine holiness, and justice, and faithfulness, as well as goodness, to bestow pardon on the guilty, and salvation on the lost children of men, believing in Jesus.

The resurrection of our Lord is represented as the result of this shedding of His blood, by which the everlasting covenant was confirmed. He was brought again from the dead by the blood of the everlasting covenant. His obedience to death was the procuring cause of His own resurrection, as well as of the salvation of His people. The Father loved the Son—had entire complacency in Him—because, in compliance with His will, He had laid down His life for the sheep; and raising Him from the dead was the appropriate manner of manifesting this complacency. Because He humbled Himself to death to do the will of God, in making expiation for the sins of men, and thus confirmed the holy covenant, God highly exalted Him; and as the first step of this high exaltation, brought Him again from the dead. It is substantially the same thought (though the connective particle is different) which is expressed, chap. ix., when Christ is said to have "entered into the true holy place by His own blood."

I proceed to remark, in the fifth place, that the words before us intimate, that in bringing again our Lord Jesus, as the great Shepherd of the sheep, from the dead by the blood of the everlasting covenant, God acted as "the God of peace." This appellation of the Divinity is peculiar to the Apostle Paul, and occurs frequently in his writings. "The God of peace be with you all." "The God of peace shall bruise Satan under your feet." "Now the Lord of peace Himself give you peace always, by all means." The word, peace, is often used as equivalent to prosperity, happiness in general; and the appellation, the God of peace, may be considered as equivalent to—the God who is the Author of happiness. The proper signification of the word peace, is reconciliation, and the tranquillity and happiness which is the result of reconciliation; and there can be little doubt that it has its primary and proper signification here. The God of peace, or reconciliation, is synonymous with the pacified, the reconciled Divinity. It is just of the same import as the more fully expressed character of God given us by the

Apostle in the Second Epistle to the Corinthians: "God was in Christ reconciling the world to Himself, not imputing to us our trespasses; for He hath made Him who knew no sin to be sin for us, that we might be made the righteousness of God in Him."

God was displeased with man on account of sin; He was angry at him. That is, in plain words, not only was man the object of His moral disapprobation, but, in the ordinary course of things, man's final happiness was inconsistent with the honour of the character of God as the wise and righteous Governor of the world, and—what is but another way of expressing the same truth—with the principles of His moral administration, and the happiness of His intelligent subjects generally. This incompatibility could be removed only by some display of the divine displeasure at sin, and of the righteousness and reasonableness of the law which man had violated, fully equivalent in moral influence to that which would have been given if the condemning sanction of the law had been allowed to take its course in reference to the offenders. Such a display has been found in the substituted obedience and sufferings of the incarnate Son. These have magnified the law, and made it honourable. God is now just and the justifier of the ungodly, united to Jesus by believing in Him—the just God and the Saviour. His righteousness is declared in His Son being set forth a propitiation in His blood. And the first display, and the satisfactory proof, that God is now the God of peace, is His raising His Son, our Surety, from the dead, and giving Him all power in heaven and earth, that He may give eternal life to as many as the Father hath given Him.

It is finely said by that master in Israel, Dr Owen, "The well-spring of the whole dispensation of grace lies in the bringing again from the dead our Lord Jesus Christ, that great Shepherd of the sheep, by the blood of the everlasting covenant. Had not the will of God been fully executed, atonement made for sin, the Church sanctified, the law accomplished, and the threatenings satisfied, Christ could not have been brought from the dead. The death of Christ, if He had not risen, would not have completed our redemption. We should have been yet in our sins; for evidence would have been thus given that atonement was not made. The bare resurrection of Christ, or the bringing Him again from the dead, would not have saved us, for so any man may be raised by the power of God; but the bringing of Christ again from the dead by the blood of the everlasting covenant, is that which gives assurance of the complete redemption and salvation of the Church."

I have only further to remark, in the sixth place, that the words before us intimate, that it is to God, manifested as the God of peace, the pacified Divinity, by bringing again from the dead our Lord Jesus, the great Shepherd of the sheep, by the blood of the everlasting covenant, that the Apostle addresses his prayers in behalf of the Hebrew Christians. Indeed, this is the only character in which the Divinity can be rationally addressed in the way of petition by sinful men for sinful men. Who durst go to God, and ask Him to deny Himself by violating His word? And this must every man do who goes to God for pardon, apart from the atonement made by the incarnate Son. Without a reference to that atonement which was completed in His death, and the perfection of which is demonstrated by His resurrection, no spiritual and saving blessing can be reasonably expected by sinners from Him who is glorious in holiness, and who can by no means clear the guilty. But from the pacified Divinity declaring, by the resurrection of His Son, who died, the just in the room of the unjust, that as it was our offences that caused His death, so, that which secured His resurrection was the laying of a foundation for our justification,—it is rendered certain that whosoever by faith becomes connected with Him cannot perish, but must have everlasting life. To him in Christ Jesus there is no condemnation,—to him in Christ Jesus there is the salvation that is in Christ, with eternal glory; and God, who is rich in mercy, through the channel of His Son's atonement, can, in perfect consistency with His righteousness, for the great love wherewith He loved us, bless us with all heavenly and spiritual blessings in Christ. In this character we may all come near to Him, and ask for ourselves and others every blessing we need, for time and for eternity. In the faith that God is the God of peace, and has proved Himself to be so, we may come boldly to the throne of grace, that we may obtain mercy, and find grace to help us in the time of need. Christ died; Christ rose again; Christ sits at the right hand of God, making intercession for us. God is well pleased for His righteousness' sake, and has showed that He is. He is well pleased with Him—well pleased with us coming to God through Him. So much for the address of the Apostle's prayer.

Such is the import of the appellation here given to God, the great object of worship: The God of peace, who brought again from the dead our Lord Jesus, that great Shepherd of the sheep, by the blood of the everlasting covenant.

It is my purpose now, somewhat more briefly, in the remaining part of this discourse, to illustrate the other two topics suggested by the text,—the Apostle's petition and doxology.

II. I proceed, therefore, in the second place, to call your attention to the Apostle's petition. He prays the God of peace that He would make the Hebrew Christians " perfect in every good work to do His will, working in them that which is well-pleasing in His sight, through Christ Jesus." The prayer, when looked at attentively, will be found to resolve itself into two petitions:—the one referring to an end—the making of them perfect in every good work, to do the will of the God of peace; the other referring to the means by which this end was to be accomplished—the God of peace working in them that which is well-pleasing in His sight. Let us attend to these petitions in their order.

The first petition is, that the God of peace would make the Hebrew Christians " perfect in every good work to do His will." The natural meaning of these English words is, ' May the God of peace make you perfect, that, being thus made perfect, you may in every good work do His will,'—a prayer which will assuredly be answered in reference to all the sheep of the great Shepherd, but not till they are brought into His heavenly fold. But this does not seem to be the Apostle's meaning. He is praying for something which he wishes to be immediately conferred on the Hebrew Christians.

The force of the petition will become apparent, if we attend to the meaning of the word rendered " make perfect." That word properly signifies, to put a thing into proper order, so that it may be fit for serving its purpose. The meaning will be made plain by attending to the manner in which it is employed in some other passages of Scripture where it occurs. In Rom. ix. 22, " the vessels of wrath" are said to be " fitted"—the same word used here—" for destruction;" *i.e.*, prepared, made ready, by their own self-depravation, for that state to which they are doomed. They have made themselves fit for nothing else but for destruction,—utterly unfit for any purpose but to be fuel for the fire unquenchable. In Heb. xi. 3, the worlds are said to have been " framed"—the same word—" by the word of God;" that is, *put in* order, reduced into fit shape, from the formless state in which these materials were called into being—without form and void,—and prepared for the several purposes which they were intended to answer. In Heb. x. 5, " a body" is said to have been " prepared"—the word before us—for our Lord, referring to the formation of a human nature fitted to serve the purposes of His mediation. In Gal. vi. 1, the spiritual are called on to " *restore*"—the same word—the brother who has fallen into a fault; that is, to employ means for fitting him again to perform his functions as a member of the body of Christ. To refer only to one passage more: in Eph. iv. 12, Christ, having ascended to heaven, is represented to have given, among other gifts to His Church, " some teachers, for the perfecting of the saints, for the work of the ministry;" *i.e.*, to put in order, to prepare the saints, *i.e.*, individual Christians, for ministering to, for promoting the welfare of the body of Christ, the Church at large.

The word seems used in the same, its ordinary meaning, in the passage before us; and the Apostle's prayer, in plain English terms, is, ' that God, as the God of peace, would fit, qualify, prepare the Hebrew Christians, for the great business of their high and holy calling, " the doing of His will in every good work."'

We are all by nature utterly unfit for obeying the will of God in any good work. We are not destitute, indeed, of any physical faculty necessary for this purpose. We have a mind and a heart, we have head and hands, to serve Him in our bodies and in our spirits, which are His. But all these are out of order, unfit for their proper purpose. In our natural state, we do not know His will, and we have no desire to know it. When urged on our attention, we discover a dislike to it, and will not do it. God alone can put to rights this disorder. God alone can make any man fit to do His will. And this is true not only in reference to men in a state of unregeneracy; it is equally true in reference to the most advanced Christian. It is God who works in him both to will and to do. God hath made us, says the Apostle, "*able,*" *i.e.,* qualified, fit ministers of the New Testament; and if any man is a strong, healthy, active Christian, fruitful in every good word and work, it is because He is God's workmanship, because God has made him fit for doing His will in every good work. Left to himself, he would not desire to do good; and even were he desiring to do good, evil would be present with him. We need not merely to be once for all put to rights. There are disordering elements in the most thoroughly renewed man. We must be kept in order as well as put in order. Without God we can do nothing: our sufficiency is of Him, of Him alone.

The Apostle's prayer is, that the Hebrew Christians may be prepared to do the will of God,—*i.e.,* to yield a cheerful obedience to the will of God, as made known in His written word and by His providential dispensations; denying ungodliness and worldly lusts; living soberly, righteously, and godly in His world; doing justly, loving mercy, walking humbly with God in His commandments and ordinances; in one word, actively doing, and patiently suffering, His will.

The Apostle's prayer is a very extensive one. He wishes not only that they may be prepared to do the will of God, but prepared to do this will in every good work. His desire is, that they may be "perfect in all the will of God,"—" entire, wanting nothing." The will of God is our sanctification—our entire, our complete sanctification—our sanctification " in the whole man, soul, body, and spirit,"—every word, every action, every thought, every feeling, being brought into entire conformity to the mind and will of God. The Apostle's prayer is, that Christians may be enabled by God to "cleanse themselves from *all* filthiness of the flesh and of the spirit, and to *perfect* holiness in the fear of God;" so that no demand of duty, however heavy, no crisis of circumstances, however unexpected, may find them unprepared, but that they may be *ready* to every good work.

The second petition refers to the means by which this most desirable end is to be accomplished. This preparation for doing the will of God in every good work, is effected by God's "working in men that which is well-pleasing in His sight, by Jesus

Christ." "Out of the heart are the issues of life." If the streams are to be clear, the fountain must be pure; and if it is defiled, it must be purified. External good works can be secured only by internal good principles. In order to conformity to the law of God in the life, there must be conformity to the will of God in the heart.

"That which is well-pleasing in God's sight" in man, is just a habitual mode of thinking and feeling in accordance with God's mind and will. The man who thinks along with God, wills along with God, chooses along with God, loves what God loves, hates what God hates, seeks and finds enjoyment in that in which God finds enjoyment,—that is the man who in his inward part is well-pleasing in God's sight. God approves of, He has complacency in, this state of mind and heart. It is His own work; and He sees it, He looks on it, contemplates it, and, behold, it is very good. This state of mind is not natural to man in his present state. God works in him this new and better frame of thought and feeling. He gives the right mind and the new heart. In the new creation, all things are of God. He does not do this, however, miraculously,—making us immediately, as by inspiration, at once, without the intervention of means, to know and love Himself and His will. I do not say that such a revolution in the inner man is impossible, but I do say that it is not in this way that we are to expect that God will "work in us that which is well-pleasing in His sight."

In this matter He honours His own work; He acts in accordance with the established laws of that intelligent and moral nature which He has given us. In His word He has given us a plain, well-accredited revelation of His mind. By the influence of His Spirit, which our depravity has rendered absolutely necessary, He leads us to understand and believe that revelation. The revealed mind of God being understood and believed by us, in the degree in which it is so, becomes our mind; and our mind being brought thus into accordance with God's mind, according to the constitution of our spiritual nature, our will is brought into conformity with God's will. It is thus that God, by His word and Spirit, "works in us that which is well-pleasing in His sight."

It is plain from these remarks, that God's "working in us

that which is well-pleasing in His sight," by no means makes us the mere passive subjects of His operation—entire recipients, in no sense agents. Christians (I am speaking, not of the origin, but the progress of inward sanctification) must study the Holy Scriptures, and accompany their study of the Scriptures with fervent believing prayer for that divine influence without which these Scriptures, given though they be by inspiration of God, never are savingly understood and really believed. While we thus use the means—and we act like madmen if we do not use them, diligently and perseveringly use them—and look for the appropriate result, we are never to forget that His working *in us* is necessary in order to our either willing or doing; and when the use of the means are effectual, and we are enabled to walk at liberty, keeping His commandments, serving Him without fear, in righteousness and holiness, let us give to Him, as is most meet, all the glory, saying, It is not I that live, it is Christ that lives in me. It is not I who work, but He, working in me, by me; not I, but the grace of God that was in me. He works all our works in us.

The expression, "by Christ Jesus," admits of a twofold connection, and, of course, of a twofold explication. It may either be connected with the phrase, "that which is well-pleasing in His sight," or with the phrase, "working in us." In the first case, the sentiment expressed is, that whatever good is wrought in the mind of man, is acceptable to God through Christ Jesus. We owe to Him not only the pardon of our sins and the sanctification of our natures, but we owe also the acceptance of our imperfectly sanctified natures and lives to His mediation. We and our services are accepted in the Beloved. God sees Christ Jesus in us, and is well pleased with us, because well pleased with Him. In the second case, the meaning is, that all God's sanctifying operations on the mind of man, while the Holy Spirit is the direct agent, are carried on with a reference to the mediation of our Lord Jesus Christ. There is no communication of sanctifying influence from the God of peace but with a reference to the atonement and intercession of our Lord Jesus, the great Shepherd of the sheep. We are washed, we are sanctified, in the name of our Lord Jesus, as well as by the Spirit of our God. God is in Christ reconciling the world to Himself; and it is as the God of peace in Christ that He blesses us in Christ with all heavenly and spiritual blessings.

III. The last topic suggested for consideration by the text is the doxology with which the Apostle's prayer concludes, "To whom be glory for ever." It is impossible, from the words or their construction, to determine with absolute certainty whether this ascription of divine honour refer to the God of peace or to Jesus Christ. We know that both are worthy of eternal honour and praise, and that both shall receive the eternal honour and praise to which they are entitled. We find that glory is ascribed to them both separately and conjointly. To the Father separately: Phil. iv. 20, "Now unto God and our Father be glory for ever and ever. Amen." To the Son separately: Rev. i. 5, 6, "Unto Him that loved us, and washed us from our sins in His own blood, and hath made us kings and priests unto God and His Father; to Him be glory and dominion for ever and ever. Amen." To the Father and the Son conjointly: "Blessing, and honour, and glory, and power, be unto Him that sitteth on the throne, and to the Lamb, for ever and ever."

It appears to me, however, that though "Jesus Christ" be the nearest antecedent, yet as "the God of peace" is directly addressed, and chiefly spoken of, that the ascription of praise ought to be considered as offered to Him. It is natural that the doxology should be addressed to the same person as the prayer.

"The bringing again from the dead our Lord Jesus, that great Shepherd of the sheep, by the blood of the everlasting covenant," the blessing acknowledged,—and the preparing Christians to "do His will in every good work, by working in them that which is well-pleasing in His sight," the blessing sought for,—are themes worthy of the songs of eternity. In these dispensations God displays a power and a wisdom, a holiness and a grace, which richly deserve everlasting praise; and as they richly deserve, so shall they certainly receive it. The Apostle's fervent wish, in which every loyal intelligence on earth and in heaven will cordially acquiesce, shall be fully accomplished. A song ever new shall be unceasingly raised by "the nations of the saved"—a number without number—with sweet voices uttering praise to the God of peace, who reconciled them to Himself by the blood of His Son, and declared the accomplishment of this reconciliation by His glorious resurrection; and who, by the instrumentality of His word and the agency of His Spirit, prepared them for doing His will in every good work, by working in them that which is well-pleasing in His sight. "Amen," says the Apostle. Eternal, universal praise be to the redeeming God! So it ought to be. O that it were so even now! So it shall be ere long, and so it shall continue to be for ever. Who does not feel disposed to reiterate the Apostle's expression of conviction, and desire, and faith—Amen and Amen!

Such is the prayer with which the Apostle closes his Epistle to the Hebrew Christians. It is a prayer which all Christians should habitually present to God for themselves and for each other. It is a prayer which cannot be presented but by Christians. They only know God as the God of peace, the reconciled Divinity—reconciled by the bloodshedding of the great Shepherd, showing Himself reconciled in His resurrection from the dead. Till men know God and Jesus Christ in these characters, they cannot come to God by Christ—they cannot come boldly to the throne of grace to seek spiritual and heavenly blessings, either for themselves or for others; and it will be in proportion to the firmness of their faith respecting the completed and sealed reconciliation in the blood of the everlasting covenant, that they will be desirous and hopeful of obtaining, either for the one or the other, a personal interest in its benefits. Let every Christian, then, present this petition for himself. Let progressive holiness, the blessing here asked for —holiness of heart and of life—be the great object of his desire and pursuit. In our times there is a very eager thirst, indeed a diseased appetite, for what is called comfort among professors of Christianity;—a very good thing if it rest on solid foundations, and be obtained in the right way. Comfort is to be sought in increased faith and holiness; or rather, faith and holiness are to be sought, and comfort, in the measure that will do us good, will follow as a matter of course. That Christian enjoys the most comfort who thinks more of his duty than of his comfort—more of God's glory than his own inward satisfaction. Believe what God says—do what God commands, and you will never want a due measure of comfort. Seek to grow in faith—seek to grow in holiness : that is the way to secure that the peace of God shall keep the heart and mind. Sensible at once of the obligation that lies on him, to be perfect in all the will of God,—of the close connection there is between his doing the will of God and enjoying tokens of the favour of God,—of his own utter incapacity to do God's will in *every* good work—in *any* good work, and of the disposition of God to give good gifts to them who ask them, let his prayer be : " O that my ways were directed to keep Thy statutes. Teach me the way of Thy statutes. Enlarge my heart, that I may run in the way of Thy commandments. Make me to go in the path of Thy commandments. Hold Thou me up ; so shall I be safe. Let Thine hand help me. And that it may be so, work all my work in me. Work in me to will and to do of Thy good pleasure. Incline my heart to Thy testimonies. Put Thy law in my heart; write it on my inward parts. Make Thy grace sufficient for me, and perfect Thy strength in my weakness."

And let us remember that we are but mocking God in presenting such supplications to Him for ourselves, if we are not diligent in the use of all the means appointed by God for obtaining that preparation of the mind that is necessary for the acceptable service of God. He who expects these blessings, while neglectful of, or negligent in, the duties of reading the word of God, meditation, careful observance of the dispensations of divine providence, and regular waiting on the instituted public ordinances of divine worship, cherishes a presumptuous expectation. He is like a man professing to have a great desire to reach a particular place, who, though the road lies plain before him, stands still or moves in an opposite direction. It is in spiritual as in worldly affairs. The hand of the diligent makes rich ; the mere talk of the lips, however specious, tends to poverty. It is they who " wait on the Lord" in prayer, and in the use of means, that " renew their strength." It is they who "put on the whole armour prepared by God," and prove it by habitual exercise, that will approve themselves good soldiers of Jesus Christ, be made more than conquerors, and meet the complacent smile and kind invitation of their Lord at last : " Well done, good and faithful servant," thou hast done My will ; enter into My joy.

And while we present this prayer for ourselves as individuals, let us also present it for all our brethren in Christ Jesus. How often did the Apostle show his love to his brethren by praying for their progressive sanctification! Let us imitate his example. If we do not, is there not indicated either a want of love for the brethren, or an unduly low estimate of the value of spiritual blessings, or a deficiency in our confidence in prayer, or rather in the Hearer of prayer, or something of all these united? Let us often " bow our knees unto the Father of our Lord Jesus Christ," the common Father of us all, for " the whole family on earth called by the same name," that they may be "filled with the fruits of righteousness, which are by Christ Jesus, to the praise and glory of God;" that they may " walk worthy of the Lord unto all pleasing, being fruitful in every good work, and increasing in the knowledge of God ;" and that for this purpose they may be " strengthened with all might, according to God's glorious power ;" that God may " work in them, both to will and to do of His good pleasure ;" that " the very God of peace may sanctify them wholly, and preserve their whole spirit and soul and body blameless unto the coming of our Lord Jesus Christ ;" that " the God of all grace may make them perfect, stablish, strengthen, and settle them ;" and that " He who is able to keep them from falling may present them faultless before the presence of His glory, with exceeding joy." Such prayers for the brotherhood would bring down blessings on ourselves.

And let us be encouraged, in presenting such prayers for ourselves and others, by remembering that God is the God of peace—who was angry, but whose anger is turned away—and who delights in bestowing benefits, especially spiritual benefits; that the blood of the covenant which sprinkles His throne is of infinite atoning virtue; that Christ, the great Shepherd of the sheep, has laid down His life for us—has risen from the dead—ever lives to make intercession—able to save to the uttermost all coming to God by Him. With full assured faith, and with confident hope, let us thus draw near to the throne of grace, and ask these and all other heavenly and spiritual blessings in the all-prevailing name.

And while we seek blessings, let us not neglect to render praise. In all our prayers, as our Catechism teaches us, let us praise the great object of our worship, "ascribing kingdom, power, and glory to Him." Let us declare our sense of His infinite excellence, and our desire that that excellence may be universally perceived and felt, and worthily acknowledged by all intelligent beings. And in testimony, equally of our confidence that our prayers for ourselves and our brethren shall be heard, and that our earnest desire that the universe may be filled with His glory as the God of peace shall be fully gratified, —let us say, AMEN, AMEN, and AMEN. Nor let Christians, when praying for themselves and one another, that God would prepare them for doing His will in every good work, by working in them that which is well-pleasing in His sight, forget those who still are what they once were—vessels "self-fitted for destruction." He who has made you what you are, can create them anew. He can make them, too, vessels fitted for glory. He can arrest a man in the full career of rebellion, and convert him into a loyal subject. He converted Saul the persecutor into Paul the Apostle, and made him who seemed, if ever man did, bent on fitting himself for destruction, "a chosen vessel to Him, to bear His name before the Gentiles, and kings, and the children of Israel." And what He has done, He can do. His power and His grace are unchanged, unchangeable; and the prayers of the Church are one of the means to be employed for the conversion of the world. Lift up, then, unceasing, ardent prayers in behalf of your perishing brethren, who are every day becoming fitter for destruction. Oh Thou who canst do all things! of these stones raise up children to Abraham. The valley is full of bones—very many, very dry. But these dry bones can live. For thus saith the Lord, Behold, I will cause breath to enter into them, and they shall live. But we, who by God's mercy already live, must prophesy unto these bones, and must say to the Spirit, Come! come from the four winds, O Spirit, and breathe upon these slain, that they may live. And as we prophesy and pray, we have reason to hope that the breath will come into them, and they shall live and stand up on their feet, an exceeding great army—prepared by the God of peace, who brought again from the dead our Lord Jesus, that great Shepherd of the sheep, working in them that which is well-pleasing in His sight, through Jesus Christ—prepared to do His will in every good work—all ready to give glory for ever and ever to their divine Benefactor. O that it were so! "Our Father who art in heaven, hallowed be Thy name. Thy kingdom come. Thy will be done on earth as it is in heaven. For Thine *is* the kingdom, and the power, and the glory, for ever. Amen."

INDEX.

I.

PRINCIPAL MATTERS.

Abel's sacrifice better than Cain's, ii. 40.
Abraham, the promise and oath to, i. 313; his faith, ii. 55.
Altar, Christian, ii. 243, 399.
Angels called "spirits, and a flame of fire," i. 52; "a little lower than," the meaning of, 93; ministry of, 144; ministering spirits, 69; not the objects of Christ's incarnation, 130.
Assurance of faith, ii. 8; of hope, i. 311.
Author of salvation, i. 258.

"Baptism and laying on of hands, doctrine of," i. 279.
Barak's faith, ii. 127.
"Better things provided for Christians," what, ii. 387.
"Blood of Abel," ii. 203.
"Blood of the covenant," meaning of, i. 418.
"Body, a, hast Thou prepared Me," signification of, i. 441.
"Boldness to enter into the holiest," the meaning of, i. 6.
Brotherly love, ii. 219.
"Built by God, all things," its import, i. 163.

Christ, the Apostle and High Priest of our profession, i. 150; addressed as God, 54; brightness of God's glory, and express image of His person, 29; Creator, 60; counted worthy of more glory than Moses, ii. 161; entered into the holy place by a greater and more perfect tabernacle, 327; Forerunner, i. 327; "Heir of all things," 25; *a High Priest*, and great High Priest, 226; who has passed through the heavens, 228; who can sympathize, 231, ii. 288; without sin, i. 233; such as became us, 353; in heaven, 365; of a superior covenant, 367; our High Priest, ii. 282; of good things to come, i. 391, ii. 323; "He learned obedience by the things He suffered," what it means, i. 249; made perfect by suffering, 108, 257; become the Author of eternal salvation, ii. 318; a merciful and faithful High Priest, i. 135; obtained eternal redemption, ii. 325; offered up prayers and supplications in the days of His flesh, 309; *a Priest* by divine appointment, i. 242; like unto Melchisedec, 261; by an oath, 349; for ever, 350; His *priesthood* similar to Melchisedec's, a proof of superiority, 335; superior to the Levitical, from the solemnity of its institution, 345; more efficacious than the Levitical, 398; He received a more excellent ministry than the angels, 39; His *sacrifice* more efficacious than the Levitical, ii. 341; offered through the Eternal Spirit, 347; is the Captain of salvation, i. 105; *superior* to the angels, 36, 42; to Moses, 148; to the Aaronical priesthood, 222; He is a successful Priest, 248; by suffering, brings many sons to glory, 146; suffering, being tempted, 138.

Christians, holy brethren, and partakers of the heavenly calling, i. 152.
Chastening, not joyous, but grievous, ii. 177.
"City which hath foundations," what it is, ii. 59.
Cloud of witnesses, surrounded by, ii. 147.
Confidence, not to be cast away, ii. 31; of hope, 168.
"Conscience, evil, sprinkled from," meaning of the expression, ii. 50.
Consuming fire, God is a, ii. 218.
"Country," meaning of the word, ii. 65.
"Covenant, everlasting," ii. 416; new, different from the old, i. 373; old, what it had, 376.
Covetousness, the Scripture meaning of, ii. 229.

David's faith, ii. 128.
"Dead works," the meaning of, i. 403.
"Death, the power of," its import, i. 126; of Christ, the extent of, 101; and judgment, analogy between men's and Christ's, 428.
Destroyer of the first-born, ii. 106.
"Divers doctrines," what these were, ii. 240.
Doxology, ii. 425.

Epistle, author of, i. 5; canonicity, 8; interpretation, 9; language, style, and place, 7; subject and division, 8; to whom written, 6.
"End of the world," meaning of the phrase, ii. 427.
Enoch's faith, ii. 45.
"Entrance into the holiest," signification of, ii. 2.
Esau's finding no place of repentance, ii. 190.
"Eternal Spirit," meaning of, i. 401.

Faith, the substance of things hoped for, ii. 36.
"Falling away, so as not to be renewed to repentance," in what case, i. 289.
First principles of the doctrine of Christ, what, i. 275.
Fear of entering into God's rest, inculcated, i. 200.

"Field often rained upon," what it is, i. 299.
Gideon's faith, ii. 126.
"Grace given us," what it means, ii. 216.
"God of peace," the import of, ii. 417.
"Him that speaketh from heaven," who, ii. 204.
Holiness, its proper meaning in Scripture, ii. 185.
Hope, an anchor of the soul, i. 320; confidence of, 168; rejoicing of, 169.
Hospitality, duty of, ii. 224.

Incarnation of Christ, its design and end, i. 124.
Isaac's offering up, ii. 67; blessing Jacob and Esau, 75.
Israelitish history improved, i. 172.

Jacob's faith, ii. 80.
Jephthah's faith, ii. 128.
Jericho, the falling of its walls, ii. 117.
Jesus, the Author and Finisher of our faith, ii. 159.
Joseph's faith, ii. 84.

"Kingdom which cannot be moved," what, ii. 213.

Law, the, a shadow of good things to come, i. 432.
Levitical priesthood, its nature, design, and functions, i. 237; sacrifices efficacious, ii. 338.

"Majesty in the heavens," meaning of the phrase, i. 362.
Marriage honourable in all, ii. 227.
"Mediator of the new covenant," meaning of, ii. 358.
Melchisedec, who and what he was, i. 261; a type of Christ, in what respects, 322.
Messiah, as promised, not a Levitical priest, i. 343.
Moses, faithful as a servant, i. 165; faith, ii. 89; and Christ faithful over their house, 165; parents, their faith, 85.
Mount that might be touched, ii.

192; Zion, the city of the living God, 199.

Noah's faith, ii. 49.

"Obedience by the things He suffered," learned by Christ, ii. 305; to spiritual rulers, 257.
"Oracles of God," what are they? i. 266.

Passover, keeping of, ii. 105.
"Patience, running with," the meaning of, ii. 153.
Patterns of things in the heavens, what these were, i. 420.
"Perfect, made," meaning of, ii. 145.
Perfection not by the Levitical priesthood, i. 337.
Postscript to the Epistle, ii. 273.
"Priest taken from among men," meaning of, i. 239.
Profession, holding fast, ii. 296; our, what the expression means, i. 154, 229.
Promise made to Israel conditional, i. 193; of eternal inheritance, 411; Gospel, its nature, 195; not received, meaning of, ii. 140, 384.
Psalm Eighth, the bearing of it, as quoted by the Apostle, i. 90.

Race, Christian, ii. 152.
Rahab's faith, ii. 122.
"Recompense of reward," meaning of, ii. 95.
"Redemption of transgressions," what the phrase means, i. 412, ii. 361.
Red Sea, passing through, ii. 111.
Repentance from dead works, what it is, i. 277; no more, for those who sin wilfully, ii. 16.
Reproach of Christ, what it means, ii. 92.
Resemblance between Christ and Moses, i. 158.
Rest of God, what it is not, i. 206; left to the people of God under the Gospel, 198; remaining, what it is, 208.
Rulers, Church, to be remembered, ii. 234.
Revelation, the Jewish, described, i. 16; the Christian, described, 21.

Revelations, the two, contrasted, i. 15.

Sacrifice of Christ, ii. 253.
Salvation, the great, i. 76.
Samson's faith, ii. 128.
Samuel's faith, ii. 129.
"Sanctify," the meaning of the word in the Epistle, ii. 22.
Sanctifier and sanctified, of one, i. 115.
"Shaking heaven and earth," the meaning of, ii. 209.
Shepherd of the sheep, Christ, ii. 262, 412.
Short, coming, and seeming to come short, meaning of, i. 199.
Sitting down at the right hand of God, what it is, i. 11, 446.
"Slip, lest we let," meaning of the phrase, i. 73.
Son of God, what it means, i. 22.
Spirit of grace, ii. 23.
Spirits of just men made perfect, ii. 202.
Superiority of Christ to angels, i. 37; to Moses, 160; to Aaron, 224.
"Surety," the meaning of the word, ii. 347.

Tabernacle, first, what it means, i. 385; greater and more perfect, by which Christ entered, 391.
Tasting of death, i. 101; of the good word of life, 285.
Testament, Mediator of, the rendering of the word, i. 407.
Testator, meaning of the original word so rendered, i. 414.
Throne of grace, what it means, i. 234; come boldly to, ii. 299.
Translations necessarily imperfect, ii. 354.

"Vail, that is to say, the flesh of Christ," meaning of, ii. 3, 371.

Walking with God, what it means, ii. 45.
Word of God, quick and powerful, i. 214; of righteousness, meaning of, 270.
"World to come," signification of the phrase, i. 87.

II.

GREEK WORDS AND PHRASES REMARKED ON.

Ἀγαγόντα, i. 143.
Ἀγγέλοις, i. 17.
Ἄγγελος, i. 37.
Ἁγιάζειν, i. 114.
Ἁγιασμόν, ii. 186.
Ἅγιον, i. 379.
Ἀδόκιμος, i. 301.
Ἀθετήσας, ii. 19.
Αἰών, i. 26.
Αἰωνίου, i. 401.
Ἀληθινὴ καρδία, ii. 7.
Ἀλλά, i. 188.
Ἀλυσιτελές, ii. 260.
Ἀναλογίσασθε, ii. 164.
Ἀναστήσας, i. 44.
Ἀνατέταλκεν, i. 341.
Ἀντιλογία εἰς αὐτόν, ii. 164.
Ἀντίτυπα, i. 425.
Ἄνω, i. 324.
Ἀπαράβατος, i. 351.
Ἀπειθείας, i. 212.
Ἀπό, i. 257.
Ἀπολείπεται, i. 211.
Ἀπόστολον καὶ ἀρχιερέα τῆς ὁμολογίας ἡμῶν, i. 155.
Ἀρχηγός, i. 107; ii. 160.
Ἀρχὴν λαβοῦσα λαλεῖσθαι, i. 79.
Ἀρχὴν τῆς ὑποστάσεως, i. 185.
Ἀρχιερεύς, i. 227.
Ἀστεῖος, ii. 86.
Αὐτό τε τὸ βιβλίον, i. 418.
Αὐτός, i. 446.
Αὐτοῦ, i. 32.
Αὐτοῦ, i. 82.
Αὐτῷ, i. 105.
Ἀφαιρεῖν ἁμαρτίας, i. 438.
Ἀφιέναι, i. 276.
Ἀφωμοιωμένος, i. 328.

Βασιλείαν παραλαμβάνοντες, ii. 214.
Βεβαίαν, i. 170.
Βλέπομεν, i. 97.
Βρώματα, ii. 243.

Γάρ, i. 88, 94, 161, 313, 353.
Γεγονότες, i. 348.
Γενόμενος, i. 41.
Γεύεσθαι, i. 101, 286.
Γῆ, i. 298.

Δέ, i. 55, 175, 232; ii. 228.
Δεδεκάτωται, i. 334.
Δεσμίοις, ii. 29.
Δήπου, i. 130.
Δι᾽ αὑτοῦ, i. 33.
Διὰ βραχέων, ii. 273.
Δι᾽ ἧς, ii. 42, 48.
Δι᾽ ὃν καὶ δι᾽ οὗ, i. 28.
Δι᾽ οὕς, i. 299.
Διὰ παθημάτων, i. 108.
Διὰ παντὸς τοῦ ζῆν, i. 129.
Διὰ πίστεως καὶ μακροθυμίας, i. 311.
Διὰ πνεύματος αἰωνίου, i. 402.
Διὰ τὸν χρόνον, i. 266.
Διαθέμενος, i. 408.
Διαθήκη, i. 346, 407.
Διάκρισιν καλοῦ τε καὶ κακοῦ, i. 272.
Διάνοια, i. 373.
Δοκῇ, i. 200.
Δυνάμεις, i. 288.
Δυνάμενον, i. 232.
Δύνασθαι, i. 139.
Δῶρα, i. 240.

Ἑαυτοῖς, i. 294; ii. 30.
Ἑαυτούς, i. 182.
Ἔγγυος, i. 347.
Ἐγγὺς ἀφανισμοῦ, i. 374.
Ἐγενήθησαν, ii. 135.

INDEX.   435

Ἐγκεκαίνισται, i. 417.
Ἐγὼ ἔσομαι αὐτῷ εἰς πατέρα καὶ αὐτὸς ἔσται μοι εἰς υἱόν, i. 45.
Ἔθηκεν, i. 25.
Εἰ παιδείαν ὑπομένετε, ii. 171.
Εἰς, i. 387; ii. 176.
Εἰς γῆν, ii. 57.
Εἰς ἡμᾶς, i. 81.
Εἶχε, i. 378.
Ἐκάθισεν ἑαυτόν, i. 34.
Ἔνλκιαν, ii. 135.
Ἐκλυόμενοι, ii. 163.
Ἐκφέρουσα, i. 301.
Ἐλαττόω, i. 91.
Ἐλεήμων, i. 136.
Ἔμαθεν, ἔπαθεν, i. 249.
Ἐμπεσεῖν εἰς τὰς χεῖρας, ii. 25.
Ἐμφανίζουσιν, ii. 65.
Ἐν, i. 17.
Ἐν παραβολῇ, ii. 71.
Ἐν τοῖς προφήταις, i. 17.
Ἐν υἱῷ, i. 23.
Ἐν ᾧ, i. 137, 316.
Ἔνοχος, i. 129.
Ἐξ ἑνὸς πάντες, i. 115, 116.
Ἐπαγγελία, ii. 32.
Ἐπαγγελία τῆς αἰωνίου κληρονομίας, i. 411.
Ἐπαγγελίας ἰδόντες, ii. 64.
Ἐπεὶ οὐκ ἄν, i. 436.
Ἐπειράσθησαν, ii. 138.
Ἐπί, i. 166, 278, 338, 368; ii. 7, 19.
Ἐπ' ἐσχάτου τῶν ἡμερῶν, i. 21.
Ἐπὶ νεκροῖς, i. 408.
Ἐπιθυμία, ii. 229.
Ἐπικείμενα, i. 389.
Ἐπιλαμβάνεται, i. 130.
Ἐπισκοποῦντες, ii. 189.
Ἐπισυναγωγήν, ii. 13.
Ἔπρεπε, i. 109.
Ἔστηκε, i. 445.
Εὐάρεστον ἐνώπιον αὐτοῦ, ii. 270.
Εὔκαιρον βοήθειαν, i. 235.
Εὐλογεῖν, ii. 77.
Εὐπερίστατον, ii. 157.

Ἔχεσθαι, i. 306.
Ἔχων, i. 125.

Ζῶντος, ii. 25.

Ἡ κατὰ πίστιν δικαιοσύνη, ii. 53.
Ἡμεῖς, ii. 151.
Ἡμεῖς οὐκ ἐσμὲν ὑποστολῆς εἰς ἀπώλειαν, ii. 35.
Ἡμῶν, i. 16, 33.
Ἤν, ii. 2.
Ἧς, i. 302, 308.

Θεράπων, i. 165.
Θυμιατήριον, i. 380.
Θυσίαι, i. 240.

Ἱλάσκεσθαι τὰς ἁμαρτίας, i. 135.
Ἱλαστήριον, i. 234.

Καθ' ἡμέραν, i. 358.
Καθ' ὁμοιότητα, i. 233.
Καθ' ὅσον, i. 161.
Καθαρισμὸν ποιεῖσθαι, i. 33.
Καθαρισμός, i. 33.
Καθώς, i. 205.
Καθὼς ἔθος τισίν, ii. 14.
Καθὼς λέγει τὸ Πνεῦμα τὸ Ἅγιον, i. 172.
Καί, i. 75, 165, 174, 175, 334.
Καὶ κατέστησας αὐτὸν ἐπὶ τὰ ἔργα τῶν χειρῶν σου, i. 93.
Καὶ τροχιὰς ὀρθὰς ποιήσατε τοῖς ποσὶν ὑμῶν, ii. 181.
Καίπερ ὢν υἱός, i. 252, 253.
Καίτοι, i. 206.
Καλεῖται, i. 182.
Καλούμενος Ἀβραάμ, ii. 55.
Καρδία, i. 373.
Καρδία ἀπιστίας, i. 177.
Κατὰ καιρόν, i. 355.
Κατὰ τὸ δοκοῦν, ii. 175.
Καταβολὴ σπέρματος, ii. 62.
Καταλειπομένης ἐπαγγελίας, i. 198.
Κατανοήσατε, i. 157.
Καταργεῖν, i. 128.

Καταρτίζειν, ii. 38.
Κατασκόπους, ii. 122.
Κατέκρινε τὸν κόσμον, ii. 51.
Καύχημα, i. 169.
Κληρονομεῖν, i. 39.
Κληρονόμος, i. 25.
Κοσμικόν, i. 378.
Κρατῆσαι, i. 320.
Κρατῶμεν, i. 229.
Κρείττοσι θυσίαις, i. 422.
Κτίσις, i. 219.

Λαλεῖν, i. 16.
Λαμβάνειν, i. 244.
Λαμβανόμενος, i. 239.
Λαός, i. 135, 159.
Λατρεύωμεν, ii. 217.
Λέγει, i. 49.
Λέγειν κατὰ μέρος, i. 382.
Λειτουργός, i. 363.
Λογικὴ λατρεία, ii. 217.
Λόγος δυσερμήνευτος, i. 263.
Λόγος τῆς ἀκοῆς, i. 203.

Μεγαλωσύνης ἐν ὑψηλοῖς, i. 34.
Μείνῃ τὰ μὴ σαλευόμενα, ii. 212.
Μέλλοντα, i. 391, 432.
Μένουσαν, ii. 30.
Μερισμοῖς, i. 82.
Μετάνοια, ii. 190.
Μετόχους, i. 58.
Μετριοπαθεῖν δυνάμενος, i. 241.
Μέχρι τέλους, i. 170.
Μέχρις αἵματος, ii. 166.
Μὴ ἐκ φαινομένων, ii. 39.

Ναός, i. 159.
Νέας, ii. 203.
Νέφος μαρτύρων, ii. 150.
Νῦν, i. 425.

Ὁ Θεός, i. 55.
Ὁ λόγος τῆς ὀρκωμοσίας, i. 358.
Ὄγκος, ii. 154, 155.
Ὅθεν, i. 134; ii. 71.
Οἱ ἀπὸ τῆς Ἰταλίας, ii. 275.

Οἱ πιστεύσαντες, i. 204.
Οἰκονομία τοῦ πληρώματος τῶν καιρῶν, i. 22.
Οἰκουμένη, i. 89.
Οἴκῳ αὐτοῦ, i. 159.
Ὅν, i. 388.
Ὀνειδισμὸς τοῦ Χριστοῦ, ii. 93.
Ὅπως, i. 100.
Ὀργή, i. 175.
Ὁρισθείς, i. 44.
Ὁρῶμεν, i. 97.
Ὅταν δὲ πάλιν, i. 47.
Οὐ μή—οὐδ᾽ οὐ μή, ii. 231.
Οὗ ἡ φωνὴ τὴν γῆν ἐσάλευσε τότε, ii. 208.
Οὗ οἶκος, i. 167.
Οὐκ ἐπαισχύνεται, i. 116.
Οὖν, i. 185, 336; ii. 3.

Πάλιν, i. 47, 291.
Πάντα ὑπέταξας, i. 94.
Παρά, i. 41.
Παρ᾽ αὐτούς, i. 39.
Παρὰ τὸν Ἄβελ, ii. 203.
Παραγενόμενος, i. 390.
Παραπίπτειν, i. 289.
Παραπλησίως, i. 122.
Παραρρυῶμεν, i. 74.
Παρόντα, ii. 230.
Παρρησία, i. 169.
Παρρησία εἰς, ii. 2.
Πατέρες, ii. 85.
Πατὴρ τῶν πνευμάτων, ii. 175.
Πέπεισμαι, i. 306.
Πεποίηκε, ii. 105.
Πεποιημένων, ii. 211.
Πέπονθε πειρασθείς, i. 138.
Περίκειται ἀσθένειαν, i. 241.
Περισσοτέρως, i. 71.
Πίσῃ, i. 212.
Πίστει, ii. 48.
Πίστει μέγας γενόμενος Μωϋσῆς ἀνεῖλεν, κ.τ.λ., ii. 89.
Πιστός, i. 136.
Πλείονα, i. 162; ii. 40.
Πλείονος, i. 161.

Πλεονεξία, ii. 229.
Πνεῦμα, i. 37, 215.
Πνευματικῶς, ii. 199.
Ποιεῖν, i. 160.
Πολλοί, i. 429.
Πολυμερῶς καὶ πολυτρόπως, i. 19.
Πού, i. 90.
Πρέπει, i. 110.
Πρεσβύτεροι, ii. 38.
Πρόδρομος, i. 321; ii. 5.
Πρός, i. 52, 55, 60; ii. 175.
Προσενήνοχεν, ii. 71.
Προσέχειν, i. 71.
Πρώτη, i. 376.
Πρωτότοκος, i. 49.
Πυρὸς φλόγα, i. 52.

Ῥῆμα, i. 32.

Σαββατισμός, i. 209.
Σαρκικῆς, i. 342.
Σκιά, i. 365.
Στοιχεῖα τῆς ἀρχῆς, i. 267.
Συγκεκραμένος, i. 204.
Συνεπιμαρτυρεῖ, i. 82.
Συντέλεια τῶν αἰώνων, i. 22.
Σωτηρία, i. 78, 106, 143.

Τὰ παιδία, i. 122.
Τὰ πάντα, i. 164.
Τὰ πρὸς τὸν Θεόν, i. 135, 240.
Τί, i. 285, 287.
Τελείων, i. 271.
Τελειωτής, ii. 160.
Τελευτῶν, ii. 84.
Τέλη τῶν αἰώνων, i. 22.
Τέλος, i. 302.
Τεχνίτης καὶ δημιουργός, ii. 61.
Τῆς δόξης, i. 29.

Τίκτουσα, i. 299.
Τιμή, i. 243.
Τίμιος ὁ γάμος, ii. 227.
Τινές, i. 187.
Τὸ πλήρωμα τοῦ χρόνου, i. 22.
Τόν, i. 48.
Τὸν τῆς ἀρχῆς τοῦ Χριστοῦ λόγον, i. 276.
Τοῦ οἴκου, i. 162.
Τούτων, i. 21.
Τύμπανον, ii. 136.
Τῷ προσώπῳ τοῦ Θεοῦ, i. 425.
Τῶν ἁγίων, i. 363.
Τῶν ἡγουμένων ὑμῶν, ii. 233.

Ὑπέρ, i. 215.
Ὑπόδειγμα, i. 365.
Ὑπομονή, ii. 32, 153.
Ὑστερεῖν, i. 199, 200.
Ὕστερον, ii. 179.
Ὕψιστος, i. 325.

Φέρειν, i. 31.
Φιλαργυρία, ii. 229.
Φοβερὰ ἐκδοχὴ κρίσεως, ii. 17.
Φοβηθῶμεν, i. 200.
Φωνὴ ῥημάτων, ii. 205.

Χαρακτὴρ ὑποστατικός, i. 30.
Χάριν, ii. 216.
Χάρις Θεοῦ, ii. 187.
Χωρίς, i. 431.
Χωρὶς Θεοῦ, i. 103.

Ψηλαφωμένῳ ὄρει, ii. 192, 193.
Ψυχή, i. 215.

Ὧδε μέν, ἐκεῖ δέ, i. 332.
Ὡς ἔπος εἰπεῖν, i. 335.

III.

AUTHORS REFERRED TO.

Abresch, i. 9, 37, 42, 81, 89, 116, 119, 129, 164, 165, 167, 169, 176, 205, 206, 211, 222, 228, 283, 299, 387.
Alexander (Dr W. L.), i. 21, 43.
Alleine, ii. 260.
Anacreon, i. 298.

Appian, i. 409.
Aquila, i. 55.
Aquinas, i. 155.
Athanasius, i. 44.
Athenæus, ii. 260.
Augustine, i. 44.

Basil, i. 30.
Bauldry, ii. 212.
Baumgarten, i. 6.
Bengel, i. 6, 33, 103, 166, 228, 358.
Bertholdt, i. 7.
Beza, ii. 39.
Bleek, i. 7.
Bloomfield, ii. 34.
Böhme, i. 9, 32, 294, 407; ii. 39, 62.
Braunius, i. 6, 9, 10.
Bretschneider, ii. 57.
Burmann, ii. 204.

Cajetan, i. 8.
Calmet, i. 380.
Calovius, i. 155.
Calvin, i. 48, 101, 201, 205, 212, 311; ii. 39, 225.
Camerarius, i. 246.
Capellus, i. 9, 332; ii. 197.
Carpzov, i. 9, 90, 138, 163, 205, 211, 289, 338, 351, 422; ii. 15, 131, 151, 205, 208, 212, 230.
Catullus, ii. 94.
Chrysostom, i. 9, 23, 31, 107, 122, 139, 155, 157, 161, 376, 417; ii. 39, 155, 250.
Cicero, i. 118, 268; ii. 160.
Clement (of Alexandria), i. 7.
Clement (of Rome), i. 8.
Cramer, i. 6; ii. 62.
Crellius, i. 17.
Cunæus, i. 8.

De Rhoer, i. 129.
Dick, i. 18.
Dindorf, ii. 119.
Diodorus Siculus, ii. 150.
Doddridge, i. 18.
Drusius, i. 9.
Duncan, i. 9, 402.

Ebrard, i. 9, 16, 87, 90, 100, 114, 120, 121, 125, 140, 143, 197, 200, 240, 334, 344, 346, 347, 365, 366, 378, 380, 409; ii. 38.
Eliezer (Rabbi), i. 54.
Elsner, i. 301.
Erasmus, i. 8, 9, 166.

Ernesti, i. 9, 81, 228, 230, 371; ii. 62.
Euripides, ii. 62, 85, 150.
Eusebius, i. 6, 7, 8, 210, 325.

Forster, i. 6.
Frommann, i. 131.

Gellius (Aulus), i. 239.
Gesenius, i. 371.
Gouge, i. 9.
Greverus, ii. 68.
Griesbach, i. 28, 33, 93, 166, 204, 388, 436, 446; ii. 203, 228.
Grigentius Sephrenensis, ii. 83.
Grotius, i. 9, 135, 164, 239, 301, 347, 438.

Haldane, i. 18.
Hall (Robert), i. 382; ii. 109.
Hallett, i. 7, 9; ii. 41, 276.
Hasæus, i. 7.
Heinrichs, i. 6, 9, 81, 371.
Hemsterhusius, i. 10.
Henderson, i. 18, 19.
Hengstenberg, i. 44.
Henley, i. 55.
Henry, ii. 254.
Herodian, i. 243; ii. 150.
Herodotus, i. 249.
Homer, ii. 135, 150.
Horace, i. 267.
Hutchinson, ii. 190.
Hyperius, i. 9, 378.

Jahn, i. 64.
Jay, ii. 226.
Jebb (Bp.), i. 358.
Jerome, i. 7; ii. 15.
Johnston (Arthur), i. 174.
Josephus, i. 324, 379; ii. 86, 87, 88.
Justin Martyr, i. 8.
Juvenal, i. 243; ii. 94.

Kimchi, i. 208.
Knapp, i. 93, 436, 446.
Kohler, i. 7.
Kuinoel, i. 6, 9, 206, 228, 301, 391, 407, 422; ii. 36, 39, 62.
Kypke, i. 19; ii. 35.

Lachmann, ii. 228.
Lactantius, i. 176.
Lawson, i. 9.
Limborch, i. 9, 407.
Livy, i. 342; ii. 150.

Lucretius, i. 241, 299.
Ludwig, i. 7.
Luther, i. 155.

M'Crie, ii. 41, 292.
Macknight, i. 88.
M'Lean, i. 9, 202, 382, 437; ii. 219.
Maimonides, ii. 245.
Martial, ii. 94.
Matthiæ, i. 94, 204, 436.
Meyer, i. 18.
Michaelis, i. 7, 57, 65, 78, 115, 125, 209, 217, 219, 246, 294, 348, 395.
Middleton, i. 57.
Mill, i. 33, 93, 204, 436; ii. 89.
Morus, i. 33.
Munburgh, i. 44.

Nemethus, i. 9.

Oecumenius, i. 90, 363, 436; ii. 39.
Oederus, i. 94.
Olshausen, i. 347.
Origen, i. 6, 8.
Owen, i. 9, 107, 136, 209, 210, 228, 285. 294, 448; ii. 8, 136, 167, 222, 259, 268, 273.

Parry, i. 18.
Peirce, i. 9, 102, 115, 116, 120, 186, 228, 332, 409, 442.
Philo, i. 29, 90, 268, 269, 437; ii. 43, 196.
Photius, i. 116.
Pothill, i. 145.
Proclus, ii. 175.
Prudentius, ii. 136.
Pye Smith, i. 29, 406, 422, 441; ii. 253.

Quintilian, i. 267.

Rosenmüller, i. 18, 64.

Salvian, ii. 71.
Sampson, i. 212.
Sanconiathon, i. 325.

Schlichting, i. 347.
Schmid (C. F.), i. 6, 9, 200, 418; ii. 39, 62, 71.
Schmid (Sebastian), i. 423.
Schmidt, i. 7.
Schoetgen, i. 90, 118; ii. 83, 190.
Schott, i. 7, 94, 294, 436.
Schulz, i. 130, 363; ii. 39.
Seneca, i. 31, 241; ii. 172.
Sophocles, i. 101.
Stanley, i. 6, 7. 11; ii. 186, 188.
Stephens, i. 166.
Storr, i. 6, 155, 292, 294; ii. 39.
Stow, i. 56.
Strabo, i. 301.
Stuart, i. 6, 9, 57, 82, 100, 102, 139, 206, 253, 294, 320, 387, 407, 442; ii. 22, 82, 274.
Sykes, i. 9.

Theodoret, i. 31, 90, 322; ii. 39. 55.
Theophylact, i. 9, 25, 122, 220, 335, 389, 417, 436, 445; ii. 7, 39, 155.
Tholuck, ii. 3, 39, 64, 72, 202, 243, 275.
Turner, i. 9, 201.

Valcknaer, i. 15, 31, 39, 48, 76, 88, 360, 445; ii. 2.
Vater, i. 93, 436.
Vaughan (Dr), i. 18.
Virgil, i. 221, 298, 302, 320, 348, 377; ii. 64, 150.
Vitringa, i. 262.

Wakefield, ii. 61.
Wardlaw, i. 209, 210.
Weber, i. 7, 44.
Wetstein, i. 7, 93, 166, 204; ii. 197.
Wickelius, i. 166.
Winer, i. 338; ii. 39, 253.
Wolfius, i. 135.

Xenophon, i. 135, 243.

Zeller, i. 129.

IV.

TEXTS OF SCRIPTURE.

Genesis iv. 1, 5,	. . . .	II. 40
,, v. 24,	. . . .	II. 44
,, vi. 12–18,	. . .	II. 49
,, xii. 1–4,	. . . .	II. 55
Genesis xiv. 18, 19,	. . .	I. 325
,, xv. 14,	. . . .	II. 25
,, xix. 24,	. . . .	I. 28
,, xxii. 1–18,	. . .	II. 67

Genesis xxiv. 3, 7, 8,	I. 417	Isaiah l. 50, ... I. 441
,, xlviii. 8–20, .	II. 82	Jeremiah i. 10, ... I. 45
,, l. 24, 25, .	II. 84	,, xxxi. 31–34, . . I. 371
Exodus i. 21, ...	I. 162	Hosea i. 1–7, ... I. 28
,, ii. 1, ...	II. 86	Habakkuk, ii. 2–4, . . II. 33
,, iii. iv. v. vi. .	II. 101	Haggai ii. 7, ... II. 209
,, xii. 1, .	II. 105	Zechariah vi. 12, . . . I. 163
,, xiv. 1, ...	II. 112	Matthew xix. 26, . . . I. 292
,, xix. 1–20, . .	II. 196	,, xxvi. 28, . . . II. 357
Numbers xiv. 14, 21, 29, .	I. 176	Mark xiv. 24, ... II. 357
,, xv. 30, 31,	I. 384	Luke xxii. 20, ... II. 357
,, xxxv. 11, 12, .	I. 319	,, xxii. 24, ... I. 199
Deuteronomy i. 35, . .	II. 176	Acts xv. 10, ... I. 389
,, iv. 11, . .	II. 196	Romans viii. 39, . . . I. 220
,, v. 22, . .	II. 196	,, ix. 22, . . . II. 420
,, xiii. 6–9, .	II. 20	1 Corinthians i. 9, . . I. 153
,, xvii. 2–7,	II. 20	,, ix. 7, . . I. 42
Joshua ii. 9–11, ...	II. 123	,, x. 11, . . I. 22
,, v. 13–15, . .	II. 119	,, xi. 25, . . II. 357
,, vi. 1–20, . .	II. 119	2 Corinthians iii. 6–14, . II. 357
Judges vi. 25, 27, . .	II. 127	Galatians iv. 4, ... I. 22
1 Samuel xii. 16, 18, . .	II. 129	,, iv. 26, ... I. 261
,, xvii. 46, 47, . .	II. 129	,, vi. 1, ... II. 421
2 Samuel vii. 14, . .	I. 45	Ephesians i. 10, ... I. 22
1 Chronicles xvii. 13, . .	I. 45	1 Thessalonians ii. 12, . . I. 411
2 Chronicles xx. 12, . .	II. 25	Titus ii. 11, ... I. 78
Psalms, ii. 7, ...	I. 245	Hebrews iv. 14, ... II. 373
,, viii. 5, 6, 7, .	I. 90	,, iv. 14–16, . . . I. 279
,, xviii. 2, . . .	I. 118	,, iv. 16, . . . I. 382
,, xxii. 22, . . .	I. 117	,, v. 7–9, . . . II. 303
,, xl. 6, ...	I. 438	,, vi. 12, . . . II. 385
,, xlv. 6, 7, . .	I. 54	,, vii. 22, . . . II. 357
,, lxxxvii. 1, . . .	II. 60	,, ix. 11, 12, . . II. 323
,, xcv. 7, ...	II. 172	,, ix. 13, 14, . . II. 337
,, xcv. 7, 8, . . .	I. 173	,, ix. 15, . . . II. 353
,, xcvii. 7, . . .	I. 46	,, ix. 26, . . . I. 22
,, cii. 24–27, . . .	I. 59	,, x. 5, ... II. 421
,, civ. 4, ...	I. 52	,, x. 19–22, . . II. 369
,, cx. 1, ...	I. 64	,, xi. 3, . . . II. 421
,, cx. 3, ...	I. 322	,, xi. 39, 40, . . II. 383
,, cx. 4, ...	I. 246	,, xiii. 10, . . . II. 397
Proverbs iii. 26, ...	II. 181	,, xiii. 20, 21, . . II. 409
Isaiah vi. 10, ...	I. 45	1 Peter i. 12, ... I. 382
,, viii. 18, ...	I. 119	Revelation i. 12, 13, 20, . I. 382
,, ix. 8, ...	I. 214	,, viii. 3, 4, . . I. 382
,, xxxv. 3, ...	II. 181	,, xi. 19, . . . II. 357
,, xlviii. 12, ...	I. 411	

FINIS.

Works Published

BY

WILLIAM OLIPHANT AND CO., EDINBURGH.

THEOLOGICAL AND EXPOSITORY WORKS

BY THE LATE

REV. PROFESSOR JOHN BROWN, D.D.,
EDINBURGH.

I.

Discourses and Sayings of our Lord Jesus Christ. Illustrated in a Series of Expositions. Second Edition. Three large volumes, 8vo, 31s. 6d.

II.

Analytical Exposition of the Epistle to the Romans. One large volume, 8vo, 14s.

III.

Exposition of the Epistle to the Galatians. In one large volume, 8vo, 12s.

IV.

Expository Discourses on the First Epistle of Peter. Second Edition. Two large volumes, 8vo, 21s.

V.

Parting Counsels. An Exposition of Second Peter, First Chapter. With four additional Discourses. 8vo, 8s.

VI.

Sufferings and Glories of the Messiah. Signified beforehand to David and Isaiah: An Exposition of Psalm xviii., and Isaiah lii. 13-liii. 12. 8vo, 8s.

VII.

Discourses Suited to the Administration of the Lord's Supper. Third Edition, 8vo, 8s.

VIII.

Hints on the Lord's Supper, and Thoughts for the Lord's Table. Foolscap 8vo, 2s.

IX.

Hints to Students of Divinity. Foolscap 8vo, 1s. 6d.

KITTO'S DAILY BIBLE ILLUSTRATIONS:

Being Original Readings for a Year, on subjects relating to Sacred History, Biography, Geography, Antiquities, and Theology. Especially designed for the Family Circle. By JOHN KITTO, D.D. In eight volumes, foolscap 8vo, with fine Frontispieces, Vignettes, and numerous Engravings.

VOL.
MORNING SERIES.
I. THE ANTEDILUVIANS AND PATRIARCHS. Eighth Edition.
II. MOSES AND THE JUDGES. Seventh Edition.
III. SAMUEL, SAUL, AND DAVID. Sixth Edition.
IV. SOLOMON AND THE KINGS. Sixth Edition.

EVENING SERIES.
V. JOB AND THE POETICAL BOOKS. Sixth Edition.
VI. ISAIAH AND THE PROPHETS. Sixth Edition.
VII. LIFE AND DEATH OF OUR LORD. Sixth Edition.
VIII. THE APOSTLES AND THE EARLY CHURCH. Sixth Edition.

The last volume contains an elaborate Index. Each volume is complete in itself, and is sold separately, price 6s., cloth. The set forms an appropriate and useful present, in cloth, bevelled boards, L.2, 8s.; in half morroco, L.3; handsomely bound in antique calf, L.3, 12s.; or in antique morocco, L.4, 4s.

'I cannot lose this opportunity of recommending, in the strongest language and most emphatic manner I can command, this invaluable series of books. I believe, for the elucidation of the historic parts of Scripture, there is nothing comparable with them in the English or any other language.'—Rev. JOHN ANGELL JAMES.

'Dr KITTO's usefulness, and, perhaps, his fame, will permanently rest on his Daily Bible Illustrations, completed just before his death, in eight small 8vo volumes. They contain an immense body of information on biblical subjects, historical, archæological, and physical, and are particularly serviceable to the clergy, as containing illustrations which may be appropriately introduced into their discourses. To young persons they have been found of extraordinary attraction; while persons of all ages rise from their perusal refreshed and charmed with the light they throw upon the Scripture.'—*Clerical Journal.*

'This work has obtained, as it merits, a wide popularity. The topics are selected with admirable skill, and are usually founded on some striking scene or novel adventure, some fact or sentiment, some attractive feature of character, or remarkable incident in eastern life and enterprise. Thus, in the first volume, you pass from the manners of the tent to the bravery of the camp, from the fire on the hearth to the flame of the altar; and whether the paper be on a marriage or a funeral, a sacrifice or a scene of revelry; whether the theme be Abel's death, Lamech's polygamy, Jubal's harp, Enoch's piety, Noah's ark, Sarah's veil, Hagar's flight, Lot's escape, Jacob's pillar, Joseph's bondage, or Pharaoh's signet, each is told with a charming simplicity, surrounded with numerous and beautiful illustrations, and interspersed or closed with pointed and just reflections. Dr Kitto throws light throughout the series on many obscure allusions, says many tender and many startling things, opens his heart to the reader, as he unfolds the stores of his learning—all his utterances being in harmony with his avowed design, to make this work "really interesting, as a reading book, to the family circle, for which it is primarily intended."'—*Professor Eadie,* in his 'Life of Dr Kitto.'

LIFE OF JOHN KITTO, D.D., Editor of the

'Pictorial Bible,' Author of 'Daily Bible Illustrations,' etc. By JOHN EADIE, D.D., LL.D. Sixth Thousand. With Portrait and Illustrations. Extra foolscap 8vo, 6s.; foolscap 8vo, 3s. 6d.; cloth boards, 2s. 6d.

'Full of the noblest lessons of faith, and patience, and indomitable self-control. Would that it were in the hands of every young man in our country.'—*Christian Treasury.*

Opinions concerning Jesus Christ. Containing the Statement and Examination of the Jewish, Infidel, Socinian, Arian, and Catholic Opinions; with an Appendix and Copious Notes. By the Rev. P. Davidson, D.D., Edinburgh. Second Edition. Extra foolscap 8vo, 4s. 6d.

The Law of Moses; its Character and Design. By the Rev. David Duncan of Howgate. Foolscap 8vo, 6s.

Exposition of the Epistle to the Romans. By Robert Haldane, Esq. With remarks on the Commentaries of Dr Macknight, Professor Moses Stuart, and Professor Tholuck. Eighth Edition. 3 vols. foolscap 8vo, 15s.

The Pilgrim Psalms: a Practical Exposition of the Songs of Degrees, Psalms cxx.-cxxxiv. By Professor M'Michael, D.D., Dunfermline. Foolscap 8vo, 4s. 6d.

The Edenic Dispensation; with Strictures on the Rev Dr Payne's Opinions on Original Sin. By the Rev. James Meikle, D.D., Beith. Foolscap 8vo, 3s. 6d.

The Nature of the Mediatorial Dispensation. Post 8vo 5s.

The Administration of the Mediatorial Dispensation. Post 8vo, 5s.

Practical Exposition of the Book of Jonah, in Ten Lectures. By the late James Peddie, D.D. Foolscap 8vo, 1s. 6d.

Old Truths and Modern Speculations. By the late Rev. James Robertson, D.D., Glasgow. Second Edition. Crown 8vo, 6s.

One Hundred Addresses and Meditations suited to the Administration of the Lord's Supper. By the late Henry Belfrage, D.D., Falkirk. Sixth Edition, complete in one volume, 6s.

The Scripture Testimony to the Messiah. By John Pye Smith, D.D., F.R.S. Fifth Edition. With Biographical and Critical Estimate of the Author, by John Eadie, D.D., LL.D. 2 large vols. 8vo, 21s.

The Sacrifice and Priesthood of Jesus Christ, in Four Discourses. By the same Author. Fourth Edition. Foolscap 8vo, 5s.

The Communicant's Manual. By the late Rev. Henry Thomson, D.D., Penrith. Foolscap 8vo, 5s.

The Song of Songs Unveiled: a New Translation and Exposition of the Song of Solomon. By the Rev. Benjamin Weiss, Algiers. 12mo, 2s. 6d.

New Translation, Exposition, and Chronological Arrangement of the Book of Psalms. By the same Author. 8vo, 5s.

New Translation and Exposition of the Book of Ecclesiastes. By the same Author. Foolscap 8vo, 2s.

Just published, with Portrait, in handsome crown 8vo, price 7s. 6d.,

THE LIFE AND TIMES OF
GEORGE LAWSON, D.D., SELKIRK,
PROFESSOR OF THEOLOGY TO THE ASSOCIATE SYNOD.
With Glimpses of Scottish Character from 1720 to 1820.
By the Rev. JOHN MACFARLANE, LL.D., Author of 'The Night Lamp,' etc., etc.

Opinions of the Press.

'We were not prepared for a volume of such singular interest as this which Dr Macfarlane has produced. Students of divinity will find a model for their imitation in acquisition, and professors a model for imitation in teaching. Seldom have we taken up a volume so full of anecdote, fresh and racy. To those to whom such books as the "Autobiography of Jupiter Carlyle" and the lively *facetiæ* of Dean Ramsay have any interest, this will be the very book.'—*Eclectic Review.*

'Scottish character has of late received ample illustration in the autobiographies of Drs Carlyle and Sommerville, and in the collections of anecdotes and *ana* which Dean Ramsay, Dr Rogers, Alexander Leighton, and Mr Kennedy, have given to the press. Dr Macfarlane has cultivated a distinct field of the same period, and has produced a work of equal interest, full of anecdote, thoroughly Scottish, and delineating the life and labours of a man of high scholarship.'—*Meliora.*

'One of the best biographies we have read for long—one of the best, if not the very best, Dr Macfarlane has yet written. The work is professedly a collection of memorabilia; and when we remember what Xenophon did for Socrates, and Boswell for Johnson, we feel perfectly persuaded that, in adopting the plan he has pursued, Dr Macfarlane has chosen by far the best he could have followed. In its general style it is correct, chaste, and simple; nay, some of its descriptions are most beautiful, and there is over it all a rich glow of affectionate interest, which gilds the whole horizon of the heart, as a fine sunset does the evening sky.'—*The Scottish Review.*

'Our opinion is, that this is the most spirited of all the author's productions. He has fairly risen to the height of his subject. His (Dr Lawson) memorial is still like fragrance on the breeze; and this volume, like a golden casket, has collected within it much of the perfume, which will be there retained to regale generations to come. We have little doubt of the coming popularity of this work, and of the high esteem in which it will be held by all classes. No minister, no student, and no congregational library in the United Presbyterian Church, should be without it.'—*United Presbyterian Magazine.*

Life and Correspondence of the Rev. Henry Belfrage, D.D.,
Falkirk. By the Rev. Drs M'KERROW and MACFARLANE. With Portrait. 8vo, 3s. 6d.

Memoir and Remains of the Rev. John Brown of Haddington.
Edited by the Rev. WILLIAM BROWN, M.D. Foolscap 8vo, 1s. 6d.

Memoir of the Rev. John Brown of Whitburn; with his
Letters on Sanctification. By the Rev. D. SMITH, D.D., of Biggar. With Portrait. Foolscap 8vo, 2s. 6d.

Life and Diary of the Rev. Ralph Erskine, Author of
'Gospel Sonnets.' By the Rev. Dr FRASER. With Portrait. 12mo, 3s. 6d.

Life of the Rev. Hugh Heugh, D.D., of Glasgow. By his
Son-in-law, the Rev. H. M. MACGILL. New Edition. 12mo, 6s. 6d.

'A work full of interest to all Christians; to ministers, perhaps the most truly valuable biographical volume that has been published since "Orton's Life of Doddridge."'—*Late* Rev. JOHN BROWN, D.D.

Memoir of the Rev. Alexander Waugh, D.D., London. By
the late Drs HAY and BELFRAGE. Third Edition. With Portrait. Post 8vo, 5s.

www.ingramcontent.com/pod-product-compliance
Lightning Source LLC
Chambersburg PA
CBHW022140300426
44115CB00006B/281